NEWSPAPER DAYS

AMERICAN NEWSPAPERMEN 1790-1933

THEODORE DREISER

NEWSPAPER DAYS

BEEKMAN PUBLISHERS INC.

NEW YORK   1974

Library of Congress Cataloging in Publication Data

Dreiser, Theodore, 1871-1945.
    Newspaper Days.

    (American Newspapermen, 1790-1933)
    First published under title: A book about myself.
    Reprint of the ed. published by H. Liveright, New
York, which was issued as v. 2 of the author's A history
of myself.
    1. Dreiser, Theodore, 1871-1945. I. Title.
PS3507.R55Z5   1974   070.4'092'4 (B) 74-531
ISBN 0-8464-0023-5

AUTHOR'S NOTE

THIS BOOK was originally published under the title "A Book About Myself." My own title, which accurately embraces its content, was "Newspaper Days." Publisher and author disagreeing, I permitted for the time being the publisher's title. Since it was only Volume Two in a series of four or five to be entitled "A History of Myself" and since now, under the title "Dawn," Volume One of that series has appeared, it is fitting that Volume Two (now called "A Book About Myself") should resume its proper title. And that is "Newspaper Days."

Two more books covering the incidents and influences of my later life are—time and chance agreeing—to follow.

THEODORE DREISER

July, 1931

THEODORE DREISER

NEWSPAPER DAYS

CHAPTER I

DURING the year 1890 I had been formulating my first dim notion as to what it was I wanted to do in life. For two years and more I had been reading Eugene Field's "Sharps and Flats," a column he wrote daily for the Chicago *Daily News*, and through this, the various phases of life which he suggested in a humorous though at times romantic way, I was beginning to suspect, vaguely at first, that I wanted to write, possibly something like that. Nothing else that I had so far read—novels, plays, poems, histories—gave me quite the same feeling for constructive thought as did the matter of his daily notes, poems, and aphorisms, which were of Chicago principally, whereas nearly all others dealt with foreign scenes and people.

But this comment on local life here and now, these trenchant bits on local street scenes, institutions, characters, functions, all moved me as nothing hitherto had. To me Chicago at this time seethed with a peculiarly human or realistic atmosphere. It is given to some cities, as to some lands, to suggest romance, and to me Chicago did that hourly. It sang, I thought, and in spite of what I deemed my various troubles —small enough as I now see them—I was singing with it. These seemingly drear neighborhoods through which I walked each day, doing collecting for an easy-payment furniture company, these ponderous regions of large homes where new-wealthy packers and manufacturers dwelt, these curiously foreign neighborhoods of almost all nationalities; and, lastly, that great downtown area, surrounded on two sides by the river, on the east by the lake, and on the south by railroad yards and stations, the whole set with these new tall buildings, the wonder of the western world, fascinated me. Chicago was so young, so blithe, so new, I thought. Florence in its best days must have been something like this to young Florentines, or Venice to the young Venetians.

Here was a city which had no traditions but was making them, and this was the very thing that every one seemed to understand and rejoice in. Chicago was like no other city in the world, so said they all. Chicago would outstrip every other American city, New York included, and become the first of all American, if not European or world, cities. . . . This dream many hundreds of thousands of its citizens held dear. Chicago would be first in wealth, first in beauty, first in art achievement. A great World's Fair was even then being planned that would bring people from all over the world. The Auditorium, the new Great Northern Hotel, the amazing (for its day) Masonic Temple twenty-two stories high, a score of public institutions, depots, theaters and the like, were being constructed. It is something wonderful to witness a world metropolis springing up under one's very eyes, and this is what was happening here before me.

Nosing about the city in an inquiring way and dreaming half-formed dreams of one and another thing I would like to do, it finally came to me, dimly, like a bean that strains at its enveloping shell, that I would like to write of these things. It would be interesting, so I thought, to describe a place like Goose Island in the Chicago River, a mucky and neglected realm then covered with shanties made of upturned boats sawed in two, and yet which seemed to me the height of the picturesque; also a building like the Auditorium or the Masonic Temple, that vast wall of masonry twenty-two stories high and at that time actually the largest building in the world; or a seething pit like that of the Board of Trade, which I had once visited and which astonished and fascinated me as much as anything ever had. That roaring, yelling, screaming whirlpool of life! And then the lake, with its pure white sails and its blue water; the Chicago River, with its black, oily water, its tall grain elevators and black coal pockets; the great railroad yards, covering miles and miles of space with their cars.

(2)

How wonderful it all was! As I walked from place to place collecting I began betimes to improvise rhythmic, vaguely formulated word-pictures or rhapsodies anent these same and many other things—free verse, I suppose we should call it now—which concerned everything and nothing but somehow expressed the seething poetry of my soul and this thing to me. Indeed I was crazy with life, a little demented or frenzied with romance and hope. I wanted to sing, to dance, to eat, to love. My word-dreams and maunderings concerned my day, my age, poverty, hope, beauty, which I mouthed to myself, chanting aloud at times. Sometimes, because on a number of occasions I had heard the Reverend Frank W. Gunsaulus and his like spout rocket-like sputterings on the subjects of life and religion, I would orate, pleading great causes as I went. I imagined myself a great orator with thousands of people before me, my gestures and enunciation and thought perfect, poetic, and all my hearers moved to tears or demonstrations of wild delight.

After a time I ventured to commit some of these things to paper, scarcely knowing what they were, and in a fever for self-advancement I bundled them up and sent them to Eugene Field. In his column and elsewhere I had read about geniuses being occasionally discovered by some chance composition or work noted by one in authority. I waited for a time, with great interest but no vast depression, to see what my fate would be. But no word came and in time I realized that they must have been very bad and had been dropped into the nearest waste basket. But this did not give me pause nor grieve me. I seethed to express myself. I bubbled. I dreamed. And I had a singing feeling, now that I had done this much, that some day I should really write and be very famous into the bargain.

But how? How? My feeling was that I ought to get into newspaper work, and yet this feeling was so nebulous that I thought it would never come to pass. I saw mention in the papers of reporters calling to find out this, or being sent to do that, and so the idea of becoming a reporter gradually formulated itself in my mind, though how I was to get such a place I had not the slightest idea. Perhaps reporters had to have a special training of some kind; maybe they had to begin as clerks behind a counter, and this made me very somber, for those glowing business offices always seemed so far removed from anything to which I could aspire. Most of them were ornate, floreate, with onyx or chalcedony wall trimmings, flambeaux of bronze or copper on the walls, imitation mother-of-pearl lights in the ceilings—in short, all the gorgeousness of a sultan's court brought to the outer counter where people subscribed or paid for ads. Because the newspapers were always dealing with signs and wonders, great functions, great commercial schemes, great tragedies and pleasures, I began to conceive of them as wonderlands in which all concerned were prosperous and happy. I painted reporters and newspaper men generally as receiving fabulous salaries, being sent on the most urgent and interesting missions. I think I confused, inextricably, reporters with ambassadors and prominent men generally. Their lives were laid among great people, the rich, the famous, the powerful; and because of their position and facility of expression and mental force they were received everywhere as equals. Think of me, new, young, poor, being received in that way!

Imagine then my intense delight one day, when, scanning the "Help Wanted: Male" columns of the Chicago *Herald,* I encountered an advertisement which ran (in substance):

Wanted: A number of bright young men to assist in the business department during the Christmas holidays. Promotion possible. Apply to Business Manager between 9 and 10 a. m.

"Here," I thought as I read it, "is just the thing I am looking for. Here is this great paper, one of the most prosperous in Chicago, and here is an opening for me. If I can only get this my fortune is made. I shall rise rapidly." I conceived of myself as being sent off the same day, as it were, on some brilliant mission and returning, somehow, covered with glory.

I hurried to the office of the *Herald,* in Washington Street near Fifth Avenue, this same morning, and asked to see the business manager. After a short wait I was permitted

(4)

to enter the sanctuary of this great person, who to me, because of the material splendor of the front office, seemed to be the equal of a millionaire at least. He was tall, graceful, dark, his full black whiskers parted aristocratically in the middle of his chin, his eyes vague pools of subtlety. "See what a wonderful thing it is to be connected with the newspaper business!" I told myself.

"I saw your ad in this morning's paper," I said hopefully.

"Yes, I did want a half dozen young men," he replied, beaming upon me reassuringly, "but I think I have nearly enough. Most of the young men that come here seem to think they are to be connected with the *Herald* direct, but the fact is we want them only for clerks in our free Christmas gift bureau. They have to judge whether or not the applicants are impostors and keep people from imposing on the paper. The work will only be for a week or ten days, but you will probably earn ten or twelve dollars in that time——" My heart sank. "After the first of the year, if you take it, you may come around to see me. I may have something for you."

When he spoke of the free Christmas gift bureau I vaguely understood what he meant. For weeks past, the *Herald* had been conducting a campaign for gifts for the poorest children of the city. It had been importuning the rich and the moderately comfortable to give, through the medium of its scheme, which was a bureau for the free distribution of all such things as could be gathered via cash or direct donation of supplies: toys, clothing, even food, for children.

"But I wanted to become a reporter if I could," I suggested.

"Well," he said, with a wave of his hand, "this is as good a way as any other. When this is over I may be able to introduce you to our city editor." The title, "city editor," mystified and intrigued me. It sounded so big and significant.

This offer was far from what I anticipated, but I took it joyfully. Thus to step from one job to another, however brief, and one with such prospects, seemed the greatest luck

(5)

in the world. For by now I was nearly hypochondriacal on the subjects of poverty, loneliness, the want of the creature comforts and pleasures of life. The mere thought of having enough to eat and to wear and to do had something of paradise about it. Some previous long and fruitless searches for work had marked me with a horror of being without it.

I bustled about to the *Herald's* Christmas Annex, as it was called, a building standing in Fifth Avenue between Madison and Monroe, and reported to a brisk underling in charge of the doling out of these pittances to the poor. Without a word he put me behind the single long counter which ran across the front of the room and over which were handled all those toys and Christmas pleasure pieces which a loud tomtoming concerning the dire need of the poor and the proper Christmas spirit had produced.

Life certainly offers some amusing paradoxes at times, and that with that gay insouciance which life alone can muster and achieve when it is at its worst anachronistically. Here was I, a victim of what Socialists would look upon as wage slavery and economic robbery, quite as worthy, I am sure, of gifts as any other, and yet lined up with fifteen or twenty other economic victims, ragamuffin souls like myself, all out of jobs, many of them out at elbows, and all of them doling out gifts from eight-thirty in the morning until eleven and twelve at night to people no worse off than themselves.

I wish you might have seen this chamber as I saw it for eight or nine days just preceding and including Christmas day itself. (Yes; we worked from eight a. m. to five-thirty p. m. on Christmas day, and very glad to get the money, thank you.) There poured in here from the day the bureau opened, which was the morning I called, and until it closed Christmas night, as diverse an assortment of alleged poverty-stricken souls as one would want to see. I do not say that many of them were not deserving; I am willing to believe that most of them were; but, deserving or no, they were still worthy of all they received here. Indeed when I think of the many who came miles, carrying slips of paper on which had been listed, as per the advice of this paper, all they wished Santa Claus to bring them or their children, and then recall that, for all their pains in having their minister or doctor or the *Herald* itself visé their request, they received only a fraction of what they sought, I am inclined to think that all were even more deserving than their reward indicated.

For the whole scheme, as I soon found in talking with others and seeing for myself how it worked, was most loosely managed. Endless varieties of toys and comforts had been talked about in the paper, but only a few of the things promised, or vaguely indicated, were here to give—for the very good reason that no one would give them for nothing to the *Herald*. Nor had any sensible plan been devised for checking up either the gifts given or the persons who had received them, and so the same person, as some of these recipients soon discovered, could come over and over, bearing different lists of toys, and get them, or at least a part of them, until some clerk with a better eye for faces than another would chance to recognize the offender and point him or her out. Jews, the fox-like Slavic type of course, and the poor Irish, were the worst offenders in this respect. The *Herald* was supposed to have kept all applications written by children to Santa Claus, but it had not done so, and so hundreds claimed that they had written letters and received no answer. At the end of the second or third day before Christmas it was found necessary, because of the confusion and uncertainty, to throw the doors wide open and give to all and sundry who looked worthy of whatever was left or "handy," we, the ragamuffin clerks, being the judges.

And now the clerks themselves, seeing that no records were kept and how without plan the whole thing was, notified poor relatives and friends, and these descended upon us with baskets, expecting candy, turkeys, suits of clothing and the like, but receiving instead only toy wagons, toy stoves, baby brooms, Noah's Arks, story books—the shabbiest mess of cheap things one could imagine. For the newspaper, true to that canon of commerce which demands the most for the least, the greatest show for the least money, had gathered all the odds and ends and left-overs of toy bargain sales and had dumped

(7)

them into the large lofts above, to be doled out as best we could. We could not give a much-desired article to any one person because, supposing it were there, which was rarely the case, we could not get at it or find it; yet later another person might apply and receive the very thing the other had wanted.

And we clerks, going out to lunch or dinner (save the mark!), would seek some scrubby little restaurant and eat ham and beans, or crullers and coffee, or some other tasteless dish, at ten or fifteen cents per head. Hard luck stories, comments on what a botch the *Herald* gift bureau was, on the strange characters that showed up—the hooded Niobes and dusty Priams, with eyes too sunken and too dry for tears— were the order of the day. Here I met a young newspaper man, gloomy, out at elbows, who told me what a wretched, pathetic struggle the newspaper world presented, but I did not believe him although he had worked in Chicago, Denver, St. Paul.

"A poor failure," I thought, "some one who can't write and who now whines and wastes his substance in riotous living when he has it!"

So much for the sympathy of the poor for the poor.

But the *Herald* was doing very well. Daily it was filling its pages with the splendid results of its charity, the poor relieved, the darkling homes restored to gayety and bliss. . . . Can you beat it? But it was good advertising, and that was all the *Herald* wanted.

Hey, Rub-a-dub! Hey, Rub-a-dub-dub!

CHAPTER II

On Christmas Eve there came to our home to spend the next two days, which chanced to be Saturday and Sunday, Alice Kane, a friend and fellow-clerk of one of my sisters in a department store. Because the store kept open until ten-thirty or eleven that Christmas Eve, and my labors at the *Herald* office detained me until the same hour, we three arrived at the house at nearly the same time.

I should say here that the previous year, my mother having died and the home being in dissolution, I had ventured into the world on my own. Several sisters, two brothers and my father were still together, but it was a divided and somewhat colorless home at best. Our mother was gone. I was already wondering, in great sadness, how long it could endure, for she had made of it something as sweet as dreams. That temperament, that charity and understanding and sympathy! We who were left were like fledglings, trying our wings but fearful of the world. My practical experience was slight. I was a creature of slow and uncertain response to anything practical, having an eye single to color, romance, beauty. I was but a half-baked poet, romancer, dreamer.

As I was hurrying upstairs to take a bath and then see what pleasures were being arranged for the morrow, I was intercepted by my sister with a "Hurry now and come down. I have a friend here and I want you to meet her. She's awful nice."

At the mere thought of meeting a girl I brightened, for my thoughts were always on the other sex and I was forever complaining to myself of my lack of opportunity, and of lack of courage when I had the opportunity, to do the one thing I most craved to do: shine as a lover. Although at her suggestion of a girl I pretended to sniff and be superior, still I bustled to the task of embellishing myself. On coming into the general livingroom, where a fire was burning brightly, I beheld a pretty dark-haired girl of medium height, smooth-cheeked and graceful, who seemed and really was guileless, good-natured and sympathetic. For a while after meeting her I felt stiff and awkward, for the mere presence of so pretty a girl was sufficient to make me nervous and self-conscious. My brother, E——, had gone off early in the evening to join the family of some girl in whom he was interested; another brother, A——, was out on some Christmas Eve lark with a group of fellow-employees; so here I was alone with C—— and this stranger, doing my best to appear gallant and clever.

I recall now the sense of sympathy and interest which I felt for this girl from the start. It must have been clear to my sister, for before the night was over she had explained, by way of tantalizing me, that Miss Kane had a beau. Later I learned that Alice was an orphan adopted by a fairly comfortable Irish couple, who loved her dearly and gave her as many pleasures and as much liberty as their circumstances would permit. They had made the mistake, however, of telling her that she was only an adopted child. This gave her a sense of forlornness and a longing for a closer and more enduring love.

Such a mild and sweet little thing she was! I never knew a more attractive or clinging temperament. She could play the banjo and guitar. I remember marveling at the dexterity of her fingers as they raced up and down the frets and across the strings. She was wearing a dark green blouse and brown corduroy skirt, with a pale brown ribbon about her neck; her hair was parted on one side, and this gave her a sort of maidenish masculinity. I found her looking at me slyly now and then, and smiling at one or another of my affected remarks as though she were pleased. I recounted the nature of the work I was doing, but deliberately attempted to confuse it in her mind and my sister's with the idea that I was regularly employed by the *Herald* as a newspaper man and that this was merely a side task. Subsequently, out of sheer vanity and a desire to appear more than I was, I allowed her to believe that I was a reporter on this paper.

It was snowing. We could see great flakes fluttering about the gas lamps outside. In the cottage of an Irish family across the street a party of merrymakers was at play. I proposed that we go out and buy chestnuts and popcorn and roast them, and that we make snow punch out of milk, sugar and snow. How gay I felt, how hopeful! In a fit of great daring I took one hand of each of my companions and ran, trying to slide with them over the snow. Alice's screams and laughter were disturbingly musical, and as she ran her little feet twinkled under her skirts. At one corner, where the stores were brightly lighted, she stopped and did a graceful little dance under the electric light.

"Oh, if I could have a girl like this—if I could just have her!" I thought, forgetting that I was nightly telling a Scotch girl that she was the sweetest thing I had ever known or wanted to know.

Bedtime came, with laughter and gayety up to the last moment. Alice was to sleep with my sister, and preceded me upstairs, saying she was going to eat salt on New Year's Eve so that she would dream of her coming lover. That night I lay and thought of her, and next morning hurried downstairs hoping to find her, but she had not come down yet. There were Christmas stockings to be examined, of course, which brought her, but before eight-thirty I had to leave in order to be at work at nine o'clock. I waved them all a gay farewell and looked forward eagerly toward evening, for she was to remain this night and the next day.

Through with my work at five-thirty, I hurried home, and then it was that I learned—and to my great astonishment and gratification—that she liked me. For when I arrived, dressed, as I had been all day, in my very best, E—— and A—— were there endeavoring to entertain her, E——, my younger brother, attempting to make love to her. His method was to press her toe in an open foolish way, which because of the jealousy it waked in me seemed to me out of the depths of dullness. From the moment I entered I fancied that

Alice had been waiting for me. Her winning smile as I entered reassured me, and yet she was very quiet when I was near, gazing romantically into the fire.

During the evening I studied her, admiring every detail of her dress, which was a bit different from that of the day before and more attractive. She seemed infinitely sweet, and I flattered myself that I was preferred over my two brothers. During the evening, we two being left together for some reason, she arose and went into the large front room and standing before one of the three large windows looked out in silence on the homelike scene that our neighborhood presented. The snow had ceased and a full moon was brightening everything. The little cottages and flat-buildings nearby glowed romantically through their drawn blinds, a red-ribboned Christmas wreath in every window. I pumped up my courage to an unusual point and, heart in mouth, followed and stood beside her. It was a great effort on my part.

She pressed her nose to the pane and then breathed on it, making a misty screen between herself and the outside upon which she wrote my initials, rubbed them out, then breathed on the window again and wrote her own. Her face was like a small wax flower in the moonlight. I had drawn so close, moved by her romantic call, that my body almost touched hers. Then I slipped an arm about her waist and was about to kiss her when I heard my sister's voice:

"Now, Al and Theo, you come back!"

"We must go," she said shamefacedly, and as she started I ventured to touch her hand. She looked at me and smiled, and we went back to the other room. I waited eagerly for other solitary moments.

Because the festivities were too general and inclusive there was no other opportunity that evening, but the next morning, church claiming some and sleep others, there was a half-hour or more in which I was alone with her in the front room, looking over the family album. I realized that by now she was as much drawn to me as I to her, and that, as in the case of my Scotch maid, I was master if I chose so to be. I was so wrought up in the face of this opportunity, however, that I scarcely had courage to do that which I earnestly believed I could do. As we stood over the album looking at the pictures I toyed first with the strings of her apron and then later, finding no opposition, allowed my hand to rest gently at her waist. Still no sign of opposition or even consciousness. I thrilled from head to toe. Then I closed my arm gently about her waist, and when it became noticeably tight she looked up and smiled.

"You'd better watch out," she said. "Some one may come."

"Do you like me a little?" I pleaded, almost choking.

"I think so. I think you're very nice, anyhow. But you mustn't," she said. "Some one may come in," and as I drew her to me she pretended to resist, maneuvering her cheek against my mouth as she pulled away.

She was just in time, for C—— came into the back parlor and said: "Oh, there you are! I wondered where you were."

"I was just looking over your album," Alice said.

"Yes," I added, "I was showing it to her."

"Oh yes," laughed my sister sarcastically. "You and Al— I know what you two were trying to do. You!" she exclaimed, giving me a push. "And Al, the silly! She has a beau already!"

She laughed and went off, but I, hugely satisfied with myself, swaggered into the adjoining room. Beau or no beau, Alice belonged to me. Youthful vanity was swelling my chest. I was more of a personage for having had it once more proved to me that I was not unattractive to girls.

CHAPTER III

WHEN I asked Alice when I should see her again she suggested the following Tuesday or Thursday, asking me not to say anything to C——. I had not been calling on her more than a week or two before she confessed that there was another suitor, a telegraph operator to whom she was engaged and who was still calling on her regularly. When she came to our house to spend Christmas, she said, it was with no intention of seeking a serious flirtation, though in order not to embarrass the sense of opportunity we boys might feel she had taken off her engagement, ring. Also, she confessed to me, she never wore it at the store, for the reason that it would create talk and make it seem that she might leave soon, when she was by no means sure that she would. In short, she had become engaged thus early without being certain that she was in love.

Never were happier hours than those I spent with her, though at the time I was in that state of unrest and change which afflicts most youths who are endeavoring to discover what they want to do in life. On Christmas day my job was gone and the task of finding another was before me, but this did not seem so grim now. I felt more confident. True, the manager of the *Herald* had told me to call after the first of the year, and I did so, but only to find that his suggestion of something important to come later had been merely a ruse to secure eager and industrious service for his bureau. When I told him I wanted to become a reporter, he said: "But, you see, I have nothing whatsoever to do with that. You must see the managing editor on the fourth floor."

To say this to me was about the same as to say: "You must see God." Nevertheless I made my way to that floor, but at that hour of the morning, I found no one at all. Another day, going at three, so complete was my ignorance of newspaper hours, I found only a few uncommunicative individuals at widely scattered desks in a room labeled "City Room." One of these, after I had asked him how one secured a place as a reporter, looked at me quizzically and said: "You want to see the city editor. He isn't here now. The best times to see him are at noon and six. That's the only time he gives out assignments."

"Aha!" I thought. " 'Assignments'—so that's what reportorial work is called! And I must come at either twelve or six." So I bustled away, to return at six, for I felt that I must get work in this great and fascinating field. When I came at six and was directed to a man who bent over a desk and was evidently very much concerned about something, he exclaimed: "No vacancies. Nothing open. Sorry," and turned away.

So I went out crestfallen and more overawed than ever. Who was I to attempt to venture into such a wonderland as this—I, a mere collector by trade? I doubt if any one ever explored the mouth of a cave with more feeling of uncertainty. It was all so new, so wonderful, so mysterious. I looked at the polished doors and marble floors of this new and handsome newspaper building with such a feeling as might have possessed an Ethiopian slave examining the walls and the doors of the temple of Solomon. How wonderful it must be to work in such a place as this! How shrewd and wise must be the men whom I saw working here, able and successful and comfortable! How great and interesting the work they did! Today they were here, writing at one of these fine desks; tomorrow they would be away on some important mission somewhere, taking a train, riding in a Pullman car, entering some great home or office and interviewing some important citizen. And when they returned they were congratulated upon having discovered some interesting fact or story on which, having reported to their city editor or managing editor, or having written it out, they were permitted to retire in comfort with more compliments. Then they resorted to an excellent hotel or restaurant, to refresh themselves among interested and interesting friends before retiring to rest. Some such hodge-podge as this filled my immature brain.

Despite the discouraging reception of my first overture, I visited other newspaper offices, only to find the same, and even colder, conditions. The offices in most cases were by no means so grand, but the atmosphere was equally chill, and the city editor was a difficult man to approach. Often I was stopped by an office boy who reported, when I said I was looking for work, no vacancies. When I got in at all, nearly all the city editors merely gave me a quick glance and said: "No vacancies." I began to feel that the newspaper world must be controlled by a secret cult or order until one lithe bony specimen with a pointed green shade over his eyes and dusty red hair looked at me much as an eagle might look at a pouter pigeon, and asked:

"Ever worked on a paper before?"

"No, sir."

"How do you know you can write?"

"I don't; but I think I could learn."

"Learn? Learn? We haven't time to teach anybody here! You better try one of the little papers—a trade paper, maybe, until you learn how—then come back," and he walked off.

This gave me at least a definite idea as to how I might begin, but just the same it did not get me a position.

Meanwhile, looking here and there and not finding anything, I decided, since I had had experience as a collector and must live while I was making my way into journalism, to return to this work and see if I might not in the meantime get a place as a reporter.

Having been previously employed by an easy-payment instalment house, I now sought out another, the Corbin Company, in Lake Street, not very far from the office of the firm for which I had previously worked. From this firm, having been hard pressed for a winter overcoat the preceding fall, I had abstracted or held out twenty-five dollars, intending to restore it. But before I had been able to manage that a slack up in the work occurred, due to the fact that wandering street agents sold less in winter than in summer, and

I had to confess that I was short in my account and was laid off.

The manager and owner, who had seemed to take a fancy to me, said nothing other than that I was making a mistake, taking the path that led to social hell. I do not recall that he even requested that the money be returned. But I was so nervous that I was convinced that some day, unless I returned the money, I should be arrested, and to avoid this I had written him a letter after leaving promising that I would pay up. He never even bothered to answer the letter, and I believe that if I had returned in the spring, paid the twenty-five dollars and asked for work he would have taken me on again. But I had no such thought in mind. I held myself disgraced forever and only wished to get clear of this sort of work. It was a vulture game at best, selling trash to the ignorant for twelve and fourteen times its value. Now that I was out of it I hated to return. I feared that the first thing my proposed employer would do would be to inquire of my previous employer, and that being informed of my stealing he would refuse to employ me.

With fear and trembling I inquired of the firm in Lake Street and was told that there was a place awaiting some one—"the right party." The manager wanted to know if I could give a bond for three hundred dollars; they had just had one collector arrested for stealing sixty dollars. I told him I thought I could and decided to explain the proposition to my father and obtain his advice since I knew little about how a bond was secured. When I learned that the bonding company investigated one's past, however, I was terrorized. My father, an honest, worthy and defiant German, on being told that a bond was required, scouted the idea with much vehemence. Why should any one want a bond from me? he demanded to know. Hadn't I worked for Mr. M—— in the same line? Couldn't they go there and find out? At thought of M—— I shook, and, rather than have an investigation, dropped the whole matter, deciding not to go near the place again.

But the manager, taken by my guileless look, I presume,

called one evening at our house. He had taken a fancy to me, he said; I looked to be honest and industrious; he liked the neighborhood I lived in. He proposed that I should go to one of the local bonding companies and get a three hundred dollar bond for ten dollars a year, his company paying for the bond out of my first week's salary, which was to be only twelve dollars to start with. This promised to involve explaining about M——, but I decided to go to the bonding company and refer only to two other men for whom I had worked and see what would happen. For the rest, I proposed to say that school and college life had filled my years before this. If trouble came over M—— I planned to run away.

But, to my astonishment and delight, my ruse worked admirably. The following Sunday afternoon my new manager called and asked me to report the following morning for work.

Oh, those singing days in the streets and parks and showplaces of Chicago, those hours when in bright or thick lowery weather I tramped the highways and byways dreaming chaotic dreams. I had all my afternoons to myself after one or two o'clock. The speed with which I worked and could walk would soon get me over the list of my customers, and then I was free to go where I chose. Spring was coming. I was only nineteen. Life was all before me, and the feel of plenty of money in my pocket, even if it did not belong to me, was comforting. And then youth, youth—that lilt and song in one's very blood! I felt as if I were walking on tinted clouds, among the highlands of the dawn.

How shall I do justice to this period, which for perfection of spirit, ease of soul, was the very best I had so far known? In the first place, because of months of exercise in the open air, my physical condition was good. I was certain to get somewhere in the newspaper world, or so I thought. The condition of our family was better than it had ever been in my time, for we four younger children were working steadily. Our home life, in spite of bickerings among several of my brothers and sisters, was still pleasing enough. Altogether we were prospering, and my father was looking forward to a day when all family debts would be paid and the soul of my mother, as well as his own when it passed over, could be freed from too prolonged torments in purgatory! For, as a Catholic, he believed that until all one's full debts here on earth were paid one's soul was held in durance on the other side.

For myself, life was at the topmost toss. I was like some bird poised on a high twig, teetering and fluttering and ready for flight. Again, I was like those flying hawks and buzzards that ride so gracefully on still wings above a summer landscape, seeing all the wonders of the world below. Again, I was like a song that sings itself, the spirit of happy music that by some freak of creation is able to rejoice in its own harmonies and rhythms. Joy was ever before me, the sense of some great adventure lurking just around the corner.

How I loved the tonic note of even the grinding wheels of the trucks and cars, the clang and clatter of cable and electric lines, the surge of vehicles in every street! The palls of heavy manufacturing smoke that hung low over the city like impending hurricanes; the storms of wintry snow or sleety rain; the glow of yellow lights in little shops at evening, mile after mile, where people were stirring and bustling over potatoes, flour, cabbages—all these things were the substance of songs, paintings, poems. I liked the sections where the women of the town were still, at noon, sleeping off the debauches of the preceding night, or at night were preparing for the gaudy make-believes of their midnight day. I liked those sections crowded with great black factories, stockyards, steel works, Pullman yards, where in the midst of Plutonian stress and clang men mixed or forged or joined or prepared those delicacies, pleasures and perfections for which the world buys and sells itself. Life was at its best here, its promise the most glittering. I liked those raw neighborhoods where in small, unpainted, tumbledown shanties set in grassless, canstrewn yards drunken and lecherous slatterns and brawlers were to be found mooning about in a hell of their own. And, for contrast, I liked those areas of great mansions set upon the great streets of the city in spacious lawns, where liveried servants stood by doors and carriages turned in at spacious gates and under heavy porte-cochères.

I think I grasped Chicago in its larger material if not in its more complicated mental aspects. Its bad was so deliciously bad, its good so very good, keen and succulent, reckless, inconsequential, pretentious, hopeful, eager, new. People cursed or raved or snarled—the more fortunate among them, but they were never heavy or dull or asleep. In some neighborhoods the rancidity of dirt, or the stark icy bleakness of poverty, fairly shouted, but they were never still, decaying pools of misery. On wide bleak stretches of prairie swept by whipping winds one could find men who were tanning dog or cat hides but their wives were buying yellow plush albums or red silk-shaded lamps or blue and green rugs on time, as I could personally testify. Churches with gaudy altars and services rose out of mucky masses of shanties and gas-tanks; saloons with glistening bars of colored glass and mirrors stood as the centers and clubs of drear, bleak masses of huts. There were vice districts and wealth districts hung with every enticing luxury that the wit of a commonplace or conventional mind could suggest. Such was Chicago.

In the vice districts I had been paid for shabby rugs and lamps, all shamelessly overpriced, by plump naked girls striding from bed to dresser to get a purse, and then offered certain favors for a dollar, or its equivalent—a credit on the contract slip. In the more exclusive neighborhoods I was sent around to a side entrance by comfortably dressed women who were too proud or too sly to have their neighbors know that they were buying on time. Black negresses leered at me from behind shuttered windows at noon; plump wives drew me into risqué situations on sight; death-bereaved weepers mourned over their late lost in my presence—and postponed paying me. But I liked the life. I was crazy about it. Chicago was like a great orchestra in a tumult of noble harmonies. I was like a guest at a feast, eating and drinking in a delirium of ecstasy.

CHAPTER IV

BUT if I was wrought up by the varying aspects of the city, I was equally wrought up by the delights of love, which came for the first time fully with the arrival of Alice. Was I in love with her? No, as I understand myself now. I doubt that I have ever been in love with any one, or with anything save life as a whole. Twice or thrice I have developed stirring passions but always there was a voice or thought within which seemed to say over and over, like a bell at sea: "What does it matter? Beauty is eternal. . . . Beauty will come again!" But this thing, *life*, this picture of effort, this colorful panorama of hope and joy and despair—that *did* matter! Beauty, like a tinkling bell, the tintings of the dawn, the whispering of gentle winds and waters in summer days and Arcadian places, was in everything and everywhere. Indeed the appeal of this local life was its relationship to eternal perfect beauty. That it should go! That never again, after a few years, might I see it more! That love should pass! That youth should pass! That in due time I should stand old and grizzled, contemplating with age-filmed eyes joys and wonders whose sting and color I could no longer feel or even remember—out on it for a damned tragedy and a mirthless joke!

Alice proved to be in love with me. She lived in a two-flat frame house in what was then the far middle-south section of the city, a region about Fifty-first and Halsted streets. Her foster-father was a railroad watchman, and had saved up a few thousand dollars by years of toil. This little apartment represented his expenditures plus her taste, such as it was: a simple little place, with red plush curtains shielding a pair of folding-doors which separated two large rooms front and back. There were lace curtains and white shades at the windows, a piano (a most soothing luxury for me to contemplate), and then store furniture: a red velvet settee, a red plush rocker, several other new badly designed chairs.

Quaint little soul! How cheery and dreamful and pulsating with life she was when I met her! Her suitor, as I afterwards came to know, was a phlegmatic man of thirty-five, who had found in her all that he desired and was eager to marry her, as he eventually did. He was wont to call regularly on Wednesday and Sunday evenings, taking her occasionally to a theater or to dinner downtown. When I arrived on the scene I must have disrupted all this, for after a time, because I manifested some opposition, leaving her no choice indeed, Wednesdays and Sundays became my evenings, and any others that I chose. Regardless of my numerous and no doubt asinine defects, she was in love with me and willing to accept me on my own terms.

Yes, Alice saw something she wanted and thought she could hold. She wanted to unite with me for this little span of existence, to go with me hand in hand into the ultimate nothingness. I think she was a poet in her way, but voiceless. When I called the first night she sat primly for a little while on one of her red chairs near the window, while I occupied a rocker. I had hung up my coat and hat with a flourish and had stood about for a while examining everything, with the purpose of estimating it and her. It all seemed cozy and pleasing enough and, curiously, I felt more at ease on this my first visit than I ever did at my Scotch maid's home. There her thrifty, cautious, religious though genial and well-meaning mother, her irritable blind uncle and her more attractive young sister disturbed and tended to alienate me. Here, for weeks and weeks, I never saw Alice's foster-parents. When finally I was introduced to them, they grated on me not at all. This first night she played a little on her piano, then on her banjo, and because she seemed especially charming to me I went over and stood behind her chair, deciding to take her face in my hands and kiss her. Perhaps a touch of remorse and in consequence a bit of indecision now swayed her, for she got up before I could do it. On the instant my assurance became less and yet my mood hardened, for I thought she was trifling with me. After the previous Sunday it seemed to me that she could do no less than permit me to embrace her. I was deciding that the evening was about to be a failure, when she came up behind me and said: "Don't you think it's rather nice across there, between those houses?"

Over the way a gap between peaked-roofed houses revealed a long stretch of prairie, now covered with snow, gas lamps flickering in orderly rows, an occasional frame house glowing in the distance.

"Yes," I admitted moodily.

"This is a funny neighborhood," she ventured. "People are always moving in and out in that row of houses over there."

"Are they?" I said, not very much interested now that I felt myself defeated. There was a silence and then she laid one hand on my arm.

"You're not mad at me, Dorse?" she asked, using a name which my sister had given me.

The sound of it on her lips, soft and pleading, moved me.

"Oh, no," I replied loftily. "Why should I be?"

"I was thinking that maybe I oughtn't to be doing this. There's been some one else up to now, you know."

"Yes."

"I guess I don't care for him any more or I wouldn't be doing what I am."

"I thought you cared for me. Why did you invite me down here?"

"Oh, Dorse, I do," she said, placing both her hands on my folded arms and looking up into my face with a kind of tenseness. "I know it isn't right but I can't help it. You have such nice hair and eyes, and you're so tall. Do you care for me at all?"

"Yes," I said, smiling cynically over my victory. "I think you're beautiful." I smoothed her cheek with one hand while I held her about the waist with the other.

We went over to the red settee and I took her in my arms

and held her and kissed her mouth and eyes and neck. She clung to me and laughed and told me bits about her work and her pompous floor-walker and her social companions, and even her fiancé. She danced for me when I asked her, doing a running overstep clog, sidewise to and fro, her skirts lifted to her shoetops. She was sweetly feminine, in no wise aggressive or bold. I stayed until nearly one in the morning. I had nine or ten miles to go by owl cars, arriving home at nearly three; but at this time I was not working and so my time was my own.

The thing that troubled me was what my Scotch girl would think if she found out (which she never would), and how I could extricate myself from a situation which, now that I had Alice, was not as interesting as it had been.

CHAPTER V

As spring approached this affair moved on apace. The work of the Corbin Company was no harder than that of the Lovell Company, and I had more time to myself. Because of an ingrowing sense of my personal importance and because I thought it such a wonderful thing to be a newspaper man and so very much less to be a collector, I lied to Alice as to what I was doing. When should I be through with collecting and begin reporting? I was eager to know all about music, painting, sculpture, literature, and to be in those places where life is at its best. I was regretful now that I had not made better use of my school and college days, and so in my free hours I read, visited the art gallery and library, went to theaters and concerts. The free intellectual churches, or ethical schools, were my favorite places on Sunday mornings. I would sometimes take Alice or my Scotch girl to the Theodore Thomas concerts, which were just beginning at the Auditorium, or to see the best plays and actors: Booth, Barrett, Modjeska, Fannie Davenport, Mary Anderson, Joseph Jefferson, Nat Goodwin. Thinking of myself as a man with a future, I assumed a kind of cavalier attitude toward my two sweethearts, finally breaking with N—— on the pretext that she was stubborn and superior and did not love me, whereas I really wanted to assume privileges which she, with her conventional notions, could not permit and which I was not generous enough not to want. As for Alice she was perfectly willing to yield, with a view, I have always thought, to moving me to marry her. But being deeply touched by her very obvious charm, I did nothing.

Once my work was done of an afternoon, I loitered over many things waiting for evening to come, when I should see Alice again. Usually I read or visited a gallery or some park. Alice was intensely sweet to me. Her eyes were so soft, so liquid, so unprotesting and so unresenting. She was usually gay, with at times a suggestion of hidden melancholy. At night, in that great world of life which is the business heart of Chicago I used to wait for her, and together, once we had found each other in the crowds, we would make our way to the great railway station at the end of Dearborn Street, where a tall clock-tower held a single yellow clock-face. If it chanced to be Tuesday or Thursday I would go home with her. On other nights she would sometimes stay down to dine with me at some inexpensive place.

I never knew until toward the end of the following summer, when things were breaking up for me in Chicago and seemingly greater opportunities were calling me elsewhere, that during all this time she had really never relinquished her relationship with my predecessor, fearing my instability perhaps. By what necessary lies and innocent subterfuges she had held him against the time when I might not care for her any more I know not. The thing has poignance now. Was she unfaithful? I do not think so. At any rate she was tender, clinging and in need of true affection. She would take my hand and hold it under her arm or against her heart and talk of the little things of the day: the strutting customers and managers, the condescending women of social pretensions, the other girls, who sometimes spied upon or traitorously betrayed each other. Usually her stories were of amusing things, for she had no heart for bitter contention. There was a note of melancholy running all through her relationship with me, however, for I think she saw the unrest and uncertainty of my point of view. Already my mind's eye was scanning a farther horizon, in which neither she nor any other woman had a vital part. Fame, applause, power, possibly, these were luring me. Once she said to me, her eyes looking longingly into mine:

"Do you really love me, Dorse?"

"Don't you think I do?" I replied evasively, and yet saying to myself that I truly cared for her in my fashion, which was true.

"Yes, I think you do, in your way," she said, and the

correct interpretation shocked me. I saw myself a stormy petrel hanging over the yellowish-black waves of life and never really resting anywhere. I could not; my mind would not let me. I saw too much, felt too much, knew too much. What was I, what any one, but a small bit of seaweed on an endless sea, flotsam, jetsam, being moved hither and thither—by what subterranean tides?

Oh, Alice, dead or living, eternally sleeping or eternally waking, listen to these few true words! You were beautiful to me. My heart was hungry. I wanted youth, I wanted beauty, I wanted sweetness, I wanted a tender smile, wide eyes, loveliness—all these you had and gave.

Peace to you! I do not ask as much for myself.

My determination to leave the Corbin Company was associated with other changes equally important and of much more emotional interest. Our home life, now that my mother was gone, was most unsatisfactory. What I took to be the airs and plotting domination of my sister M——, toward whom I had never borne any real affection, had become unbearable. I disliked her very much, for though she was no better than the rest of us, or so I thought at the time, she was nevertheless inclined to dogmatize as to the duty of others. Here she was, married yet living at home and traveling at such times and to such places as suited her husband's convenience, obtaining from him scarcely enough to maintain herself in the state to which she thought she was entitled, contributing only a small portion to the upkeep of the home, and yet setting herself and her husband up as superiors whose exemplary social manners might well be copied by all. Her whole manner from morning to night, day in and day out, was one of superiority. Or, so I thought at the time. "I am Mrs. G. A——, if you please," she seemed to say. "G—— is doing this. I am going to do so-and-so. It can scarcely be expected that we, in our high state, should have much to do with the rest of you."

Yet whenever A—— was in or near Chicago he made our home his abiding place. Two of the best rooms on the second floor were set aside for his and M——'s use. The most stirring preparations were made whenever he was coming, the house swept, flowers bought, extra cooking done and what not; the moment he had gone things fell to their natural and rather careless pace. M—— retired to her rooms and was scarcely seen for days. T——, another sister, who despised her heartily, would sulk, and when she thought the burden of family work was being shouldered on to her would do nothing at all. My father was left to go through a routine of duties such as fire-building, care of the furnace, marketing, which should have facilitated the housework but which in these quarreling conditions made it seem as if he were being put upon. C——, another sister, who was anything but a peacemaker, added fuel to the flames by criticizing the drift of things to the younger members: A——, E—— and myself.

The thing that had turned me definitely against M—— followed a letter which my brother Paul once sent to my mother, enclosing a check for ten dollars and intended especially for her. Because it was sent to her personally she wanted to keep it secret from the others, and to do this she sent me to the general postoffice, on which it was drawn, with her signature filled in and myself designated as the proper recipient. I got the money and returned it to her, but either because of her increasing illness or because she still wanted to keep it a secret, when Paul mentioned it in another letter she said she had not received it. Then she died and the matter of the money came up. It was proved by inquiry at the postoffice that the money had been paid to me. I confirmed this and asserted, which was true, that I had given it to mother. M—— alone, of all the family, felt called upon to question this. She visited an inspector at the general postoffice (a friend of A——'s by the way) and persuaded him to make inquiry, with a view no doubt to frightening me. The result of this was a formal letter asking me to call at his office. When I went and found that he was charging me with the detention of this money and demanding its return on pain of my being sent to prison, I blazed of course and told him to go to the devil. When I reached home I was furious. I called out my sister M—— and told her—well, many things.

For weeks and even months I had a burning desire to strike her, although nothing more was ever done or said concerning it. For over fifteen years the memory of this one thing divided us completely, but after that, having risen, as I thought, to superior interests and viewpoints, I condescended to become friendly.

The first half of 1891 was the period of my greatest bitterness toward her, and in consequence, when my sister C—— came to me with her complaints and charges we brewed between us a kind of revolution based primarily on our opposition to M—— and her airs, but secondarily on the inadequate distribution of the family means and the inability of the different sisters to agree upon the details of the home management. According to C——, who was most bitter in her charges, both M—— and T—— were lazy and indifferent. As a matter of fact, I cared as little for C—— and her woes as I did for any of the others. But the thought of this home, dominated by M—— and T—— and supported by us younger ones, with father as a kind of pleading watchdog of the treasury, weeping in his beard and moaning over the general recklessness of our lives, was too much.

Indeed this matter of money, not idleness or domination, was the crux of the whole situation, for if there had been plenty of money, or if each of us could have retained his own earnings, there would have been little grieving. C—— was jealous of M—— and T——, and of the means with which their marital relations supplied them, and although she was earning eight dollars a week she felt that the three or four which she contributed to the household were far too much. A——, who earned ten and contributed five, had no complaint to make, and E——, who earned nine and supplied four-and-a-half, also had nothing to say. I was earning twelve, later fourteen, and gave only six, and very often I begrudged much of this. So between us C—— and I brewed a revolution, which ended unsatisfactorily for us all.

Late in March, a crisis came because of a bitter quarrel that sprung up between M—— and C——. C—— and I now proposed, with the aid of A—— and E—— if we could get it, either to drive M—— from the house and take charge ourselves, or rent a small apartment somewhere, pool our funds and set up a rival home of our own, leaving this one to subsist as best it might. It was a hard and cold thing to plan, and I still wonder why I shared in it; but then it seemed plausible enough.

However that may be, this revolutionary program was worked out to a definite conclusion. With C—— as the whip and planner and myself as general executive, a small apartment only a few blocks from our home was fixed upon, prices of furniture on time studied, cost of food, light, entertainment gone into. C——, in her eagerness to bring her rage to a cataclysmic conclusion, volunteered to do the cooking and housekeeping alone, and still work downtown as before. If each contributed five dollars a week, as we said, we would have a fund of over eighty dollars a month, which should house and feed us and buy furniture on the instalment plan. A—— was consulted as to this and refused, saying, which was the decent thing to say and characteristic of him, that we ought to stay here and keep the home together for father's sake, he being old and feeble. E——, always a lover of adventure and eager to share in any new thing, agreed to go with us. We had to revise our program, but even with only sixty dollars a month as a general fund we thought we could get along.

And so we three, C—— being the spokesman, had the cheek to announce to my father that either M—— should leave and allow us to run the house as we wished or we would leave. The ultimatum was not given in any such direct way: charges and counter charges were first made; long arguments and pleadings were indulged in by one side and the other. Finally, seeing that there was no hope of forcing M—— to leave, C—— announced that she was going, alone or with others. I said I would follow. E—— said he was coming— and there you were. I never saw a man more distressed than my father, one more harassed by what he knew to be the final dissolution of the family. He pleaded, but his pleas fell on youthful, inconsiderate ears. I went and rented the flat, had the gas turned on and some furniture installed; and then, toward the end of March, in blustery weather, we moved.

Never was a man more distrait than my father during these last two or three days of our stay. Having completed the details, C——, E—— and I were busy marching to and fro at spare moments, carrying clothes, books, pictures and the like to the new home. There were open squabbles now between C—— and M—— as to the possession of certain things, but these were finally adjusted without blows. At last we were ready to leave, and then came our last adieux to my father and A——. When my turn came I marched out with a hard, cheery, independent look on my face, but I was really heavy with a sense of my unfairness and brutality. A—— and my father were the two I really preferred. My father was so old and frail.

"Well," he said with his German accent when I came to say good-by, "you're going, are you? I'm sorry, Dorsch. I done the best I could. The girls, they won't ever agree, it seems. I try, but it don't seem to do any good. I have prayed these last few days. . . . I hope you don't ever feel sorry. It's C—— who stirs up all these things."

He waved his hands in a kind of despairing way and after some pointless and insincere phrases I went out. The cold March winds were blowing from the West, and it was raw, blowy, sloppy, gray. Tomorrow it would be brighter, but tonight——

CHAPTER VI

As April advanced I left the Corbin Company, determined to improve my condition. I was tired of collecting—the same districts, the same excuses, innocences, subterfuges. By degrees I had come to feel a great contempt for the average mind. So many people were so low, so shifty, so dirty, so nondescript. They were food for dreams; little more. Owing to my experience with the manager of the Lovell Company in the matter of taking what did not belong to me I had become very cautious, and this meant that I should be compelled to live from week to week on my miserable twelve dollars.

In addition, home life had become a horrible burden. The house was badly kept and the meals were wretched. Being of a quarrelsome, fault-finding disposition and not having M—— or T—— to fight with, C—— now turned her attentions to E—— and myself. We did not do this and that; the burden of the work was left to her. By degrees I grew into a kind of servant. Being told one April Friday of some needs that I must supply, and having decided that I could not endure either this abode or my present work, I took my fate in my hands and the next day resigned my job, having in my possession sixty-five dollars. I was now determined, come what might, never to take another job except one of reporting unless I was actually driven to it by starvation, and in this mood I came home and announced that I had lost my position and that this "home" would therefore have to be given up. And how glad I was! Now I should be rid of this dull flat, which was so colorless and burdensome. As I see it now, my sister sensibly enough from her point of view, perhaps, was figuring that E—— and I, as dutiful brothers, should support her while she spent all her money on clothes. I came to dislike her almost as much as I did M——, and told her gladly this same day that we could not live here any longer. In consequence the furniture company was notified to come and get the furniture. Our lease of the place being only from month to month, it was easy enough to depart at once. E—— and I were to share a room at the de G——s for a dollar and a half a week each, such meals as I ate there to be paid for at the rate of twenty-five cents each.

Then and there, as I have since noted with a kind of fatalistic curiosity, the last phase of my rather troublesome youth began. Up to and even including this last move to Taylor Street I had been intimately identified, in spirit at least, with our family and its concentrated home life. During my mother's life, of course, I had felt that wherever she was was home; after her death it was the house in which she had lived that held me, quite as much as it was my father and those of us who remained together to keep up in some manner the family spirit. When the spell of this began to lessen, owing to bitter recrimination and the continuous development of individuality in all of us, this new branch home established by three of us seemed something of the old place and spiritually allied to it; but when it fell, and the old home broke up at about the same time, I felt completely adrift.

What was I to do with myself now? I asked. Where go? Here I was, soon (in three months) to be twenty-one years old, and yet without trade or profession, a sort of nondescript dreamer without the power to earn a decent living and yet with all the tastes and proclivities of one destined to an independent fortune. My eyes were constantly fixed on people in positions far above my own. Those who interested me most were bankers, millionaires, artists, executives, leaders, the real rulers of the world. Just at this time the nation was being thrown into its quadrennial ferment, the presidential election. The newspapers were publishing reams upon reams of information and comment. David B. Hill, then governor of New York, Grover Cleveland of New York, Thomas B. Hendricks of Indiana, and others were being widely and favorably discussed by the Democratic party, whose convention was to be held here in Chicago the coming June.

(33)

Among the Republicans, Benjamin Harrison of Indiana, James G. Blaine of Maine, Thomas B. Allison of Iowa, and others were much to the fore.

If by my devotion to minor matters I have indicated that I was not interested in public affairs I have given an inadequate account of myself. It is true that life at close range fascinated me, but the general progress of Europe and America and Asia and Africa was by no means beyond my intellectual inquiry. By now I was a reader of Emerson, Carlyle, Macaulay, Froude, John Stuart Mill and others. The existence of Nietzsche in Germany, Darwin, Spencer, Wallace and Tyndall in England, and what they stood for, was in part at least within the range of my intuition, if not my exact knowledge. In America, Washington, Jefferson, Jackson, Lincoln, the history of the Civil War and the subsequent drift of the nation to monopoly and so to oligarchy, were all within my understanding and private philosophizing.

And now this national ferment in regard to political preferment and advancement, the swelling tides of wealth and population in Chicago, the upward soaring of names and fames, stirred me like whips and goads. I wanted to get up— oh, how eagerly! I wanted to shake off the garments of the commonplace in which I seemed swathed and step forth into the public arena, where I should be seen and understood for what I was. "No common man am I," I was constantly saying to myself, and I would no longer be held down to this shabby world of collecting in which I found myself. The newspapers —the newspapers—somehow, by their intimacy with everything that was going on in the world, seemed to be the swiftest approach to all this of which I was dreaming. It seemed to me as if I understood already all the processes by which they were made. Reporting, I said to myself, must certainly be easy. Something happened—one car ran into another; a man was shot; a fire broke out; the reporter ran to the scene, observed or inquired the details, got the names and addresses of those immediately concerned, and then described it all. To reassure myself on this point I went about looking for accidents on my own account, or imagining them, and then wrote out what I saw or imagined. To me the result, compared with what I found in the daily papers, was quite satisfactory. Some paper must give me a place.

CHAPTER VII

PICTURE a dreamy cub of twenty-one, long, spindling, a pair of gold-framed spectacles on his nose, his hair combed *à la pompadour,* a new spring suit consisting of light check trousers and bright blue coat and vest, a brown fedora hat, new yellow shoes, starting out to force his way into the newspaper world of Chicago. At that time, although I did not know it, Chicago was in the heyday of its newspaper prestige. Some of the nation's most remarkable editors, publishers and newspaper writers were at work there: Melville E. Stone, afterward general manager of the Associated Press; Victor F. Lawson, publisher of the *Daily News;* Joseph Medill, editor and publisher of the *Tribune;* Eugene Field, managing editor of the *Morning Record;* William Penn Nixon, editor and publisher of the *Inter-Ocean;* George Ade; Finley Peter Dunne; Brand Whitlock; and a score of others subsequently to become well known.

Having made up my mind that I must be a newspaper man, I made straight for the various offices at noon and at six o'clock each day to ask if there was anything I could do. Very soon I succeeded in making my way into the presence of the various city and managing editors of all the papers in Chicago, with the result that they surveyed me with the cynical fishy eye peculiar to newspaper men and financiers and told me there was nothing.

One day in the office of the *Daily News* a tall, shambling, awkward-looking man in a brown flannel shirt, without coat or waistcoat, suspenders down, was pointed out to me by an office boy who saw him slipping past the city editorial door.

"Wanta know who dat is?" he asked.

"Yes," I replied humbly, grateful even for the attention of office boys.

"Well, dat's Eugene Field. Heard o' him, ain'tcha?"

"Sure," I said, recalling the bundle of incoherent MS. which I had once thrust upon him. I surveyed his retreating figure with envy and some nervousness, fearing he might psychically detect that I was the perpetrator of that unsolicited slush and abuse me then and there.

In spite of my energy, manifested for one solid week between the hours of twelve and two at noon and five-thirty and seven at night I got nothing. Indeed it seemed to me as I went about these newspaper offices that they were the strangest, coldest, most haphazard and impractical of places. Gone was that fine ambassadorial quality with which a few months before I had invested them. These rooms, as I now saw, were crowded with commonplace desks and lamps, the floors strewn with newspapers. Office boys and hirelings gazed at you in the most unfriendly manner, asked what you wanted and insisted that there was nothing—they who knew nothing. By office boys I was told to come after one or two in the afternoon or after seven at night, when all assignments had been given out, and when I did so I was told that there was nothing and would be nothing. I began to feel desperate.

Just about this time I had an inspiration. I determined that, instead of trying to see all of the editors each day and missing most of them at the vital hour, I would select one paper and see if in some way I could not worm myself into the good graces of its editor. I now had the very sensible notion that a small paper would probably receive me with more consideration than one of the great ones, and out of them all chose the *Daily Globe,* a struggling affair financed by one of the Chicago politicians for political purposes only.

You have perhaps seen a homeless cat hang about a doorstep for days and days meowing to be taken in: that was I. The door in this case was a side door and opened upon an alley. Inside was a large, bare room filled with a few rows of tables set end to end, with a railing across the northern one-fourth, behind which sat the city editor, the dramatic and sporting editors, and one editorial writer. Outside this railing, near the one window, sat a large, fleshy gelatinous, round-faced round-headed young man wearing gold-rimmed spectacles.

He had a hard, keen, cynical eye, and at first glance seemed to be most vitally opposed to me and everybody else. As it turned out, he was the *Daily Globe's* copy-reader. Nothing was said to me at first as I sat in my far corner waiting for something to turn up. By degrees some of the reporters began to talk to me, thinking I was a member of the staff, which eased my position a little during this time. I noticed that as soon as all the reporters had gone the city editor became most genial with the one editorial writer, who sat next him, and the two often went off together for a bite.

Parlous and yet delicious hours! Although I felt all the time as though I were on the edge of some great change, still no one seemed to want me. The city editor, when I approached after all the others had gone, would shake his head and say: "Nothing today. There's not a thing in sight," but not roughly or harshly, and therein lay my hope. So here I would sit, reading the various papers or trying to write out something I had seen. I was always on the alert for some accident that I might report to this city editor in the hope that he had not seen it, but I encountered nothing.

The ways of advancement are strange, so often purely accidental. I did not know it, but my mere sitting here in this fashion eventually proved a card in my favor. A number of the employed reporters, of whom there were eight or nine (the best papers carried from twenty to thirty), seeing me sit about from twelve to two and thinking I was employed here also, struck up occasional genial and enlightening conversations with me. Reporters rarely know the details of staff arrangements or changes. Some of them, finding that I was only seeking work, ignored me; others gave me a bit of advice. Why didn't I see Selig of the *Tribune*, or Herbst of the *Herald*? It was rumored that staff changes were to be made there. One youth learning that I had never written a line for a newspaper, suggested that I go to the editor of the City Press Association or the United Press, where the most inexperienced beginners were put to work at the rate of eight dollars a week. This did not suit me at all. I felt that I could write.

Finally, however, my mere sitting about in this fashion brought me into contact with that copy-reader I have described, John Maxwell, who remarked one day out of mere curiosity:

"Are you doing anything special for the *Globe?*"

"No," I replied.

"Just looking for work?"

"Yes."

"Ever work on any paper?"

"No."

"How do you know you can write?"

"I don't. I just feel that I can. I want to see if I can't get a chance to try."

He looked at me, curiously, amusedly, cynically.

"Don't you ever go around to the other papers?"

"Yes, after I find out there's nothing here."

He smiled. "How long have you been coming here like this?"

"Two weeks."

"Every day?"

"Every day."

He laughed now, a genial, rolling, fat laugh.

"Why do you pick the *Globe?* Don't you know it's the poorest paper in Chicago?"

"That's why I pick it," I replied innocently. "I thought I might get a chance here."

"Oh, you did!" he laughed. "Well, you may be right at that. Hang around. You may get something. Now I'll tell you something: this National Democratic Convention will open in June. They'll have to take on a few new men here then. I can't see why they shouldn't give you a chance as well as anybody else. But it's a hell of a business to be wanting to get into," he added.

He began taking off his coat and waistcoat, rolling up his sleeves, sharpening his blue pencils and taking up stacks of copy. The while I merely stared at him. Every now and then he would look at me through his round glasses as though I were some strange animal. I grew restless and went out.

But after that he greeted me each day in a friendly way, and because he seemed inclined to talk I stayed and talked with him.

What it was that finally drew us together in a minor bond of friendship I have never been able to discover. I am sure he considered me of little intellectual or reportorial import and yet also I gathered that he liked me a little. He seemed to take a fancy to me from the moment of our first conversation and included me in what I might call the *Globe* family spirit. He was interested in politics, literature, and the newspaper life of Chicago. Bit by bit he informed me as to the various editors, who were the most successful newspaper men, how some reporters did police, some politics, and some just general news. From him I learned that every paper carried a sporting editor, a society editor, a dramatic editor, a political man. There were managing editors, Sunday editors, news editors, city editors, copy-readers and editorial writers, all of whom seemed to me marvelous—men of the very greatest import. And they earned—which was more amazing still —salaries ranging from eighteen to thirty-five and even sixty and seventy dollars a week. From him I learned that this newspaper world was a seething maelstrom in which clever men struggled and fought as elsewhere; that some rose and many fell; that there was a roving element among newspaper men that drifted from city to city, many drinking themselves out of countenance, others settling down somewhere into some fortunate berth. Before long he told me that only recently he had been copy-reader on the Chicago *Times* but due to what he characterized as "office politics," a term the meaning of which I in no wise grasped, he had been jockeyed out of his place. He seemed to think that by and large newspaper men while interesting and in some cases able, were tricky and shifty and above all, disturbingly and almost heartlessly inconsiderate of each other. Being young and inexperienced this point of view made no impression on me whatsoever. If I thought anything I thought that he must be wrong, or that, at any rate, this heartlessness would never trouble me in any way, being the live and industrious person that I was.

CHAPTER VIII

It made me happy to know that whether or not I was taken on I had at least achieved one friend at court. Maxwell advised me to stick.

"You'll get on," he said a day or two later. "I believe you've got the stuff in you. Maybe I can help you. You'll probably be like every other damned newspaper man once you get a start: an ingrate; but I'll help you just the same. Hang around. That convention will begin in three or four weeks now. I'll speak a good word for you, unless you tie up with some other paper before then."

And to my astonishment really, he was as good as his word. He must have spoken to the city editor soon after this, for the latter asked me what I had been doing and told me to hang around in case something should turn up.

But before a newspaper story appeared for me to do a new situation arose which tied me up closer with this prospect than I had hoped for. The lone editorial writer previously mentioned, a friend and intimate of the city editor, had just completed a small work of fiction which he and the city editor in combination had had privately printed, and which they were very eager to sell. It was, as I recall it, very badly done, an immature imitation of *Tom Sawyer* without any real charm or human interest. The author himself, Mr. Gissel, was a picayune yellow-haired person. He spent all his working hours, as I came to know, writing those biased, envenomed and bedeviling editorials which are required by purely partisan journals. I gathered as much from conversations that were openly carried on before me between himself and the city editor, the managing editor and an individual who I later learned was the political man. They were "out" as I heard the managing editor say, one day "to get" some one—on orders from some individual of whom at that time I knew nothing, and Mr. Gissel was your true henchman or editorial mercenary, a "peanut" or "squeak" writer, penning what he was ordered to pen. Once I understood I despised him but at first he amused me though I could not like him. Whenever he had concocted some particularly malicious or defaming line as I learned in time, he would get up and dance about, chortling and cackling in a disconcerting way. So for the first time I began to see how party councils and party tendencies were manufactured or twisted or belied, and it still further reduced my estimate of humanity. Men, as I was beginning to find— all of us—were small, irritable, nasty in their struggle for existence. This little editor, for instance, was not interested in the Democratic party (which this paper was supposed to represent), or indeed in party principles of any kind. He did not believe what he wrote, but, receiving forty dollars a week, he was anxious to make a workmanlike job of it. Just at this time he was engaged in throwing mud at the national Republican administration, the mayor and the governor, as well as various local politicians, whom the owner of the paper wished him to attack.

What a pitiful thing journalism or our alleged "free press" was, I then and there began to gather—dimly enough at first I must admit. What a shabby compound of tricky back-room councils, public professions, all looking to public favors and fames which should lead again to public contracts and financial emoluments! Journalism, like politics, as I was now soon to see, was a slough of muck in which men were raking busily and filthily for what their wretched rakes might uncover in the way of financial, social, political returns. I looked at this dingy office and then at this little yellow-haired rat of an editor one afternoon as he worked, and it came to me what 'a desperately subtle and shifty thing life was. Here he was, this little runt, scribbling busily, and above him were strong, dark, secretive men, never appearing publicly perhaps but paying him his little salary privately, dribbling it down to him through a publisher and an editor-in-chief and a managing editor, so that he might be kept busy misconstruing, lying, intellectually cheating.

But the plan he had in regard to his book: The graduating class of the Hyde Park High School, of which he had been a member a few years before, had numbered about three hundred students. Of these two hundred were girls, one hundred and fifty of whom he claimed to have known personally. One afternoon as I was preparing to leave after all the assignments had been given out, the city editor called me over and, with the help of this scheming little editorial writer, began to explain to me a plan by which, if I carried it out faithfully, I could connect myself with the *Daily Globe* as a reporter. I was to take a certain list of names and addresses and as many copies of *The Adventures of Harry Munn,* or some such name, as I could carry and visit each of these quondam schoolmates of Mr. Gissel at their homes, where I was to recall to their minds that he was an old schoolmate of theirs, that this his first book related to scenes with which they were all familiar, and then persuade them if possible to buy a copy for one dollar. My reward for this was to be ten cents a copy on all copies sold, and in addition (and this was the real bait) I was to have a tryout on the *Globe* as a reporter at fifteen dollars a week if I succeeded in selling one hundred and twenty copies within the next week or so.

I took the list and gathered up an armful of the thin cloth-covered volumes, fired by the desire thus to make certain my entrance into the newspaper world. I cannot say that I was very much pleased with my mission, but my necessity or aspiration was so great that I was glad to do it just the same. I was nervous and shamefaced as I approached the first home on my list, and I suffered aches and pains in my vanity and my sense of the fitness of things. The only salve I could find in the whole thing was that Mr. Gissel actually knew these people and that I could say I came personally from him as a friend and fellow-member of the *Globe* staff. It was a thin subterfuge, but apparently it went down with a few of those pretty unsophisticated girls. The majority of them lived in the best residences of the south side, some of them mansions of the truly rich whose democratic parents had insisted upon sending their children to the local high school. In each case, upon inquiring for a girl, with the remark that I came from Mr. Gissel of the *Globe*, I was received in the parlor or reception-room and told to wait. Presently the girl would come bustling in and listen to my tactful story, smiling contemptuously perhaps at my shabby mission or opening her eyes in surprise or curiosity.

"Mr. Gissel? Mr. Gissel?" said one girl inquiringly. "Why, I don't recall any such person——" and she retired, leaving me to make my way out as best I might.

Another exclaimed: "Harry Gissel! Has that little snip written a book? The nerve—to send you around to sell his book! Why do you do it? I will take one, because I am curious to see the kind of thing he has done, but I'll wager right now it's as silly as he is. He's invented some scheme to get you to do this because he knows he couldn't sell the book in any other way."

Others remembered him and seemed to like him; others bought the book only because he was a member of their class. Some struck up a genial conversation with me.

In spite of my distress at having to do this work there were compensations. It gave me a last fleeting picture of that new, sunny prosperity which was the most marked characteristic of Chicagoans of that day, and contrasted so sharply with the scenes of poverty which I had recently seen. In this region, for it was June, newly fledged collegians, freshly returned from the colleges of the East and Europe, were disporting themselves about the lawns and within the open-windowed chambers of the houses. Traps and go-carts of many of the financially and socially elect filled the south side streets. The lawn tennis suit, the tennis game, the lawn party and the family croquet game were everywhere in evidence. The new-rich and those most ambitious financially at that time were peculiarly susceptible I think to the airs and manners of the older and more pretentious regions of the world. They were bent upon interpreting their new wealth in terms of luxury as they had observed it elsewhere. Hence these strutting youths in English suits with turned-up trousers, swagger sticks and flori-colored ties and socks intended to suggest the spirit of London, as they imagined it to be; hence the high-headed girls in flouncy, lacy dresses, their cheeks and eyes bright with color, who no doubt imagined themselves to be great ladies, and who carried themselves with an air of remote disdain. The whole thing had the quality of a play well staged: really the houses, the lawns, the movements of the people, their games and interests all harmonizing after the fashion of a play. They saw this as a great end in itself, which, perhaps, it is. To me in my life-hungry, love-hungry state, this new-rich prosperity with its ease, its pretty women and its effort at refinement was quite too much. It set me to riotous dreaming and longing made me ache to lounge and pose after this same fashion.

CHAPTER IX

In due course of time, I having performed my portion of the contract, it became the duty of the two editors to fulfill their agreement with me. Every day for ten days I had been turning in the cash for from five to fifteen books, thereby establishing my reputation for industry and sobriety. Mr. Gissel was very anxious to know at the end of each day whom I had seen and how the mention of his name was received. Instead of telling him of the many who laughed or sniffed or bought to get rid of me gracefully, I gave him flattering reports. Lately, by way of reward I presume, he had taken to reading to me the cleverest passages in his editorials. Mr. Sullivan, the city editor, confided to me one day that he was from a small town in central Illinois not unlike the Warsaw from which I hailed, and which I then roughly and jestingly sketched to him, and from then on we were on fairly good terms. He dug up a number of poems and granted me the favor of reading them. Some of them were almost as good as similar ones by Whittier and Bryant, after whom they were obviously modeled. Today I know them to be bad, or mediocre; then I thought they were excellent and grieved to think that any one should be going to make a reputation as a great poet, while I, the only real poet extant (although I had done nothing as yet to prove it), remained unrecognized.

I did not know until later that I might not have secured a place even now, so numerous were the applications of clever and experienced newspaper men, had it not been for the influence of my friend Maxwell. For one reason or another, my errant youth perhaps, my crazy persistence and general ignorance of things journalistic, he had become interested in me and seemed fairly anxious to see me get a start. Out of the tail of his eye he had been watching. When I arrived of an evening and there was no one present he sometimes inquired what I was doing, and by degrees, although I had been cautioned not to tell, he extracted the whole story of Gissel's book. I even loaned him a copy of the book, which he read and pronounced rot, adding: "They ought to be ashamed of themselves, sending you out on a job of this kind. You're better than that."

As the end of my task drew near and I was dreading another uncertain wait, he put in a good word for me. But even then I doubt if I should have had a trial had it not been for the convention which was rapidly drawing near. On the day the newspapers were beginning to chronicle the advance arrival of various leaders from all parts of the country, I was taken on at fifteen dollars a week, for a week or two anyhow, and assigned to watch the committee rooms in the hotels Palmer, Grand Pacific, Auditorium and Richelieu. There was another youth who was set to work with me on this, and he gave me some slight instruction. Over us was the political man, who commanded other men in different hotels and whose presence I had only noted when the convention was nearly over.

If ever a youth was cast adrift and made to realize that he knew nothing at all about the thing he was so eager to do, that youth was I. "Cover the hotels for political news," were my complete instructions, but what the devil was political news? What did they want me to do, say, write? At once I was thoroughly terrified by this opportunity which I had so eagerly sought, for now that I had it I did not know how to make anything clear.

For the first day or two or three therefore I wandered like a lost soul about the corridors and parlor floors and "committee rooms" of these hotels which I was supposed to cover, trying to find out where the committee rooms were, who and what were the men in them, what they were trying to do. No one seemed to want to tell me anything, and, as dull as it may seem, I really could not guess. I had no clear idea of what was meant by the word "politics" as locally used. Various country congressmen and politicians brushed past me in a most secretive manner; when I hailed them with the information that I was from the *Globe* they waved me off with: "I am only a delegate; you can't get anything out of me. See the chairman.'' Well, what was a chairman? I didn't know. I did not even know that there had been lists published in all the papers, my own included, giving the information which I was so anxiously seeking!

I had no real understanding of politics or party doings or organization. I doubt if I knew how men came to be nominated, let alone elected. I did not know who were the various State leaders, who the prospective candidates, why one candidate might be preferred to another. The machinations of such an institution as Tammany Hall, or the things called property interests, were as yet beyond me. My mind was too much concerned with the poetry of life to busy itself with such minor things as politics. However, I did know that there was a bitter feud on between David Bennett Hill, governor of New York, and Grover Cleveland, ex-President of the United States, both candidates for nomination on the Democratic ticket, and that the Tammany organization of New York City was for Hill and bitterly opposed to Cleveland. I also knew that the South was for any good Southerner as opposed to Cleveland or Hill, and that a new element in the party was for Richard Bland, better known as "Silver Dick," of Missouri. I also knew by reputation many of the men who had been in the first Cleveland administration.

Imagine a raw youth with no knowledge of the political subtleties of America trying to gather even an inkling of what was going on! The nation and the city were full of dark political trafficking, but of it all I was as innocent as a baby. The bars and lobbies were full of inconsequential spouting delegates, who drank, swore, sang and orated at the top of their lungs. Swinging Southerners and Westerners in their long frock-coats and wide-brimmed hats amused me. They were forever pulling their whiskers or mustachios, drinking, smoking, talking or looking solemn or desperate. In many cases they knew no more of what was going on than I did. I was told to watch the movements of Benjamin Ryan Tillman, senator from South Carolina, and report any conclusions or rumors of conclusions as to how his delegation would vote. I had a hard time finding where his committee was located, and where and when if ever it deliberated, but once I identified my man I never left him. I dogged his steps so persistently that he turned on me one afternoon as he was going out of the Palmer House, fixed me with his one fiery eye and said:

"Young man, what do you want of me anyhow?"

"Well, you're Senator Tillman, aren't you?"

"Yes, sir. I'm Senator Tillman."

"Well, I'm a reporter from the *Globe*. I've been told to learn what conclusions your delegation has reached as to how it will vote."

"You and your editor of the *Globe* be damned!" he replied irritably. "And I want you to quit following me wherever I go. Just now I'm going for my laundry, and I have some rights to privacy. The committee will decide when it's good and ready, and it won't tell the *Globe* or any other paper. Now you let me alone. Follow somebody else."

I went back to the office the first evening at five-thirty and sat down to write, with the wild impression in my mind that I must describe the whole political situation not only in Chicago but in the nation. I had no notion that there was a supervising political man who, in conjunction with the managing editor and editor-in-chief, understood all about current political conditions.

"The political pot," I began exuberantly, "was already beginning to seethe yesterday. About the lobbies and corridors of the various hotels hundreds upon hundreds of the vanguard of American Democracy—etc., etc."

I had not scrawled more than eight or nine pages of this mush before the city editor, curious as to what I had discovered and wondering why I had not reported it to him, came over and picked up the many sheets which I had turned face down.

"No, no, no!" he exclaimed. "You mustn't write on both sides of the paper! Don't you know that? For heaven's sake. And all this stuff about the political pot boiling is as old as the hills. Why, every country jake paper for thousands of miles East and West has used it for years and years. You're not to write the general stuff. Here, Maxwell, see if you can't find out what Dreiser has discovered and show him what to do with it. I haven't got time." And he turned me over to my gold-spectacled mentor, who eyed me very severely. He sat down and examined my copy with knitted brows. He had a round, meaty, cherubic face which seemed all the more ominous because he could scowl fiercely, and his eyes could blaze with a cold, examining, mandatory glance.

"This is awful stuff!" he said as he read the first page. "He's quite right. You want to try and remember that you're not the editor of this paper and just consider yourself a plain reporter sent out to cover some hotels. Now where'd you go today?"

I told him.

"What'd you see?"

I described as best I could the whirling world in which I had been.

"No, no! I don't mean that! That might be good for a book or something but it's not news. Did you see any particular man? Did you find out anything in connection with any particular committee?"

I confessed that I had tried and failed.

"Very good!" he said. "You haven't anything to write," and he tore up my precious nine pages and threw them into the waste basket. "You'd better sit around here now until the city editor calls you," he added. "He may have something special he wants you to do. If not, watch the hotels for celebrities—Democratic celebrities—or committee meetings, and if you find any try to find out what's going on. The great thing is to discover beforehand who's going to be nominated—see? You can't tell from talking to four or five people, but what you find out may help some one else to piece out what is to happen. When you come back, see me. And unless you get other orders, come back by eleven. And call up two or three times between the time you go and eleven."

Because of these specific instructions I felt somewhat encouraged, although my first attempt at writing had been thrown into the waste basket. I sat about until nearly seven, when I was given an address and told to find John G. Carlisle, ex-Secretary of the Treasury, and see if I could get an interview with him. Failing this, I was to "cover" the Grand Pacific, Palmer House and Auditorium, and report all important arrivals and delegations.

Even if I had secured the desired interview I am sure I should have made an awful botch of it, but fortunately I could not get it. Only one thing of importance developed for me during the evening, and that was the presence of a Democratic United States Supreme Court Justice at the Grand Pacific who, upon being intercepted by me as he was going to his room for the night and told that I was from the *Globe*, eyed me genially and whimsically.

"My boy," he said, "you're just a young new reporter, I can see that. Otherwise you wouldn't waste your time on me. But I like reporters: I was one myself years ago. Now this hotel and every other is full of leaders and statesmen discussing this question of who's to be President. I'm not discussing it, first of all because it wouldn't become a Justice of the United States Supreme Court to do so, and in the next place because I don't have to: my position is for life. I'm just stopping here for one day on my way to Denver. You'd better go around to these committee rooms and see if they can't tell you something," and, smiling and laying one hand on my shoulder in a fatherly way, he dismissed me.

"My!" I thought. "What a fine thing it is to be a reporter! All I have to do is to say I'm from the *Globe* and even a Justice of the United States Supreme Court is smiling and agreeable to me!"

I hurried to a phone to tell Maxwell, and he said: "He don't count. Write a stick of it if you want to, and I'll look it over."

"How much is a stick?" I asked eagerly and curiously.

"About a hundred and fifty words."

So much for a United States Supreme Court Justice in election days.

CHAPTER X

I CANNOT say that I discovered anything of import this night or the next or the next, although I secured various interviews which, after much wrestling with my spirit and some hard, intelligent, frank statements from my friend, were whipped into shape for fillers.

"The trouble with you, Dreiser," said Maxwell as I was trying to write out what the Supreme Court Justice had said to me, "is that you haven't any training and you're trying to get it now when we haven't the time. Over in the *Tribune* office they have a sign which reads: WHO OR WHAT? HOW? WHEN? WHERE? All those things have to be answered in the first paragraph—not in the last paragraph, or the middle paragraph, but in the first. Now come here. Gimme that stuff," and he cut and hacked, running thick lines of blue lead through my choicest thoughts and restating in a line or two all that I thought required ten. A sardonic smile played about his fat mouth, and I saw by his twinkling eyes that he felt that it was good for me.

"News is information," he went on as he worked. "People want it quick, sharp, clear—do you hear? Now you probably think I'm a big stiff, chopping up your great stuff like this, but if you live and hold this job you'll thank me. As a matter of fact, if it weren't for me you wouldn't have this job now. Not one copy-reader out of a hundred would take the trouble to show you," and he looked at me with hard, cynical and yet warm gray eyes.

I was wretched with the thought that I should be dropped once the convention was over, and so I bustled here and there, anxious to find something. Of a morning, from six o'clock until noon, I studied all the papers, trying to discover what all this fanfare was about and just what was expected of me. The one great thing to find out was who was to be nominated and which delegations or individuals would support the successful candidate. Where could I get the information? The third day I talked to Maxwell about it, and as a favor he brought out a paper in which a rough augury was made which showed that the choice lay between David Bennett Hill and Grover Cleveland, with a third man, Senator McEntee, as a dark horse. Southern sentiment seemed to be centering about him, and in case no agreement could be reached by the New York delegation as to which of its two opposing candidates it would support their vote might be thrown to this third man.

Of course this was all very confusing to me. I did my best to get it straight. Learning that the Tammany delegation, two thousand strong, was to arrive from New York this same day and that the leaders were to be quartered at the Auditorium, I made my way there, determined to obtain an interview with no less a person than Richard Croker, who, along with Bourke Cochran, and a hard-faced, beefy individual by the name of John F. Carroll seemed to be the brains and mouthpiece of the Tammany organization. In honor of their presence, the Auditorium was decorated with flags and banners, some of them crossed with tomahawks or Indian feathers. Above the onyx-lined bar was a huge tiger with a stiff projecting tail which when pulled downward, as it was every few seconds by one bartender and another, caused the *papier mâché* image to emit a deep growl. This delighted the crowd, and after each growl there was another round of drinks. Red-faced men in silk hats and long frockcoats slapped each other on the back and bawled out their joy or threats or prophecies.

On the first floor above the office of the hotel, were Richard Croker, his friend and adviser, Carroll, and Bourke Cochran. They sat in the center of a great room on a huge red plush divan, receiving and talking.

As a representative of the *Globe,* a cheap nickel star fastened to one of the lapels of my waistcoat and concealed by my coat, my soul stirred by being allowed to mingle in affairs of great import, I finally made my way to the footstool of this imposing group and ventured to ask for an interview with

Croker himself. The great man, short, stocky, carefully, almost too carefully, dressed, his face the humanized replica of that of a tiger, looked at me in a genial, quizzical, condescending way and said: "No interviews." I remember the patent leather button shoes with the gray suède tops, the heavy gold ring on one finger, and the heavy watch-chain across his chest.

"You won't say who is to be nominated?" I persisted nervously.

"I wish I could," he grinned. "I wouldn't be sitting here trying to find out." He smiled again and repeated my question to one of his companions. They all looked at me with smiling condescension and I beat a swift retreat.

Defeated though I was, I decided to write out the little scene, largely to prove to the city editor that I had actually seen Croker and been refused an interview.

I went down to the bar to review the scene being enacted there. While I was standing at the bar drinking a lemonade there came a curious lull. In the midst of it the voices of two men near me became audible as they argued who would be nominated, Cleveland, Hill or some third man, not the one I have mentioned. Bursting with my new political knowledge and longing to air it, I, at the place where one of the strangers mentioned the third man as the most likely choice, solemnly shook my head as much as to say: "You are all wrong."

"Well, then, who do you think?" inquired the stranger, who was short, red-faced, intoxicated.

"Senator McEntee, of South Carolina," I replied, feeling as though I were stating an incontrovertible truth.

A tall, fair-complexioned, dark-haired Southerner in a wide-brimmed white hat and flaring frockcoat paused at this moment in his hurried passage through the room and, looking at the group, exclaimed:

"Who does me the honah to mention my name in connection with the Presidency? I am Senator McEntee of South Carolina. No intrusion, I hope?"

I and the two others stared in confusion.

"None whatever," I replied with an air, thinking how interesting it was that this man of all people should be passing through the room at this time. "These gentlemen were saying that —— of —— would be nominated, and I was going to say that sentiment is running more in your favor."

"Well, now, that is most interesting, my young friend, and I'm glad to hear you say it. It's an honah to be even mentioned in connection with so great an office, however small my qualifications. And who are you, may I ask?"

"My name in Dreiser. I represent the Chicago *Globe*."

"Oh, do you? That makes it doubly interesting. Won't you come along with me to my rooms for a moment? You interest me, young man, you really do. How long have you been a reporter?"

"Oh, for nearly a year now," I replied grandly.

"And have you ever worked for any other paper?"

"Yes; I was on the *Herald* last fall."

He seemed elated by his discovery. He must have been one of those swelling nonentities flattered silly by this chance discussion of his name in a national convention atmosphere. An older newspaper man would have known that he had not the least chance of being seriously considered. Somebody from the South had to be mentioned, as a compliment, and this man was fixed upon as one least likely to prove disturbing later.

He bustled out to a shady balcony overlooking the lake, ordered two cocktails and wanted to know on what I based my calculation. In order to not seem a fool I now went over my conversation with Maxwell. I spoke of different delegations and their complexions as though these conclusions were my own, when as a matter of fact I was quoting Maxwell verbatim. My hearer seemed surprised at my intelligence.

"You seem to be very well informed," he said genially, "but I know you're wrong. The Democratic party will never go to the South for a candidate—not for some years anyway. Just the same, since you've been good enough to champion me in this public fashion, I would like to do something for you in return. I suppose your paper is always anxious for advance news, and if you bring it in you get the credit. Now at this very moment, over in the Hotel Richelieu, Mr. William C. Whitney and some of his friends—Mr. Croker has just gone over there—are holding a conference. He is the one man who holds the balance of power in this convention. He represents the moneyed interests and is heart and soul for Grover Cleveland. Now if you want a real beat you'd better go over there and hang about. Mr. Whitney is sure to make a statement some time today or tomorrow. See his secretary, Mr. ——, and tell him I sent you. He will do anything for you he can.''

I thanked him, certain at last I had a real piece of news. This conference was the most important event that would or could take place in the whole convention. I was so excited that I wanted to jump up and run away.

"It will keep,'' he said, noting my nervousness. "No other newspaper man knows of it yet. Nothing will be given out yet for several hours because the conference will not be over before that time.''

"But I'd like to phone my office,'' I pleaded.

"All right, but come back.''

I ran to the nearest telephone. I explained my beat to the city editor and, anxious lest I be unable to cover it, asked him to inform the head political man. He was all excitement at once, congratulated me and told me to follow up this conference. Then I ran back to my senator.

"I see,'' he said, "that you are a very industrious and eager young man. I like to see that. I don't want to say anything which will set up your hopes too much, because things don't always work out as one would wish, but did any one ever suggest to you that you would make a good private secretary?''

"No, sir,'' I replied, flattered and eager.

"Well, from what I have seen here today I am inclined to think you would. Now I don't know that I shall be returned to the Senate after this year—there's a little dispute in my State—but if I am, and you want to write me after next January, I may be able to do something for you. I've seen a lot of bright young fellows come up in the newspaper profession, and I've seen a lot go down. If you're not too much attached to it, perhaps you would like this other better.''

He smiled serenely, and I could have kissed his hands. At the same time, if you please, I was already debating whether one so promising as myself should leave the newspaper profession!

But even more than my good fortune at gleaning this bit of news or beat, as it proved, I was impressed by the company I was keeping and the realm in which I now moved as if by right—great hotels, a newspaper office with which I was connected, this senator, these politicians, the display of comfort and luxury on every hand. Only a little while back I was an inexperienced, dreaming collector for an ''easy-payment'' company, and now look at me! Here I sat on this grand balcony, the senator to my right, a table between us, all the lovely panorama of the lake and Michigan Drive below. What a rise! From now on, no doubt, I would do much better. Was I not even now being offered the secretaryship to a senator?

In due time I left and ran to the Richelieu, but my brain was seething with my great rise and my greater achievement in being the first to know of and report to my paper this decisive conference. If that were true I should certainly have discovered what my paper and all papers were most eager to know.

CHAPTER XI

WHAT the senator had told me was true. The deciding conference was on, and I determined to hang about the corridors of the Richelieu until it was over. The secretary, whom I found closeted with others (not newspaper men) in a room on the second floor, was good enough to see me when I mentioned Senator McEntee's name, and told me to return at six-thirty, when he was sure the conference would be over and a general statement be issued to the press. If I wished, I might come back at five-thirty. This dampened my joy in the thought that I had something exclusive, though I was later cheered by the thought that I had probably saved my paper from defeat anyhow for we were too poor to belong to the general news service. As a matter of fact, my early information was a cause of wonder in the office, the political man himself coming down late in the night to find out how I had learned so soon. I spoke of my friend Senator McEntee as though I had known him for years. The political man merely looked at me and said: "Well, you ought to get along in politics on one of the papers, if nowhere else."

The capture of this one fact, as I rather felt at the time, was my making in this newspaper office and hence in the newspaper world at large, in so far as I ever was made.

At five-thirty that afternoon I was on hand, and, true to his word, the secretary outlined exactly what conclusions the conference had reached. Afterward he brought out a type-written statement and read from it such facts as he wished me to have. Cleveland was to be nominated. Another man, Adlai Stevenson of Illinois, of whom I had never heard, was to be nominated for Vice-President. There were other details, so confusing that I could scarcely grasp them, but I made some notes and flew to the office and tried to write out all I had heard. I know now that I made a very bad job of it, but

Maxwell worked so hard and so cheerfully that he saved me. From one source and another he confirmed or modified my statements, wrote an intelligent introduction and turned it in.

"You're one of the damnedest crack-brained loons I ever saw," he said at one place, cutting out a great slice of my stuff, "but you seem to know how to get the news just the same, and you're going to be able to write. If I could just keep you under my thumb for four or five weeks I think I could make something out of you."

At this I ventured to lay one hand over his shoulder in an affectionate and yet appealing way, but he looked up frowningly and said: "Cut the gentle con work, Theodore. I know you. You're just like all other newspaper men, or will be: grateful when things are coming your way. If I were out of a job or in your position you'd do just like all the others: pass me up. I know you better than you know yourself. Life is a God-damned stinking, treacherous game, and nine hundred and ninety-nine men out of every thousand are bastards. I don't know why I do this for you," and he cut some more of my fine writing, "but I like you. I don't expect to get anything back. I never do. People always trim me when I want anything. There's nobody home if I'm knocking. But I'm such a God-damned fool that I like to do it. But don't think I'm not on, or that I'm a genial ass that can be worked by every Tom, Dick and Harry." And after visiting me with that fat superior smile he went on working. I stared, nervous, restless, resentful, sorrowful, trying to justify myself to life and to him.

"If I had a real chance," I said, "I would soon show you."

The convention opened its sessions the next day, and because of my seeming cleverness I was given a front seat in the press-stand, where I could hear all speeches, observe the crowd, trade ideas with the best newspaper men in the city and the country. In a day, if you will believe it, and in spite of the fact that I was getting only fifteen dollars a week, my stock had risen so that, in this one office at least, I was looked upon as a newspaper man of rare talent, an extraordinarily bright boy sure to carve out a future for himself, one to be made friends with and helped. Here in this press-stand I was now being coached by one newspaper man and another in the intricacies of convention life. I was introduced to two other members of our staff who were supposed to be experienced men, both of them small, clever, practical-minded individuals well adapted to the work in hand. One of them, Harry L. Dunlap, followed my errant fortunes for years, securing a place through me in St. Louis and rising finally to be the confidential adviser of one of our Presidents, William Howard Taft—a not very remarkable President to be adviser to at that. The other, a small brown-suited soul, Brady by name, came into my life for a very little while and then went, I know not where.

But this convention, how it thrilled me! To be tossed into the vortex of national politics at a time when the country was seething over the possible resuscitation of the old Democratic party to strength and power was something like living. I listened to the speeches, those dully conceived flights and word gymnastics and pyrotechnics whereby backwoods statesmen, district leaders and personality-followers seek to foist upon the attention of the country their own personalities as well as those of the individuals whom they admire. Although it was generally known that Cleveland was to be nominated (the money power of America having fixed upon him) and it was useless to name any one else, still as many as ten different "statesmen" great leaders, saviors were put in nomination. Each man so mentioned was the beau ideal of a nation's dream of a leader, a statesman, a patriot, lover of liberty and of the people. This in itself was a liberal education and slowly but surely opened my eyes. I watched with amazement this love of fanfare and noise, the way in which various delegations and individual followers loved to shout and walk up and down waving banners and blowing horns. Different States or cities had sent large delegations, New York a marching club two thousand strong, all of whom had seats in this hall, and all were plainly instructed to yell and demonstrate at the mention of a given name.

The one thing I heard which seemed rather important at the time, beautiful, because of a man's voice and gestures, was a speech by Bourke Cochran, exhorting the convention to nominate his candidate, David Bennett Hill, and save the party from defeat. Indeed his speech, until later I heard William Jennings Bryan, seemed to me the best I had ever heard, clear, sonorous, forcible, sensible. He had something to say and he said it with art and seeming conviction. He had presence too, a sort of Herculean, animal-like effrontery. He made his audience sit up and pay attention to him, when as a matter of fact it was interested in talking privately, one member to another. I tried to take notes of what he was saying until one of my associates told me that the full minutes of his speech could soon be secured from the shorthand reporters.

Being in this great hall cheek by jowl with the best of the Chicago newspaper world thrilled me. "Now," I said to myself, "I am truly a newspaper man. If I can only get interesting things to write about, my fortune is made." At once, as the different forceful reporters of the city were pointed out to me (George Ade, Finley Peter Dunne, "Charlie" Seymour, Charles d'Almy), my neck swelled as does a dog's when a rival appears on the scene. Already, at mere sight of them, I was anxious to try conclusions with them on some important mission and so see which of us was the better man. Always, up to the early thirties, I was so human as to conceive almost a deadly opposition to any one who even looked as though he might be able to try conclusions with me in anything. At that time, I was ready for a row, believing, now that I had got thus far, that I was destined to become one of the greatest newspaper men that ever lived!

But this convention brought me no additional glory. I did write a flowery description of the thing as a whole, but only a portion of it was used. I did get some details of committee work, which were probably incorporated in the political man's general summary. The next day, Cleveland being nominated, interest fell off. Thousands packed their bags and departed.

I was used for a day or two about hotels gathering one bit of news and another, but I could see that there was no import to what I was doing and began to grow nervous lest I should be summarily dropped. I spoke to Maxwell about it.

"Do you think they'll drop me?" I asked.

"Not by a damned sight!" he replied contentiously. "You've earned a show here; it's been promised you; you've made good, and they ought to give it to you. Don't you say anything; just leave it to me. There's going to be a conference here tomorrow as to who's to be dropped and who kept on, and I'll have my say then. You saved the day for us on that nomination stuff, and that ought to get you a show. Leave it to me."

The conference took place the next day and of the five men who had been taken on to do extra work during the convention I and one other were the only ones retained, and this at the expense of two former reporters dropped. At that, I really believe I should have been sent off if it had not been for Maxwell. He had been present during most of the transactions concerning Mr. Gissel's book and thought I deserved work on that score alone, to say nothing of my subsequent efforts. I think he disliked the little editorial writer very much. At any rate when this conference began Maxwell, according to Dunlap who was there and reported to me, sat back, a look of contented cynicism on his face not unlike that of a fox about to devour a chicken. The names of several of the new men were proposed as substitutes for the old ones when, not hearing mine mentioned, he inquired:

"Well, what about Dreiser?"

"Well, what about him?" retorted Sullivan, the city editor. "He's a good man, but he lacks training. These other fellows are experienced."

"I thought you and Gissel sort of agreed to give him a show if he sold that book for you?"

"No, I didn't," said Sullivan. "I only promised to give him a tryout around convention time. I've done that."

"But he's the best man on the staff today," insisted Maxwell. "He brought in the only piece of news worth having. He's writing better every day."

He bristled, according to Dunlap, and Sullivan and Gissel, taking the hint that the quarrel might be carried higher up or aired inconveniently, changed their attitude completely.

"Oh, well," said Sullivan genially, "let him come on. I'd just as lief have him. He may pan out."

And so on I came, at fifteen dollars a week, and thus my newspaper career was begun in earnest.

CHAPTER XII

THIS change from insecurity to being an accredited news-paper man was delightful. For a very little while, a year or so, it seemed to open up a clear straight course which if followed energetically must lead me to great heights. Of course I found that beginners were very badly paid. Salaries ranged from fourteen to twenty-five dollars for reporters; and as for those important missions about which I had always been reading, they were not even thought of here. The best I could learn of them in this office was that they did exist— on some papers. Young men were still sent abroad on mis-sions, or to the West or to Africa (as Stanley), but they had to be men of proved merit or budding genius and con-nected with papers of the greatest importance. How could one prove oneself to be a budding genius?

Salary or no salary, however, I was now a newspaper man, with the opportunity eventually to make a name for myself. Having broken with the family and with my sister C——, I was now quite alone in the world and free to go anywhere and do as I pleased. I found a front room in Ogden Place overlooking Union Park (in which area I afterwards placed one of my heroines). I could walk from here to the office in a little over twenty minutes. My route lay through either Madison Street or Washington Boulevard east to the river, and morning and night I had ample opportunity to speculate on the rancid or out-at-elbows character of much that I saw. Both Washington and Madison, from Halsted east to the river, were lined with vile dens and tumbledown yellow and gray frame houses, slovenly, rancorous, unsolved and possibly unsolvable misery and degeneracy, whole streets of degraded, dejected, miserable souls. Why didn't society do better by them? I often asked of myself then. Why didn't they do better by themselves? Did God, who, as had been drummed into me up to that hour was all wise, all merciful, omnipresent and omnipotent make people so or did they themselves have something to do with it? Was government to blame, or they themselves? Always the miseries of the poor, the scandals, corruptions and physical deteriorations which trail folly, weakness, uncontrolled passion fascinated me. I was never tired of looking at them, but I had no solution and was not willing to accept any, suspecting even then that man is the victim of forces over which he has no control. As I walked here and there through these truly terrible neighborhoods, I peered through open doors and patched and broken windows at this wretchedness and squalor, much as a man may tread the poisonous paths of a jungle, curious and yet fearsome.

It was this nosing and speculative tendency, however, which helped me most, as I soon found. Journalism, even in Chicago, was still in that discursive stage which loved long-winded yarns upon almost any topic. Nearly all news stories were padded to make more of them than they deserved, especially as to color and romance. All specials were being written in imitation of the great novelists, particularly Charles Dickens, who was the ideal of all newspaper men and editors as well as magazine special writers (how often have I been told to imitate Charles Dickens in thought and manner!). The city editors wanted not so much bare facts as feature stories, color, romance; and, although I did not see it clearly at the time, I was their man.

Write?

Why, I could write reams upon any topic when at last I discovered that I could write at all. One day some one— Maxwell, I suppose—hearing me speak of what I was seeing each day as I came to or went from the office to my room, suggested that I do an article on Chicago's vilest slum, which lay between Halsted and the river, Madison and Twelfth streets, for the next Sunday issue, and this was as good as meat and drink for me. I visited this region a few times between one and four in the morning, wandering about its clattering boardwalks, its dark alleys, its gloomy mire and muck atmosphere. Chicago's wretchedness was never utterly tame, disconsolate or hang-dog, whatever else it might be; rather, it was savage, bitter and at times larkish and impish. The vile slovens, slatterns, prostitutes, drunkards and drug fiends who infested this region all led a strident if beggarly or horrible life. Saloon lights and smells and lamps gleaming smokily from behind broken lattices and from below wooden sidewalk levels, gave it a shameless and dangerous color. Accordions, harmonicas, jew's-harps, clattering tin-pan pianos and stringy violins were forever going; paintless rotting shacks always resounded with a noisy blasphemous life between twelve and four; oaths, foul phrases; a Hogarthian shamelessness and reconciliation to filth everywhere—these were some of the things that characterized it. Although there was a closing-hour law there was none here as long as it was deemed worth while to keep open. Only at four and five in the morning did a heavy peace seem to descend, and this seemed as wretched as the heavier vice and degradation which preceded it.

In the face of such a scene or picture as this my mind invariably paused in question. I had been reared on dogmatic religious and moral theory, or at least had been compelled to listen to it all my life. Here then was a part of the work of an omnipotent God, who nevertheless tolerated, apparently, a most industrious devil. Why did He do it? Why did nature, when left to itself, devise such astounding slums and human muck heaps? Harlots in doorways or behind windows or under lamp-posts in these areas, smirking and signaling creatures with the dullest or most fox-like expression and with heavily smeared lips and cheeks and blackened eyebrows, were ready to give themselves for one dollar, or even fifty cents, and this in the heart of this budding and prosperous West, a land flowing with milk and honey! What had brought that about so soon in a new, rich, healthy, forceful land—God? devil? or both working together toward a common end? Near at hand were huge and rapidly expanding industries. The street-cars and trains, morning and evening, were crowded with earnest, careful, saving, seeking, moderately well-dressed people who were presumably anxious to work and lay aside a competence and own a home. Then why was it that these others lived in such a hell? Was God to blame? Or society?

I could not solve it. This matter of being, with its differences, is permanently above the understanding of man, I fear.

I smiled as I thought of my father's attitude to all this. There he was out on the west side demanding that all creatures of the world return to Christ and the Catholic Church, see clearly, whether they could or not, its grave import to their immortal souls; and here were these sows and termagants, wretched, filthy, greasy. And the men low-browed, ill-clad, rum-soaked, body-racked! Mere bags of bones, many of them, blue-nosed, scarlet-splotched, diseased—if God should get them what would He do with them? On the other hand, in the so-called better walks of life, there were so many strutting, contentious, self-opinionated swine-masters whose faces were maps of gross egoism and whose clothes were almost a blare of sound.

I think I said a little something of all this in the first newspaper special I ever wrote. It seemed to open the eyes of my superiors.

"You know, Theodore," Maxwell observed to me as he read my copy the next morning between one and three, "you have your faults, but you do know how to observe. You bring a fresh mind to bear on this stuff; anyhow I think maybe you're cut out to be a writer after all, not just an ordinary newspaper man." He lapsed into silence, and then at periods as he read he would exclaim: "Jesus Christ!" or "That's a hell of a world!" Then he would fall foul of some turgid English and with a kind of malicious glee would cut and hack and restate and shake his head despairingly, until I was convinced that I had written the truckiest rot in the world. At the close, however, he arose, dusted his lap, lit a pipe and said: "Well, I think you're nutty, but I believe you're a writer just the same. They ought to let you do more Sunday specials." And then he talked to me about phases of the Chicago he knew, contrasting it with a like section in San Francisco, where he had once worked.

"A hell of a fine novel is going to be written about some of these things one of these days," he remarked; and from now on he treated me with such equality that I thought I must indeed be a very remarkable man.

CHAPTER XIII

THIS world of newspaper men who now received me on terms of social equality, who saw life from a purely opportunistic, and yet in the main sentimentally imaginative, viewpoint broadened me considerably and finally liberated me from moralistic and religionistic qualms. So many of them were hard, gallant adventurers without the slightest trace of the nervousness and terror of fortune which agitated me. They had been here, there, everywhere—San Francisco, Los Angeles, New York, Calcutta, London. They knew the ways of the newspaper world and to a limited extent the workings of society at large. The conventional-minded would have called them harsh, impracticable, impossible, largely because they knew nothing of trade, that great American standard of ability and force. Most of them, as I soon found, were like John Maxwell, free from notions as to how people were to act and what they were to think. To a certain extent they were confused by the general American passive acceptance of the Sermon on the Mount and the Beatitudes as governing principles, but in the main they were nearly all mistrustful of these things, and of conventional principles in general.

They did not believe, as I still did, that there was a fixed moral order in the world which one contravened at his peril. Heaven only knows where they had been or what they had seen, but they misdoubted the motives, professed or secret, of nearly every man. No man, apparently, was utterly and consistently honest, that is, no man in a powerful or dominant position; and but few were kind or generous or truly public-spirited. As I sat in the office between assignments, or foregathered with them at dinner or at midnight in some one of the many small restaurants frequented by newspaper men, I heard tales of all sorts of scandals: robberies, murders, fornications, incendiarisms, not only in low life but in our so-called high life. Most of these young men looked upon life as a fierce, grim struggle in which no quarter was either given or taken, and in which all men laid traps, lied, squandered, erred through illusion: a conclusion with which I now most heartily agree. The one thing I would now add is that the brigandage of the world is in the main genial and that in our hour of success we are all inclined to be more or less liberal and warm-hearted.

But at this time I was still sniffing about the Sermon on the Mount and the Beatitudes, expecting ordinary human flesh and blood to do and be those things. Hence the point of view of these men seemed at times a little horrific, at other times most tonic.

"People make laws for other people to live up to," Maxwell once said to me, "and in order to protect themselves in what they have. They never intend those laws to apply to themselves or to prevent them from doing anything they wish to do."

There was a youth whose wife believed that he did not drink. On two occasions within six weeks I was sent as envoy to inform his wife that he had suddenly been taken ill with indigestion and would soon be home. Then Maxwell and Brady would bundle him into a hack and send him off, one or two of us going along to help him into his house. So solemnly was all this done and so well did we play our parts that his wife believed it for a while—long enough for him to pull himself together a year later and give up drinking entirely. Another youth boasted that he was syphilitic and was curing himself with mercury; another there was whose joy it was to sleep in a house of prostitution every Saturday night, and so on. I tell these things not because I rejoice in them but merely to indicate the atmosphere into which I was thrown. Neither sobriety nor virtue nor continence nor incontinence was either a compelling or preventive cause of either success or failure or had anything to do with true newspaper ability; rather men succeeded by virtue of something that was not intimately related to any of these. If one could do anything which the world really wanted it would not trouble itself so much about one's private life.

Another change that was being brought about in me was that which related to my personal opinion of myself, the feeling I was now swiftly acquiring that after all I amounted to something, was somebody. A special or two that I wrote, thanks largely to Maxwell's careful schooling, brought me to the forefront among those of the staff who were writing for the Sunday supplement. A few news stories fell to my lot and I handled them with a freedom which won me praise on all sides. Not that I felt at the time that I was writing them so well or differently as that I was most earnestly concerned to state what I saw or felt or believed. I even essayed a few parables of my own, mild, poetic commentaries on I scarcely recall what, which Maxwell scanned with a scowling eye at first but later deigned to publish, affixing the signature of Carl Dreiser because he had decided to nickname me "Carl." This grieved me, for I was dying to see my own name in print; but when they appeared I had the audacity to call upon the family and show them, boasting of my sudden rise in the world and saying that I had used the name Carl as a compliment to a nephew.

During this time I was taking a rather lofty hand with Alice because of my great success, unmindful of the fact that I had been boasting for months that I was connected with one of the best of the local papers and telling her that I did not think it so wonderful. But now I began to think that I was to be called to much higher realms, and solemnly asked myself if I should ever want to marry. A number of things helped to formulate this question in me. For one thing, I had no sooner been launched into general assignments than one afternoon, in seeking for the pictures of a group of girls who had taken part in some summer-night festival, I encountered one who seemed to be interested in me, a little blonde of about my own age, very sleek and dreamy. She responded to my somewhat timid advances when I called on her and condescended to smile as she gave me her photograph. I drew close to her and attempted a flirtation, to which she was not averse, and on parting I asked if I might call some afternoon or evening, hoping to crowd it in with my work. She agreed, and for several Sundays and week-nights I was put to my utmost resources to keep my engagements and do my work, for the newspaper profession that I knew, tolerated neither week-days nor Sundays off. I had to take an assignment and shirk it in part or telephone that I was delayed and could not come at all. Thus early even I began to adopt a cavalier attitude toward this very exacting work. Twice I took her to a theater, once to an organ recital, and once for a stroll in Jackson Park; by which time she seemed inclined to yield to my blandishments to the extent of permitting me to put my arms about her and even to kiss her, protesting always that I was wanton and forward and that she did not know whether she cared for me so much or not. Charming as she was, I did not feel that I should care for her very much. She was beautiful but too lymphatic, too carefully reared. Her mother, upon hearing of me, looked into the fact of whether I was truly connected with the *Globe* and then cautioned her daughter to be careful about making new friends. I saw that I was not welcome at that house and thereafter met her slyly. I might have triumphed in this case had I been so minded and possessed of a little more courage, but as I feared that I should have to undergo a long courtship with marriage at the end of it, my ardor cooled. Because she was new to me and comfortably stationed and better dressed than either Alice or N—— had ever been, I esteemed her more highly, made invidious comparisons from a material point of view, and wished that I could marry some such well-placed girl without assuming all the stern obligations of matrimony.

During the second month of my work on the *Globe* there arrived on the scene a man who was destined to have a very marked effect on my career. He was a tall, dark, broad-shouldered, slender-legged individual of about forty-five or fifty, with a shock of curly black hair and a burst of smuggler-like whiskers. He was truly your Bret Harte gold-miner type, sloven, red-eyed at times, but amazingly intelligent and genial, reminding me not a little of my brother Rome in his best hours. He wore a long dusty, brownish-black frockcoat and a pair of black trousers specked, gummed, shined and worn by tobacco, food, liquor and rough usage. His feet were incased in wide-toed shoes of the old "boot-leather" variety, and the swirl of Jovian locks and beard was surmounted by a wide-brimmed black hat such as Kentucky colonels were wont to affect. His nose and cheeks were tinted a fiery red by much drinking, the nose having a veinous, bulbous, mottled and strawberry texture.

This man was John T. McEnnis, a well-known middle-West newspaper man of that day, a truly brilliant writer whose sole fault was that he drank too much. Originally from St. Louis, the son of a well-known politician there, he had taken up journalism as the most direct avenue to fame and fortune. At forty-five he found himself a mere hanger-on in this profession, tossed from job to job because of his weakness, his skill equaled if not outrivaled by that of younger men! It was commonly said that he could drink more and stand it better than any other man in Chicago.

"Why, he can't begin to work unless he's had three or four drinks to limber him up," Harry Dunlap once said to me. "He has to have six or seven more to get through till evening." He did not say how many were required to carry him on until midnight, but I fancy he must have consumed at least a half dozen more. He was in a constant state of semi-intoxication, which was often skillfully concealed.

During my second month on the *Globe* McEnnis was made city editor in place of Sullivan, who had gone to a better paper. Later he was made managing editor. I learned from Maxwell that he was well known in Chicago newspaper circles for his wit, his trenchant editorial pen, and that once he had been considered the most brilliant newspaper editor in St. Louis. He had a small, spare, intellectual wife, very homely and very dowdy, who still adored him and had suffered God knows what to be permitted to live with him.

The first afternoon I saw him sitting in the city editorial chair I was very much afraid of him and of my future. He looked raucous and uncouth, and Maxwell had told me that new editors usually brought in new men. As it turned out, however, much to my astonishment, he took an almost immediate fancy to me which ripened into a kind of fatherly affection and even, if you will permit me humbly to state a fact, a kind of adoration. Indeed he swelled my head by the genial and hearty manner in which almost at once he took me under his guidance and furthered my career as rapidly as he could, the while he borrowed as much of my small salary as he could. Please do not think that I begrudged this then or that I do now. I owe him more than a dozen such salaries borrowed over a period of years could ever repay. My one grief is, that I had so little to give him in return for the very great deal he did for me.

The incident from which this burst of friendship seemed to take its rise was this. One day shortly after he arrived he gave me a small clipping concerning a girl on the south side who had run away or had been kidnaped from one of the dreariest homes it has ever been my lot to see. The girl was a hardy Irish creature of about sixteen. A neighborhood street boy had taken her to some wretched dive in South Clark Street and seduced her. Her mother, an old, Irish Catholic woman whom I found bending over a washtub when I called, was greatly exercised as to what had become of her daughter, of whom she had heard nothing since her disap· pearance. The police had been informed, and from clews picked up by a detective I learned the facts first mentioned. The mother wept into her wash as she told me of the death of her husband a few years before, of a boy who had been injured in such a way that he could not work, and now this girl, her last hope——

From a newspaper point of view there was nothing much to the story, but I decided to follow it to the end. I found the house to which the boy had taken the girl, but they had just left. I found the parents of the youth, simple, plain working people, who knew nothing of his whereabouts. Something about the wretched little homes of both families, the tumbledown neighborhoods, the poverty and privation which would ill become a pretty sensuous girl, impelled me to write it out as I saw and felt it. I hurried back to the office that afternoon and scribbled out a kind of slum romance, which in the course of the night seemed to take the office by storm. Maxwell, who read it, scowled at first, then said it was interesting, and then fine.

"Carl," he interpolated at one point as he read, "you're letting your youthful romantic mood get the best of you, I see. This will never do, Carl. Read Schopenhauer, my boy, read Schopenhauer."

The city editor picked it up when he returned, intending, I presume, to see if there was any sign of interest in the general introduction; finding something in it to hold him, he read on carefully to the end, as I could see, for I was not a dozen feet away and could see what he was reading. When he finished he looked over at me and then called me to come to him.

"I want to say to you," he said, "that you have just done a fine piece of writing. I don't go much on this kind of story, don't believe in it as a rule for a daily paper, but the way you have handled this is fine. You're young yet, and if you just keep yourself well in hand you have a future."

Thereafter he became very friendly, asked me out one lunch-time to have a drink, borrowed a dollar and told me of some of the charms and wonders of journalistic work in St. Louis and elsewhere. He thought the *Globe* was too small a paper for me, that I ought to get on a larger one, preferably in another city, and suggested how valuable would be a period of work on the St. Louis *Globe-Democrat,* of which he had once been city editor.

"You haven't any idea how much you need all this," he said. "You're young and inexperienced, and a great paper like the *Globe-Democrat* or the New York *Sun* starts a boy off right. I would like to see you go first to St. Louis, and then to New York. Don't settle down anywhere yet, don't drink, and don't get married, whatever you do. A wife will be a big handicap to you. You have a future, and I'm going to help you if I can." Then he borrowed another dollar and left me.

CHAPTER XIV

TAKEN up by this man in this way and with Maxwell as my literary guide and mentor still, I could not help but prosper to an extent at this task, and I did. I cannot recall now all the things that I was called upon to do, but one of the things that shortly after the arrival of McEnnis was assigned to me and that eventually brought my Chicago newspaper career to a close in a sort of blaze of glory as I saw it, at least, was a series of articles or rather a campaign to close a group of fake auction shops which were daily fleecing hundreds by selling bogus watches, jewelry, diamonds and the like, yet which were licensed by the city and from which the police were deriving a very handsome revenue. Although so new at this work the task was placed in my hands as a regular daily assignment by Mr. McEnnis with the comment that I must make something out of it, whether or not I thought I could put a news punch in it and close these places. That would be a real newspaper victory and ought to do me some good with my chief the managing editor. Campaigns of this kind are undertaken not in a spirit of righteousness as a rule but because of public pressure or a wish to increase circulation and popularity; yet in this case no such laudable or excusable intent could be alleged.

This paper was controlled by John B. MacDonald, an Irish politician, gambler, racer of horses, and the owner of a string of local houses of prostitution, saloons and gambling dens, all of which brought him a large income and made him influential politically. Recently he had fallen on comparatively difficult days. His reputation as a shady character had become too widespread. The pharisees and influential men generally who had formerly profited by his favor now found it expedient to pass by on the other side. Public sentiment against him had been aroused by political attacks on the part of one newspaper and another that did not belong to his party. The last election having been lost to him, the police and other departments of the city were now supposed to work in harmony to root out his vile though profitable vice privileges.

Everybody knows how these things work. Some administration attacks were made upon his privileges, whereupon, not finding suitable support in the papers of his own party in the city, they having axes of their own to grind, he had started a paper of his own, the *Globe*. He had brought on a capable newspaper man from New York, who was doing his best to make of the paper something which would satisfy MacDonald's desire for circulation and influence while he lined his own pockets against a rainy day. For this reason, no doubt, our general staff was underpaid, though fairly capable. During my stay the police and other departments, under the guidance of Republican politicians and newspapers, were making an attack on Mr. MacDonald's preserves; to which he replied by attacking through the medium of the *Globe* anything and everything he thought would do his rivals harm. Among these were a large number of these same mock auction shops in the downtown section. Evidently the police were deriving a direct revenue from these places, for they let them severely alone but since the administration was now anti-MacDonald and these were not Mr. MacDonald's property nothing was left undone by us to stop this traffic. We charged, and it was true, that though victims daily appeared before the police to complain that they had been swindled and to ask for restitution, nothing was done by the police.

I cannot now recall what it was about my treatment of these institutions that aroused so much interest in the office and made me into a kind of *Globe* hero. I was innocent of all knowledge of the above complications which I have just described when I started, and almost as innocent when I concluded. Nevertheless now daily at ten in the morning and again in the afternoon I went to one or another of these shops, listened to the harangue of the noisy barkers, saw tin-gilt jewelry knocked down to unsuspecting yokels from the South and West who stood open-mouthed watching the hypnotizing movements of the auctioneer's hands as he waved a glistering gem or watch in front of them and expatiated on the beauties and perfections of the article he was compelled to part from for a song. These places were not only deceptions and frauds in what they pretended to sell but also gathering-places for thieves, pick-pockets, footpads who, finding some deluded bystander to be possessed of a watch, pin or roll of money other than that from which he was parted by the auctioneer or his associates, either then and there by some legerdemain robbed him or followed him into a dark street and knocked him down and did the same. At this time Chicago was notorious for this sort of thing, and it was openly charged in the *Globe* and elsewhere that the police connived at and thrived by the transactions.

My descriptions of what was going on, innocent and matter of fact as they were at first and devoid of guile or make-believe, so pleased Mr. McEnnis beyond anything I had previously done that he was actually fulsome and yet at the same time mandatory and restraining in his compliments. I have no desire to praise myself at this time. Such things and so much that seemed so important then have since become trivial beyond words but it is only fair to state that he was seemingly immensely pleased and amused as was Maxwell.

"Upon my word," I once heard him exclaim, as he read one of my daily effusions. "The rascals. Who would think that such scamps would be allowed to run at large in a city like this! They certainly ought to be in jail. Every one of them. And the police along with them." Then he chuckled, slapped his knee and finally came over and made some inquiries in regard to a certain dealer whom I had chanced to picture. I was cautioned against overstating anything; also against detection and being beaten up by those whom I was offending. For I noticed after the first day or two that the barkers of some of the shops occasionally studied me curiously or ceased their more shameful effronteries in my presence and produced something of more value. The facts which my articles presented, however, finally began to attract a little attention to the paper. Either because the paper sold better or because this was an excellent club wherewith to belabor his enemies, the publisher now decided to call the attention of the public via the billboards, to what was going on in our columns, and McEnnis himself undertook to frighten the police into action by swearing out warrants against the different owners of the shops and thus compelling them to take action.

I became the center of a semi-literary, semi-public reform hubbub. The principal members of the staff assured me that the articles were forceful in fact and color and highly amusing. One day, by way of the license bureau and with the aid of McEnnis, I secured the names of the alleged owners and managers of nearly all of these shops and thereafter attacked them by name, describing them just as they were, where they lived, how they made their money, etc. In company with a private detective and several times with McEnnis, I personally served warrants of arrest, accompanied the sharpers to police headquarters, where they were immediately released on bail, and then ran to the office to write out my impressions of all I had seen, repeating conversations as nearly as I could remember, describing uncouth faces and bodies of crooks, policemen and detectives, and by sly innuendo indicating what a farce and sham was the whole seeming interest of the police.

One day McEnnis and I called on the chief of police, demanding to know why he was so indifferent to our crusade and the facts we put before him. To my youthful amazement and enlightenment he shook his fist in our faces and exclaimed: "You can go to the devil, and so can the *Globe!* I know who's back of this campaign, and why. Well, go on and play your little game! Shout all you want to. Who's going to listen to you? You haven't any circulation. You're not going to make a mark of me, and you're not going to get me fired out of here for not performing my duty. Your paper is only a dirty political rag without any influence."

"Is it!" taunted McEnnis. "Well, you just wait and see. I think you'll change your mind as to that," and we stalked solemnly out.

And in the course of time he did change his mind. Some

of the fakers had to be arrested and fined and their places closed up, and the longer we talked and exposed the worse it became for them. Finally a dealer approached me one morning and offered me an eighteen-carat gold watch, to be selected by me from any jewelry store in the city and paid for by him, if I would let his store alone. I refused. Another, a dark, dusty, most amusing little Jew, offered me a diamond pin, insisting upon sticking it in my cravat, and said: "Go see! Go see! Ask any jeweler what he thinks, if that ain't a real stone! If it ain't—if he says no—bring it back to me and I'll give you a hundred dollars in cash for it. Don't you mention me no more now. Be a nice young feller now. I'm a hard-workin' man just like anybody else. I run a honest place."

I carried the pin back to the office and gave it to McEnnis. He stared at me in amazement.

"Why did you do this?" he exclaimed. "You shouldn't have taken this, at all. It may get the paper in trouble. They may have had witnesses to this—but maybe not. Perhaps this fellow is just trying to protect himself. Anyway, we're going to take this thing back to him and don't take anything more, do you hear, money or anything. You can't do that sort of thing. If I didn't think you were honest I'd fire you right now."

He took me into the office of the editor-in-chief, who looked at me with still, gray-blue eyes and listened to my story. He dismissed me and talked with McEnnis for a while. When the latter came out he exclaimed triumphantly: "He sees that you're honest, all right, and he's tickled to death. Now we'll take this pin back, and then you'll write out the whole story just as it happened."

On the way we went to a magistrate to swear out a charge of attempted bribery against this man, and later in the same day I went with the detective to serve the warrant. To myself I seemed to be swimming in a delicious sea of life. "What a fine thing life is!" I thought. "Here I am getting along famously because I can write. Soon I will get more money, and maybe some day people will begin to hear of me. I will get a fine reputation in the newspaper world."

Thanks to this vigorous campaign, of which McEnnis was the inspiration and guiding spirit, all these auction shops were eventually closed. In so much at least John B. MacDonald had achieved a revenge.

As for myself, I felt that there must be some serious and favorable change impending for me; and true enough, within a fortnight after this the change came. I had noticed that McEnnis had become more and more friendly. He introduced me to his wife one day when she was in the office and told her in my presence what splendid work I was doing. Often he would take me to lunch or to a saloon for drinks (for which I would pay), and would then borrow a dollar or two or three, no part of which he ever returned. He lectured me on the subject of study, urging me to give myself a general education by reading, attending lectures and the like. He wanted me to look into painting, music, sculpture. As he talked the blood would swirl in my head, and I kept thinking what a brilliant career must be awaiting me. One thing he did was to secure me a place on the St. Louis *Globe-Democrat.*

Just at this time a man whose name I have forgotten—Leland, I think—the Washington correspondent of the St. Louis *Globe-Democrat,* came to Chicago to report the preliminary preparations for the great World's Fair which was to open the following spring. Already the construction of a number of great buildings in Jackson Park had been begun, and the newspapers throughout the country were on the alert as to its progress. Leland, as I may as well call him, a cool, capable observer and writer, was an old friend of McEnnis. McEnnis introduced me to him and made an impassioned plea in my behalf for an opportunity for me to do some writing for the *Globe-Democrat* in St. Louis under his direction. The idea was to get this man to allow me to do some World's Fair work for him, on the side, in addition to my work on the *Globe,* and then later to persuade Joseph B. McCullagh of the former paper to make a place for me in St. Louis.

"As you see," he said when he introduced me, "he's a mere

boy without any experience, but he has the makings of a first-rate newspaper man. I'm sure of it. Now, Henry, as a favor to me, I want you to help him. You're close to Mac'' (Joseph B. McCullagh, editor-in-chief of the St. Louis *Globe-Democrat*), ''and he's just the man this boy ought to go to to get his training. Dreiser has just completed a fine piece of journalistic work for me. He's closed up the fake auction shops here, and I want to reward him. He only gets fifteen a week here, and I can't do anything for him in Chicago just now. You write and ask Mac to take him on down there, and I'll write also and tell him how I feel about it.''

The upshot of this was that I was immediately taken into the favor of Mr. Leland, given some easy gossip writing to do, which netted me sixteen dollars the week for three weeks in addition to the fifteen I earned on the *Globe*. At the end of that time, some correspondence having ensued between the editor of the *Globe-Democrat* and his two Chicago admirers, I one day received a telegram which read:

''You may have reportorial position on this paper at twenty dollars a week, beginning next Monday. Wire reply.''

I stood in the dusty little *Globe* office and stared at this, wondering what so great an opportunity portended. Only six months before I had been jobless and hanging about this back door; here I was tonight with as much as fifty dollars in my pocket, a suit of good clothes on my back, good shoes, a good hat and overcoat. I had learned how to write and was already classed here as a star reporter. I felt as though life were going to do wonderful and beautiful things for me. I thought of Alice, that now I should have to leave her and this familiar and now comfortable Chicago atmosphere, and then I went over to McEnnis to ask him what I ought to do.

When he read the telegram he said: ''This is the best chance that could possibly come to you. You will be working on one of the greatest papers and under one of the greatest editors that ever lived. Make the most of your chance. Go? Of course go! Let's see—it's Tuesday; our regular week ends Friday. You hand in your resignation now, to take effect then, and go Sunday. I'll give you some letters that will help you," and he at once turned to his desk and wrote out a series of instructions and recommendations.

That night, and for four days after, until I took the train for St. Louis, I walked on air. I was going away. I was going out in the world to make my fortune. Withal I was touched by the pathos of the fact that life and youth and everything which now glimmered about me so hopefully was, for me as well as for every other living individual, insensibly slipping away.

CHAPTER XV

THIS sudden decision to terminate my newspaper life in Chicago involved the problem of what to do about Alice. During these spring and summer days I had been amusing myself with her, imagining sometimes, because of her pretty face and figure and her soft clinging ways, that I was in love with her. By the lakes and pagodas of Chicago's parks, on the lake shore at Lincoln Park where the white sails were to be seen, in Alice's cozy little room with the windows open and the lights out, or of a Sunday morning when her parents were away visiting and she was preparing my breakfast and flouring her nose and chin in the attempt—how happy we were! How we frivoled and kissed and made promises to ourselves concerning the future! We were like two children at times, and for a while I half decided that I would marry her. In a little while we were going everywhere together and she was planning her wedding trousseau, the little fineries she would have when we were married. We were to live on the south side near the lake in a tiny apartment. She described to me the costume she would wear, which was to be of satin of an ivory shade, with laces, veils, slippers and stockings to match.

But as spring wore on and I grew so restless I began to think not so much less of Alice as more of myself. I never saw her as anything but beautiful, tender, a delicate, almost perfect creature for some one to love and cherish. Once we went hand-in-hand over the lawns of Jackson Park of a Sunday afternoon. She was enticing in a new white flannel dress and dark blue hat. The day was warm and clear and a convoy of swans was sailing grandly about the little lake. We sat down and watched them and the ducks, the rowers in green, blue and white boats, with the white pagoda in the center of the lake reflected in the water. All was colorful, gay.

"Oh, Dorse," she said at one place, with a little gasping sigh which moved me by its pathos, "isn't it lovely?"

"Beautiful."

"We are so happy when we are together, aren't we?"

"Yes."

"Oh, I wish we were married! If we just had a little place of our own! You could come home to me, and I could make you such nice things."

I promised her happy days to come, but even as I said it I knew it would not be. I did not think I could build a life on my salary . . . I did not know that I wanted to. Life was too wide and full. She seemed to sense something of this from the very beginning, and clung close to me now as we walked, looking up into my eyes, smiling almost sadly. As the hours slipped away into dusk and the hush of evening suggested change and the end of many things she sighed again.

"Oh, Dorse," she said as we reached her doorstep, "if we could just be together always and never part!"

"We will be," I said, but I did not believe my own words.

It was on this spring night that she attempted to persuade me, not by words or any great craft but merely by a yielding pressure, to take her and make her fully mine. I fancy she thought that if she yielded to me physically and found herself with child my sympathy would cause me to marry her. We in her own home threw some pillows on the floor, and there in my arms she kissed and hugged me, begging me to love her; but I had not the wish. I did not think that I ought to do that thing, then.

It was after this that the upward turn of my fortunes began. I was involved in the mock auction war for over three weeks and for two weeks following that with my buzzing dreams of leaving Chicago. In this rush of work, and in paying some attentions to Miss Winstead, I neglected Alice shamefully, once for ten days, not calling at her house or store or writing her a note. One Sunday morning, troubled about me and no doubt heartsick, she attended the ethical culture lecture in the Grand Theater, where I often went. On coming out she met me and I greeted her affectionately, but she only looked at me with sad and reproachful eyes and said: "Oh, Dorse, you don't really care any more, do you? You're just a little sorry when you see me. Well, you needn't come any more. I'm going back to Harry. I'm only too glad that I can."

She admitted that, misdoubting me, she had never dropped him entirely but had kept him calling occasionally. This angered me and I said to myself: "What is she that I should worry over her?" Imagine. And this double-dealing, essential as it was then, cut me to the quick, although I had been doing as much and more. When I thought it out I knew that she was entitled to protect herself against so uncertain a love as mine. Even then I could have taken her—she practically asked me to—but I offered reasons and excuses for delay. I went away both angry and sad, and the following Sunday, having received the telegram from St. Louis, I left without notifying her. Indeed I trifled about on this score debating with myself until Saturday night, when McEnnis asked me to go to dinner with him; afterwards when I hurried to her home she was not there. This angered me groundlessly, even though I knew she never expected me any more of a Saturday night. I returned to my room, disconsolate and gloomy, packed my belongings and then decided that I would go back after midnight and knock at her door. Remembering that my train left at seven-thirty next morning and having no doubt that she was off with my rival, I decided to punish her. After all, I could come back if I wished, or she could come to me. I wrote her a note, then went to bed and slept fitfully until six-thirty, when I arose and hurried to make my train. In a little while I was off, speeding through those wide flat yards which lay adjacent to her home, and with my nose pressed against the window, a driving rain outside, I could see the very windows and steps by which we had so often sat. My heart sank and I ached. I decided at once to write her upon my arrival in St. Louis and beg her to come—not to become my wife perhaps but my mistress. I brooded gloomily all day as

I sped southward, picturing myself as a lorn youth without money, home, family, love, anything. I tried to be sad, thinking at the same time what wonderful things might not be going to befall me. But I was leaving Alice! I was leaving Chicago, my home, all that was familiar and dear! I felt as though I could not stand it, as though when I reached St. Louis I should take the next train and return.

CHAPTER XVI

THE time was November, 1892. St. Louis, as I stepped off the train that Sunday evening, after leaving Chicago in cold dreary state, seemed a warmer clime. The air was soft, almost balmy; but St. Louis could be cold enough too, as I soon discovered. The station, then at Twelfth and Poplar (the new Union Station at Eighteenth and Market was then building), an antiquated affair of brick and stone, with the tracks stretching in rows in front of it and reached by board walks laid at right angles to them, seemed unspeakably shabby and inconvenient to me after the better ones of Chicago. St. Louis, I said to myself, was not as good as Chicago. Chicago was rough, powerful, active; St. Louis was sleepy and slow. This was due, however, to the fact that I entered it of a Sunday evening and all its central portion was still. Contrasted with Chicago it was not a metropolis at all. While rich and successful it was a creature of another mood and of slower growth. I learned in time to like it very much, but for the things that set it apart from other cities, not for the things by which it sought to rival them.

But on that evening how dull and commonplace it seemed—how slow after the wave-like pulsation of energy that appeared to shake the very air of Chicago.

I made my way to a hotel called The Silver Moon, recommended to me by my mentor and sponsor, where one could get a room for a dollar, a meal for twenty-five cents. Outside of Joseph B. McCullagh, editor of the *Globe-Democrat,* and Edmond O'Neill, former editor of the *Republic* to whom I bore a letter, there was no one to whom I might commend myself. I did not care. I was in a strange city at last! I was out in the world now really, away from my family. My great interest was in life as a spectacle, this singing, rhythmic, mystic state in which I found myself. Life, the great sea! Life, the wondrous, colorful riddle!

After eating a bite in the almost darkened restaurant of this hotel I at once went out into Pine Street and stared at the street-cars, yellow, red, orange, green, brown, labeled Choteau Avenue, Tower Grove, Jefferson Avenue, Carondelet. My first business was to find the *Globe-Democrat* building, a prosperous eight-story brownstone and brick affair standing at Sixth and Pine. I stared at this building in the night, looking through the great plate glass windows at an onyx-lined office, and finally went in and bought a Sunday paper.

I went to my room and studied this paper—then slept, thinking of my coming introduction in the morning. I was awakened by the clangor of countless cars. Going to the stationary washstand I was struck at once by the yellowness of the water, a dark yellowish-brown, which deposited a yellow sediment in the glass. Was that the best St. Louis could afford? I asked myself in youthful derision. I drank it just the same, went down to breakfast and then out into the city to see what I should see. I bought a *Globe-Democrat* (a Republican party paper, by the way: an anachronism of age and change of ownership) and a *Republic*, the one morning Democratic paper, and then walked to Sixth and Pine to have another look at the building in which I was to work. I wandered along Broadway and Fourth Street, the street of the old courthouse; sought out the Mississippi River and stared at it, that vast river lying between banks of yellow mud; then I went back to the office of the *Globe-Democrat*, for it was nearing the time when its editor-in-chief might choose to put in an appearance.

Joseph B. McCullagh ("Little Mac" of Eugene Field's verse) was a short, thick, aggressive, rather pugnacious and defensive person of Irish extraction. He was short, sturdy, Napoleonic, ursine rather than leonine. I was instantly drawn and thrown back by his stiff reserve. A negro elevator boy had waved me along a marble hall on the seventh floor to a room at the end, where I was met by an office boy who took in my name and then ushered me into the great man's presence. I found him at a roll-top desk in a minute office, and he was almost buried in discarded newspapers. I learned afterward that he would never allow these to be removed until he was all but crowded out. I was racked with nervousness. Whatever high estimate I had conceived of myself had oozed out by the time I reached his door. I was now surveyed by keen gray Irish eyes from under bushy brows.

"Um, yuss! Um, yuss!" was all he deigned to say. "See Mr. Mitchell in the city-room, Mr. Mitchell—um, yuss. Your salary will be—um—um—twenty dollars to begin with" (he was chewing a cigar and mumbled his words), and he turned to his papers.

Not a word, not a sign, that he knew I had ever written a line worth while. I returned to the handsome city-room, and found only empty desks. I sat down and waited fully three-quarters of an hour, examining old papers and staring out of the windows over the roofs until Mr. Mitchell appeared.

Like his employer, he was thick-set, a bigger man physically but less attractive. He had a round, closely-cropped head and a severe and scowling expression. He reminded me of Squeers in *Nicholas Nickleby*. A savage fat man—can anything be worse? He went to his desk with a quick stride when he entered, never noticing me. When I approached and explained who I was and why I was there he scarcely gave me a glance.

"The afternoon assignments won't be ready till twelve-thirty," he commented drily. "Better take a seat in the next room."

It was then only eleven-thirty, and I went into the next room and waited. It was empty but deliciously warm on this chilly day. How different from McEnnis, I thought. Evidently being called to a newspaper by telegram was not to be interpreted as auguring that one was to lie on a bed of roses.

A little bit afraid to leave for this hour, in case he might call, I hung about the two windows of this room staring at the new city. How wonderful it seemed, now this morning, after the quiet of the night before, how strong and forceful in this November air. The streets and sky were full of smoke; there was a clangor of street-car gongs below and the rumble of endless trucks. A block or two away loomed up a tall building of the newer order, twelve stories at least. Most of the buildings were small, old family dwellings turned into stores. I wondered about the life of the city, its charms, its prospects. What did it hold for me? How long would I remain here? Would this paper afford me any real advancement? Could I make a great impression and rise?

As I was thus meditating several newspaper men came in. One was a short bustling fellow with a golden-brown mustache and a shock of curly brown hair, whose name I subsequently learned was Hazard—a fitting name for a newspaper reporter. He wore a fedora hat, a short cream-colored overcoat which had many wrinkles about the skirts in the back, and striped trousers. He came in with a brisk air, slightly skipping his feet as he walked, and took a desk, which was nothing more than a segment of one long desk fastened to the wall and divided by varnished partitions of light oak. As soon as he was seated he opened a drawer and took out a pipe, which he briskly filled and lighted, and then began to examine some papers he had in his pockets. I liked his looks.

There sauntered in next a pale creature in a steel-gray suit of not too new a look, who took a seat directly opposite the first comer. His left hand, in a brown glove, hung at his side; apparently it was of wood or stuffed leather. Later there arrived a negro of very intellectual bearing, who took a seat next the second arrival; then a stout, phlegmatic-looking man with dark eyes, dark hair and skin, which gave me a feeling of something saturnine in his disposition. The next arrival was a small skippity man, bustling about like a little mouse, and having somewhat of a mousy look in his eyes, who seemed to be attached to the main city editorial room in some capacity.

A curious company gradually filed in, fourteen or fifteen all told. I gave up trying to catalogue them and turned to look out the window. The little bustling creature came through the room several times, looked at me without deigning to speak however, and finally put his head in at the door and whispered to the attendant group: "The book's ready." At this there was an immediate stir, nearly all of the men got up and one by one they filed into the next room. Assuming that they were going to consult the assignment book, I followed, but my name was not down. In Chicago my city editor usually called each individual to him in person; here each man was supposed to discover his assignment from a written page. I returned to the reporters' room when I found my name was not down, wondering what I should be used for.

The others were not long gone before I was sought by the mouse—Hugh Keller Hartung by name—who whispered: "The city editor wants to see you"; and then for the second time I faced this gloomy man, whom I had already begun not only to dislike but to fear. He was dark and savage, in his mood to me at least, whether unconsciously so or not I do not know. His broad face, set with a straight full nose and a wide thin-lipped mouth, gave him a frozen Cromwellian outline. He seemed a queer, unliterary type to be attached to so remarkable a journalist as McCullagh.

"There's been some trouble down at this number," he said, handing me a slip of paper on which an address was written. "A fight, I think. See if you can find out anything about it."

I hurried out, immensely relieved to get into the fresh air of the city. I finally made my way to the place, only to find a vacant lot. Thinking there might be some mistake, I went to the nearest police station and inquired. Nothing was known. Fearing to fall down on my first assignment, I returned to the lot, but could learn nothing. Gradually it began to dawn upon me that this might be merely a trial assignment, a bright idea of the frowning fat man, a bearings-finder. I had already conceived a vast contempt for him, a stumbling-block in my path, I thought. No wonder he came to hate me, as I learned afterward he did.

I wandered back through the city, looking at the strange little low houses (it was the region between the river and North Broadway, about a mile above the courthouse), and marveling at the darksome character of the stores. Never in my life had I seen such old buildings, all brick and all crowded together, with solid wood or iron shutters, modeled after those of France from whence its original settlers came and having something of the dourness of the poorer quarters of Paris about them, and windows composed of very small panes of glass, evidences of the influence of France, I am sure. Their interiors seemed so dark, so redolent of an old-time life. The streets also appeared old-fashioned with their cobblestones, their twists and turns and the very little space that lay between the curbs. I felt as though the people must be different from those in Chicago, less dynamic, less aggressive.

When I reached the office I found that the city editor, Mr. Mitchell, had gone. The little mousy individual was at one of the parti-divisions of the wall desk, near Mr. Mitchell's big one, diving into a mass of copy the while he scratched his ear or trifled with his pencil or jumped mousily about in his seat.

"Is Mr. Mitchell about?" I inquired.

"No," replied the other briskly; "he never gets in much before four o'clock. Anything you want to know? I'm his assistant."

He did not dare say "assistant city editor"; his superior would not have tolerated one.

"He sent me out to this place, but it's only a vacant lot."

"Did you look all around the neighborhood? Sometimes you can get news of these things in the neighborhood, you know, when you can't get it right at the spot. I often do that."

"Yes," I answered. "I inquired all about there."

"It would be just like Tobe to send you out there, though," he went on feverishly and timidly, "just to break you in. He does things like that. You're the new man from Chicago, aren't you—Dreiser?"

"Yes, but how did you know?"

"He said you were coming," he replied, jerking his left thumb over his shoulder. "My name's Hartung, Hugh Keller Hartung."

He was so respectful, almost fearsome in his references

to his superior that I could not help smiling. Now that I had my bearings, I did not feel so keenly about Mr. Mitchell. He seemed dull.

"I suppose you'll find St. Louis a little slower than Chicago," he went on, "but we have some of the biggest newspaper stories here you ever saw. You remember the Preller Trunk Mystery, don't you, and that big Missouri-Pacific train robbery last year?"

I recalled both distinctly. "Is that so?" I commented, thinking of my career in Chicago and hoping for a duplication of it here.

Heavy steps were heard in the hall just outside, and Mr. Hartung jumped to his work like a frightened mouse; on the instant his head was fairly pulled down between his shoulders and his nose pressed over his work. He seemed to shrivel and shrink, and I wondered why. I went into the next room just as Mr. Tobias Mitchell entered. When I explained that the address he had given me was a vacant lot he merely looked up at me quizzically, suspiciously.

"Couldn't find it, eh? Somebody must have given me the wrong tip. Wait in the next room. I'll call you when I want you."

I returned to that empty room, from which I could hear the industrious pencil of Mr. Hartung and the occasional throat-clearing cough of Mr. Mitchell brooding among his papers.

CHAPTER XVII

THIS reporters' room, for all its handsome furnishings, never took on an agreeable atmosphere to me; it was too gloomy—and solely because of the personality next door. The room was empty when I entered, but in a short while an old drunken railroad reporter with a red nose came in and sat down in a corner seat, taking no notice of me. I read the morning paper and waited. The room gradually filled up, and all went at once to their desks and began to write industriously. I felt very much out of tune; a reporter's duty at this hour of the night was to write.

However, I made the best of my time reading, and finally went out to supper alone, returning as quickly as possible in case there should be an assignment for me. When I returned I found my name on the book and I set out to interview a Chicago minister who was visiting in the city. Evidently this city editor thought it would be easier for me to interview a Chicago minister than any other. I found my man, after some knocking at wrong doors, and got nothing worth a stick—mere religious drive—and returned with my "story," which was never used. '

While I was writing it up, however, the youth of the Jovian curls returned from an assignment, hung up his little wrinkled overcoat and sat down in great comfort next me. His evening's work was apparently futile for he took out his pipe, rapped it sonorously on his chair, lighted it and then picked up an evening paper.

"What's doing, Jock, up at police headquarters?" called the little man over his shoulder.

"Nothing much, Bob," replied the other, without looking up.

"By jing, you police reporters have a cinch!" jested the first. "All you do is sit around up there at headquarters and get the news off the police blotters, while we poor devils are chasing all over town. *We* have to earn our money." His voice had a peculiarly healthy, gay and bantering ring to it.

"That's no joke," put in a long, lean, spectacled individual who was sitting in another corner. "I've been tramping all over south St. Louis, looking for a confounded robbery story."

"Well, you've got long legs, Benson," retorted the jovial Hazard. "You can stand it. Now I'm not so well fixed that way. Bellairs, there, ought to be given a chance at that. He wouldn't be getting so fat, by jing!"

The one called Jock also answered to the name of Bellairs.

"You people don't do so much," he replied, grinning cheerfully. "If you had my job you wouldn't be sitting here reading a newspaper. It takes work to be a police reporter."

"Is that so?" queried the little man banteringly. "You're proof of it, I suppose? Why, you never did a good day's work in your life!"

"Give us a match, Bob, and shut up," grinned the other. "You're too noisy. I've got a lot of work ahead of me yet tonight."

"I got your work! Is she over sixteen? Wish I had your job."

Jock folded up some copy paper and put it into his pocket and walked into the next room, where the little assistant was toiling away over the night's grist of news.

I still sat there, looking curiously on.

"It's pretty tough," said the spirited Hazard, turning to me, "to go out on an assignment and then get nothing. I'd rather work hard over a good story any day, wouldn't you?"

"That's the way I feel about it," I replied. "It's not much fun, sitting around. By the way, do you know whose desk this is? I've been sitting at it all evening."

"It doesn't belong to anybody at present. You might as well take it if you like it. There's a vacant one over there next to Benson's, if you like that better." He waved toward the tall awkward scribe in the corner.

"This is good enough," I replied.

"Take your choice. There's no trouble about desks just now. The staff's way down anyhow. You're a stranger here, aren't you?"

"Yes; I only came down from Chicago yesterday."

"What paper'd jeh work on up there?"

"The *Globe* and *News*," I answered, lying about the latter in order to give myself a better standing than otherwise I might have.

"They're good papers, aren't they?"

"Yes, pretty fair. The *News* has the largest evening circulation."

"We have some good papers here too. This is one of the biggest. The *Post-Dispatch* is pretty good too; it's the biggest evening paper."

"Do you know how much circulation this paper has?" I inquired.

"Oh, about fifty thousand, I should say. That's not so much, compared to Chicago circulation, but it's pretty big for down here. We have the biggest circulation of any paper in the Southwest. McCullagh's one of the greatest editors in this country, outside of Dana in New York, the greatest of any. If McCullagh were in New York he'd be bigger than he is, by jing!"

"Do you run many big news stories?"

"Sometimes; not often. The *Globe* goes very light on local news. They play up the telegraph on this paper because we go into Texas and Arkansas and Louisiana and all these other States around here. We use $400,000 worth of telegraph news here every year," and he said it as though he were part owner of the paper. I liked him very much.

I opened my eyes at this news and thought dubiously of it in relation to my own work. It did not promise much for a big feature, on which I might spread myself.

We talked on, becoming more and more friendly. In spite of the city editor, whom I did not like, I now began to like this place, although I could feel that these men were more or less browbeaten, held down and frozen. The room was much too quiet for a healthy Western reportorial room, the atmosphere too chill.

We talked of St. Louis, its size (450,000), its principal hotels, the Southern, the Lindell and the La Clede (I learned that its oldest and best, the Planter, had recently been torn down and was going to be rebuilt some day), what were the chief lines of news. It seemed that fires, murders, defalcations, scandals were here as elsewhere the great things, far overshadowing most things of national and international import. Recently a tremendous defalcation had occurred, and this new acquaintance of mine had been working on it, had "handled it alone," as he said. Like all citizens of an American city he was pro-St. Louis, anxious to say a good word for it. The finest portion of it, he told me, was in the west end. I should see the wonderful new residences and places. There was a great park here, Forrest, over fourteen hundred acres in size, a wonderful thing. A new bridge was building in north St. Louis and would soon be completed, one that would relieve traffic on the Eads Bridge and help St. Louis to grow. There was a small city over the river in Illinois, East St. Louis, and a great Terminal Railroad Association which controlled all the local railroad facilities and taxed each trunk line six dollars a car to enter and each passenger twenty-five cents. "It's a great graft and a damned shame, but what can you do?" was his comment. Traffic on the Mississippi was not so much now, owing to the railroads that paralleled it, but still it was interesting.

The already familiar noise of a roll-top desk broke in upon us from the next room, and I noticed a hush fall on the room. What an atmosphere! I thought. After a few moments of silence my new friend turned to me and whispered very softly:

"That's Tobe Mitchell, the city editor, coming in. He's a proper ——, as you'll find." He smiled wisely and began scribbling again.

"He didn't look so pleasant to me," I replied as softly.

"I've quit here twice," he whispered. "The next time I go I won't come back. I don't have to stay here, and he knows it. I can get a job any day on the *Chronicle,* and wouldn't have to work so hard either. That's an evening paper. I stay here because I like a morning paper better, that's all. There's more to it. Everything's so scrappy and kicked together on an evening paper. But he doesn't say much to me any more, although he doesn't like me. You'd think we were a lot of kids, and this place a schoolroom.'' He frowned.

We dropped into silence again. I did not like this thought of difficulty thrust upon me. What a pity a man like McEnnis was not here!

''He doesn't look like much of a newspaper man to me,'' I observed.

''And he isn't either. McCullagh has him here because he saved his life once in a fight somewhere, down in Texas, I think —or that's what they tell me.''

We sat and read; the sound of city life below had died out and one could hear the scratching of reporters' pens. Assignments were written up and turned in, and then the reporters idled about, dangling their legs from spring-back chairs, smoking pipes and whispering. As the clock registered eleven-thirty the round body of Mitchell appeared in the doorway, his fair-tinted visage darkened by a faint scowl.

''You boys can go now,'' he pronounced solemnly.

All arose, I among them, and went to a closet where were our hats and overcoats. I was tired, and this atmosphere had depressed me. What a life! Had I come down here for this? The thought of the small news end which the local life received depressed me also. I could not see how I was to make out.

I went down to a rear elevator, the only one running at this time of night, and came out into the dark street, where a carriage was waiting. I assumed that this must be for the famous editor. It looked so comfortable and sedate, waiting at the door in the darkness for an editor who, as I later learned, might not choose to leave until two. I went on to my little room at the hotel, filled with ideas of how, some day, I should be a great editor and have a carriage waiting for me. Yes; I felt that I was destined for a great end. For the present I must be content to look around for a modest room where I could sleep and bide my time and opportunity.

CHAPTER XVIII

I FOUND a room the next morning in Pine Street, only a few doors from this hotel and a block from my new office. It was a hall bedroom, one of a long series which I was to occupy, dirty and grimy. I recall it still with a sickening sense of its ugliness; and yet its cheapness and griminess did not then trouble me so much. Did I not have the inestimable boon of youth and ambition, which make most material details unimportant? Some drab of a woman rented it to me, and outside were those red, yellow, blue, green and orange street-cars clanging and roaring and wheezing by all night long. Inside were four narrow gray walls, a small wooden bed, none too clean sheets and pillow-cases, a yellow washstand. I brought over my bag, arranged the few things I thought need not be kept under lock and key, and returned to the streets. I need not bother about the office until twelve-thirty, when the assignments were handed out—or "the book," as Hartung reverently called it, was laid out for our inspection.

And now, spread before me for my survey and entertainment was the great city of St. Louis, and life itself as it was manifesting itself to me through this city. This was the most important and interesting thing to me, not my new position. Work? Well, that was important enough, considering the difficulty I had had in securing it. What was more, I was always driven by the haunting fear of losing this or any other position I had ever had, of not being able to find another (a left-over fear, perhaps, due to the impression that poverty had made on me in my extreme youth). Just the same, the city came first in my imagination and desires, and I now began to examine it with care, its principal streets, shops, hotels, its residence district. What a pleasure to walk about, to stare, to dream of better days and great things to come.

Just at this time St. Louis seemed to be upon the verge of

change and improvement. An old section of mansions bordering on the business center was rapidly giving way to a rabble of small stores and cheap factories. Already several new buildings of the Chicago style of skyscraper were either contemplated or in process of construction. There was a new club, the Mercantile, the largest in the city, composed entirely of merchants in the downtown section, which had just been opened and about which the papers were making a great stir. There was a new depot contracted for, one of the finest in all the country, so I was told, which was to house all the roads entering the city. A new city hall was being talked of, an enormous thing-to-be. Out in the west end, where progress seemed the most vital, were new streets and truly magnificent residence "places," parked and guarded areas these, in which were ranged many residences of the ultra-rich. The first time I saw one of these *places* I was staggered by its exclusive air and the beauty and even grandeur of some of the great houses in it—newly manufactured exclusiveness. Here were great gray or white or brownstone affairs, bright, almost gaudy, with great verandas, astonishing doorways, flights of stone steps, heavily and richly draped windows, immense carriage-houses, parked and flowered lawns.

By degrees I came to know the trade and poor sections of the city. Here were long throbbing wholesale streets, crowded with successful companies; along the waterfront was a mill area backed up by wretched tenements, as poor and grimy and dingy as any I have ever seen; elsewhere were long streets of middle-class families, all alike, all with white stone doorsteps or windowsills and tiny front yards.

The atmosphere of the *Globe-Democrat* after a time came to have a peculiar appeal for me because it was dominated so completely by the robust personality of McCullagh. He was so natural, unaffected, rugged. As time passed he steadily grew in my estimation and by degrees, as I read his paper, his powerful, brilliant editorials, and saw how systematically and forcefully he managed all things in connection with himself and his men, the very air of St. Louis became redolent of him. He was a real force, a great man. So famous was he already that men came to St. Louis from the Southwest and elsewhere just to see him and his office. I often think of him in that small office, sitting waist-deep among his papers, his heavy head sunk on his pouter-like chest, his feet incased in white socks and low slipper-like shoes, his whole air one of complete mental and physical absorption in his work. A few years later he committed suicide, out of sheer weariness, I assume, tired of an inane world. Yet it was not until long after, when I was much better able to judge him and his achievements, that I understood what a really big thing he had done: built up a journal of national and even international significance in a region which, one would have supposed, could never have supported anything more than a mediocre panderer to trade interests. As Hazard had proudly informed me, the annual bill for telegraph news alone was $400,000: a sum which, in the light of subsequent journalistic achievements in America, may seem insignificant but which at that time meant a great deal. He seemed to have a desire to make the paper not only good (as that word is used in connection with newspapers) but great, and from my own memory and impression I can testify that it was both. It had catholicity and solidity in editorials and news. The whole of Europe, as well as America, was combed and reflected in order that his readers might be entertained and retained, and each day one could read news of curious as well as of scientific interest from all over the world. Its editorials were in the main wise and jovial, often beautifully written by McCullagh himself. Of assumed Republican tendencies, it was much more a party leader than follower, both in national and in State affairs. The rawest of raw youths, I barely sensed this at the time, and yet I felt something of the wonder and beauty of it all. I knew him to be a great man because I could feel it. There was something of dignity and force about all that was connected with him. Later it became a fact of some importance to me that I had been called to a paper of so much true worth, by a man so wise, so truly able.

The only inharmonious note at this time was my intense loneliness. In Chicago, in spite of the gradual breaking up of our home and the disintegration of the family, I had managed to build up that spiritual or imaginative support which comes to all of us from familiarity with material objects. I had known Chicago, its newspaper world, its various sections, its places of amusement, some dozen or two of newspaper men. Here I knew no one at all.

And back in Chicago there had been Alice and N—— and K——, whereas here whom had I? Alice was a living pain for years, for in my erratic way I was really fond of her. I am of that peculiar disposition, which will not let memories of old ties and old pleasures die easily. I suffer for things which might not give another a single ache or pain. Alice came very close to me, and now she was gone. Without any reasonable complaint, save that I was slightly weary, did not care for her as much as I had, and that my mind was full of the world outside and my future, I had left her. It had not been more than four weeks since I had visited her in her little *parlor* in Chicago, sipping of those delights which only youth and ecstatic imagination can conjure; now I was three hundred miles away from her kisses and the warmth of her hands. At the same time there was this devil or angel of ambition which quite in spite of myself was sweeping me onward. I fancied some vast Napoleonic ending for myself, which of course was moonshine. I could not have gone back to Chicago then if I had wished; it was not spiritually possible. Something within kept saying "On—on!" Besides, it would have done no good. The reaction would have been more irritating than the pain it satisfied. As it was, I could only walk about the city in this chilling November weather and speculate about myself and Alice and N—— and K—— and my own future. What an odd beginning, I often thought to myself. Scandalous, perhaps, in one so young: three girls in as many years, two of them deeply and seriously wounded by me.

"I shall write to her," I thought. "I will ask her to come down here. I can't stand this. She is too lovely and precious to me. It is cruel to leave her so."

There is this to be said for me in regard to my not writing to her: I was uncertain as to the financial practicability of it.

In Chicago I had been telling her of my excellent position, boasting that I was making more than I really was. So long as I was there and not married the pretense could easily be sustained. Here, three hundred miles away, where she would and could not come unless I was prepared to support her, it was a different matter. To ask her now meant a financial burden which I did not feel able, or at least willing, to assume. No doubt I could have starved her on twenty dollars a week; had I been desperately swayed by love I would have done so. I could even have had her, had I so chosen, on conditions which did not involve marriage; but I could not bring myself to do this. I did not think it quite fair. I felt that she would have a just claim to my continuing the relation with her. . . . And outside was the wide world. I told myself that I would marry her if I had money. If she had not been of a soft yielding type she could easily have entrapped me, but she had not chosen to do so. Anyhow, here I was, and here I stayed, meditating on the tragedy of it all.

By this time of course it is quite obvious that I was not an ethically correct and moral youth, but a sentimental boy of considerable range of feeling who, facing the confusing evidences of life, was not prepared to accept anything as final. I did not know then whether I believed that the morality and right conduct preached by the teachers of the world were important or not. The religious and social aphorisms of the day had been impressed upon me, but they did not stick. Something whispered to me that apart from theory there was another way which the world took and which had little in common with the strait and narrow path of the doctrinaires. Not all men swindle in little things, or lie or cheat, but how few fail to compromise in big ones. Perhaps I would not have deliberately lied about anything, at least not in important matters, and I would not now under ordinary circumstances after the one experience in Chicago have stolen. Beyond this I could not have said how I would have acted under given circumstances. Women were not included in my moral speculations as among those who were to receive strict justice—not pretty women. In that, perhaps, I was right: they did not always wish it. I was anxious to meet with many of them, as many as I might, and I would have conducted myself as joyously as their own consciences would permit. That I was to be in any way punished for this, or that the world would severely censure me for it, I did not yet believe. Other boys did it; they were constantly talking about it. The world—the world of youth at least—seemed to be concerned with libertinage. Why should not I be?

CHAPTER XIX

No picture of these my opening days in St. Louis would be of the slightest import if I could not give a fairly satisfactory portrait of myself and of the blood-moods or so-called spiritual aspirations which were animating me. At that time I had already attained my full height, six feet one-and-one-half inches, and weighed only one hundred and thirty-seven pounds, so you can imagine my figure. Aside from one eye (the right) which was turned slightly outward from the line of vision, and a set of upper teeth which because of their exceptional size were crowded and so stood out too much, I had no particular blemish except a general homeliness of feature. It was a source of worry to me all the time, because I imagined that it kept me from being interesting to women; which, apparently, was not true—not to all women at least.

Spiritually I was what might be called a poetic melancholiac, crossed with a vivid materialistic lust of life. I doubt if any human being, however poetic or however material, ever looked upon the scenes of this world, material or spiritual, so called, with a more covetous eye. My body was blazing with sex, as well as with a desire for material and social supremacy —to have wealth, to be in society—and yet I was too cowardly to make my way with women readily; rather, they made their way with me. Love of beauty as such—feminine beauty first and foremost, of course—was the dominating characteristic of all my moods: joy in the arch of an eyebrow, the color of an eye, the flame of a lip or cheek, the romance of a situation, spring, trees, flowers, evening walks, the moon, the roundness of an arm or a hip, the delicate turn of an ankle or a foot, spring odors, moonlight under trees, a lighted lamp over a dark lawn—what tortures have I not endured because of these! My mind was riveted on what love could bring me, once I had the prosperity and fame which somehow I foolishly fancied commanded love; and at the same time I was horribly depressed by the thought that I should never have them, never; and that thought, for the most part, has been fulfilled.

In addition to this I was filled with an intense sympathy for the woes of others, life in all its helpless degradation and poverty, the unsatisfied dreams of people, their sweaty labors, the things they were compelled to endure—nameless impositions, curses, brutalities—the things they would never have, their hungers, thirsts, half-formed dreams of pleasure, their gibbering insanities and beaten resignations at the end. I have sobbed dry sobs looking into what I deemed to be broken faces and the eyes of human failures. A shabby tumbledown district or doorway, a drunken woman being arraigned before a magistrate, a child dying in a hospital, a man or woman injured in an accident—the times unbidden tears have leaped to my eyes and my throat has become parched and painful over scenes of the streets, the hospitals, the jails! I have cried so often that I have felt myself to be a weakling; at other times I have been proud of them and of my great rages against fate and the blundering, inept cruelty of life. If there is a God, conscious and personal, and He considers the state of man and the savagery of His laws and His indifferences, how He must smile at little insect man's estimate of Him! It is so flattering, so fatuously unreasoning, that only a sardonic devil could enjoy it.

I was happy enough in my work although at times despondent lest all the pleasures that can come to youth from health, courage, wealth and opportunity should fail me while I was working and trying to get somewhere. I had health yet I imagined I had not because I was not a Sandow, an athlete, and my stomach, due to an undiscovered appendix, gave me some trouble. As to courage, when I examined myself in that direction I fancied that I had none at all. Would I slip out if a dangerous brawl were brewing anywhere? Certainly. Well, then, I was a coward. Could I stand up and defend myself against a man of my own height and weight? I doubted it, particularly if he were well-trained. In consequence, I was again a coward. There was no hope for me among decently courageous men. Could I play tennis, base-ball, football? No; not successfully. Assuredly I was a weakling of the worst kind. Nearly everybody could do those things, and nearly all youths were far more proficient in all the niceties of life than was I: manners, dancing, knowledge of dress and occasions. Hence I was a fool. The dullest ath-lete of the least proficiency could overcome me; the most minute society man, if socially correct, was infinitely my superior. Hence what had I to hope for? And when it came to wealth and opportunity, how poor I seemed! No girl of real beauty and force would have anything to do with a man who was not a success; and so there I was, a complete failure to begin with.

The aches and pains that went with all this, the amazing depression, all but suicidal. How often have I looked into comfortable homes and wished that some kindly family would give me shelter! And yet half knowing that had it been offered I would have refused it. How often have I looked through the windows of some successful business firm and wished I had achieved ownership or stewardship, a position similar to that of any of the officers and managers inside! To be president or vice-president or secretary of something, some great thrashing business of some kind. Great God, how sublime it seemed! And yet if I had only known how cen-trally controlling the tool of journalism could be made! It mattered not then that I was doing fairly well, that most of my employers had been friendly and solicitous as to my wel-fare, that the few girls I had approached had responded freely enough—still I was a failure.

I rapidly became familiar with the city news department of the *Globe-Democrat*. Its needs, aside from great emergencies, were simple enough: interviews, the doings of conventions of various kinds (wholesale grocers, wholesale hardware men, wholesale druggists), the plans of city politicians when those could be discovered, the news of the courts, jails, city hospi-tals, police courts, the deaths of well-known people, the goings-on in society, special functions of one kind and another, fires, robberies, defalcations. For the first few weeks nothing of importance happened. I was given the task evenings of looking in at the North Seventh Street police station, a slow district, to see if anything had happened, and was naturally able to add to my depression by contemplating the life about there. Again, I attended various churches to hear sermons, interviewed the Irish boss of the city, Edward Butler, an amazing person with a head like that of a gnome or ogre, who immediately took a great fancy to me and wanted me to come and see him again (which I did once).

He has always stuck in my mind as one of the odd experiences of my life. He lived in a small red brick family dwelling just beyond the prostitution area of St. Louis, which stretched out along Chestnut Street between Twelfth and Twenty-second, and was the city's sole garbage contractor (out of which he was supposed to have made countless thousands) as well as one of its principal horse-shoers, having many blacksmithing shops, and was incidentally its Democratic or Republican boss, I forget which, a position he retained until his death.

I first saw him at a political meeting during my first few weeks in St. Louis, and the manner in which he arose, the way in which he addressed his hearers, the way in which they listened to him, all impressed me. Subsequently, being sent to his house, I found him in his small front parlor, a yellow plush album on the marble-topped center table, horse-hair furniture about the room, a red carpet, crayon enlargements of photographs of his mother and father. But what force in the man! What innate gentility of manner and speech! He seemed like a prince disguised as a blacksmith.

"So ye've come to interview me," he said soothingly. "Ye're from the *Globe-Democrat*—well, that paper's no particular friend of mine, but ye can't help that, can ye?" and then he told me whatever it was I wanted to know, giving me no least true light, you may be sure. At the conclusion he offered me a drink, which I refused. As I was about to leave he surveyed me pleasantly and tolerantly.

"Ye're a likely lad," he said, laying an immense hand or one of my lean shoulders, "and ye're jest startin' out in life,

I can see that. Well, be a good boy. Ye're in the newspaper business, where ye can make friends or enemies just as ye choose, and if ye behave yerself right ye can just as well make friends. Come an' see me some time. I like yer looks. I'm always here av an evenin', when I'm not attendin' a meetin' av some kind, right here in this little front room, or in the kitchen with me wife. I might be able to do something fer ye sometime—remember that. I've a good dale av influence here. Ye'll have to write what ye're told, I know that, so I won't be offended. So come an' see me, an' remember that I want nothin' av ye,'' and he gently ushered me out and closed the door behind me.

But I never went, at least not for anything for myself. The one time I asked him for a position for a friend who wanted to work on the local street-cars as a conductor he wrote across the letter: ''Give this man what he wants.'' It was wretchedly scrawled (the man brought it back to me before presenting it) and was signed ''edward butler.'' But the man was given the place at once.

Although Butler was an earnest Catholic, he was supposed to control and tax the vice of the city; which charge may or may not have been true. One of his sons owned and managed the leading vaudeville house in the city, a vulgar burlesque theater, at which the ticket taker was Frank James, brother of the amazing Jesse who terrorized Missouri and the Southwest as an outlaw at one time and enriched endless dime novel publishers afterward. As dramatic critic of the *Globe-Democrat* later I often saw him. Butler's son, a more or less stodgy type of Tammany politician, popular with a certain element in St. Louis, was later elected to Congress.

I wrote up a labor meeting or two, and at one of these saw for the first time Terence V. Powderly, the head of the dominant labor organization—the Knights of Labor. This meeting was held in a dingy hall at Ninth or Tenth and Walnut, a dismal institution known as the Workingman's Club or some such thing as that, which had a single red light hanging out over its main entrance. This long, lank leader, afterward so much discussed in the so-called ''capitalistic press,'' was sitting on a wretched platform surrounded by local labor leaders and discussed in a none too brilliant way, I thought, the need of a closer union between all classes of labor.

In regard to all matters relating to the rights of labor and capital I was at this time perfectly ignorant. Although I was a laborer myself in a fair sense of the word I was more or less out of sympathy with laborers, not as a class struggling for their "rights" (I did not know what their rights or wrongs were) but merely as individuals. I thought, I suppose, that they were not quite as *nice* as I was, not as refined and superior in their aspirations, and therefore not as worthy or at least not destined to succeed as well as I. I even then felt dimly what subsequently, after many rough disillusionments, I came to accept as a fact: that some people are born dull, some shrewd, some wise and some undisturbedly ignorant, some tender and some savage, *ad infinitum*. Some are silk purses and others sows' ears and cannot be made the one into the other by any accident of either poverty or wealth. At this time, however, after listening to Mr. Powderly and taking notes of his speech, I came to the conclusion that all laborers had a just right to much better pay and living conditions, and in consequence had a great cause and ought to stick together. I also saw that Mr. Powderly was a very shrewd man and something of a hypocrite, very simple-seeming and yet not so. Something he said or did—I believe it was a remark to the effect that "I always say a little prayer whenever I have a stitch in my side"—irritated me. It was so suave, so English-chapel-people-like; and he was an Englishman, as I recall it. Anyhow, I came away disliking him and his local labor group, and yet liking his cause and believing in it, and wrote as favorable a comment as I dared. The *Globe* was not pro-corporation exactly, at least I did not understand so, and yet it was by no means pro-workingman either. If I recall correctly, it merely gave the barest facts and let it go at that.

CHAPTER XX

My connection with the *Globe-Democrat* had many aspects, chief among which was my rapidly developing consciousness of the significance of journalism and its relation to the life of the nation and the state. My journalistic career had begun only five months before and preceding that I had had no newspaper experience of any kind. The most casual reader of a newspaper would have been as good as I in many respects. But here I rather sensed the significance of it all, the power of a man like McCullagh, for instance, for good or evil, the significance of a man like Butler in this community. I still had a lot to learn: the extent of graft in connection with politics in a city, the power of a newspaper to make sentiment in a State and so help to carry it for a Governor or a President. The political talk I heard on the part of one newspaper man and another "doing politics," as well as the leading editorials in this and other papers, which just at this time were concerned with a coming mayoralty fight and a feud in the State between rival leaders of the Republican party, completely cleared up the situation for me. I listened to all the gossip, read the papers carefully, wondered over the personalities and oddities of State governments in connection with our national government. Just over the river in Illinois everybody was concerned with the administration of John P. Altgeld, governor of the State, and whether he would pardon the Chicago anarchists whose death sentences, recorded a few years before, had been commuted to life imprisonment. On this side of the river everybody was interested in the administration of William Joel Stone, who was the governor. A man by the name of Cyrus H. Walbridge was certain to be the next mayor if the Republicans won, and according to the *Globe*, they ought to win because the city needed to be reformed. The local Democratic board of aldermen was supposed to be the

most corrupt in all America (how many cities have yearly
thought that, each of its governing body, since the nation began!), and Edward Noonan, the mayor, was supposed to
be the lowest and vilest creature that ever stood up in shoes.
The chief editorials of the *Globe* were frequently concerned
with blazing denunciations of him. As far as I could make
out, he had joined with various corporations and certain members of council to steal from the city, sell its valuable fran-
chises for a song and the like. He had also joined with the
police in helping bleed the saloons, gambling dens and houses
of prostitution. Gambling and prostitution were never so
rampant as now, so our good paper stated. The good people
of the city should join and help save the city from destruction.

How familiar it all sounds, doesn't it? Well, this was 1892,
and I have heard the same song every year since, in every
American city in which I have ever been. Gambling, prostitution, graft, *et cetera*, must be among our national weaknesses, not?

Just the same, in so far as this particular office and the
country about St. Louis were concerned, Joseph McCullagh
was of immense significance to his staff and the natives.
Plainly he was like a god to many of them, the farmers and
residents in small towns in States like Texas, Iowa, Missouri,
Arkansas and in Southern Illinois, where his paper chiefly cir-
culated, for they came to the office whenever they were in the
city merely to get a glimpse of him. He was held in high esteem by his staff, and was one of the few editors of his day
who really deserved to be. Within his office he had an ador-
ing group of followers, which included everyone from the
managing editor down. "The chief says——," "The chief
thinks——," "The old man looks a little grouchy this morning—what do you think?" "Gee, wait'll the old man hears
about that! He'll be hopping!" "That ought to please the
old man, don't you think? He likes a bit of good writing."
Yet for all this chatter, "the old man" never seemed to notice
much of anything or have much to say to any one, except possibly to one or two of his leading editorial writers and his telegraph editor. If he ever conferred with his stout city editor

for more than one moment at a time I never saw or heard of it. And if anything seen or heard by anybody in connection with him was not whispered about the reporters' room before nightfall or daybreak it was a marvel of concealment. Occasionally he might be seen ambling down the hall to the lavatory or to the room of his telegraph chief, but most always it was merely to take his carriage or walk to the Southern Hotel at one o'clock for his luncheon or at six for his dinner, his derby hat pulled over his eyes, his white socks gleaming, a cane in his hand, a cigar between his lips. If he ever had a crony it was not known in the reporters' room. He was a solitary or eccentric, and a few years later, as I have said, he leaped to his death from the second story window of his home, where he had lived in as much privacy and singularity as a Catholic priest.

There were silent figures slipping about—Captain King, a chief editorial writer; Casper S. Yost, a secretary of the corporation, assistant editor and what not; several minor editors, artists, reporters, the city editor, the business manager—but no one or all of them collectively seemed to amount to a hill of beans. Only "the old man" or J. B., as he was occasionally referred to, counted. Under him the paper had character, succinctness and point, not only in its news but in its editorial columns. Although it was among the conventional of the conventional of its day (what American newspaper of that period could have been otherwise?), still it had an awareness which made one feel that "the old man" knew much more than he ever wrote. He seemed to like to have it referred to as "the great religious daily" and often quoted that phrase, but with the saving grace of humor behind it.

And he seemed to understand just how to supply that region with all it desired in the shape of news. Though in the main the paper published mere gossip, oddities about storms, accidents, eccentricities, still there was something about the way the thing was done, the crisp and brief manner in which the material was edited, which made it palatable—very much so, I should say, to the small-town store-lounger or owner—and nearly all had humor, naïveté or pathos. The drift of things politically was always presented in leaders in such a way that even I, a mere stripling, began to get a sense of things national and international. States, the adjacent ones in particular, which supplied the bulk of the *Globe's* circulation, were given special attention and yet in such a way as not to irritate the general reader, leaving it optional with him whether he should read or not. The editorials, sometimes informing, sometimes threatening and directive, sometimes mere fol-de-rol and foolery, and intended as such, had a delicious whimsy in them. Occasionally "the old man" himself wrote one and then everybody sat up and took notice. One could easily single it out even if it had not been passed around, as it nearly always was. "The old man wrote that." "Have you read the old man's editorial in this morning's paper? Gee! Read it!" Then you expected brilliant, biting words, a luminous phraseology, sentences that cracked like a whip, and you were rarely disappointed. The paragraphs exploded at times, burst like a torpedo; at others the whole thing ended like music, the deep, sonorous bass of an organ. "The old man" could write, there was no doubt of that. He also seemed to believe what he wrote, for the time being anyhow. That was why his staff, to a man, revered him. He was a real editor, as contrasted with your namby-pamby "business man" masquerading as editor. He had been a great reporter and war correspondent in his day, one of the men who were with Farragut on the Mississippi and with Sherman and others elsewhere during the great Civil War.

Wandering about this building at this time was an old red-faced, red-nosed German, with a protuberant stomach, very genial, dull and apparently unimportant. He was, as I later learned, the real owner of the paper, the major portion of the stock being in his name; and yet, as every one seemed to understand, he never dared pose as such but must slip about, as much overawed as the rest of us. I was a mere underling and new to the place, and yet I could see it. A more apologetic mien and a more obliging manner was never worn by any mortal, especially when he was in the vicinity of McCullagh's office. His name was Daniel M. Hauser. For the most part he wandered about the building like a ghost, seeming to wish to be somebody or to say something but absolutely without meaning. The short, stout Napoleonic editor ruled supreme.

By degrees I made friends with a number of those that worked here: Bob Hazard; Jock Bellairs, son of the Captain Bellairs who presided over the city zoo; Charlie Benson, and a long list of others whose names escape me now. Of all those on the city staff I was inclined to like Hazard most, for he was a personage, a character, quick, gay, intellectual, literary, forceful. Why he never came to greater literary fame I do not know, for he seemed to have all the flair and feeling necessary for the task. He was an only son of some man who had long been a resident of St. Louis and was himself well known about town. He lived with a mother and sister in southwest St. Louis in a small cottage which always pleased me because of its hominess, and supported that mother and sister in loyal son-like fashion. I had not been long on the paper before I was invited there to dinner, and this in spite of a rivalry which was almost immediately and unconsciously set up between us the moment I arrived and which endured in a mild way even after our more or less allied literary interests had drawn us socially together. At his home I met his sister, a mere slip of a tow-headed girl, whom later on I saw in vaudeville as a headliner. Hazard I encountered years later as a blasé correspondent in Washington, representing a league of papers. He had then but newly completed a wild-West thriller, done in cold blood and with an eye to a quick sale. Assuming that I had influence with publishers and editors, he invoked my aid. I gave him such advice and such letters as I could. But only a few months later I read that Robert Hazard, well-known newspaper correspondent, living with his wife and child in some Washington residence section, had placed a revolver to his temple and ended it all. Why, I have often wondered. He was seemingly so well fitted mentally and physically to enjoy life. . . . Or is it mental fitness that really kills the taste for life?

I would not dwell on him at such length save for some other things which I propose later to narrate. For the moment

I wish to turn to another individual, "Jock" Bellairs, who impressed me as a most curious compound of indifference, wisdom, literary and political sense and a hard social cunning. He had a capacity for (as some one in the office once phrased it) a "lewd and profane life." He was the chief police reporter at a building known as the "Four Courts," an institution which housed, among other things, four judicial chambers of differing jurisdiction, as well as the county jail, the city detention wards, the office of the district attorney, the chief of police, chief of detectives, the city attorney, and a "reporters' room" where all the local reporters were permitted to gather and were furnished paper, ink, tables.

A more dismal atmosphere than that which prevailed in this building, and in similar institutions in all the cities in which I ever worked, would be hard to find. In Chicago it was the city hall and county courthouse, with its police attachment; in Pittsburgh the county jail; in New York the Tombs and Criminal Courts Building, with police headquarters as a part of its grim attachment. I know of nothing worse. These places, essential as they are, are always low in tone, vile, and defile nearly all they touch. They have a corrupting effect upon those with whom they come in contact and upon those who are employed to administer law or "justice." Harlots, criminals, murderers, buzzard lawyers, political judges, detectives, police agents, and court officials generally—what a company! I have never had anything to do with one of these institutions in any city as reporter, plaintiff or assisting friend, without sensing anew the brutality and horror of legal administration. The petty tyrannies that are practiced by underlings and minor officials! The "grafting" of low, swinish brains! The tawdry pomp of ignorant officials! The cruelty and cunning of agents of justice! "Set a thief to catch a thief." Clothe these officials as you will, in whatsoever uniforms of whatsoever splendor or sobriety; give them desks of rosewood and walls of flowered damask; entitle them as you choose, High and Mightiness This and That—still they remain the degraded things they have always been, equals of the criminals and the crimes they are supposed to do away with. It cannot be helped; it is a law of chemistry, of creation. Offal breeds maggots to take care of it, to nullify its stench; carrion has its buzzards, carrion crows and condors. So with criminals and those petty officials of the lower courts and jails who are set to catch them.

But this is a wandering paragraph and has little to do with "Jock" Bellairs, except that he was of and yet not of this particular atmosphere. The first time I saw him I felt compelled to study him, for he seemed somehow to suggest this atmosphere to which he was appointed as reporter. He was in a way, and yet with pleasing reservations, the man for this task. He had a sense of humor and a devil-may-care approach to all this. Whenever anything of real import broke loose he was always the one to be called upon for information or aid, because he was in close touch with the police and detectives, who were his cronies and ready to aid him. And whenever anything happened that was beyond his power to manage he called up the office for aid. On more than one occasion, some "mystery" coming up, I was the one delegated to help him, the supposition being that it was likely to yield a "big" story, bigger than he had time for, being a court fixture. I then sought him out at the Four Courts and was given what he knew, whereupon I began investigations on my own account. Nearly always I found him lolling about with other reporters and detectives, a chair tilted back, possibly a game of cards going on between him and the reporters of other papers, a bottle of whisky in his pocket —"to save time," as he once amusingly remarked—and a girl or two present, friends of one or other of these newspaper men, their "dollies." He would rise and explain to me just what was going on, whisper confidentially in my ear the name of some other newspaper man who had been put on the case by one of the other papers, perhaps ask me to mention the name of some shabby policeman or detective who had been assigned to the case, one who was "a good fellow" and who could be depended upon to help us in the future.

I often had to smile, he was so naïve and yet so wise in his position, so matter-of-fact and commonplace about it all.

Sometimes he would give me the most befuddling information as to how the news got out: he and John Somebody or Other were down at Maggie Sanders's place in Chestnut Street the other night, where he heard from a detective, who was telling somebody else, who told somebody else, and so on. Then, if there was a prisoner in the case, he would take me to him, or tell me where some individual or the body was to be found if there was a body. Then, after I had gone about my labors, he would return to his card-game, his girl and his bottle. There were stories afloat of outings with these girls, or the using of some empty room in this building for immoral purposes, with the consent of complaisant officials. And all about, of course, was this atmosphere of detained criminals, cases at trial, hurrying parents and members of families, weeping mothers and sisters—a mess.

On an average of twice a month during my stay in St. Louis I was called to this building on one errand and another, and always I went with a sicky and sinking sensation, and always I came away from it breathing a sigh of relief. To me it was a horrible place, a pest-hole of suffering and error and trickery, and yet necessary enough, I know.

CHAPTER XXI

I was walking down the marble hall of our editorial floor one day not long after I arrived when I noted on a door at its extreme end the words: "Art Department." The *Globe* in Chicago had no art department, at least I never discovered it. The mere word *art*, although I had no real understanding of it, was fascinating to me. Was it not on every tongue? A man who painted or drew was an artist; Doré was one, for instance, and Rembrandt. (I classed the two together.) In Chicago I had of course known that each paper should have an art department, and that interested me in this one. What were artists like? I had never known one.

Another day I was on my way to the lavatory when I discovered that I had come away without the key, a duplicate of which every department possessed. The art department door being nearest, I entered to borrow theirs. Behold, three distinctive if not distinguished looking individuals at work upon drawings laid upon drawing-boards. Two of these looked up, the one nearest me with a look of criticism in his eye, I thought. The one who answered me when I asked for the key, and who swiftly arose to get it for me, was short and stocky, with bushy, tramp-like hair and beard. There was something that savored of opera bouffe about him, and yet, as I could see, he took himself seriously enough. There was something pleasing in his voice too as he said, "Certainly; here it is," and smiled.

The one who had looked up at first and frowned but made no move was much less cheery. I recall the long, thin, sallow face, the coal-black hair, long and coarse, which was parted most carefully in the middle and slicked down at the sides and back over the ears until it looked as though it had been oiled, and the eyes, black and small and querulous and petulant, as was the mouth, with drawn lines at each corner, as

(120)

though he had endured much pain. That long, loose, flowing black tie! And that soft white or blue or green or brown linen shirt!—would any Quartier Latin denizen have been without them? He had thin, pale bony hands, long and graceful, and an air of "touch thou me not, O defiled one." The man appealed to and repelled me at a glance, appealing to me much more later, and ever remained a human humoresque, something to coddle, endure, decipher, laugh at. Surely Dick Wood, or "Richard Wood, Artist," as his card read, might safely be placed in any pantheon of the unconventionally ridiculous and delicious.

This visit provided a mere glance, however. When I returned the key I was given no encouragement. A little later, my ability to write having been fairly established, I was given a rather large order for one so new: a double-page spread, with illustrations, for the Sunday issue, relating to the new depot then under construction. I was told to see that the art department supplied several drawings—one in particular of a proposed iron and glass train-shed which was to cover thirty-two tracks. Also one of a clock-tower two hundred and thirty-two feet high. This assignment seemed a very honorable one, since it was to carry drawings, and I went about it with energy and enthusiasm. It was Mitchell who told me to look to the art department for suitable illustrations.

Evidently the art department knew all about it before my arrival, for upon inquiry I found that P. B. McCord, he of the tramp-like hair and whiskers, was scheduled to make the pictures. His manner pleased me. He was so cordial, so helpful. Together we visited the depot, and a few days later he called upon me in the reportorial room to ask me to come and see what he had done. Having in regard to most things the same point of view, we were soon the best of friends. A more or less affectionate relationship was then and there established, which endured until his death sixteen years later. During all of that period we were scarcely out of touch with each other, and through him I was destined to achieve some of my sanest conceptions of life. (See *Peter*. Twelve Men.)

And the amazing Wood! I have never encountered another

like him, possibly because for years I have not been associated
with young people, who are frequently full of eccentricities.
A more romantic ass than Wood never lived, nor one with
better sense in many ways. In regard to newspaper drawing
he was only a fairly respectable craftsman, if so much, but
in other ways he was fascinating enough. He and McCord
were compelled at that time to use the old chalk plate process
for much of their hurried work, a thing which required the
artist to scratch with a steel upon a chalk-covered surface,
blowing the chalk away from his outlines as he made them.
This created a dust which both McCord and Wood complained of as being disagreeable and "hard on the lungs."
Wood, who pretended to be dying of consumption, and did die
of it sixteen years later within a month of his friend McCord,
made an awful row about it, although he could easily have
done much to mend matters by taking a little exercise and
keeping out of doors as much as possible; but he preferred
to hover over a radiator or before a fire. Always, on every
occasion, he was given to playing the rôle of the martyr.

Spiritually he was morbid, as was I, only he showed it
much more in his manner. He had much the same desire as
I had at the time: to share in the splendors of marble halls
and palaces and high places generally; and, like myself, he
had but little chance. Fresh from Bloomington, Illinois, a
commonplace American town, he was obsessed by the commonplace dream of marrying rich and coming into the imaginary
splendors of that west end life of St. Louis which was so
interesting to both of us. Far more than myself, I am sure,
he seemed to be seething with an inward rebellion against
the fact that he was poor, not included in the exclusive pleasures of the rich. At the same time he was glowing with
a desire to make other people imagine that he was or soon
would be of them. What airs! what shades of manner! He,
like myself, was forever dreaming of some gorgeous maiden,
rich, beautiful, socially elect, who was to solve all his troubles
for him. But there was this difference between us, or so I
imagined at the time, Dick being an artist, rather remote and
disdainful in manner and handsome as well as poetic and

better-positioned than myself, as I fancied, was certain to achieve this gilded and crystal state whereas I, not being so handsome, nor an artist, nor sufficiently poetic, could hardly aspire to so gorgeous an end. I might perchance arrive at some such goal if I sought it eagerly enough, but the probabilities were that I should not unless I waited a long while, and besides, my dreams and plans varied so swiftly from day to day that I couldn't be sure what I wanted to do, whereas Wood, being so stable in this, that and the other (all the things I was not), was certain to arrive quickly.

Sometimes around dinner time when I would see him leaving the office arrayed in the latest mode, as I assumed— dark blue suit, patent leather boots, dark, round, soft felt hat, loose tie blowing idly about his neck, neat thin cane in his hand—I was fairly convinced that this much-anticipated fortune had already arrived or was about to arrive, this very evening perhaps, and that I should never see him more, never even be permitted to speak to him. Somewhere (out in the west end, of course) was *the* girl, wondrous, rich, beautiful, with whom he was to elope and be forgiven by her wealthy parents. Even now he was on his way to her, while I, poor oaf that I was, was moiling here over some trucky task. Would my ship never come in, my great day arrive?

And Wood was just the type of person who would take infinite delight in creating such an impression. Ten years later, when McCord and I were in the East together and Wood was still in St. Louis, we were never weary of discussing this histrionic characteristic of his, laughing sympathetically with and at him. Later he married—but I shall not anticipate. Mentally, at this time, he was living a dream and in so far as possible acting it, playing the part of some noble Algernon Charles Claude Vere de Vere, heir to or affianced to some maid with an immense fortune which was to make them both eternally happy and allow him to travel, pose, patronize as he chose. A laudable dream, verily.

But I—I confess that I was bitter with envy. What, never to shine thus? Never to be an artist? Never to have beauty

in my lap? For me there were other stings, in connection
with him—stings sharp as serpents' teeth. Dick had a wrist-
watch, the envy of my youthful days (oh, wondrous watch!)
Also a scarf pin made of some strange stone brought from the
Orient and with a cabalistic sign or word on it (enough in
itself to entice any heiress)—and that *boutonnière* of violets!
He was never without them.

And along with all this, that sad, wan, reproachful, dying
smile! And that mysterious something of manner which
seemed to say: "My boy! My boy! The things you will
never know!"

And yet after a time Dick condescended to receive me into
his confidence and into his "studio," a very picturesque
affair, situated in the heart of the downtown district. Also
he condescended to bestow upon me some of his dreams as
well as his friendly presence; a thing which exalted me, being
so new to this art world. I was *permitted* (note the word) to
gather dimly, as neophyte from priest, the faintest outlines of
these wondrous dreams of his, and to share with him the
hope that they might be realized. I was so set up by this
great favor that I felt certain great things must flow from it.
Assuredly we three could do great things if only we would
stick together. But was I worthy? There were already rumors of books, plays, stories, poems, to come from a certain
mighty pen—as a matter of fact, it was already hard upon the
task of writing them—which were to set the world aflame by-
and-by. Certain editors in New York were already receiving (and sending back, alas!) certain preliminary masterpieces along with carefully worded suggestions in regard to
slight but necessary changes which would perfect them and
so inaugurate the new era. Certain writers, certain poets,
certain playwrights were already better than any that had
ever been—the best ever, in short. Dick knew, of course,
and I was allowed to share this knowledge, to be thrilled by it.

CHAPTER XXII

ONCE the ice was broken in this way intimacy with these twain came fast enough, although I never became quite as intimate with Dick as I did with Peter, largely because I could not think him as important. Wood had some feminine characteristics; he could be very jealous of anybody's interest in Peter as well as Peter's interest in anybody else. He was big enough, at times, to see the pettiness of this and try to rise above it, but at other times it would show. Years later McCord confided to me in the most amused way how, when I first appeared on the scene, Dick at once began to belittle me and to resent my obvious desire to "break in," as he phrased it, these two, according to Dick, having established some excluding secret union.

But the union was not exclusive, in so far as Peter was concerned. Shortly after my arrival young Hartung had begun running into the art room (so Peter told me) with amazing tales of the new man, his exploits in Chicago. I had been sent for to come to this paper—that was the great thing. I was vouched for by no less a person than John T. McEnnis, one of the famous newspaper men of St. Louis and a former city editor of this same paper; also by a Mr. Somebody (the Washington correspondent of the paper), for whom I had worked in Chicago on the World's Fair. He had hurried to the art department with his tales of me, wishing, I fancy, to be on friendly and happy terms there. Dick, however, considered Hartung's judgment as less than nothing, himself an upstart, a mere office rat; to have him endeavor to introduce anybody was too much. At first he received me very coldly, then finding me perhaps better than he thought, he hastened to make friends with me.

The halcyon hours with these two that followed. Not infrequently Peter and Dick would dine together at some downtown restaurant; or, if a rush of work were on and they were compelled to linger, they had a late supper in some German saloon. It was Peter who first invited me to one of these late séances, and later Wood did the same, but this last was based on another development in connection with myself which I should narrate here.

The office of the *Globe* proved a sprouting-bed for incipient literary talent. Hazard had, some fifteen or eighteen months before, in company with another newspaper man of whom later I heard amazing things, written a novel entitled *Theo*, which was plainly a bog-fire kindled by those blazing French suns, Zola and Balzac. The scene was laid in Paris (imagine two Western newspaper men who had never been out of America writing a novel of French life and laying it in Paris!) and had much of the atmosphere of Zola's *Nana*, plus the delicious idealism of Balzac's *The Great Man from the Provinces*. Never having read either of these authors at this time, I did not see the similarity, but later I saw it plainly. One or both of these men had fed up on the French realists to such an extent that they were able to create the illusion of France (for me at least) and at the same time to fire me with a desire to create something, perhaps a novel of this kind but preferably a play. It seemed intensely beautiful to me at the time, this book, with its frank pictures of raw, greedy, sensual human nature, and its open pictures of self-indulgence and vice.

The way this came about was interesting but I would not relate it save that it had such a marked effect on me. I was sitting in the city reportorial room later one gloomy December afternoon, having returned from a fruitless assignment, when a letter was handed me. It was postmarked Chicago and addressed in the handwriting of Alice. Up to then I had allowed matters to drift, having, as I have said, written but one letter in which I apologized rather indifferently for having come away without seeing her. But my conscience had been paining me so much that when I saw her writing I started. I tore the letter open and read with a sense of shame:

"Dear Theo:

"I got your letter the day you left, but then it was too late. I know what you say is true, about your being called away, and I don't blame you. I'm only sorry our quarrel" (there had been none save of my making) "didn't let you come to see me before you left. Still, that was my fault too, I guess. I can't blame you entirely for that.

"Anyhow, Theo, that isn't what I'm writing you for. You know that you haven't been just the same to me as you once were. I know how you feel. I have felt it too. I want to know if you won't send me back the letters I wrote you. You won't want them now. Please send them, Theo, and believe I am as ever your friend,

"ALICE."

There was a little blank space on the paper, and then:

"I stood by the window last night and looked out on the street. The moon was shining and those dead trees over the way were waving in the wind. I saw the moon on that little pool of water over in the field. It looked like silver. Oh, Theo, I wish I were dead."

As I read this I jumped up and clutched the letter. The pathos of it cut me to the quick. To think I should have left her so! To think I should be here and she there! Why hadn't I written? Why had I shilly-shallied these many days? Of course she wished to die. And I—what of me?

I went over the situation and tried to figure out what I should do. Should I send for her? Twenty dollars a week was very little for two. My legitimate expenses made a total of eleven a week. I wished to keep myself looking well, to have a decent room, to eat three fair meals a day. And I was in no position to return to Chicago, where I had earned less. Then my new friendships with Wood and McCord as well as with other newspaper men, nearly all of whom liked to drink, were costing me something extra; I could not associate with them without buying an occasional drink. I did not see where I was to save much or how I could support a wife. In addition, there was the newness of my position here. I could not very well leave it now, having just come from Chicago. By nature where things material of futurial were concerned I was timid, but little inclined to battle for my rights or desires, and consequently not often realizing them. I was in a trying situation, for I had, as I have said, let it appear to Alice that money was no object. With the vanity of youth, I had always talked of my good salary and comfortable position, and now that this salary and comfortable position were to be put to the test I did not know what to do about it. Honesty would have dictated a heartfelt confession, of course.

But I made none. Instead I wavered between two horns of an ever-recurring dilemma. Sympathizing with the pain which Alice was suffering, and alive to my own loss of honor and happiness, still I hesitated to pull down the fine picture of myself which I had so artistically built up, to reveal myself as I really was, a man unable to marry on his present salary. If I had loved her more, if I had really respected her, if I had not looked upon her as one who might be so easily put aside, I would have done something about it. My natural tendency was to drift, to wait and see, suffering untold agonies in the meanwhile. This I was preparing to do now.

These mental stresses were always sufficient, however, to throw me into a soulful mood. And now as I looked out of the window on the "fast widowing sky" it was with an ache that rivaled in intensity those melancholy moods we sometimes find interpreted by music. Indeed my heart was torn by the inextricable problems which life seemed ever to present and I fairly wrung my hands as I looked into the face of the hurrying world. How it was hastening away! How swiftly and insensibly my own life was slipping by! The few sweets which I had thus far tasted were always accompanied by such bitter repinings. No pleasure was without pain, as I had already seen, and life offered no solution. Only silence and the grave ended it all.

My body was racked with a fine tremor, my brain ached. I went to my desk and took up a pencil. I sat looking into the face of the tangle as one might into the gathering front of a storm. Words moved in my brain, then bubbled, then marshaled themselves into curious lines and rhythms. I put my pencil to paper and wrote line after line.

Presently I saw that I was writing a poem but that it was rough and needed modifying and polishing. I was in a great fever to change it and did so but more eager to go on with my idea, which was about this tangle of life. I became so moved and interested that I almost forgot Alice in the process. When I read it over it seemed but a poor reflection of the thoughts I had felt, the great sad mood I was in. Then I sat there, dissatisfied and unhappy, resolving to write Alice and tell her all.

I took a pen and wrote her that I could not marry her now, that I was in no position to do so. Later, if I found myself in better shape financially, I would come back. I told her that I did not want to send back her letters, that I did not wish to think our love was at an end. I had not meant to run away. I closed by saying that I still loved her and that the picture she had painted of herself standing at the window in the moonlight had torn my heart. But I could not write it as effectually as I might have, for I was haunted by the idea that I should never keep my word. Something kept telling me that it was not wise, that I didn't really want to.

While I was writing Hazard came into the room and glanced over my shoulder to where the poem was lying. "What you doing, Dreiser? Writing poetry?"

"Trying to," I replied a little shamefacedly. "I don't seem to be able to make much of it, though." The while I was wondering at the novelty of being taken for a poet. It seemed such a fine thing to be.

"There's no money in it," he observed helpfully. "You can't sell 'em. I've written tons of 'em, but it don't do any good. You'd better be putting your time on a book or a play."

A book or a play! I sat up. To be considered a writer, a dramatist—even a possible dramatist—raised me in my own estimation. Why, at this rate I might become one—who knows?

"I know it isn't profitable," I said. "Still, it might be if I wrote them well enough. It would be a great thing to be a great poet."

Hazard smiled sardonically. From his pinnacle of twenty-six years such aspirations seemed ridiculous. I might be a good newspaper man (I think he was willing to admit that), but a poet!

The discussion took the turn of book-and play-writing. He had written a book in connection with Young, I think his name was. He had lately been thinking of writing a play. He expatiated on the money there was to be made out of this, the great name some playwrights achieved. Look at Augustus Thomas now, who had once worked on the *Star* here. One of his pieces was then running in St. Louis. Look at Henry Blossom, once a St. Louis society boy, one of whose books was now in the local bookstore windows, a hit. To my excited mind the city was teeming with brilliant examples. Eugene Field had once worked here, on this very paper; Mark Twain had idled about here for a time, drunk and hopeless; W. C. Brann had worked on and gone from this paper; William Marion Reedy the same.

I returned to my desk after a time, greatly stirred by this conversation. My gloom was dissipated. Hazard had promised to let me read this book. This world was a splendid place for talent, I thought. It bestowed success and honor upon those who could succeed. Plays or books, or both, were the direct entrance to every joy which the heart could desire. Something of the rumored wonder and charm of the lives of successful playwrights came to me, their studios, their summer homes and the like. Here at last, then, was the equivalent of Dick's wealthy girl!

I sat thinking about plays somewhat modified in my grief over Alice for the nonce, but none the less aware of its tremendous sadness. I read over my poem and thought it good, even beautiful. I must be a poet! I copied it and put a duplicate in Alice's letter, and folded my own copy and put it in my pocket, close to my heart. It seemed as though I had just forged a golden key to a world of beauty and light where sorrow and want could never be.

CHAPTER XXIII

THE central character of Hazard's book was an actress, young and very beautiful. Her lover was a newspaper man, deeply in love with her and yet not faithful, in one instance anyhow. This brought about a Zolaesque scene in which she spanked another actress with a hairbrush. There was treacherous plotting on the part of somebody in regard to a local murder, which brought about the arrest and conviction of the newspaper man for something he knew nothing about. This entailed a great struggle on the part of Theo to save him, which resulted in her failure and his death on the guillotine. A priest figured in it in some way, grim, jesuitical.

To this day some of the scenes of this book come back to me as having been forcefully done—the fight between the two actresses, for one thing, a midnight feast with several managers, the gallows scene, a confession. I am not sure of the name of the newspaper man who collaborated with Hazard on this work, but the picture of his death in an opium joint later, painted for me by Hazard, and the eccentricities of his daily life, stand out even now as Poe-like. He must have been blessed or cursed with some such temperament as that of Poe, dark, gloomy, reckless, poetic, for he was a dope-fiend and died of dope.

Be that as it may, this posthumous work, never published, so far as I know, was the opening wedge for me into the realm of realism. Being distinctly imitative of Balzac and Zola, the method was new and to me impressive. It has always struck me as curious that the first novel written by an American that I read in manuscript should have been one which by reason of its subject matter and the puritanic character of the American mind could never be published. These two youths knew this. Hazard handed it to me with the statement: "Of course a thing like this could never be published over here. We'd have to get it done abroad." That struck me as odd at the time—the fact that if one wrote a fine thing nevertheless because of an American standard I had not even thought of before, one might not get it published. How queer, I thought. Yet these two incipient artists had already encountered it. They had been overawed to the extent of thinking it necessary to write of French, not American life in terms of fact. Such things as they felt called upon to relate occurred only in France, never here—or at least such things, if done here, were never spoken of. I think it nothing less than tragic that these men, or boys, fresh, forceful, imbued with a burning desire to present life as they saw it, were thus completely overawed by the moral hypocrisy of the American mind and did not even dare to think of sending their novel to an American publisher. Hazard was deeply impressed with the futility of attempting to do anything with a book of that kind. The publishers wouldn't stand for it. You couldn't write about life as it was; you had to write about it as somebody else thought it was, the ministers and farmers and dullards of the home. Yet here he was, as was I, busy in a profession that was hourly revealing the fact that this sweetness and light code, this idea of a perfect world which contained neither sin nor shame for any save vile outcasts, criminals and vagrants, was the trashiest lie that was ever foisted upon an all too human world. Not a day, not an hour, but the pages of the very newspaper we were helping to fill with our scribbled observations were full of the most incisive pictures of the lack of virtue, honesty, kindness, even average human intelligence, not on the part of a few but of nearly everybody. Not a business, apparently, not a home, not a political or social organization or an individual but in the course of time was guilty of an infraction of some kind of this seemingly perfect and unbroken social and moral code. But in spite of all this, judging by the editorial page, the pulpit and the noble mouthings of the average citizen speaking for the benefit of his friends and neighbors, all men were honest—only they weren't; all women were virtuous and without evil intent or design—but they weren't; all mothers were gentle, self-sacrificing slaves, sweet pictures for songs and Sunday Schools—only they weren't; all fathers were kind, affectionate, saving, industrious—only they weren't. But when describing actual facts for the news columns, you were not allowed to indicate these things. Side by side with the most amazing columns of crimes of every kind and description would be other amazing columns of sweet mush about love, undying and sacrificial, editorials about the perfection of the American man, woman, child, his or her sweet deeds, intentions and the like—a wonderful dose. And all this last in the face of the other, which was supposed to represent the false state of things, merely passing indecencies, accidental errors that did not count. If a man like Hazard or myself had ventured to transpose a true picture of facts from the news columns of the papers, from our own reportorial experiences, into a story or novel, what a howl! Ostracism would have followed much more swiftly in that day than in this, for today turgid slush approximating at least some of the facts is tolerated. Fifteen years later Hazard told me he still had his book buried in a trunk somewhere, but by then he had turned to adventurous fiction, and a year later, as I have said, be blew his brains out.

Just the same the book made a great impression on me! It gave me a great respect for Hazard, made me really fond of him. And it fixed my mind definitely on this matter of writing—not a novel, curiously, but a play, a form which from the first seemed easier for me and which I still consider so, one in which I work with greater ease than I do in the novel. I mentioned to Wood and McCord that Hazard and another man had written a novel and that I had read it. I must have enthused over it for both were impressed, and I myself seemed to gain standing, especially with Wood. It was generally admitted then that Hazard was one of the best reporters in the city, and my being taken into his confidence in this fashion seemed to Wood to be a significant thing.

And not long after that I had something else to tell these two which carried great weight. There was at that time on the editorial page of the paper a column entitled "Heard in the Corridors," which was nothing more than a series of imaginary interviews with passing guests at the various hotels, or interviews condensed into short tales, about six to the column, one at least being accredited to a guest at each of the three principal hotels, the others standing accredited as things heard at the Union Station or upon the street somewhere. Previous to my arrival this column had been written by various men, the last one having been the already famous W. C. Brann, then editor of the brilliant *Iconoclast*. By the time I arrived, however, Brann had departed, and the column had sagged. Hazard was doing a part of it, Bellairs another, but both were tired of it. At first when I considered it (a little extra work added to my daily reporting) I was not so pleased; indeed it seemed an all but impossible thing to do. Later, however, after a trial, I discovered that it gave free rein to my wildest imaginings, which was exactly what I wanted. I could write any sort of story I pleased, romantic, realistic or lunatic, and credit it to some imaginary guest at one of the hotels, and if it was not too improbable it was passed without comment. At any rate, when this was assigned to me I went forth to get names of personages stopping at the hotels. I inquired for celebrities. As a rule, the clerks could give me no information or were indifferent, and seemed to take very little interest in having the hotel advertised. I returned and racked my brain, decided that I could manufacture names as well as stories, and forthwith scribbled six marvels, attaching such names as came into my mind. The next day these were all duly published and I was told to do the column regularly as well as my regular assignments. My asinine ebullience had won me a new task without any increase in pay.

However, it seemed an honor to have a whole column assigned to me, and this honor I communicated to McCord and Wood. It was then that either Wood or McCord informed me that Brann had done it previously and had written snake stories for the paper into the bargain. This flattered me, for they pictured him for what he was, a rare soul, and I felt myself growing. Peter had illustrated some of these tales for him, for, as he said with mock dignity: "I am the official snake artist of this paper." That very night, as a reward for my efficiency I was invited by Dick to come to his room—*the* room, the studio—where he inflicted about nine of his horrible masterpieces upon me.

I would not make so much of this great honor if it were not for what it meant to me then. The room was large and dark, on Broadway between Market and Walnut, with the cars jangling below. It contained one great white bed, a long table covered with the papers and literary compositions of Mr. Richard Wood, and was decorated and reinforced with that gentleman's conception of what constituted literary insignia. On the walls hung dusty engravings representing the death of Hamlet and the tempting of Faust. In one corner, over a chest of drawers, was the jagged blade of a sword-fish, and in another a most curious display of oriental coins. The top of the wardrobe was surmounted by a gruesome *papier-mâché* head representing that somewhat demented creature known in England as Ally Sloper. A clear space at one corner of the table held a tin pail for carrying beer, and the floor, like the walls, was covered with some dusty brown material which might once have been a carpet. Owing to the darkness of the furnishings and the brightness of the fire, the room had a very cheery look.

"Say, Dick, did you see where one of ——'s plays had made a great hit in New York?" asked McCord. "He's made a strike this time."

"No," replied Dick solemnly, poking among the coals of the grate and drawing up a chair. "Sit down, Dreiser. Pull up a chair, Peter. This confounded grate smokes whenever the wind's from the South. Still there's nothing like a grate fire."

We drew up chairs. I was revolving in my mind the charm of the room and a vision of greatness in play-writing. These two men seemed subtly involved with the perfection of the arts. In this atmosphere, with such companions, I felt that I could accomplish anything, and soon.

"I'll tell you how it is with the game of play-writing," observed Dick sententiously. "You have to have imagination and feeling and all that, but what's more important than anything is a little business sense, to know how to get in with those fellows. You might have the finest play in the world in your pocket, but if you didn't know how to dispose of it what good would it do you? None at all. You got to know that end first."

He reached over and pulled the coal-scuttle into position as a footrest and then looked introspectively at the ceiling.

"The play's the thing," put in Peter. "If you could write a real good play you wouldn't need to worry about getting it staged."

"Aw, wouldn't I? Listen to that now!" commented Dick irascibly. "I tell you, Peter, you don't know anything about it. You only think you do; that's all. Say, did Campbell have a good play in his pocket or didn't he? You betcher neck he did. Did he get it staged? No, you betcher boots he didn't. Don't talk to me; I know."

By his manner you would have thought he had a standing bone to pick with Peter, but this was only his way. It made me laugh.

"Well, the play's the first thing to worry about anyhow," I observed. "I wish I were in a position to write one."

"Why don't you try?" suggested McCord. "You ought to be able to do something in that line. I bet you could write a good one."

We fell to discussing dramatists. Peter, with his eye for gorgeous effects, costuming and the like, immediately began to describe the ballet effects and scenery of a comic opera laid in Algeria which was then playing in St. Louis.

"You ought to go and see that, Dreiser," he urged. "It's something wonderful. The effect of the balconies in the first act, with the muezzins crying the prayers from the towers in the distance, is great. Then the harmony of the color work in the stones of the buildings is something exquisite. You want to see it."

I felt myself glowing. This intimate conversation with men

of such marked artistic ability, in a room, too, which was the reflection of an artist's personality, raised my sense of latent ability to the highest point. Not that I felt I was not fit to associate with these people—I felt that I was more than fit, their equal at every point, conceal it as I might—but it was something to come in touch with your own, to find real friends to the manner born who were your equals and able to sympathize with you and appreciate your every mood. A man who had found such friends as these so quickly surely need never worry.

"I'll tell you what I propose to do, Peter, while you people are talking," observed Dick. "I propose to go over to Frank's and get a can of beer. Then I'll read you that story."

This proposal to read a story was new to me; I had not heard Wood had written one before. I looked at him more keenly, and a little flame of envy leaped to life in me. To be able to write a short story—or any kind of a story!

He went to his wardrobe, whence he extracted a medium-length black cape of broadcloth, which he threw about his shoulders, and a soft hat which he drew rakishly over his eyes, then took the tin pail and a piece of money from a plate, after the best fashion of the artistic romances of the day, and went out. I gazed admiringly after him, touched by the romance of it all. That face, waxen, drawn, sensitive, with deep burning eyes, and that frail body! That cape! That hat! That plate of coins! Yes, this was Bohemia! I was now a part of that happy middle world which was superior to wealth and poverty. I was in that serene realm where moved freely talent, artistic ability, noble thought, ingenious action, unhampered by conventional thought and conduct. A great man should so live, an artist certainly. These two could and did do as they pleased. They were not as others, but wise, sensitive, delicately responsive to all that was best in life; and as yet the great world was not aware of their existence!

Wood came back with the beer and then Peter insisted that he read us the story. I noticed that there was something impish in his manner. He assured me that all of Dick's stories were masterpieces, every one; that time alone was required for world-wide recognition.

Dick picked up a single manuscript from a heap. "I don't want to inflict this on you, Dreiser," he said sweetly and apologetically. "We had planned to do this before I knew you were coming."

"That's the way he always talks," put in Peter banteringly. "Dick loves to stage things. But they're great stories just the same."

I leaned back, prepared to be thrilled. Dick drew up his chair to the table and adjusted a green-shaded gas lamp close to the table's edge. He then unfolded his MS. and began reading in a low, well-modulated, semi-pathetic voice, which seemed very effective in the more sentimental passages. Reverently I sat and listened. The tale was nothing, a mere daub, but, oh, the wonder of it! Was I not in the presence and friendship of artists? Was not this Bohemia? Had I not long heard and dreamed of it? Well, then, what difference whether the tales were good or bad? They were by one whom I was compelled to admire, an artist, pale, sensitive, recessive, one who at the slightest show of inattention or lack of appreciation might leave me and never see me more.

I listened to about nine without dying, declaring each and every one to be the best I had ever heard—perfect.

CHAPTER XXIV

FROM now on, because of this companionship, my life in St. Louis took on a much more cheerful aspect. Hitherto, in spite of my work and my natural interest in a strange city, I had had intensely gloomy moments. My favorite pastime, when I was not out on an assignment or otherwise busy, was to walk the streets and view the lives and activities of others, not thinking so much how I might advantage myself and my affairs as how, for some, the lightning of chance was always striking in somewhere and disrupting plans, leaving destruction and death in its wake, for others luck or fortune. I never was blinded to the gross favoritism practiced by nature, and this I resented largely, it may be, because it was not, or I thought it was not, practiced in my behalf. Later in life I began to suspect that a gross favoritism, in regard to certain things at least, was being practiced in my behalf. I was never without friends, never without some one to do me a good turn at a critical moment, never without love and the sacrifice of beauty on the part of some one in my behalf, never without a certain amount of applause or repute. Was I worthy of it? I knew I was not and I felt that the powers that make and control life did not care two whoops whether I was or not.

Life, as I had seen and felt from my earliest thinking period, used people, sometimes to their advantage, sometimes not. Occasionally, as I could see, I was used to my advantage as well as to that of some one or something else. Occasionally I was used, as I thought, to my disadvantage. Now and then when I imagined I was being used most disadvantageously it was not so at all, as when for a period I found myself unable to write and so compelled to turn to other things—a turning which resulted in better material later on. At this time, however, I felt that whatever the quality of the gifts handed me or the favors done me, they were as nothing compared to some; and, again, I was honestly and sympathetically interested in the horrible deprivations inflicted upon others, their weaknesses of mind and body, afflictions of all sizes and sorts, the way so often they helplessly blundered or were driven by internal chemic fires, as in the case of the fascinating and beautiful-minded John T. McEnnis, to their own undoing. That great idealistic soul, that warm, ebullient heart!

The opportunity for indulging in these moods was due to the fact that I had plenty of time on my hands, that just at this time I was more interested in seeing than in reading, and that the three principal hotels here, Southern-fashion, were most hospitable, equipping their lobbies and even their flanking sidewalks with comfortable rocking-chairs where one might sit and dream or read or view the passing scene with idle or analytic eye. My favorite hotel was the Lindell, rather large and not impressive but still successful and popular, which stood at the northwest corner of Sixth and Washington Avenue. Here I would repair whenever I had a little time and rock in peace and watch the crowd of strangers amble to and fro. The manager of this hotel, a brisk, rather interesting and yet job-centered American, seeing me sit about every afternoon between four-thirty and six and knowing that I was from the *Globe*, finally began to greet me and ask occasionally if I did not want to go up to dinner. (How lonely and forlorn I must have looked!) On Thanksgiving and Christmas afternoons of this my first season there, seeing me idle and alone, he asked me to be his guest. I accepted, not knowing what else to do. To make it seem like a real invitation he came in after I was seated at the table and sat down with me for a few minutes. He was so charming and the hotel so brisk and crowded that I soon felt at home.

The daily routine of my work seemed to provide ample proof of my suspicions that life was grim and sad. Regularly it would be a murder, a suicide, a failure, a defalcation which I would be assigned to cover, and on the same day there would be an important wedding, a business or political banquet, a ball or a club entertainment of some kind, which would provide just the necessary contrast to prove that life is haphazard and casual and cruel; to some lavish, to others niggardly.

Mere money, often unworthily inherited or made by shabby methods, seemed to throw commonplace and even wretched souls into such glittering and condescending prominence, in this world at least. Many of the business men with whom I came in contact were vulgarians, their wives and daughters vain and coarse and inconsiderate. I was constantly impressed by the airs of the locally prominent, their craving for show and pleasure, their insane greed for personal mention, their hearty indifference to anything except money plus a keen wish to seem to despise it. I remember going one afternoon to an imposing residence where some function was in progress. I was met by an ostentatious butler who exclaimed most nobly: "My dear sir, who sent you here? The *Globe* knows we never give lists to newspaper men. We never admit reporters," and then stiffly closed the door on me. I reported as much to the city editor, who remarked meekly, "Well, that's all right," and gave me something else to do. But the next day a list of the guests at this function was published, and in this paper. I made inquiry of Hartung, who said: "Oh, the society editor must have turned that in. These society women send in their lists beforehand and then say they don't receive reporters."

Another time it was the residence of the Catholic archbishop of St. Louis, a very old but shrewd man whom, so it was rumored in newspaper circles, the local priests were plotting to make appear infirm and weakminded in order that a favorite of theirs might be made coadjutor. I was sent to inquire about his health, to see him if possible. At the door I was met by a sleek dark priest who inquired what I wished, whereupon he assured me that the archbishop was too feeble to be seen.

"That is exactly why I am here," I insisted. "The *Globe* wishes to inform the public of his exact condition. There seems to be a belief on the part of some that he is not as ill as is given out."

"What! You accuse us of concealing something in connection with the archbishop! This is outrageous!" and he firmly shut me out.

It seemed to me that the straightforward thing would have been to let me meet the archbishop. He was a public official, the state of whose health was of interest to thousands. But no; official control regulated that. Shortly afterward he was declared too feeble to perform his duties and a coadjutor was appointed.

Again I was sent to a fashionable west end hotel to interview a visiting governor who was attending a reception of some kind and who, as we understood, was leaving the next day.

"My dear young fellow," said a functionary connected with the entertainment committee, "you cannot do anything of the sort. This is no time to be coming around for anything of this kind."

"But he is leaving tomorrow. . . ."

"I cannot help that. You cannot see him now."

"How about taking him my card and asking him about tomorrow?"

"No, no, no! I cannot do anything of the sort. You cannot see him," and once again I was shunted briskly forth.

I recall being sent one evening to attend a great public ball of some kind—The Veiled Prophets—which was held in the general selling-room of the stock exchange at Third and Walnut, and which followed as a rule some huge autumnal parade. The city editor sent me for a general view or introduction or pen picture to be used as a lead to the full story, which was to be done by others piecemeal. For this occasion I was ordered to hire a dress-suit (the first I had ever worn), which cost the paper three dollars. I remember being greatly disturbed by my appearance once I got in it and feeling very queer and conspicuous. I was greatly troubled as to what sort of impression my garb would make on the various members of the staff. As to the latter I was not long in doubt.

"Say, look at our friend in the claw-hammer, will you?"

this from Hazard. "He looks like a real society man to me!"

"Usher, you mean," called Bellairs. "Who is he? I don't seem to remember him."

"Those pants come darned near being a fit, don't they?" this from some one who had laid hold of the side lines of the trousers.

I could not make up my mind whether I wanted to fight or laugh or whether I was startlingly handsome or a howling freak.

But the thing that weighed on me most was the luxury, tawdry enough perhaps to those intimately connected with it, which this ball presented, contrasted with my own ignoble state. After spending three hours there bustling about examining flowers, decorations, getting names, details of costumes, and drinking various drinks with officiating floormasters whose sole duty appeared to be to look after the press and see that they got all details straight, I returned to the office and began to pour forth a glowing account of how beautiful it all was, how gorgeous, how perfect the women, how marvelous their costumes, how gracious and graceful the men, how oriental or occidental or Arabic, I forget which, were the decorations, outdoing the Arabian Nights or the fabled splendors of the Caliphate. Who does not recognize this indiscriminate newspaper tosh, poured forth from one end of America to another for everything from a farmers' reunion or an I. O. O. F. Ladies' Day to an Astor or a Vanderbilt wedding?

As I was writing, my head whirring with the imaginary and impossible splendors of the occasion, I was informed by my city editor that when I was done I should go to a number in South St. Louis where only an hour before a triple or quadruple murder had been committed. I was to go out on a street-car and if I could not get back in time by street-car I was to get a carriage and drive back at breakneck speed in order to get the story into the last edition. The great fear was that the rival paper, the *Republic,* would get it or might already have it and we would not. And so, my head full of pearls, diamonds, silks, satins, laces, a world of flowers and lights, I was now hustled out along the dark, shabby, lonely streets of South St. Louis to the humblest of cottages, in the humblest of streets where, among unpainted shacks with lean-tos at the back for kitchens, was one which contained this story.

An Irish policeman, silent and indifferent, was already at the small dark gate in the dark and silent street, guarding it against intruders; another was inside the door, which stood partially open, and beyond in the roadway in the darkness, their faces all but indistinguishable, a few horrified people. A word of explanation and I was admitted. A faint glow from a small smoky glass lamp illuminated the front room darkly. It turned out that a very honest, simple, religious and good-natured Irish-American of about fifty, who had been working by the day in this neighborhood, had recently been taken ill with brain fever and had on this night arisen from his fever-ish sickbed, seized a flatiron, crept into the front room where his wife and two little children slept and brained all three. He had then returned to the rear room, where a grown daughter slept on a couch beside him, and had first felled her with the iron and then cut her throat with a butcher knife. Murderous as the deed seemed, and apparently premeditated, it was the result of fever. The policeman at the gate in-formed me that the father had already been taken to the Four Courts and that a hospital ambulance was due any moment.

"But he's out av his mind," he insisted blandly. "He's crazy, sure, or sick av the fever. No man in his right sinses would do that. I tried to taalk to him but he couldn't say naathin', just mumble like."

After my grand ball this wretched front room presented a sad and ghastly contrast. The house and furniture were very poor, the dead wife and children homely and seemingly work-worn. I noticed the dim, smoky flame cast by the lamp, the cheap bed awry and stained red, the mother and two children lying in limp and painful disorder, the bedding dragged half off. It was evident that a struggle had taken place, for a chair and table were upset, the ironing-board thrown down, a bureau and the bed pushed sidewise.

Shocked beyond measure, yet with an eye to color and to the zest of the public for picturesque details, I examined the three rooms with care, the officer in the house following me. Together we looked at the utensils in the kitchen, what was in the cupboard to eat, what in the closet to wear. I made notes of the contents of the rooms, their cheapness, then went to the neighbors on either hand to learn if they had heard anything. Then in a stray owl-car, no carriages being available, I hurried to the Four Courts, several miles cityward, to see the criminal. I found him, old, pale, sick, thin, walking up and down in his small iron cell, plainly out of his mind, a picture of hopeless, unconscious misery. His hands trembled idly about his mouth; his shabby trousers bagged about his shoes; he was unshaven and weak-looking, and all the while he mumbled to himself some unintelligible sounds. I tried to talk with him but could get nothing. He seemed not even to know that I was there, so brain-sick was he. Then I questioned the jail attendants, those dull wiseacres of the law. Had he talked? Did they think he was sane? With the usual acumen and delicacy of this tribe, they were inclined to think he was shamming.

I hurried through dark streets to the office. It was an almost empty reportorial room in which I scribbled my dolorous picture. With the impetuosity of youth and curiosity and sorrow and wonder I told it all, the terror, the pity, the inexplicability. As I wrote, each page was taken up by Hartung, edited and sent up. Then, having done perhaps a column and a half (Bellairs having arrived with various police theories), I was allowed finally to amble out into a dark street and seek my miserable little room with its creaky bed, its dirty coverlets, its ragged carpets and stained walls. Nevertheless, I lay down with a kind of high pride and satisfaction in my story of the murder and my description of the ball, and with my life in consequence! I was not so bad. I was getting along. I must be thought an exceptional man to be picked for two such difficult tasks in the same evening. Life itself was not so bad; it was just higgledy-piggledy, catch-as-catch-can, that was all. If one were clever, like myself, it was all right. Next morning, when I reached the office, McCord and Hazard and some others pronounced my stuff "pretty good," and I was beside myself with glee. I strolled about as though I owned the earth, pretending simplicity and humility but actually believing that I was the finest ever, that no one could outdo me at this game of reporting.

CHAPTER XXV

THINGS relatively interesting, contrasts nearly as sharp and as well calculated to cause one to meditate on the wonder, the beauty, the uncertainty, the indifference, the cruelty and the rank favoritism of life, were daily if not hourly put before me. Now it would be some such murder as this or a social scandal of some kind, often of a gross and revolting character, in some ultra-respectable neighborhood, or a suicide of peculiarly sad or grim character. Or, again, it would be a fine piece of chicane, as when a certain "board-and-feed" stable owner of the west end, about to lose his property because of poor business and anxious to save himself by securing the insurance, set fire to the stable and destroyed seventeen healthy horses as well as one stable attendant and "got away with it," legally anyhow. His plan had probably been to save the horses and the man, but the plan miscarried. I gathered as much from him when I interviewed him. I put some pertinent questions at him but could get no admissions on which to base a charge. He was a shrewd, calculating, commercial type, vigorous and semi-savage. He evaded me blandly and I had to write the fire up as a sad accident, thereby aiding him to get his insurance, the while I was convinced that he was guilty, a hard-hearted scoundrel.

Another thing that I sensed very clearly at this time was the fact that the average newspaper reporter was a far better detective in his way than the legitimate official detective, and not nearly so well paid. The average so-called "headquarters man," was a loathsome thing, as low in his ideas and methods as the lowest criminal he was set to trap. The criminal was at least shrewd and dynamic enough to plot and execute a crime, whereas the detective had no brains at all, merely a low kind of cunning. Often red-headed, freckled, with big hands and feet, store clothes, squeaky shoes—why does such a picture of the detective come back to me? Pop-eyed, with a ridiculous air of mystery and profundity in matters requiring neither, dirty, offensive, fish-eyed and merciless, the detectives floundered about in different cases without a grain of humor; whereas the average reporter was, by contrast anyhow, intelligent or shrewd, cleanly nearly always, if at times a little slouchy, inclined to drink and sport perhaps but genial, often gentlemanly, a fascinating story-teller, a keen psychologist (nearly always one of the best), frequently well read, humorous, sympathetic, amusing or gloomy as the case might be, but generally to be relied upon in such emergencies for truly skillful work. Naturally there was some enmity between the two, a contempt on the part of the newspaper man for the detective, a fear and dislike and secret opposition on the part of the detective. The reporter would go forth on a mystifying case and as a rule, given time enough, would solve it, whereas the police detectives would be tramping about often trailing the reporters, reading the newspapers to discover what had been discovered, and then, when the work had been done and the true clew furnished, would step forward at the grand moment to do the arresting and get their pictures and names in the papers. The detectives were constantly playing into the hands of the police reporters in unimportant matters during periods between great cases, doing them little favors, helping them in small cases, in order that when a big case came along they might have favors done unto them. The most important of all these favors, of course, was that of seeing that their names were mentioned in the papers as being engaged in solving a mystery or having done thus and so, when in all likelihood some newspaper man had done it.

Sometimes the tip as to where the criminal was likely to be found would be furnished by the papers and later credited to the police. Sometimes the newspaper men would lash the police, sometimes flatter them, but always they were seeking to make the police aid them to get various necessary things done, and not always succeeding. Sometimes the police were hand-in-glove with certain crooks or evil-doers, and you could all but prove it, but until you did so, and sometimes afterward, they were stubborn and would defy you and the papers. But not for long. They loved publicity too much; offer them sufficient publicity, and they would act. It was nearly always my experience that the newspapers, which meant the reporters of course plus an efficient city editor and possibly a managing editor, would be the first to worm out the psychology of any given case and then point an almost unerring finger at the criminal; then the police or detectives would come in and do the arresting and get the credit.

Another thing that impressed me greatly at this time was the kaleidoscopic character of newspaper work, which, in its personal significance to me, cannot be too much emphasized. As I have said, one day it would be a crime of a lurid or sensational character that would arrest and compel me to think, and the same day, within the hour perhaps, it would be a lecturer or religionist with some finespun theory of life, some theosophist like Annie Besant, who in passing through St. Louis on a lecture tour would be at one of the best hotels, usually the Southern, talking transmigration and Nirvana. Again, it would be some mountebank or quack of a low order— a spiritualist, let us say, of the Eva Fay stripe, or a mind-reader like Bishop, or a third-rate religionist like the Reverend Sam Jones, who was then in his heyday preaching unadulterated hell, or the arrival of a prize-fighter-actor like John L. Sullivan, then only recently defeated by Corbett, or a novelist of the quack order, such as Hall Caine.

And there were distinguished individuals, including such excellent lecturers as Henry Watterson and Henry M. Stanley, or a musician like Paderewski, or a scientist of the standing of Nikola Tesla. I was sent to interview my share of these, to get their views on something—anything or nothing really, for my city editor, Mr. Mitchell, seemed at times a little cloudy as to their significance, and certainly I had no clear insight into what most of them stood for. I wondered, guessed, made vague stabs at what I thought they represented, and in the main took them seriously enough. My favorite question was what did they think of life, its meaning, since this was uppermost in my mind at the time, and I think I asked it of every one of them, from John L. Sullivan to Annie Besant. And what a jangle of doctrines! What a noble burst of ideas! Annie Besant, in a room at the Southern delicately scented with flowers, arrayed in a cool silken gray dress, informed me that the age was material, that wealth and show were an illusion based on nothing at all (I wrote that down without understanding what she meant), that the Hindu Swamis had long since solved all this seeming mystery of living, Madame Blavatsky being the most recent and the greatest apostle of wisdom in this matter, and that the great thing to do in this world or the next was to improve oneself spiritually and so eventually attain to Nirvana, nothingness—a word I had to look up afterward. (When I told Dick Wood about her he seemed greatly impressed and said: "Oh, there's more to that stuff than you think, Dreiser. You're just not up on all that yet. These mystics see more than we think they do," and he looked very wise.)

And Henry Watterson—imagine me at the age of twenty-one trying to interview him when he was in the heyday of his fame and mental powers! Short, stocky, with a protuberant belly, slightly gray hair, gruff and simple in his manner and joyously secure in his fame (he had just the preceding summer said that Cleveland, Democratic candidate of the hour and later elected, was certain to "walk up an alley to a slaughter-house and an open grave," and had of course seen his prediction fail), he was convinced that the country was in bad hands, not likely to go to the "demnition bow-wows" as yet but in for a bad corporation-materialistic spell. And when I asked *him* what he thought of life——

"My son, when you get as old as I am you probably won't think so much of it, and you won't be to blame. It's good enough in its way, but it's a damned ticklish business. You may say that Henry Watterson said that if you like. Do the best you can, and don't crowd the other fellow too hard, and you'll come out as well as anybody, I suppose."

And then John L. Sullivan, raw, red-faced, big-fisted, broad-shouldered, drunken, with gaudy waistcoat and tie, and rings and pins set with enormous diamonds and rubies—what an impression he made! Surrounded by local sports and politicians of the most rubicund and degraded character (he was a great favorite with them), he seemed to me, sitting in his suite at the Lindell, to be the apotheosis of the humorously gross and vigorous and material. Cigar boxes, champagne buckets, decanters, beer bottles, overcoats, collars and shirts littered the floor, and lolling back in the midst of it all in ease and splendor his very great self, a sort of prize-fighting J. P. Morgan.

"Aw, haw! haw! haw!" I can hear him even now when I asked him my favorite question about life, his plans, the value of exercise (!), etc. "He wants to know about exercise! You're all right, young fella, kinda slim, but you'll do. Sit down and have some champagne. Have a cigar. Give 'im some cigars, George. These young newspaper men are all all right to me. I'm for 'em. Exercise? What I think? Haw! haw! Write any damned thing yuh please, young fella, and say that John L. Sullivan said so. That's good enough for me. If they don't believe it bring it back here and I'll sign it for yuh. But I know it'll be all right, and I won't stop to read it neither. That suit yuh? Well, all right. Now have some more champagne and don't say I didn't treat yuh right, 'cause I did. I'm ex-champion of the world, defeated by that little dude from California, but I'm still John L. Sullivan—ain't that right? Haw! haw! They can't take that away from me, can they? Haw! haw! Have some more champagne, boy."

I adored him. I would have written anything he asked me to write. I got up the very best article I could and published it, and was told afterward that it was fine.

Another thing that interested me about newspaper work was its pagan or unmoral character, as contrasted with the heavy religionistic and moralistic point of view seemingly prevailing in the editorial office proper (the editorial page, of course), as well as the world outside. While the editorial office might be preparing the most flowery moralistic or religionistic editorials regarding the worth of man, the value of progress, character, religion, morality, the sanctity of the home, charity and the like, the business office and news rooms were concerned with no such fine theories. The business office was all business, with little or no thought of anything save success, and in the city news room the mask was off and life was handled in a rough-and-ready manner, without gloves and in a catch-as-catch-can fashion. Pretense did not go here. Innate honesty on the part of any one was not probable. Charity was a business with something in it for somebody. Morality was in the main for public consumption only. "Get the news! Get the news!"—that was the great cry in the city editorial room. "Don't worry much over how you get it, but get it, and don't come back without it! Don't fall down! Don't let the other newspapers skin us—that is, if you value your job! And write—and write well. If any other paper writes it better than you do you're beaten and might as well resign." The public must be entertained by the writing of reporters.

But the methods and the effrontery and the callousness necessary at times for the gathering of news—what a shock even though one realized that it was conditional with life itself! At most times one needed to be hard, cold, jesuitical. For instance, one of the problems that troubled me most, and to which there was no solution save to act jesuitically or get out, was how to get the facts from a man or woman suspected of some misdeed or error without letting him know that you were so doing. In the main, if you wanted facts of any kind, especially in connection with the suspected, you did not dare tell them that you came as an enemy or were bent on exposing them. One had to approach all, even the worst and most degraded, as a friend and pretend an interest, perhaps even a sympathy one did not feel, to apply the oil of flattery to the soul. To do less than this was to lose the news, and while a city editor might readily forgive any form of trickery he would never forgive failure. Cheat and win and you were all right; be honest and lose and you were fired. To appear wise when you were ignorant, dull when you were not, disinterested when you were interested, brutal or severe when you might be just the reverse—these were the essential tricks of the trade.

And I, being sent out every day and loafing about the corridors of the various hotels at different times, soon encountered other newspaper men who were as shrewd and wily as ferrets, who had apparently but one motive in life: to trim their fellow newspaper men in the matter of news, or the public which provided the news. There being only two morning papers here (the *Globe* and the *Republic*), the reporters of each loved the others not, even when personally they were inclined to be friendly. They did not dare permit their personal likes to affect their work. It was every man for himself. Meet a reporter of the *Republic* or the *Globe* on a story: he might be friendly enough but he would tell you nothing. He wished either to shun you or worm your facts out of you. Meet him in the lobby of the La Clede, where by common consent, winter or summer, most seemed to gather, or at the corner drugstore outside, and each would be friendly with the other, trading tales of life, going together to a saloon for a drink or to the "beanery," a famous eating-place on Chestnut between Fourth and Broadway, perhaps borrowing a dime, a quarter or a dollar until pay day—but never repaying with news or tips; quite the reverse, as I soon found. One had to keep an absolutely close mouth as to all one might be doing.

The counsel of all of these men was to get the news in any way possible, by hook or by crook, and to lose no time in theorizing about it. If a document was lying on an official's table, for instance, and you wanted to see it and could not persuade him to give it to you—well, if he turned his back it was good business to take it, or at least read it. If a photograph was desired and the one concerned would not give it and you saw it somewhere, take it of course and let them complain afterward if they would; your city editor was supposed to protect you in such matters. You might know of certain conditions of which a public official was not aware and the knowledge of which would cause him to talk in one way, whereas lack of that knowledge would cause him to talk in another. Personally you might think it your duty to tell him, but as a newspaper man you could not. It was your duty to your paper to sacrifice him. If you didn't some one else would. I was not long in learning all this and more, and although I understood the necessity I sometimes resented having to do it. There were times when I wanted to treat people better than I did or could. Sometimes I told myself that I was better in this respect than other newspaper men; but when the test came I found that I was like the others, as eager to get the news. Something akin to a dog's lust of the chase would in critical moments seize upon me and in my eagerness to win a newspaper battle I would forget or ignore nearly every tenet of fairness and get it. Then, victorious, I might sigh over the sadness of it all and decide that I was going to get out of the business—as I eventually did, and for very much this reason—but at the time I was weak or practical enough.

One afternoon I was sent to interview the current Democratic candidate for mayor, an amiable soul who conducted a wholesale harness business and who was supposed to have an excellent chance of being elected. The city had long been sick of Republican misrule, or so our office seemed to think. When I entered his place he was in the front part of the store discussing with several friends or politicians the character of St. Louis, its political and social backwardness, its narrowness, slowness and the like, and for some reason, possibly due to the personality of his friends, he was very severe. Local religionists, among others, came in for a good drubbing. I did not know him but for some unexplainable reason I assumed at once that the man talking was the candidate. Again, I instinctively knew that if what he was saying were published it would create a sensation. The lust of the hunter stalking a wild animal immediately took possession of me. What a beat, to take down what this man was saying! What a stir it would make! Without seeming to want anything in particular, I stood by a showcase and examined the articles within. Soon he finished his tirade and came to me.

"Well, sir?"

"I'm from the *Globe*," I said. "I want to ask you——"
and I asked him some questions.

When he heard that I was from the *Globe* he became visibly
excited.

"Did you hear what I was saying just now?"

"Yes, sir."

"Well, you know that I was not speaking for publication." . . .

"Yes, I know."

"And you're not to forget that."

"I understand."

Just the same I returned to the office and wrote up the
incident just as it had occurred. My city editor took it,
glanced over it, and departed for the front office. I could tell
by his manner that he was excited. The next day it was published in all its crude reality, and the man was ruined politically. There were furious denials in the rival Democratic
papers. A lying reporter was denounced, not only by Mr.
Bannerman, the candidate, but by all the other papers editorially. At once I was called to the front office to explain
to Mr. McCullagh, which I did in detail. "He said it all,
did he?" he asked, and I insisted that he had. "I know it's
true," he said, "for other people have told me that he has
said the same things before."

Next day there was a defiant editorial in the *Globe* defend-
ing me, my truthfulness, the fact that the truth of the interview was substantiated by previous words and deeds of the
candidate. Various editors on the paper came forward to
congratulate me, to tell me what a beat I had made; but
to tell the truth I felt shamefaced, dishonest, unkind. I was
an eavesdropper. I had taken an unfair advantage, and I
knew it. Still, something in me made me feel that I was
fortunate. As a reporter I had done the paper a great service.
My editor-in-chief, as I could see, appreciated it. No other
immediate personal reward came to me, but I felt that I had
strengthened my standing here a little. Yet for that I had
killed that man politically. Youth, zest, life, the love of the
chase—that is all that explains it to me now.

CHAPTER XXVI

MY standing as a local newspaper man seemed to grow by leaps and bounds—I am not exaggerating. Certain almost fortuitous events (how often they have occurred in my life!) seemed to assist me, far above my willing or even my dreams. Thus, one morning I had come down to the *Globe* city room to get something, a paper or a book I had left, before going to my late breakfast, when a tall, broad-shouldered man, wearing a slouch hat and looking much like the typical Kentucky colonel, hurried into the office and exclaimed:

"Is the city editor here?"

"He isn't down yet," I replied. "Anything I can do for you?"

"I just stopped to tell you there's a big wreck on the road up here near Alton. I saw it from the train as I passed coming down from Chicago. A half-dozen cars are burning. If you people get a man up there right away you can get a big lead on this."

I grabbed a piece of paper, for I felt instinctively that this was important. Some one ought to attend to it right away. I looked around to see if there was any one to appeal to, but there was no one.

"What did you say the name of the place was?" I inquired.

"Wann," relied the stranger, "right near Alton. You can't miss it. Better get somebody up there quick. I think it's something big. I know how important these things are to you newspaper boys: I used to be one myself, and I owe the *Globe* a few good turns anyhow." He smiled and bustled out.

I did not wait to see the city editor. I felt that I was taking a big risk, going out without orders, but I also felt that something terrible had happened and that the occasion warranted it. I had never seen a big wreck. It must be wonderful. The newspapers always gave them so much space. I wrote a note to the city editor explaining that the wreck was reported to be a great one and added that I felt it to be my duty to go at once. Perhaps he had better send an artist after me—imagine me advising him!

On the way to the depot I thought of what I must do: telegraph for an artist if the wreck was really important, and then get my story and get back. It was over an hour's run. I got off at the nearest station to the wreck and walked the remaining distance, which was a little more than a mile. As I neared it I saw a crowd of people gathered about what was evidently the smoldering embers of a train, and on the same track, not more than a hundred feet away, were three oil-tank cars, those evidently into which the passenger train had crashed. These cars were also surrounded by a crowd, citizens of nearby towns, as it proved, who were staring at them as the fire blazed about them. As I learned later, a fourth oil-tank car had been smashed and the contents had poured out about these others of the oil group as well as the passenger train itself. The oil had taken fire and consumed the train, although no people were killed.

The significance of the scene had not yet quite dawned upon me, however, when for the second time in my life I was privileged to behold one of those terrible catastrophes which it is given to few of us to see. The oil-tank cars about which the crowd was gathered, having become overheated by the burning oil beneath, exploded all at once with a muffled report which to me (I was no more than fifteen hundred feet away) sounded like a deep breath exhaled by some powerful man. The earth trembled, the heavens instantly appeared to be surcharged with flame. The crowd, which only a moment before I had seen solidly massed about the cars, was now hurled back in confusion, and I beheld men running, some toward me, some from me, their bodies on fire or being momentarily ignited. I saw flames descending toward me, long, red, licking things, and realizing the danger I turned and in a panic ran as fast as I could, never stopping until I deemed myself at a safe distance. Then I halted and gazed back, hearing at the same time a chorus of pitiful wails and screams which tore my heart.

Death is here, I said to myself. I am witnessing a real tragedy, a horror. The part of the great mysterious force which makes and unmakes our visible scene is here and now magnificently operative. But, first of all, I was a newspaper man; I must report this, run to it, not away.

I saw dashing toward me a man whose face I could not make out clearly, for at times it was partially covered by his hands, which seemed aflame, at other times the hands waved in the air like flails, and were burning. His body was being consumed by a rosy flame which partially enveloped him. His face, whenever it became visible as he moved his hands to and fro, was screwed into a horrible grimace. Unconscious of me as he ran, he dashed like a fiery force to the low ditch which paralleled the railroad, where he rolled and twisted like a worm.

I could scarcely believe my eyes or my senses. My hair rose on end. My hands twitched convulsively. I ran forward, pulling off my coat, and threw it over him to smother the spots of flame—but it was of no use—my coat began to burn. With my bare hands I tore grass and earth from the ditch and piled them upon the sufferer. For the moment I was beside myself with terror and misery and grief. Tears came to my eyes and I choked with the sense of helpless misery. When I saw my own coat burning I snatched it away and stamped the fire out.

The man was burned beyond recovery. The oil had evidently fallen in a mass upon the back of his head and shoulders and back and legs. It had burnt his clothes and hair and cooked the skin. His hands were scorched black, as well as his neck and ears and face. Finally he ceased to struggle and lay still, groaning heavily but unconscious. He was alive, but that was all.

Oppressed by the horror of it I looked about for help, but seeing many others in the same plight I realized the futility of further labor here. I could do nothing more. I had stopped the flames in part, the man's rolling in the ditch had done the rest, but to what end! Hope of life was ridiculous, I could see that plainly. I turned, like a soldier in battle, and looked after the rest of the people.

To this hour I can see it all—some running over the fields in the distance away from the now entirely exploded tanks, others approaching the fallen victims. A house a little beyond the wreck was burning. A small village, not a thousand feet away, was blazing in spots, bits of oil having fallen upon the roofs. People were running hither and thither like ants, bending over and examining prostrate forms.

My first idea of course when I recovered my senses was that I must get in touch with my newspaper and get it to send an artist—Wood, if possible—and then get the news. These people here would do as much for the injured as I could. Why waste my newspaper's time on them? I ran to a little road-crossing telegraph station a few hundred feet farther on where I asked the agent what was being done.

"I've sent for a wreck-train," he replied excitedly. "I've telegraphed the Alton General Hospital. There ought to be a train and doctor here pretty soon, any minute now." He looked at his watch. "What more can I do?"

"Have you any idea how many are killed?"

"I don't know. You can see for yourself, can't you?"

"Will you take a message to the *Globe-Democrat?* I want to send for an artist."

"I can't be bothered with anything like that now," he replied roughly. I felt that an instant antagonism and caution enveloped him. He hurried away.

"How am I to do this?" I thought, and then I ran, studying and aiding with the victims where aid seemed of the slightest use, wondering how I should ever be able to report all this, and awaiting the arrival of the hospital and wrecking train.

CHAPTER XXVII

I<small>T</small> was not long before the wreck-train arrived, a thing of flat cars, box-cars and cabooses of an old pattern, with hospital cots made ready en route, and a number of doctors and nurses who scrambled out with the air and authority of those used to scenes of this kind. Meanwhile I had been wondering how long it would be before the wreck-train would arrive and had set about getting my information before the doctors and authorities were on the scene, when it might not be so easy. I knew that names of the injured and their condition were most important, and I ran from one to another of the groups that had formed here and there over one dying or dead, asking them who it was, where he lived, what his occupation was (curiously, there were no women), and how he came to be at the scene of the wreck. Some, I found, were passengers; some residents of the nearby village of Wann or Alton who had hurried over to see the wreck. Most of the passengers had gone on a train provided for them.

I had a hard enough time getting information, even from those who were able to talk. Citizens from the nearby town and those who had not been injured were too much frightened by the catastrophe or were lending a hand to do what they could . . . they were not interested in a reporter or his needs. A group carrying the injured to the platform resented my intrusion, and others searching the meadows for those who had run far away until they fell were too busy to bother with me. Still I pressed on. I went from one to another asking who they were, receiving in some cases mumbled replies, in others merely groans. With those laid out on the platform awaiting the arrival of the wreck-train I did not have so much trouble: they were helpless and there were none to attend them.

"Oh, can't you let me alone!" exclaimed one man whose

face was a black crust. "Can't you see I'm dying?"

"Isn't there some one who will want to know?" I asked softly. It struck me all at once that this was a duty these people owed to everybody, their families and friends included.

"You're right," said the man with cracked lips, after a long silence, and he gave his name and an account of his experiences.

I went to others and to each who was able to understand I put the same question. It won me the toleration of those who were watching me. All except the station agent seemed to see that I was entitled to do this, and he could have been soothed with a bribe if I had thought of it.

As I have said, however, once the wreck-train rolled in surgeons and nurses leaped down, and men brought litters to carry away the wounded. In a moment the scene changed; the authorities of the road turned a frowning face upon inquiry and I was only too glad that I had thought to make my inquiries early. However, I managed in the excitement to install myself in the train just as it was leaving so as to reach Alton with the injured and dead and witness the transfer. Some died en route, others moaned in a soul-racking way. I was beside myself with pity and excitement, and yet I could think only of the manner in which I would describe, describe, describe, once the time came. Just now I scarcely dared to make notes.

At Alton the scene transferred itself gradually to the Alton General Hospital, where in spite of the protests of railroad officials I demanded as my right that I be allowed to enter and was finally admitted. Once in the hospital I completed my canvass, being now assisted by doctors and nurses, who seemed to like my appearance and to respect my calling, possibly because they saw themselves mentioned in the morning paper. Having interviewed every injured man, obtaining his name and address where possible, I finally went out, and at the door encountered a great throng of people, men, women and children, who were weeping and clamoring for information. One glance, and I realized for all time what these tragedies of the world really mean to those dependent. The white drawn faces, the liquid appealing eyes, tragedy written in large human characters.

"Do you know whether my John is in there?" cried one woman.

"Your John?" I replied sympathetically. "Will you tell me who your John is?"

"John Taylor. He works on that road. He was over there."

"Wait a moment," I said, reaching down in my pocket for my pad and reading the names. "No, he isn't here."

The woman heaved a great sigh.

Others now crowded about me. In a moment I was the center of a clamoring throng. All wanted to know, each before the other.

"Wait a moment," I said, as an inspiration seized me. I raised my hand, and a silence fell over the little group.

"You people want to know who is injured," I called. "I have a list here which I made over at the wreck and here. It is almost complete. If you will be quiet I will read it."

A hush fell over the crowd. I stepped to one side, where was a broad balustrade, mounted it and held up my paper.

"Edward Reeves," I began, "224 South Elm Street, Alton. Arms, legs and face seriously burned. He may die."

"Oh!" came a cry from a woman in the crowd.

I decided to not say whether any one was seriously injured.

"Charles Wingate, 415 North Tenth Street, St. Louis."

No voice answered this.

"Richard Shortwood, 193 Thomas Street, Alton."

No answer.

I read on down the list of forty or more, and at each name there was a stir and in some instances cries. As I stepped down two or three people drew near and thanked me. A flush of gratification swept over me. For once I felt that I had done something of which I could honestly be proud.

The rest of the afternoon was spent in gathering outside details. I hunted up the local paper, which was getting out an extra, and got permission to read its earlier account. I went to the depot to see how the trains ran, and by accident ran into Wood. In spite of my inability to send a telegram the city editor had seen fit to take my advice and send him. He was intensely wrought up over how to illustrate it all, and I am satisfied that my description of what had occurred did not ease him much. I accompanied him back to the hospital to see if there was anything there he wished to illustrate, and then described to him the horror as I saw it. Together we visited the morgue of the hospital, where already fourteen naked bodies had been laid out in a row, bodies from which the flames had eaten great patches of skin, and I saw that there was nothing now by which they could be identified. Who were they? I asked myself. What had they been, done? The nothingness of man! They looked so commonplace, so unimportant, so like dead flies or beetles. Curiously enough, the burns which had killed them seemed in some cases pitifully small, little patches cut out of the skin as if by a pair of shears, revealing the raw muscles beneath. All those dead were stark naked, men who had been alive and curiously gaping only two or three hours before. For once Dick was hushed; he did not theorize or pretend; he was silent, pale. "It's hell, I tell you," was all he said.

On the way back on the train I wrote. In my eagerness to give a full account I impressed the services of Dick, who wrote for me such phases of the thing as he had seen. At the office I reported briefly to Mitchell, giving that solemn salamander a short account of what had occurred. He told me to write it at full length, as much as I pleased. It was about seven in the evening when we reached the office, and at eleven I was still writing and not nearly through. I asked Hartung to look out for some food for me about midnight, and then went on with my work. By that time the whole paper had become aware of the importance of the thing I was doing; I was surrounded and observed at times by gossips and representatives of out-of-town newspapers, who had come here to get transcripts of the tale. The telegraph editor came in from time to time to get additional pages of what I was writing in order to answer inquiries, and told me he thought it was fine. The night editor called to ask questions, and the reporters present sat about and eyed me curiously. I was a lion for once. The realization of my importance set me up. I wrote with vim, vanity, a fine frenzy.

By one o'clock I was through. Then after it was all over the other reporters and newspaper men gathered about me—Hazard, Bellairs, Benson, Hartung, David the railroad man, and several others.

"This is going to be a great beat for you," said Hazard generously. "We've got the *Post* licked, all right. They didn't hear of it until three o'clock this afternoon, but they sent five men out there and two artists. But the best they can have is a *cold* account. You *saw* it."

"That's right," echoed Bellairs. "You've got 'em licked. That'll tickle Mac, all right. He loves to beat the other Sunday papers." It was Saturday night.

"Tobe's tickled sick," confided Hartung cautiously. "You've saved his bacon. He hates a big story because he's always afraid he won't cover it right and it always worries him, but he knows you've got 'em beat. McCullagh'll give him credit for it, all right."

"Oh, that big stiff!" I said scornfully, referring to Tobias.

"Something always saves that big stiff," said Hazard bitterly. "He plays in luck, by George! He hasn't any brains."

I went in to report to my superior after a time, and told him very humbly that I thought I had written all I could down here but that there was considerable more up there which I was sure should be personally covered by me and that I ought to go back.

"Very well," he replied gruffly. "But don't overdo it."

"The big stiff!" I thought as I went out.

That night I stayed at a downtown hotel, since I was now charging everything to the paper and wanted to be called early, and after a feverish sleep arose at six and started out again. I was as excited and cheerful as though I had suddenly become a millionaire. I stopped at the nearest corner and bought a *Globe*, a *Republic*, and a *Post-Dispatch*, and proceeded to contrast the various accounts, scanning the columns to see how much my stuff made and theirs, and measuring the atmosphere and quality. To me, of course, mine seemed infinitely the best. There it was, occupying the whole front page, with cuts, and nearly all of the second page, with cuts! I could hardly believe my eyes. Dick's illustrations were atrocious, a mess, no spirit or meaning to them, just great blotches of weird machinery and queer figures. He had lost himself in an effort to make a picture of the original crumpling wreck, and he had done it very badly. At once, and for the first time, he began to diminish as an artist in my estimation. "Why, this doesn't look anything like it at all! He hasn't drawn what I would have drawn," and I began to see or suspect that art might mean something besides clothes and manner. "Why didn't he show those dead men, that crowd clamoring about the main entrance of the hospital?" The illustrations in the other papers seemed much better.

As for myself, I saw no least flaw in my work. It was all all right, especially the amount of space given me. Splendid! "My!" I said to myself vainly, "to think I should have written all this, and single-handed, between the hours of five and midnight!" It seemed astonishing, a fine performance. I picked out the most striking passages first and read them, my throat swelling and contracting uncomfortably, my heart beating proudly, and then I went over the whole of the article word by word. To me in my vain mood, it read amazingly well. I felt that it was full of fire and pathos and done in the right way, with facts and color. And, to cap it all and fill my cup of satisfaction to the brim, this same paper contained an editorial calling attention to the facts that the *Globe* had triumphed in the matter of reporting this story and that the skill of the *Globe-Democrat* could always be counted upon in a crisis like this to handle such things correctly, and commiserating the other poor journals on their helplessness when faced by such trying circumstances. The *Globe* was always best and first, according to this statement. I felt that at last I had justified the opinion of the editor-in-chief in sending for me.

Bursting with vanity, I returned to Alton. Despite the woes

of others I could not help glorying in the fact that nearly the whole city, a good part of it anyhow, must be reading *my* account of the wreck. It was anonymous, of course, and they could not know who had done it, but just the same I had done it whether they knew it or not and I exulted. This was the chance, apparently, that I had been longing for, and I had not failed.

This second day at Alton was not so important as I had fancied it might be, but it had its phases. On my arrival I took one more look at the morgue, where by then thirty-one dead bodies were laid out in a row, and then began to look after those who were likely to recover. I visited some of the families of the afflicted, who talked of damage suits. At my leisure I wrote a full account of just how the case stood, and wired it. I felt that to finish the thing properly I should stay until another day, which really was not necessary, and decided to do so without consulting my editor.

But by nightfall, after my copy had been filed, I realized my mistake, for I received a telegram to return. The local correspondent could attend to the remaining details. On the way back I began to feel a qualm of conscience in regard to my conduct. I had been taking a great deal for granted, as I knew, in thus attempting to act without orders. My city editor might think I was getting a "swelled head," as no doubt I was, and so complain to McCullagh. I knew he did not like me, and this gave him a good excuse to complain. Besides, my second day's story, now that it was gone, did not seem to be so important; I might as well have carried it in and saved the expense of telegraphing it. I felt that I had failed in this; also that mature consideration might decide that I had failed on the first story also. I began to think that by my own attitude I had worked up all the excitement in the office that Saturday night and that my editor-in-chief would realize it now and so be disappointed in me. Suppose, I thought, when I reached the office McCullagh were dissatisfied and should fire me—then what? Where would I go, where get another job as good as this? I thought of my various follies and my past work here. Perhaps with this

last error my sins were now to find me out. "Pride goeth before destruction," I quoted, "and a haughty spirit before
a fall."

By eight o'clock, when I reached the office, I was thoroughly depressed and hurried in, expecting the worst. Of
course the train had been late—had to be on this occasion!—
and I did not reach the office in time to take an evening assignment. Mitchell was out, which left me nothing to do
but worry. Only Hartung was there, and he seemed rather
glum. According to him, Tobe had seemed dissatisfied with
my wishing to stay up there. Why had I been so bold, I
asked myself, so silly, so self-hypnotized? I took up an
evening paper and retired gloomily to a corner to wait.
When Mitchell arrived at nine he looked at me but said
nothing. As I was about to go out to get something to eat
Hartung came in and said: "Mr. Mitchell wants to speak
to you."

My heart sank. I went in and stood before him.

"You called for me?"

"Yes. Mr. McCullagh wants to see you."

"It's all over," I thought. "I can tell by his manner.
What a fool I was to build such high hopes on that story!"

I went out to the hall and walked nervously to the office
of the chief, which was at the front end of the hall. I was
so depressed I could have cried. To think that all my fine
dreams were to have such an end!

That Napoleon-like creature was sitting in his little office,
his chin on his chest, a sea of papers about him. He did not
turn when I entered, and my heart grew heavier. He was
angry with me! I could see it! He kept his back to me,
which was to show me that I was not wanted, done for! At
last he wheeled.

"You called for me, Mr. McCullagh?" I murmured.

"Mmm, yuss, yuss!" he mumbled in his thick, gummy,
pursy way. His voice always sounded as though it were being
obstructed by something leathery or woolly. "I wanted to
say," he added, covering me with a single glance, "that I
liked that story you wrote, very much indeed. A fine piece

of work, a fine piece of work! I like to recognize a good piece of work when I see it. I have raised your salary five dollars, and I would like to give you this.'' He reached in his pocket, drew out a roll and handed over a yellow twenty-dollar bill.

I could have dropped where I stood. The reaction was tremendous after my great depression. I felt as though I should burst with joy, but instead I stood there, awed by this generosity.

"I'm very much obliged to you, Mr. McCullagh,'' I finally managed to say. "I thank you very much. I'll do the best I can.''

"It was a good piece of work,'' he repeated mumblingly, "a good piece of work,'' and then slowly wheeled back to his desk.

I turned and walked briskly out.

CHAPTER XXVIII

THE fact that I had gained the notice of a man as important as McCullagh, a man about whom a contemporaneous poet had written a poem, was almost more than I could stand. I walked on air. Yet the next morning, returning to work, I found myself listed for only "Hotels" and "Heard in the Corridors," my usual tasks, and was depressed. Why not great tasks always? Why not noble hours always? Yet once I had recovered from this I walked about the downtown streets convulsively digging my fingers into my palms and shaking myself with delight as I thought of Saturday, Sunday and Monday. That was something worth talking about. Now I was a real newspaper man. I had beaten the whole town, and in a new city, a city strange to me!

Having practically nothing to do and my excitement cooling some, I returned to the art department this same day to report on what had happened. By now I was so set up that I could scarcely conceal my delight and told both volubly, not only about my raise in salary but also that I had been given a twenty-dollar bill by McCullagh himself—an amazing thing, of course. This last was received with mingled feelings by the department: McCord was pleased, of course, but Dick naturally was inclined to be glum. He was conscious of the fact that his drawings were not good, and McCord had been twitting him about them. Dick admitted it frankly, saying that he had not been able to collect himself. "You know I can't do those things very well and I shouldn't have been sent out on it. That's Mitchell for you!" Perhaps it angered him to think that he should have been so unfortunate at the very time that I should have been so signally rewarded; anyhow he did not show anything save a generous side to me at the time although latterly I felt that it was the beginning of a renewal of that slight hostility based on his original opposition to me. He complimented me, saying: "You've done it this time. I'm glad you've made a hit, old man."

That night, however, I was not invited to his room, as I had hoped I should be, although he and Peter went off somewhere—to his room, as I assumed. I applied myself instead to "Heard in the Corridors." Then the days settled down into their old routine for me—petty assignments, minor contrasts between one thing and another. Only one thing held me up, and that was that Hazard now urged me to do a novel with him, a thing which flattered me so much that I felt my career as a great writer was at hand. For had he not done a novel already? I considered it seriously for a few days, arguing the details of the plot with him at the office and after hours, but it came to nothing. Plays rather than novels, as I fancied for some reason, were more in my line, and poems —things which I thought easier to do. Since writing that first poem a month or so before I was busy now from time to time scribbling down the most mediocre jingles relative to my depressions and dreams, and imaging them to be great verse. Truly, I thought I was to be a great poet, one of the very greatest, and so nothing else really mattered for the time being. Weren't poets always lone and lorn, as I was?

It was about this time too that, having received the gift of twenty and the raise of five, I began to array myself in manner so ultra-smart, as I thought, but fantastic, really, that I grieve to think that I should ever have been such a fool. Yet to tell the truth, I do not know whether I do or not. A foolish boyhood is as delightful as any. I had now moved into Tenth Street, and fortunately or unfortunately for me (fortunately, I now think) a change in the personnel of the *Globe's* editorial staff occurred which had a direct bearing upon my ambitions. A man by the name of Carmichael who did the dramatics on the paper had been called to a better position in Chicago, and the position he had occupied here was therefore temporarily vacant. Hazard was the logical man for the place and should have had it because he had held this position before. He was older and a much better critic. But I, as may be imagined, was in a very appropriate mood for this, having recently been thinking of writing a play, and besides, I was crazy for advancement of any kind. Accordingly the moment I heard of it I was on the alert, eager to make a plea for myself and yet not dreaming that I should ever get it. My sole qualification, as I see it now, was that I was an ardent admirer of the stage and one who, because of his dramatic instincts (as I conceived mine to be), ought to make a good enough critic. I did not know that I was neither old nor cold nor experienced enough to do justice to the art of any one. Yet I should add in all fairness that for the work here required—to write a little two-stick announcement of each new play, mostly favorable, and to prepare a weekly announcement of all the new performances—I was perhaps not so poorly equipped. At any rate, my recent triumph had given me such an excellent opinion of myself, had made me think that I stood so well in the eyes of Mr. McCullagh, that I decided to try for it. It might not mean any more salary, but think of the honor of it! Dramatic Editor of the *Globe-Democrat* of St. Louis! Ha! . . . I decided to try.

There were two drawbacks to this position, as I learned later: one was that although I might be dramatic editor I should still be under the domination of Mr. Tobias Mitchell, who ruled this department; the other was that I should have to do general reporting along with this other work, a thing which irritated me very much and took much of the savor of the task away. The department was not deemed important enough to give any one man complete control of it. It seemed a poor sort of thing to try for, once I learned of this, but still there would be the fact that I could still say I was a dramatic editor. It would give me free entrance to the theaters also.

Consequently I began to wonder how I should go about getting it. Mitchell was so obviously opposed to me that I knew it would be useless to appeal to him. McCullagh might give it to me, but how appeal to him? I thought of asking him direct, but that would be going over Mitchell's head, and he would never forgive me for that, I was sure. I debated for a day or two, and then decided, since my principal relations had been with Mr. McCullagh, that I would go to him direct. Why not? He had been very kind to me, had sent for me. Let Mitchell be angry if he would. If I made good he could not hurt me.

I began to lay my plans or rather to screw up my courage to the point where I could force myself to go and see Mr. McCullagh. He was such a chill and distant figure. At the same time I felt that this man who was the object of so much reverence was one of the loneliest persons imaginable. He was not married. Day after day he came to this office alone, sat alone, ate alone, went home alone, for he had no friends apparently to whom he would condescend to unbend. This touched me. He was too big, too lonely.

This realization drew me sympathetically toward him and made me imagine, if you please, that he ought to like me. Was I not his protégé? Had he not brought me here? Instinctively I felt that I was one who could appreciate him, one whom he might secretly like. The only trouble was that he was old and famous, whereas I was a mere boy, but he would understand that too.

The day after I had made up my mind I began to loiter about the long corridor which led to his office, in the hope of encountering him accidentally. I had often noticed him shouldering his way along the marble wainscoting of this hall, his little Napoleonic frame cloaked in a conventional overcoat, his broad, strong, intellectual face crowned by a wide-brimmed derby hat which he wore low over his eyes. Invariably he was smoking a short fat cigar, and always looked very solemn, even forbidding. However, having made up my mind, I lay in wait for him one morning, determined to see him, and walking restlessly to the empty telegraph room which lay at the other end of the hall from his office and then back, but keeping as close as I could to one door or another in order to be able to disappear quietly in case my courage failed me. Yet so determined was I to see him that I had come down early, before any of the others, in order that he should not slip in ahead of me and so rob me of this seemingly accidental encounter.

At about eleven he arrived. I was on one of my return trips from the telegraph room when I heard the elevator click and dodged into the city room only to reappear in time to meet him, ostensibly on my way to the toilet. He gave me but one sage glance, then stared straight ahead.

At sight of him I lost my courage. Arriving exactly opposite him, however, I halted, controlled by a reckless, eager impulse.

"Mr. McCullagh," I said without further ado, "I want to know if you won't make me dramatic editor. I hear that Mr. Carmichael has resigned and the position is open. I thought maybe you might give it to me." I flushed and hesitated.

"I will," he replied simply and gruffly. "You're dramatic editor. Tell Mr. Mitchell to let you be it."

I started to thank him but the stocky little figure moved in-differently away. I had only time to say, "I'm very much obliged" before he was gone.

I returned to the city editorial room tingling to the finger-tips. To think that I should have been made dramatic editor, and so quickly, in such an offhand, easy way! This great man's consideration for me was certainly portentous, I thought. Plainly he liked me, else why should he do this? If only I could now bring myself seriously to this great labor what might I not aspire to? Dramatic Editor of the *Globe-Democrat* of the great city of St. Louis, and at the age of twenty-one—well, now, that was something, by George! And this great man liked me. He really did. He knew me at sight, honored my request, and would no doubt, if I behaved myself, make a great newspaper man of me. It was something to be the favorite of a great editor-in-chief by jing—a very great thing indeed.

CHAPTER XXIX

Upon my explaining to Mitchell what had happened he looked at me coldly, as much as to say "What the devil is this now that this ass is telling me?" Then, thinking, I suppose, that I must have some secret hold on Mr. McCullagh or at least stand high in his favor, he gave me a very wry smile and said he would have made out for me a letter of introduction to the local managers. An hour later this was laid on my desk by Hartung, who congratulated me, and there I was: dramatic editor. "Gee!" exclaimed Hartung when he came in with the letter. "I bet you could have knocked Tobe over with a straw! He doesn't understand yet, I guess, how well you stand with the old man. The chief must like you, eh?" I could see that my new honor made a considerable difference in his already excellent estimate of me.

Armed with this letter I now visited the managers of the theaters, all of whom received me cordially. I can still see myself very gay and enthusiastic, sure that I was entering upon a great work of some kind. And the dreams I had in connection with the theater, my future as a great popular playwright perhaps! It was all such a wonder-world to me, the stage, such a fairyland, that I bubbled with joy as I went about thinking that now certainly I should come in touch with actors, beautiful women! Think of it—dramatic critic!—a person of weight and authority!

There were seven or eight theaters in St. Louis, three or four of them staging only that better sort of play known as a first-class attraction; the others giving melodrama, vaudeville and burlesque. The manager of the Grand, a short, thick-set, sandy-complexioned man of most jovial mien, was Mc-Manus, father of the well-known cartoonist of a later period and the prototype of his most humorous character, Mr. Jiggs. He exclaimed upon seeing me:

"So you're the new dramatic editor, are you? Well, they change around over there pretty swift, don't they? What's happened to Carmichael? First it was Hartridge, then Albertson, then Hazard, then Mathewson, then Carmichael, and now you, all in my time. Well, Mr. Dreiser, I'm glad to see you. You're always welcome here. I'll take you out and introduce you to our doormen and Mr. ——— in the box-office. He'll always recognize you. We'll give you the best seat in the house if it's empty when you come."

He smiled humorously and I had to laugh at the way he rattled off this welcome. An aura of badinage and humor encircled him, quite the same as that which makes Mr. Jiggs delightful. This was the first I had ever heard of Hazard having held this position, and now I felt a little guilty, as though I had edged him out of something that rightfully belonged to him. Still, I didn't really care, sentimentalize as I might. I had won.

"Did Bob Hazard once have this position?" I asked familiarly.

"Yes. That was when he was on the paper the last time. He's been off and on the *Globe* three or four times, you know." He smiled clownishly. I laughed.

"You and I'll get along, I guess," he smiled.

At the other theaters I was received less informally but with uniform courtesy; all assured me that I should be welcome at any time and that if I ever wished tickets for myself or a friend or anybody on the paper I could get them if they had them. "And we'll make it a point to have them," said one. I felt that this was quite an acquisition of influence. It gave me considerable opportunity to be nice to any friends I might acquire, and then think of the privilege of seeing any show I chose, to walk right into a theater without being stopped, and to be pleasantly greeted en route!

The character of the stage of that day, in St. Louis and the rest of America at least, as contrasted with what I know of its history in the world in general, remains a curious and interesting thing to me. As I look back on it now it seems inane, but then it was wonderful. It is entirely possible that nations, like plants or individuals, have to grow and obtain their full development regardless of the accumulated store of wisdom and achievement in other lands, else how otherwise explain the vast level of mediocrity which obtains in some countries and many forms of effort, and that after so much that has been important elsewhere?

The stage in other lands had already seen a few tremendous periods; even here in America the mimetic art was no mystery. A few great things had been done, in acting at least, by Booth, Barrett, Macready, Forrest, Jefferson, Modjeska, Fanny Davenport, Mary Anderson, to name but a few. I was too young at the time to know or judge of their art or the quality of the plays they interpreted, aside from those of Shakespeare perhaps, but certainly their fame for a high form of production was considerable.

And yet, during the few months that I was dramatic editor, and the following year when I was a member of another staff and had entrée to these same theaters, I saw only one or two actors worthy the name, only one or two performances which I can now deem worth while. Richard Mansfield and Felix Morris stand out in my mind as excellent, and Sol Smith Russell and Joseph Jefferson as amusing comedians, but who else? Comic and light opera, with a heavy intermixture of straight melodrama, and comedy-dramas, were about the only things that managers ventured to essay. Occasionally a serious actor of the caliber of Sir Henry Irving or E. S. Willard would appear on the scene, but many of their plays were of a more or less melodramatic character, highly sentimental, emotional and unreal. In my stay here of about a year and a half I saw Joseph Jefferson, Sol Smith Russell, Salvini junior, Wilson Barrett, Fanny Davenport, Richard Mansfield, E. S. Willard, Felix Morris, E. H. Sothern, Julia Marlowe and a score of others more or less important but too numerous to mention; comedians, light-opera singers and the like; and although at the time I was entertained and moved by some of them, I now realize that in the main they were certainly pale spindling lights. And at that, America was but then entering upon its worst period of stage sentiment or mush. The movies as such had not yet appeared, but "Mr. Frohman presents" was upon us, master of middle-class sweetness and sentimentality. I remember staring at the three-sheet lithos and thinking how beautiful and perfect they were and what a great thing it was to be of the stage. To be an author, an actor, a composer, a manager! To have "Mr. Frohman present——"!

The Empire and Lyceum theater companies, with their groups of perfect lady and gentleman actors, were then at their height, the zenith of stage art—Mr. John Drew, for instance, with his wooden face and manners, Mr. Faversham, Miss Opp, Miss Spong, Miss This, Miss That. Such excellent actors as Henry E. Dixey, Richard Mansfield or Felix Morris could scarcely gain a hearing. I recall sitting one night in Hogan's Theater, at Ninth or Tenth and Pine streets, and hearing Richard Mansfield order down the curtain at one of the most critical points in his famous play "Baron Chevreuil," or some such name, and then come before it and denounce the audience in anything but measured terms for what he considered its ignorance and lack of taste. It had applauded, it seems, at the wrong time in that asinine way which only an American audience can when it is there solely because it thinks it ought to be. By that time Mansfield had already achieved a pseudo if not a real artistic following and was slowly but surely becoming a cult. On this occasion he explained to that bland gathering that they were fools, that American audiences were usually composed of such animals or creatures and were in the main dull to the point of ennui, that they were not there to see a great actor act but to see a man called Richard Mansfield, who was said to be a great actor. He pointed out how uniformly American audiences applauded at the wrong time, how truly immune they were to all artistic values, how wooden and reputation-following. At this some of them arose and left; others seemed to consider it a great joke and remained; still others were angry but wanted to see the "show." Having finished his speech he ordered up the curtain and proceeded with his act as though nothing had happened, as though the audience were really not there. I confess I rather liked him for his stand even though I did not quite know whether he was right or wrong. But I wrote it up as though he had grossly insulted his audience, a body of worthy and respectable St. Louisans. Some one—Hazard, I think—suggested that it would be good policy to do so, and I, being green to my task, did so.

The saccharine strength of the sentiment and mush which we could gulp down at that time, and still can and do to this day, is to me beyond belief. And I was one of those who did the gulping; indeed I was one of the worst. Those perfect nights, for instance, when as dramatic critic I strolled into one theater or another, two or three in an evening possibly, and observed (critically, as I thought) the work of those who were leaders in dramatic or humorous composition and that of our leading actors! It may be that the creative spirit has no particular use for intelligence above a mediocre level, or, better yet and far more likely, creative intelligence works through supermen whose visions, by which the mob is eventually entertained and made wise, must content them. Otherwise how explain the vast level of mediocrity, especially in connection with the stage, the people's playhouse, then, today and forever, I suppose, until time shall be no more?

I recall, for instance, that I thought Mr. Drew was really a superior actor, and also that I thought that most of the plays of Henry Arthur Jones, Arthur Wing Pinero, Augustus Thomas, and others (many others), were enduring works of art. I confess it: I thought so, or at least I heard so and let it go at that. How sound I thought their interpretations of life to be! The cruel over-lords of trade in those plays, for instance, how cruel they were and how true! The virtues of the lowly workingman and the betrayed daughter with her sad, downcast expression! The moral splendor of the young minister who denounced heartless wealth and immorality and cruelty in high places and reformed them then and there or made them confess their errors! I can see him yet: slim, simple, perfect, a truly good man. The offhand on-the-spot manner in which splendid reforms were effected in an hour or a night, the wrongs righted instanter—in plays! You can still see them in any movie house in America. To this hour there is no such thing as a reckless unmarried girl in any movie exhibited in America. They are all married.

But how those St. Louis audiences applauded! *Right*, here in America at least, was always appropriately rewarded and left triumphant, wrong was quite always properly drummed out. Our better selves invariably got the better of our lower selves, and we went home cured, reformed, saved. And there was little of evil of any description which went before, in acts one and two, which could not be straightened out in the last act.

The spirit of these plays captivated my fancy at that time and elevated me into a world of unreality which unfortunately fell in with the wildest of my youthful imaginings. Love, as I saw it here set forth in all those gorgeous or sentimental trappings, was the only kind of love worth while. Fortune also, gilded as only the melodramatic stage can gild it and as shown nightly by Mr. Frohman everywhere in America, was the only type of fortune worth while. To be rich, elegant, exclusive, as in the world of Frohman and Mr. Jones and Mr. Pinero! According to what I saw here, love and youth were the only things worth discussing or thinking about. The splendor of the Orient, the social flare of New York, London and Paris, the excited sex-imaginings of such minds as Dumas junior, Oscar Wilde, then in his heyday, Jones, Pinero and a number of other current celebrities, seemed all to be built around youth and undying love. The dreary humdrum of actual life was carefully shut out from these pieces; the simple delights of ordinary living, if they were used at all, were exaggerated beyond sensible belief. And elsewhere—not here in St. Louis, but in the East, New York, London, Paris, Vienna, St. Petersburg—were all the things that were worth while. If I really wanted to be happy

I must eventually go to those places, of course. There were
the really fine clothes and the superior personalities (physically and socially), and vice and poverty (painted in such
peculiar colors that they were always divinely sad or repel-
lent) existed only in those great cities.

CHAPTER XXX

I BEGAN to dream more than ever of establishing some such perfect atmosphere for myself somehow, somewhere—but never in St. Louis, of course. That was too common, too Western, too far removed from the real wonders of the world. Love and mansions and travel and saccharine romance were the great things, but they were afar off, in New York. (It was around this time that I was establishing the atmosphere of a "studio" in Tenth street.)   Nothing could be so wonderful as love in a mansion, a palace in some oriental realm such as was indicated in the comic operas in which DeWolf Hopper, Thomas Q. Seabrooke, Francis Wilson, Eddie Foy and Frank Daniels were then appearing. How often, with McCord or Wood as companion, occasionally Hazard or a new friend introduced to me by Wood and known as Rodenberger, or Rody (a most amazing person, as I will later relate), I responded to these poetic stage scenes! With one or other of these I visited as many theaters as I could, if for no more than an hour or an act at a time, and consumed with wonder and delight such scenes as most appealed to me: the denunciation scene, for instance, in *The Middleman*, or the third act of nearly any of Henry Arthur Jones's plays. Also quite all of the light operas of Reginald de Koven and Harry B. Smith, as well as those compendiums of nondescript color and melody, the extravaganzas *The Crystal Slipper, Ali Baba, Sindbad the Sailor.* Young actresses such as Della Fox, Mabel Amber, Edna May, forerunners of a long line of comic opera soubrettes, who somehow reminded me of Alice, held me spellbound with delight and admiration. Here at last was the kind of maiden I was really craving, an actress of this hoyden, airy temperament.

I remember that one night, at the close of one of Mr. Willard's performances at the Olympic—*The Professor's Love*

Story, in which he was appearing with a popular leading woman, a very beautiful one—I was asked by the manager to wait for a few moments after the performance so that he might introduce me. Why, I don't know. It seemed that he was taking them to supper and thought they might like to meet one of the local dramatic critics or that I might like to accompany them; an honor which I declined, out of fright or bashfulness. When they finally appeared in the foyer of the theater, however, the young actress very stagy and soft and clinging and dressed most carefully after the manner of the stage, I was beside myself with envy and despair. For she appeared hanging most tenderly on her star's arm (she was his mistress, I understood) and gazing soulfully about. Such beauty! Such grace! Such vivacity! Could anything be so lovely? Think of having such a perfect creature love you, hang on your arm! And here was I, poor dub, a mere reporter, a nobody, upon whom such a splendid creature would not bend a second glance. Mr. Willard was full of the heavy hauteur of the actor, which made the scene all the more impressive to me. I think most of us like to be up-staged at one time or another by some one. I glanced at her bashfully sidewise, pretending to be but little interested, while I was really dying of envy. Finally, after a few words and a few sweety-sweet smiles cast in my direction, I was urged to come with them but instead hurried away, pleading necessity and cursing my stars and my fate. Think of being a mere reporter at twenty-five or thirty a week, while others, earning thousands, were thus basking in the sunshine of success and love! Ah, why might not I have been born rich or famous and so able to command so lovely a woman?

If I had been of an ordinary, sensible, everyday turn of mind, with a modicum of that practical wisdom which puts moderate place and position first and sets great store by the saving of money, I might have succeeded fairly well here, much better than I did anywhere else for a long period after. Unquestionably Mr. McCullagh liked me; I think he may have been fond of me in some amused saturnine way, interested to keep such a bounding, high-flown dunce about the

(182)

place. I might have held this place for a year or two and made it a stepping-stone to something better. But instead of rejoicing in the work and making it the end and aim of my daily labors, I looked upon it as a mere bauble, something I had today but might not have tomorrow. And anyhow, there were better things than working day by day and living in a small room. Life ought certainly to bring me something better, something truly splendid—and soon. I deserved it— everything, a great home, fine clothes, pretty women, the respect and companionship of famous men. Indeed all my pain and misery was plainly caused by just such a lack or lacks as this. Had I these things all would be well; without them—well, I was very miserable. I was ready to accept socialism if by that I could get what I wanted, while not ready to admit that all people were as deserving as I by any means. The sad state of the poor workingman was a constant thought with me, but nearly always I was the greatest and poorest and most deserving of all workingmen.

This view naturally tended to modify the sanity of my work. Granting a modicum of imagination and force, still any youth limited as I was at that time has a long road to go. Even in that most imaginative of all professions, the literary, the possessor of such notions as I then held is certainly debarred from accomplishing anything important until he passes beyond them. Yet the particular thought or attitude I have described appears to reign in youth. Too often it is a condition of many minds of the better sort and is retained in its worst form until by rough experience it is knocked out of them or they are destroyed utterly in the process. But it cannot be got over with quickly. Mine was a sad case. One of the things which this point of view did for me was to give my writing, at that time, a mushy and melancholy turn which would not go in any newspaper of today, I hope. It caused me to paint the ideal as not only entirely probable but necessary before life would be what it should!—the progress bug, as you see. I could so twist and discolor the most commonplace scenes as to make one think that I was writing of paradise. Indeed I allowed my imagination to run away with me at times and only the good sense of the copy-reader or the indifference of a practical-minded public saved the paper from appearing utterly ridiculous.

On one occasion, for instance, I went to report a play of mediocre quality that was running at the Olympic, and was so impressed with a love scene which was a part of it that I was entirely blinded to all the faults of construction which the remainder of the play showed, and wrote it up in the most glowing colors. And the copy-reader, Hartung, was too weary that night or too inattentive to capture it. The next day some of the other newspaper men in the office noticed it and commented on it to me or to Hartung, saying it was ridiculously high-flown and that the play itself was silly, which was true. But did that cure me? Not a bit. I was reduced for a day or two by it, but not for long. Seeing other plays of the same caliber and with much sweet love mush in them, I raved as before.

A little later a negro singer, a young woman of considerable vocal ability who was being starred as the Black Patti, was billed to appear in St. Louis. The manager of the bureau that was presenting her called my attention by letter to her "marvelous" ability, and by means of clippings and notices of her work published elsewhere had endeavored to impress me favorably. I read these notices, couched in the glowing phrases of the press-agent, and then went forth on this evening to cover this myself. To make it all the grander, I invited McCord and with him proceeded to the theater, where we were assigned a box.

As it turned out, or as I chanced to see or feel it, the young woman was a sweet and impressive singer, engaging and magnetic. McCord agreed with me that she could sing. We listened to the program of a dozen pieces, including such old favorites as *Suwanee River* and *Comin' Thro' the Rye,* and then I, being greatly moved, returned to the office and wrote an account that was fairly sizzling with the beauty which I thought was there. I did not attempt critically to analyze her art—I could not, knowing nothing of even the rudiments of music—but plunged at once into that wider realm which involved the subtleties of nature itself. "What is so beautiful as the sound which the human voice is capable of producing," I wrote in part, "especially when that voice is itself a compound of the subtlest things in nature? Here we have a young girl, black it is true, fresh from the woods and fields of her native country, yet, blessed by some strange chance with that mystic thing, a voice, and fittingly interpreting via song all that we hold to be most lovely. The purling of the waters, the radiance of the moonlight, the odor of sweet flowers, sunlight, storm, the voices and echoes of nature, all are found here, thrilling over lips which represent in their youthfulness but a few of the years which wisdom and skill would seem to require. Yes, one may sit and, in hearing Miss Jones sing, vicariously entertain all these things, because of them she is a compound, youthful, vivacious, suggestive of the elemental sweetness of nature itself."

To understand the significance of such a statement in St. Louis one would have to look into the social and political conditions of the people who dwelt there. To a certain extent they were Southern in temperament, representing the vigorous anti-negro spirit which prevailed for so many years after the war. Again, they were fairly illuminated where music was concerned. Assuming that a bit of idealism such as this was sound, it might get by; but when it is remembered that this was largely mush and written about a negro, a race more or less alien to their sympathy, would it not naturally fall upon hard ears and appear somewhat ridiculous? A negro the compound of the subtlest elements in nature! And this in their favorite paper!

By chance it went through, Hartung having come to look upon most of my stuff as the outpourings of some strange genius who could do about as he pleased. Neither Mitchell nor the editor-in-chief saw it perhaps, or if they did they gave it no attention, music, the theater and the arts being of small import here. But, depend upon it, the editors of the various rival papers that were constantly being sniffed at by the *Globe* saw it and knowing the sensitiveness of our editor-in-chief to criticism of his own paper at once set to work to make some-

(185)

thing out of it. And of all the editors in the middle West, McCullagh, by reason of his force and taste and care in editing his paper, was a shining target for a thing like this. He was, as a rule, impeccable and extremely conspicuous. Whatever he did or said, good, bad or indifferent, was invariably the subject of local newspaper comment, and when any little discrepancy or error appeared in the *Globe-Democrat* it was always charged to him personally. And so it was with this furore over the Black Patti. It was too good a thing to be lost sight of.

"The erudite editor of the *Globe-Democrat*," observed the *Post-Dispatch* editorially, "appears to have visited one of our principal concert halls last night. It is not often that that ponderous intellect can be called down from the heights of international politics to contemplate so simple a thing as a singer of songs, a black one at that; but when true art beckons even he can be counted upon to answer. Apparently the Black Patti beckoned to him last evening, and he was not deaf to her call, as the following magnificent bit of word-painting fresh from his pen is here to show." (Then followed the praise in full.) "None but the grandiloquent editor of the *Globe-Democrat* could have looked into the subtleties of nature, as represented by the person of Miss Sisseretta Jones, and there discovered the wonders of music and poetry such as he openly confesses to have done. Indeed we have here at last a measure of that great man's insight and feeling, a love of art, music, poetry and the like such as has not previously been indicated by him. And we hereby hasten to make representation of our admiration and great debt that others too may not be deprived of this great privilege." After this came more of the same gay raillery, with here and there a reference to "the great patron of the black arts" and the pure joy that must have been his at thus vicariously being able to enjoy within the precincts of Exposition Hall "the purling of the waters" bubbling from a black throat. It was a gentle satire, not wholly uncalled for since the item had appeared in the *Globe*, and directed at the one man who could least stand that sort of thing, sensitive as he was to his personal dignity.

I was blissfully unaware that any comment had been made on my effusion until about five in the afternoon, by which time the afternoon editions of the *Post-Dispatch* had been out several hours. When I entered the office at five, comfortable and at peace with myself in my new position, excited comment was running about the office as to what "the old man" would think and say and do now. He had gone at two, it appeared, to the Southern for luncheon and had not returned. Wait until he saw it! Oh me! Oh my! Wouldn't he be hopping! Hartung, who was reasonably nervous as to his own share in the matter, was the first to approach and impress me with the dreadfulness of it all, how savage "the old man" could be in any such instance. "Gee, just wait! Oh, but he'll be hot, I bet!" As he talked the "old man" passed up the hall, a grim and surly figure. I saw my dramatic honors going a-glimmering.

"Here," I said to Hartung, pretending a kind of innocence, even at this late hour, "what's all this about? What's the row, anyhow?"

"Didn't you see the editorial in the *Post-Dispatch?*" inquired Hartung gloomily. It was his own predicament that was troubling him.

"No. What about?"

"Why, that criticism you wrote about the Black Patti. They've made all sorts of fun of it. The worst of it is that they've charged it all up to the old man."

I smiled a sickly smile. I felt as if I had committed some great crime. Why had I attempted to write anything "fine" anyhow? Why couldn't I have been content and rested with a little praise? Had I no sense at all? Must I always be trying to do something great? Perhaps this would be the end of me.

Hartung brought me the *Post-Dispatch*, and sorrowfully and with falling vitals I read it, my toes curling, my stomach seeming gradually to retire to my backbone. Why had I done it!

As I was standing there, my eyes glued to the paper, near the door which looked into the main city room in which was Tobe scribbling dourly away, I heard and then saw McCullagh enter and walk up to the stout city editor. He had a copy of the selfsame *Post-Dispatch* crumpled roughly in his hand, and on his face was gathered what seemed to me a dark scowl.

"Did you see this, Mr. Mitchell?" I heard him say.

Tobe looked up, then closely and respectfully at the paper. "Yes," he said.

"I don't think a thing like that ought to appear in our paper. It's a little bit too high-flown for our audience. Your reader should have modified it."

"I think so myself," replied Tobe quietly.

The editor walked out. Tobe waited for his footsteps to die away and then growled at Hartung: "Why the devil did you let that stuff go through? Haven't I warned you against that sort of thing? Why can't you watch out?"

I could have fallen through the floor. I had a vision of Hartung burying his head in his desk, scared and mute.

After the evening assignments had been given out and Tobe had gone to dinner, Hartung crept up to me.

"Gee, the old man was as mad as the devil!" he began. "Tobe gave me hell. He won't say anything to you maybe, but he'll take it out on me. He's a little afraid of your pull with the old man, but he gives me the devil. Can't you look out for those things?"

CHAPTER XXXI

In spite of this little mishap, which did me no great harm, there was a marked improvement in my affairs in every way. I had a better room, various friends—Wood, McCord, Rodenberger, Hazard, Bellairs, a new reporter by the name of Johnson, another by the name of Walden Root, a nephew of the senator—and the growing consideration if not admiration of many of the newspaper men of the city. Among them I was beginning to be looked upon as a man of some importance, and the proof of it was that from time to time I found myself being discussed in no mild way. From now on I noticed that my noble Wood, whom I had so much looked up to at first, began to take me about with him to one or more Chinese restaurants of the most beggarly description in the environs of the downtown section, which same he had discovered and with the proprietors of which he was on the best of terms. They were really hang-outs for crooks and thieves and disreputable tenderloin characters generally (such was the beginning of the Chinese restaurant in America), but not so to Wood. He had the happy faculty of persuading himself that there was something vastly mysterious and superior about the entire Chinese race, and after introducing me to many of his new laundry friends he proceeded to assure me of the existence of some huge Chinese organization known as the Six Companies which, so far as I could make out from hearing him talk, was slowly but surely (and secretly, of course) getting control of the entire habitable globe. It had complete control of great financial and constructive ventures here, there and everywhere, and supplied on order thousands of Chinese laborers to any one who desired them, anywhere. And this organization ruled them with a rod of iron, cutting their throats and burying them head down in a bucket of rice when they failed to perform their bounden duties and transferring their remains quietly to China, in coffins made in China and brought here for that purpose. The Chinese who had worked for the builders of the Union Pacific had been supplied by this company, so he said.

Again, there were the Chinese Free Masons, a society so old and so powerful and so mysterious that one might speak of it only in whispers for fear of getting into trouble. This indeed was *the* great organization of the world, in China and everywhere else. Kings and potentates knew of it and trembled before its power. If it wished it could sweep the Chinese Emperor and all European monarchs off their thrones tomorrow. There were rites, mysteries, sanctuaries within sanctuaries in this great organization. He himself was as yet a mere outsider, snooping about, but by degrees, slowly and surely, as I was given to understand, was worming its secrets out of these Chinese restaurant-keepers and laundrymen, its deepest mysteries, whereby he hoped to profit in this way: he was going to study Chinese, then go to China. There he would get into this marvelous organization through the influence of some of his Chinese friends here. Then he was going to get next to some of the officials of the Chinese Government, and being thus highly recommended and thought of would come back here eventually as an official Chinese interpreter, attached perhaps to the Chinese Legation at Washington. How he was to profit so vastly by this I could not see, but he seemed to think that he would.

Again, there was his literary world which he was always dreaming about and slaving over, his art ambitions, into which I was now by degrees permitted to look. He was forging ahead in that realm, and since I was doing fairly well as a daily scribbler it might be that I would be able to perceive a little of all he was hoping to do. His great dream or scheme was to study the underworld life of St. Louis at first hand, those horrible, grisly, waterfront saloons and lowest tenderloin dives and brothels south of Market and east of Eighth where, listening to the patois of thieves and pimps and lechers and drug-fiends and murderers and outlaws generally, he was to extract from them, aside from their stories, some bizarre originality of phrase and scene that was to stand him in good stead in the composition of his tales. Just now, so he told me, he was content with making notes, jotting down scraps of conversation heard at bars, in sloppy urinals, cheap dance-halls, and I know not what. With a little more time and a little more of that slowly arriving sanity which comes to most of us eventually, I am inclined to think that he might have made something out of all this; he was so much in earnest, so patient; only, as I saw it, he was filled with an almost impossible idealism and romance which threw nearly everything out of proportion. He naturally inclined to the arabesque and the grotesque, but in no balanced way. His dreams were too wild, his mood at nearly all times too utterly romantic, his deductions far beyond what a sane contemplation of the facts warranted.

And relative to this period I could other tales unfold. He and Peter, long before I had arrived on the scene, had surrounded themselves with a company of wayfarers of their own: down-and-out English army officers and grafting younger sons of good families, a Frenchman or two, one of whom was a poet, several struggling artists who grafted on them, and a few weird and disreputable characters so degraded and nondescript that I could never make out just what their charm was. At least two of these had suitable rooms, where, in addition to Dick's and mine, we were accustomed to meet. There were parties, Sunday and evening walks or trips, dinners. Poems, on occasion, were read, original, first-hand compositions; Dick's stories, as Peter invariably insisted, were "inflicted," the "growler" or "duck" (a tin bucket of good size) was "rushed" for beer, and cheese and crackers and hot crawfish, sold by old ambling negroes on the streets after midnight, were bought and consumed with gusto. Captain Simons, Captain Seller, Toussaint, Benèt— these are names of figures that are now so dim as to be mere wraiths, ranged about a smoky, dimly lighted room in some downtown rooming-house. Both Dick and Peter had reached that distinguished state where they were the center of attraction as well as supports and props to these others, and between them got up weird entertainments, knockabout Dutch comedian acts, which they took down to some wretched dance-hall and staged, each "doing a turn." The glee over the memory of these things as they now narrated them to me!

Wood was so thin physically and so vigorous mentally that he was fascinating to look at. He had an idea that this bohemianism and his story work were of the utmost importance; and so they were if they had been but a prelude to something more serious, or if his dreams could only have been reduced to paper and print. There was something that lay in his eye, a ray. There was an aroma to his spirit which was delicious. As I get him now, he was a rather underdone Poe or de Maupassant or Manet, and assuredly a portion of the makings was certainly there. For at times the moods he could evoke in me were poignant, and he saw beauty and romance in many and strange ways and places. I have seen him enter a dirty, horrible saloon in one of St. Louis's lowest dive regions with the air of a Prince Charming and there seat himself at some sloppy table, his patent leather low-quarters scraping the sanded or sawdusted floor, order beer and then, smiling genially upon all, begin to transcribe from memory whole sections of conversations he had heard somewhere, in the street perhaps, all the while racking his brain to recall the exact word and phrase. Unlike myself, he had a knack of making friends with these shabby levee and underworld characters, syphilitic, sodden, blue-nosed bums mostly, whom he picked up from Heaven knows where. And how he seemed to prize their vile language, their lies and their viler thoughts!

And there was McCord, bless his enthusiastic, materialistic heart, who seemed to take fire from this joint companionship and was determined to do something, he scarcely knew what —draw, paint, write, collect—anything. His mind was so wrought up by the rich pattern which life was weaving before his eyes that he could scarcely sleep at nights. He was for prowling about with us these winter and spring days, looking at the dark city after work hours, or investigating these wretched dives with Dick and myself. Or, the three of us

(192)

would take a banjo, a mandolin and a flute (McCord could perform on the flute and Dick on the mandolin) and go to Forrest Park or one of the minor parks on the south side, and there proceed to make the night hideous with our carolings until some solid policeman, assuming that the public had rights, would interfere and bid us depart. Our invariable retort on all such occasions was that we were newspaper men and artists and as such entitled to courtesies from the police, which the thick-soled minion of the law would occasionally admit. Sometimes we would go to Dick's room or mine and chatter and sing until dawn, when, somewhat subdued, we would seek out some German saloon-keeper whom either Peter or Wood knew, rouse him out of his slumbers and demand that he come down and supply us with ham and eggs and beer.

My stage critical work having vivified my desire to write a play or comic opera on the order of *Wang* or *The Isle of Champagne,* two of the reigning successes of that day, or the pleasing *Robin Hood* of de Koven, I set about this task as best I might, scribbling scenes, bits of humor, phases of character. In this idea I was aided and abetted not only by Wood and McCord, both of whom by now seemed to think I might do something, but by the fact that the atmosphere of the *Globe* office, as well as of St. Louis itself, was, for me at least, inspirational and creative. I liked the world in which I now found myself. There were about me and in the city so many who seemed destined to do great things—Wood, McCord, Hazard, a man by the name of Bennett who was engaged in sociologic propaganda of one kind and another, William Marion Reedy, already editing the *Mirror*, Albert Johnson, a most brilliant reporter who had, preceding my coming, resigned from the *Globe* and gone over to the *Chronicle*, Alfred Robyn, composer of *Answer* and *Marizanillo*, one of whose operas was even then being given a local tryout. I have mentioned the wonderful W. C. Brann who preceded me in writing "Heard in the Corridors" and who later stirred America with the *Iconoclast.*

All this, plus the fact that Augustus Thomas had come

from here, a reporter on the *Post-Dispatch*, and that I was now seeing one of his plays, *In Missouri*, moved me to the point where I finally thought out what I considered a fairly humorous plot for a comic opera, which was to be called *Jeremiah I*. It was based on the idea of transporting, by reason of his striking accidentally a mythical Aztec stone on his farm, an old Indiana farmer of a most cantankerous and inquisitive disposition from the era in which he then was back into that of the Aztecs of Mexico, where, owing to a religious invocation then being indulged in with a view to discovering a new ruler, he was assumed to be the answer. Beginning as a cowardly refugee in fear for his life, he was slowly changed into an amazing despot, having at one time as many as three hundred ex-advisers or Aztec secretaries of state in one pen awaiting poisoning. He was to be dissuaded from carrying out this plan by his desire for a certain Aztec maiden, who was to avoid him until he repented of his crimes. She eventually persuaded him to change the form of government from that of a despotism to that of a republic, with himself as candidate for President.

There was nothing much to it. Its only humor lay in the thought or sight of a cranky, curious, critical farmer superimposed upon ancient architecture and forms of worship. Having once thought it out, however, and being pleased with it, I worked at it feverishly nights when I was not on assignments, and in a week or less had a rough outline of it, lyrics and all. I told McCord and Wood about it. And so great was their youthful encouragement that at once I saw this as the way out of my difficulties, the path to that great future I desired. I would become the author of comic opera books. Already I saw myself in New York, rich, famous.

But at that time I could not possibly write without constant encouragement, and having roughed out the opera I now burned for assistance in developing it in detail. At last I went to Peter and told him of my difficulty, my inability to go ahead. He seemed to relish the whole idea hugely, so much so that he made the thing seem far more plausible and easy for me to do and urged me to go ahead, not to faint or get cold feet. Enamored of costumes and gorgeous settings, he even went so far as to first suggest and then later work out in water color, suggestions for costumes and color schemes which I thought wonderful. I was lifted to the seventh heaven. To think that I had worked out something which he considered interesting!

Later that evening, at Peter's suggestion I outlined portions of it to Wood. He also seemed to believe that it was good. He insisted that there must be an evening at his room or mine when I would read it all to them. Accordingly a week later I read it in Dick's room, to much partial applause of course. What else could they do? Peter even went so far as to suggest that he would love to act the part of Jeremiah I, and forthwith began to give us imitations of the prospective king's mannerisms and characteristics. Whatever the merit of the manuscript itself, certainly we imagined Peter's characterizations to be funny. Later he brought me as many as fifty designs of costumes and scenes in color, which appealed to me as having novelty as well as beauty. He had evidently worked for weeks, nights after hours and mornings before coming to the office and on Sundays. By this I was so thrilled that I could scarcely believe my eyes. To think that I had written the book of a real comic opera that should be deemed worthy of this, and that it was within the range of possibility that it would some day be produced!

I began to feel myself a personage, although at bottom I mistrusted the reality of it all. Fate could not be that kind, not so swift. I should never get it produced . . . and yet, like the man in the Arabian fable who kicked over his tray of glassware, dreaming great dreams, I was tending toward the same thing. There was always in me the saving grace of doubt or self-mistrust. I was never quite sure that I should be able to do all that at times I was inclined to hope I might, and so was usually inclined to go about my work as nervously and as enthusiastically as ever, hoping that I might have some of the good fortune of which I dreamed, but never seriously depending on it.

Perhaps it would have been better for me had I.

CHAPTER XXXII

WHILE I rejoiced in the thought that I might now, and so easily, become a successful comic opera librettist, and a poet besides, still I found myself for the most part in a very gloomy frame of mind. One of the things that grieved me intensely, as I have said, was the sight of bitter poverty and failure, and the fact that I personally was not one of those solid commercial figures of which St. Louis was full at this time. They filled the great hotels, the clubs, the mansions, the social positions of importance. They were free, as I foolishly thought, to indulge in all those luxuries and pleasures which, as I so sadly saw, the poor were not privileged to enjoy, myself included. Just about that time there was something about a commercial institution—its exterior simplicity and bareness, the thrash of its inward life, its suggestion of energy, force, compulsion and need—which invariably held me spellbound. Despite my literary and artistic ambitions, I still continued to think it essential, to me, and to all men for that matter if they were to have any force and dignity in this world, that each and every one should be in control of something of this kind, something commercially and financially successful. And what was I—a pale sprout of a newspaper man, possibly an editor or author in the future, but what more?

At times this state of mind tended to make me irritable and even savage instead of sad. I thought that my very generous benefactor, the great McCullagh, ought to see what an important man I was and give me at once the dramatic editorship free and clear of any other work, or at least combine it with something better than mere reporting. I ought to be allowed to do editorials or special work. Again, my mind, although largely freed of Catholic and religious dogma generally and the belief in the workability of the Christian ideals as laid down in the Sermon on the Mount, was still swashing around among the idealistic maxims of Christ and the religionists and moralists generally, contrasting them hourly, as it were, with the selfish materialism of the day as I saw it. Look at the strong men at the top, I was constantly saying to myself, so comfortable, so indifferent, so cruelly dull. How I liked to flail them with maxims excerpted from Christ! Those large districts south of the business heart, along the river and elsewhere, which nightly or weekly Wood, McCord and myself were investigating and which were crowded with the unfit, the unsuccessful, the unhappy—how they haunted me and how I attempted (in my mind, of course) to indict society and comfort them with the poetic if helpless words of the Beatitudes and the Sermon on the Mount: "Blessed are the poor," etc. Betimes, interviewing one important citizen and another, I gained the impression that they truly despised any one who was poor, that they did not give him or his fate a second thought; and betimes I was right— other times wrong. But having been reared on maxims relative to Christian duty I thought they should devote their all to the poor. This failure on their part seemed terrible to me, for having been taught to believe in the Sermon on the Mount I thought they—not myself, for instance—were the ones to make it work out. Mr. McCullagh had begun sending me out of town on various news stories, which was in itself the equivalent of a traveling correspondentship and might readily have led to my being officially recognized as such if I had remained there long enough. Trials of murder cases in St. Joseph and Hannibal, threatened floods in lower Illinois, and train robberies (common occurrences in this region, either between St. Louis and Kansas City, or St. Louis and Louisville) made it necessary for me to make arrangements with Hazard or Wood to carry on my dramatic work while I went about these tasks; a necessity which I partly relished and partly disliked, being uncertain as to which was the more important task to me.

However, I was far from satisfied. I was too restless and dissatisfied. Life, life, life, its contrasts, disappointments, lacks, enticements, was always prodding me. The sun might shine brightly, the winds of fortune blow favorably. Nevertheless, though I might enjoy both, there was always this undertone of something that was not happiness. I was not placed right. I was not this, I was not that. Life was slipping away fast (and I was twenty-one!). I could see the tiny sands of my little life's hourglass sifting down, and what was I achieving? Soon the strength time, the love time, the gay time, of color and romance, would be gone, and if I had not spent it fully, joyously, richly what would there be left for me then? The joys of a mythical heaven or hereafter played no part in my calculations. When one was dead one was dead for all time. Hence the reason for the heartbreak over failure here and now; the awful tragedy of a love lost, a youth never properly enjoyed. Think of living and yet not living in so thrashing a world as this, the best of one's hours passing unused or not properly used. Think of seeing this tinkling phantasmagoria of pain and pleasure, beauty and all its sweets, go by, and yet being compelled to be a bystander, a mere onlooker, enhungered but never satisfied! In this mood I worked on, doing sometimes good work because I was temporarily fascinated and entertained, at other times grumbling and dawdling and moaning over what seemed to me the horrible humdrum of it all.

One day, in just such a mood as this, I received the following final letter from Alice, from whom I had not heard now in months:

"Dear Theo,

"Tomorrow is my wedding-day. Tomorrow at twelve. This may strike you as strange. Well, I have waited—I don't know how long— it has seemed like years to me—for some word, but I knew it was not to be. Your last letter showed me that. I knew that you did not intend to return, and so I went back to Mr. ———. I had to. What else have I to look forward to? You know how unhappy I am here with my family, now that you are gone, in spite of how much they care for me.

"Oh, Theo, you must think me foolish for writing this. I am ashamed of myself. Still, I wanted to let you know, and to say good-bye, for although you have been indifferent I cannot bear any hard feelings toward you. I will make Mr. ——— a good wife. He understands I do not love him, but that I appreciate him. Tomorrow I will marry him, unless—unless something happens. You ought not to have told me that you loved me, Theo, unless you could have stayed with me. You have caused me so much pain.

"But I must say good-bye. This is the last letter I shall ever write you. Don't send my letters now—tear them up. It is too late. Oh, if you only knew how hard it has been to bring myself to this!

"ALICE."

I sat and stared at the floor after reading this. The pain I had caused was a heavy weight. The implication that if I would come to Chicago before noon of this day, or telegraph for her to delay, was too much. What if I should go to Chicago and get her—then what? To her it would be a beautiful thing, the height of romance, saving her from a cruel or dreary fate; but what of me? Should I be happy? Was my profession or my present restless and uncertain state of mind anything to base a marriage on? I knew it was not. ... I also knew that Alice, in spite of my great sadness and affection for her, was really nothing more to me than a passing bit of beauty, charming in itself but of no great import to me. I was sad for her and for myself, saddest because of that chief characteristic of mine and of life which will not let anything endure permanently: love, wealth, fame. I was too restless, too changeful. There rose before me a picture of my finances as compared with what they ought to be, and of any future in marriage based on it. Actually, as I looked at it then, it was more the fault of life than mine.

These thoughts, balancing with the wish I had for greater advancement, caused me as usual to hesitate. But I was in no danger of doing anything impulsive: there was no great impelling passion in this. It was mere sentiment, growing more and more roseate and less and less operative. I groaned inwardly, but night came and the next day, and I had not answered. At noon Alice had been married, as she afterward told me—years afterward, when the fire was all gone and this romance was ended forever.

CHAPTER XXXIII

Thus it was that I dawdled about the city wondering what would become of me. My dramatic work, interesting as it was, was still so trivial in so far as the space given it and the public's interest in it were concerned as to make it all but worthless. The great McCullagh was not interested in the stage; the proof of it was that he entrusted this interesting department to me. But circumstances were bringing about an onward if not upward step. I was daily becoming so restless and unhappy that it would have been strange if something had not happened. To think that there was no more to this dramatic work for me than now appeared, and that in addition Mr. McCullagh was allowing Mr. Mitchell to give me afternoon and night or out-of-town assignments when I had important theatrical performances to report! As a matter of fact they were not important, but Mitchell had no consideration for my critical work. He continued to give me two or three things to do on nights when, as he knew or I thought he should, I should spend the evening witnessing a single performance. This was to pay me out, so I thought, for going over his head. I grew more and more resentful, and finally a catastrophe occurred.

It happened that one Sunday night late in April three shows were scheduled to arrive in the city, each performance being worthy of special attention. Nearly all new shows opened in St. Louis on Sunday night and it was impossible for me to attend them all in one evening. I might have given both Dick and Peter tickets and asked them to help me, but I decided, since this was a custom practiced by my predecessor at times, to write up the notices beforehand, the facts being culled from various press-agent accounts already in my hands, and then comment more fully on the plays in some notes which I published mid-week. It happened, however, that on this particular evening Mr. Mitchell had other plans for me. Without consulting me or my theatrical duties he handed me at about seven in the evening a slip of paper containing a notice of a street-car hold-up in the far western suburbs of the city. I was about to protest that my critical work demanded my presence elsewhere but concluded to hold my tongue. He would merely advise me to write up the notices of the shows, as I had planned, or, worse yet, tell me to let other people do them. I thought once of going to McCullagh and protesting, but finally went my way determined to do the best I could and protest later. I would hurry up on this assignment and then come back and visit the theaters.

When I reached the scene of the supposed hold-up there was nothing to guide me. The people at the car-barns did not know anything about it and the crew that had been held up was not present. I visited a far outlying police station but the sergeant in charge could tell me nothing more than that the crime was not very important, a few dollars stolen. I went to the exact spot but there were no houses in the neighborhood, only a barren stretch of track lying out in a rain-soaked plain. It was a gloomy, wet night, and I decided to return to the city. When I reached a car-line it was late, too late for me to do even a part of my critical work; the long distance out and the walks to the car-barn and the police station had consumed much time. As I neared the city I found that it was eleven o'clock. What chance had I to visit the theaters then? I asked myself angrily. How was I to know if the shows had even arrived? There had been heavy rains all over the West for the last week and there had been many wash-outs.

I finally got off in front of the nearest theater and went up to the door; it was silent and dark. I thought of asking the drugman who occupied a corner of the building, but that seemed a silly thing to be doing at this hour and I let it go. I thought of telephoning to the rival paper, the *Republic*, when I reached the office, but when I got there I had first to report to Mitchell, who was just leaving, and then, irritated and indifferent, I put it off for the moment. Perhaps Hartung would know.

"Do you know what time the first edition goes to press here, Hugh?" I asked him at a quarter after twelve.

"Twelve-thirty, I think. The telegraph man can tell you."

"Do you know whether the dramatic stuff I sent up this afternoon gets in that?"

"Sure—at least I think it does. You'd better ask the foreman of the composing-room about it, though."

I went upstairs. Instead of calling up the *Republic* at once, or any of the managers of the theaters, or knocking out the notices entirely, I inquired how matters stood with the first edition. I was not sure that there was any reason for worrying about the shows not arriving, but something kept telling me to make sure.

At last I found that the first edition had been closed, with the notices in it, and went to the telephone to call up the *Republic*. Then the dramatic editor of that paper had gone and I could not find the address of a single manager. I tried to reach one of the theaters, but there was no response. The clock registered twelve-thirty by then, and I weakly concluded that things must be all right or that if they weren't I couldn't help it. I then went home and to bed and slept poorly, troubled by the thought that something might be wrong and wishing now that I had not been so lackadaisical about it all. Why couldn't I attend to things at the proper time instead of dawdling about in this fashion? I sighed and tried to sleep.

The next morning I arose and went through the two morning papers without losing any time. To my horror and distress, there in the *Republic* was an announcement on the first page to the effect that owing to various wash-outs in several States none of the three shows had arrived the night before. And in my own paper, to my great pain was a full account of the performances and the agreeable reception accorded them!

"Oh, Lord!" I groaned. "What will McCullagh say? What will the other papers say? Three shows reviewed, and not one here!'' And in connection with one I had written: ''A large and enthusiastic audience received Mr. Sol Smith Russell'' as the Grand. And in connection with another that the gallery of Pope's Theater ''was top-heavy.'' The perspiration burst from my forehead. Remembering Sisseretta Jones and my tendency to draw the lightning of public observation and criticism, I began to speculate as to what newspaper criticism would follow this last *faux pas.* ''Great God!'' I thought. ''Wait till he sees this!'' and I was ready to weep. At once I saw myself not only the laughing-stock of the town but discharged as well. Think of being discharged now, after all my fine dreams as to the future!

Without delay I proceeded to the office and removed my few belongings, resolved to be prepared for the worst. With the feeling that I owed Mr. McCullagh an explanation I sat down and composed a letter to him in which I explained, from my point of view, just how the thing had happened. I did not attack Mr. Mitchell or seek to shield myself but merely illustrated how I had been expected to handle my critical work in this office. I also added how kind I thought he had been, how much I valued his personal regard, and asked him not to think too ill of me. This letter I placed in an envelope addressed to ''Mr. Joseph B. McCullagh, Personal,'' and going into his private office before any others had come down laid it on his desk. Then I retired to my room to await the afternoon papers and think.

They were not long in appearing, and neither of the two leading afternoon papers had failed to notice the blunder. With the most delicate, laughing raillery they had seized upon this latest error of the great *Globe* as a remarkable demonstration of what they affected to believe was its editor's lately acquired mediumistic and psychic powers. The *Globe* was regularly writing up various séances, slate-writing demonstrations and the like, in St. Louis and elsewhere, things which Mr. McCullagh was interested in or considered good circulation builders, and this was now looked upon as a fresh demonstration of his development in that line. ''Oh, Lord! Oh, Lord!'' I groaned when I read the following:

"To see three shows at once," observed the *Post-Dispatch,* "and those three widely separated by miles of country and washed-out sections of railroad in three different States (Illinois, Iowa and Missouri), is indeed a triumph; but also to see them as having arrived, or as they would have been had they arrived, and displaying their individual delights to three separate audiences of varying proportions assembled for that purpose is truly amazing, one of the finest demonstrations of mediumship—or perhaps we had better say materialization—yet known to science. Great, indeed, is McCullagh. Great the *G.-D.* Indeed, now that we think of it, it is an achievement so astounding that even the *Globe* may well be proud of it—one of the finest flights of which the human mind or the great editor's psychic strength is capable. We venture to say that no spiritualist or materializing medium has ever outrivaled it. We have always known that Mr. McCullagh is a great man. The illuminating charm of his editorial page is sufficient proof of that. But this latest essay of his into the realm of combined dramatic criticism, supernatural insight, and materialization, is one of the most perfect things of its kind and can only be attributed to genius in the purest form. It is psychic, supernatural, spooky."

The *Evening Chronicle* for its part troubled to explain how ably and interestedly the spirit audiences and actors, although they might as well have been resting, the actors at least not having any contract which compelled their subconscious or psychic selves to work, had conducted themselves, doing their parts without a murmur. It was also here hinted that in future it would not be necessary for the *Globe* to carry a dramatic critic, seeing that the psychic mind of its chief was sufficient. Anyhow it was plain that the race was fast reaching that place where it could perceive in advance that which was about to take place; in proof of this it pointed of course to the noble mind which now occupied the editorial chair of the *Globe-Democrat,* seeing all this without moving from his office.

I was agonized. Sweat rolled from my forehead; my nerves twitched. And to think that this was the second time within no more than a month that I had made my great benefactor the laughing-stock of the city! What must he think of me? I could see him at that moment reading these editorials. . . . He would discharge me. . . .

Not knowing what to do, I sat and brooded. Gone were all my fine dreams, my great future, my standing in the eyes of men and of this paper! What was to become of me now? I saw myself returning to Chicago—to do what? What would Peter, Dick, Hazard, Johnson, Bellairs, all my new found friends, think? Instead of going boldly to the office and seeing my friends, who were still fond of me if laughing at my break, or Mr. McCullagh, I slipped about the city meditating on my fate and wondering what I was to do.

For at least a week, during the idlest hours of the morning and evening, I would slip out and get a little something to eat or loiter in an old but little-frequented book-store in Walnut Street, hoping to keep myself out of sight and out of mind. In a spirit of intense depression I picked up a few old books, deciding to read more, to make myself more fit for life. I also decided to leave St. Louis, since no one would have me here, and began to think of Chicago, whether I could stand it to return there, or whether I had better drift on to a strange place. But how should I live or travel, since I had very little money—having wasted it, as I now thought, on riotous living! The unhappy end of a spendthrift!

Finally, after mooning about for a day or two more I concluded that I should have to leave my fine room and try to earn some money here so as to be able to leave. And so one morning, without venturing near the *Globe* and giving the principal meeting-places of reporters and friends a wide berth, I went into the office of the St. Louis *Republic*, then thriving fairly well in an old building at Third and Chestnut streets. Here with a heavy heart, I awaited the coming of the city editor, H. B. Wandell, of whom I had heard a great deal but whom I had never seen.

(205)

CHAPTER XXXIV

THE *Republic* was in a tumbledown old building in a fairly deserted neighborhood in that region near the waterfront from which the city proper had been steadily growing away for years. This paper, if I am not mistaken, was founded in 1808.

The office was so old and rattletrap that it was discouraging. The elevator was a slow and wheezy box, bumping and creaking and suggesting immediate collapse. The boards of the entrance-hall and the city editorial room squeaked under one's feet. The city reportorial room, where I should work if I secured a place, was larger than that of the *Globe* and higher-ceiled, but beyond that it had no advantage. The windows were tall but cracked and patched with faded yellow copy-paper; the desks, some fifteen or twenty all told, were old, dusty, knife-marked, smeared with endless ages of paste and ink. There was waste paper and rubbish on the floor. There was no sign of either paint or wallpaper. The windows facing east looked out upon a business court or alley where trucks and vans creaked all day but which at night was silent as the grave, as was this entire wholesale neighborhood. The buildings directly opposite were decayed wholesale houses of some unimportant kind where in slimsy rags of dresses or messy trousers and shirts girls and boys of from fourteen to twenty worked all day, the girls' necks in summer time open to their breasts and their sleeves rolled to their shoulders, the boys in sleeveless undershirts and tight-belted trousers and with tousled hair. What their work was I forget, but flirting with each other or with the reporters and printers of this paper occupied a great deal of their time.

The city editor, H. B. Wandell, was one of those odd, forceful characters who because of my youth and extreme impressionability perhaps and his own vigor and point of view succeeded in making a deep impression on me at once. He was such a queer little man, so different from Mitchell and McCullagh, nervous, jumpy, restless, vigorous, with eyes so piercing that they reminded one of a hawk's and a skin so swarthy that it was Italian in quality and made all the more emphatic by a large, humped, protruding nose pierced by big nostrils. His hands were wrinkled and claw-like, and he had large yellowish teeth which showed rather fully when he laughed. And that laugh! I can hear it yet, a cross between a yelp and a cackle. It always seemed to me to be a mirthless laugh, insincere, and yet also it had an element of appreciation in it. He could see a point at which others ought to laugh without apparently enjoying it himself. He was at once a small and yet a large man mentally, wise and incisive in many ways, petty and even venomous in others, a man to coddle and placate if you were beholden to him, one to avoid if you were not, but on the whole a man above the average in ability.

And he had the strangest, fussiest, bossiest love of great literature of any one I have ever known, especially in the realm of the newspapers. Zola at this time was apparently his ideal of what a writer should be, and after him Balzac and Loti. He seemed to know them well and to admire and even love them, after his fashion. He was always calling upon me to imitate Zola's vivid description of the drab and the gross and the horrible if I could, assuming that I had read him, which I had not, but I did not say so. And Balzac's and Loti's sure handling of the sensual and the poignant! How often have I heard him refer to them with admiration, giving me the line and phrase of certain stark pictures, and yet at the same time there was a sneaking bending of the knee to the middle West conventions of which he was a part, a kind of horror of having it known that he approved of these things. He was a Shriner and very proud of it, as he was of various other local organizations to which he belonged. He had the reputation of being one of the best city editors in the city, far superior to my late master. Previously he had been city editor of the *Globe* itself for many years and was still favorably spoken of in that office. After I left St. Louis he returned to the *Globe* for a time and once more became its guide in local news.

But that is neither here nor there save as it illustrates what is a cardinal truth of the newspaper world: that the best of newspaper men are occasionally to be found on the poorest of papers, and vice versa. Just at this time, as I understood, he was here because the *Republic* was making a staggering effort to build itself up in popular esteem, which it finally succeeded in doing after McCullagh's death, becoming once more the leading morning paper as it had been before the *Globe*, under McCullagh, arose to power. Just now, however, in my despondent mood, it seemed an exceedingly sad affair.

Mr. Wandell, as I now learned, had heard of me and my recent *faux pas,* as well as some of the other things I had been doing.

"Been working on the *Globe*, haven't you?" he commented when I approached him. "What did they pay you?"

I told him.

"When did you leave there?"

"About a week ago."

"Why did you leave?"

"Perhaps you saw those notices of three shows that didn't come to town? I'm the man who wrote them up."

"Oho! ho! ho!" and he began eyeing me drily and slapping his knee. "I saw those. Ha! ha! ha! Ha! ha! ha! Yes, that was very funny—very. We had an editorial on it. And so McCullagh fired you, did he?"

"No, sir," I replied indignantly. "I quit. I thought he might want to, and I put a letter on his desk and left."

"Ha! ha! ha! Quite right! That's very funny! I know just how they do over there. I was city editor there myself once. They write them up in advance sometimes. We do here. Where do you come from?"

I told him. He meditated awhile, as though he were uncertain whether he needed any one.

"You say you got thirty dollars there? I couldn't pay anybody that much here—not to begin with. We never give more than eighteen to begin with. Besides, I have a full staff just now, and it's summer. I might use another man if eighteen would be enough. You might think it over and come in and see me again some time.''

Although my spirits fell at so great a drop in salary I hastened to explain that I would be glad to accept eighteen. I needed to be at work again.

"Whatever you would consider fair would suit me," I said.

He smiled. "The newspaper market is low just now. If your work proves satisfactory I may raise you a little later on." He must have seen that he had a soft and more or less unsophisticated boy to deal with.

"Suppose you write me a little article about something, just to show me what you can do," he added.

I went away insulted by this last request. In spite of all he said I could feel that he wanted me; but I had no skill in manipulating my own affairs. To drop from thirty dollars as dramatic editor to eighteen as a mere reporter was terrible. With a grain of philosophic melancholy I faced it, however, feeling that if I worked hard I might yet get a start in some way or other. I must work and save some money and if I did not better myself I would leave St. Louis. My ability must be worth something somewhere; it had been on the *Globe*.

I went home and wrote the article (a mere nothing about some street scene), went back to the office and left it. Next day I called again.

"All right," he said. "You can go to work."

I went back into that large shabby room and took a seat. In a few minutes the place filled up with the staff, most of whom I knew and all of whom eyed me curiously—reporters, special editors, the city editor and his assistant, Mr. Williams of blessed memory, one-eyed, sad, impressive, intelligent, who had nothing but kind things to say of what I wrote and who was friendly and helpful until the day I left.

In a little while the assignment book was put out, with the task I was to undertake. Before I left I was called in and advised concerning it. I went and looked into it (I have forgotten what it was) and reported later in the day. What I wrote I turned over to Mr. Williams, and later in the day when I asked him if it was all right he said: "Yes, quite all right. It reads all right to me," and then gave me a kindly, one-eyed smile. I liked him from the first day; he was a better editor than Wandell, with more taste and discrimination, and later rose to a higher position elsewhere.

Meanwhile I strolled about thinking of my great fall. It seemed as though I should never get over this. But in a few days I was back in my old reportorial routine, depressed but secure, convinced that I could write as well as ever, and for any newspaper.

For the romance of my own youth was still upon me, my ambitions and my dreams coloring it all. Does the gull sense the terrors of the deep, or the butterfly the traps and snares of the woods and fields? Roaming this keen, new, ambitious mid-Western city, life-hungry and love-hungry and underpaid, eager and ambitious, I still found so much in the worst to soothe, so much in the best to torture me. In every scene of ease or pleasure was both a lure and a reproach; in every aspect of tragedy or poverty was a threat or a warning. I was never tired of looking at the hot, hungry, weary slums, any more than I was of looking at the glories of the mansions of the west end. Both had their lure, their charm; one because it was a state worse than my own, the other because it was a better—unfairly so, I thought. Amid it all I hurried, writing and dreaming, half-laughing and half-crying, with now a tale to move me to laughter and now another to send me to bottomless despairs. But always youth, youth, and the crash of the presses in the basement and a fresh damp paper laid on my desk of a morning with "the news" and my own petty achievements or failures to cheer or disappoint me; so it went, day in and day out.

The *Republic*, while not so successful as the *Globe-Democrat*, was a much better paper for me to work on. For one thing, it took me from under the domination of Mr. Mitchell (one can hate some people most persistently), and placed me under one who, whatever may have been his defects, provided me with far greater opportunities for my pen than ever the *Globe* had and supplied a better judgment as to what constituted a story and a news feature. Now that I think of him, Wandell was far and away the best judge of news, from a dramatic or story point of view, of any for whom I ever worked.

"A good story, is it?" I can see him smirking and rubbing his hands miser or gourmet fashion, as over a pot of gold or a fine dish. "She said that, did she? Ha! ha! That's excellent, excellent! You saw him yourself, did you? And the brother too? By George, we'll make a story of that! Be careful how you write that now. All the facts you know, just as far as they will carry you; but we don't want any libel suits, remember. We don't want you to say anything we can't substantiate, but I don't want you to be afraid either. Write it strong, clear, definite. Get in all the touches of local color you can. And remember Zola and Balzac, my boy, remember Zola and Balzac. Bare facts are what are needed in cases like this, with lots of color as to the scenery or atmosphere, the room, the other people, the street, and all that. You get me?"

And quite truly I got him, as he was pleased to admit, even though I got but little cash out of it. I always felt, perhaps unjustly, that he made but small if any effort to advantage me in any way except that of writing. But what of it? He was nearly always enthusiastic over my work, in a hard, bright, waspish way, nearly always excited about the glittering realistic facts which one might dig up and which he was quite determined that his paper should present. The stories! The scandals! That hard, cruel cackle of his when he had any one cornered! He must have known what a sham and a fake most of these mid-Western pretensions to sanctity and purity were, and yet if he did and was irritated by them he said little to me. Like most Americans of the time, he was probably confused by the endless clatter concerning personal perfection, the Christ ideal, as opposed to the actual details of life. He could not decide for himself which was true and which false, the Christ theory or that of Zola, but he preferred Zola when interpreting the news. When things were looking up from a news point of view and great realistic facts were coming to the surface regardless of local sentiment, facts which utterly contradicted all the noble fol-de-rol of the puritans and the religionists, he was positively transformed. In those hours when the loom of life seemed to be weaving brilliant dramatic or tragic patterns of a realistic, Zolaesque character he was beside himself with gayety, trotting to and fro in the local room, leaning over the shoulders of scribbling scribes and interrupting them to ask details or to caution them as to certain facts which they must or must not include, beaming at the ceiling or floor, whistling, singing, rubbing his hands—a veritable imp or faun of pleasure and enthusiasm. Deaths, murders, great social or political scandals or upheavals, those things which presented the rough, raw facts of life, as well as its tenderer aspects, seemed to throw him into an ecstasy—not over the woes of others but over the fact that he was to have an interesting paper tomorrow.

"Ah, it was a terrible thing, was it? He killed her in cold blood, you say? There was a great crowd out there, was there? Well, well, write it all up. Write it all up. It looks like a pretty good story to me—doesn't it to you? Write a good strong introduction for it, you know, all the facts in the first paragraph, and then go on and tell your story. You can have as much space for it as you want—a column, a column and a half, two—just as it runs. Let me look at it before you turn it in, though." Then he would begin whistling or singing, or would walk up and down in the city-room rubbing his hands in obvious satisfaction.

And how that reportorial room seemed to thrill or sing between the hours of five and seven in the evening, when the stories of the afternoon were coming in, or between ten-thirty and midnight, when the full grist of the day was finally being ground out. How it throbbed with human life and thought, quite like a mill room full of looms or a counting house in which endless records and exchanges are being made. Those reporters, eighteen or twenty of them, bright, cheerful, interesting, forceful youths, each bent upon making a name for himself, each working hard, each here bending over his desk scratching his head or ear and thinking, his mind lost in the mazes of arrangement and composition.

Wandell had no tolerance for any but the best of newspaper reporters and would discharge a man promptly for falling down on a story, especially if he could connect it with the feeling that he was not as good a newspaper man as he should be. He hated commonplace men, and once I had become familiar with the office and with him, he would often ask me in a spirit of unrest if I knew of an especially good one anywhere with whom he could replace some one else whom he did not like; a thought which jarred me but which did not prevent me from telling him. Somehow I had an eye and a taste for exceptional men myself, and I wanted his staff to be as good as any. So it was not long before he began to rely on me to supply him with suitable men, so much so that I soon had the reputation of being a local arbiter of jobs, one who could get men in or keep them out—a thing which made me some enemies later. And it really was not true for I could not have kept any good man out.

In the meantime, while he was trying me out to suit himself, he had been giving me only routine work: the North Seventh Street police station afternoons and evenings, where one or two interesting stories might be expected every day, crimes or sordid romances of one kind or another. Or if there was nothing much doing there I might be sent out on an occasional crime story elsewhere. Once I had handled a few of these for him, and to his satisfaction, I was pushed into the topnotch class and given only the most difficult stories, those which might be called feature crimes and sensations, which I was expected to unravel, sometimes single-handed, and to which always I was expected to write the lead. This realistic method of his plus a keen desire to unload all the heavy assignments on me was in no wise bad for me. He liked me, and this was his friendly way of showing it.

Indeed, with a ruthless inconsiderateness, as I then thought, he piled on story after story, until I was a little infuriated at first, seeing how little I was being paid. When nothing of immediate importance was to he had, he proceeded to create news, studying out interesting phases of past romances or crimes which he thought might be worth while to work up and publish on Sunday, and handing them to me to do over. He even created stories when the general news was dull, throwing me into the most delicate and dangerous fields of arson, murder, theft, marital unhappiness, and tragedies of all kinds, things not public but which by clever detective work could be made so, and where libel and other suits and damages lurked on either hand. Without cessation, Sunday and every other day, he called upon me to display sentiment, humor or cold, hard, descriptive force, as the case might be, quoting now Hugo, now Balzac, now Dickens, and now Zola to me to show me just what was to be done. In a little while, despite my reduced salary and the fact that I had lost my previous place in disgrace and was not likely to get a raise here soon, I was as much your swaggering newspaper youth as ever, strolling about the city with the feeling that I was somebody and looking up all my old friends, with the idea of letting them know that I was by no means such a failure as they might imagine. Dick and Peter of course, seeing me ambling in on them late one hot night, received me with open arms.

"Well, you're a good one!" yelped Dick in his high, almost falsetto voice when I came in. I could see that he had been sitting before his open window, which commanded Broadway, where he had been no doubt meditating—your true romancer. "Where the hell have you been keeping yourself? You're a dandy! We've been looking for you for weeks. We've been down to your place a dozen times, but you wouldn't let us in. You're a dandy, you are! McCord has some more of those opera cartoons done. Why didn't you ever come around, anyhow?"

"I'm working down on the *Republic* now," I replied, blushing, "and I've been busy."

"Oho!" laughed Dick, slapping his knees. "That's a good

one on you! I heard about it. Those shows written up, and not one in town! Oho! That's good!" He coughed a consumptive cough or two and relaxed.

I laughed with him. "It wasn't really all my fault," I said apologetically.

"I know it wasn't. Don't I know the *Globe?* Didn't Carmichael get me to work the same racket for him? Ask Hazard. It wasn't your fault. Sit down. Peter'll be here in a little while; then we'll go out and get something."

We fell to discussing the attitude of the people on the *Globe* after I had left. Wood insisted that he had not heard much. He knew instinctively that Mitchell was glad I was gone, as he might well have been. Hartung had reported to him that McCullagh had raised Cain with Mitchell and that two or three of the boys on the staff had manifested relief.

"You know who they'd be," continued Wood. "The fellows who can't do what you can but would like to."

I smiled. "I know about who they are," I said.

We talked about the world in general—literature, the drama, current celebrities, the state of politics, all seen through the medium of youth and aspiration and inexperience. While we were talking McCord came in. He had been to his home in South St. Louis, where he preferred to live in spite of his zest for Bohemia, and the ground had all to be gone over with him. We settled down to an evening's enjoyment: Dick went for beer; Peter lit a rousing pipe. Accumulated short stories were produced and plans for new ones recounted. At one point Peter exclaimed: "You know what I'm going to do, Dreiser?"

"Well, what?"

"I'm going to study for the leading rôle in that opera of yours. I can play that, and I'm going to if you don't object —do you?"

"Object? Why should I object?" I replied, doubtful however of the wisdom of this. Peter had never struck me as quite the actor type. "I'd like to see you do it if you can, Peter."

"Oh, I can, all right. That old rube appeals to me. I

bet that if I ever get on the stage I can get away with that.''
He eyed Dick for confirmation.

"I'll bet you could,'' said Dick loyally. "Peter makes a
dandy rube. Oh, will you ever forget the time we went
down to the old Nickelodeon and did a turn, Peter? Oho!''

Later the three of us left for a bite and I could see that I
was as high in their favor as ever, which restored me not a
little. Peter seemed to think that my escapades and mishaps,
coupled with the attention and discussion which my name
evoked among local newspaper men, were doing me good,
making me an interesting figure. I could scarcely believe that
but I was inclined to believe that I had not fallen as low as at
first I had imagined.

CHAPTER XXXV

The LaClede, as I have indicated, was the center of all gossiping newspaper life at this time, at least that part of it of which I knew anything. Here, in idling groups, during the course of a morning, afternoon or evening, might appear Dick or Peter, Rody, Clark, Hazard, Johnson, Root, Johns Daws, a long company of excellent newspaper men who worked on the different papers of the city from time to time and who, because of a desire for companionship in this helter-skelter world and the certainty of finding it here, hung about this corner. Here one could get in on a highly intellectual or diverting conversation of one kind or another at almost any time. So many of these men had come from distant cities and knew them much better than they did St. Louis. As a rule, being total strangers and here only for a short while, they were inclined to sniff at conditions as they found them here and to boast of those elsewhere, especially the men who came from New York, Boston, San Francisco and Chicago. I was one of those who, knowing Chicago and St. Louis only and wishing to appear wise in these matters, boasted vigorously of the superlative importance of Chicago as a city, whereas such men as Root of New York, Johnson of Boston, Ware of New Orleans, and a few others, merely looked at me and smiled.

"All I have to say to you, young fellow," young Root once observed to me genially if roughly after one of these heated and senseless arguments, "is wait till you go to New York and see for yourself. I've been to Chicago, and it's a way-station in comparison. It's the only other city you've seen, and that's why you think it's so great." There was a certain amount of kindly toleration in his voice which infuriated me.

"Ah, you're crazy," I replied. "You're like all New

Yorkers: you think you know it all. You won't admit you're beaten when you are.''

The argument proceeded through all the different aspects of the two cities until finally we called each other damned fools and left in a huff. Years later, however, having seen New York, I wanted to apologize if ever I met him again. The two cities, as I then learned, each individual and wonderful in its way, were not to be contrasted. But how sure I was of my point of view then!

Nearly all of these young men, as I now saw, presented a sharp contrast to those I had known in Chicago, or perhaps the character of the work in this city and my own changing viewpoint made them seem different. Chicago at that time had seemed to be full of exceptional young men in the reportorial world, men who in one way or another had already achieved considerable local repute as writers and coming men: Finley Peter Dunne, George Ade, Brand Whitlock, Ben King, Charles Stewart, and many others, some of whom even in that day were already signing their names to some of their contributions; whereas here in St. Louis, few if any of us had achieved any local distinction of any kind. No one of us had as yet created a personal or literary following. We could not, here, apparently; the avenues were not the same. And none of us was hailed as certain to attract attention in the larger world outside. We formed little more than a weak scholastic brotherhood or union, recognizing each other genially enough as worthy fellow-craftsmen but not offering each other much consolation in our rough state beyond a mere class or professional recognition as working newspaper men. Yet at times this LaClede was a kind of tonic bear garden, or mental wrestling-place, where unless one were very guarded and sure of oneself one might come by a quick and hard fall, as when once in some argument in regard to a current political question, and without knowing really what I was talking about, I made the statement that palaeontology indicated so-and-so, whereupon one of my sharp confrères suddenly took me up with: ''Say, what is palaeontology, anyhow? Do you know?''

I was completely stumped, for I didn't. It was a comparatively new word, outside the colleges, being used here and there in arguments and editorials, and I had glibly taken it over. I floundered about and finally had to confess that I did not know what it was, whereupon I endured a laugh for my pains. I was thereafter wiser and more cautious.

But this, in my raw, ignorant state, was a very great help to me. Many of these men were intelligent and informed to the cutting point in regard to many facts of life of which I was extremely ignorant. Many of them had not only read more but seen more, and took my budding local pretensions to being somebody with a very large grain of salt. At many of the casual meetings, where at odd moments reporters and sometimes editors were standing or sitting about and discussing one phase of life and another, I received a back-handed slap which sometimes jarred my pride but invariably widened my horizon.

One of the most interesting things in my life at this time was that same North Seventh Street police station previously mentioned, to which I went daily and which was a center for a certain kind of news at least—rapes, riots, murders, fantastic family complications of all kinds, so common to very poor and highly congested neighborhoods. This particular station was the very center of a mixed ghetto, slum and negro life, which even at this time was still appalling to me in some of its aspects. It was all so dirty, so poor, so stuffy, so starveling. There were in it all sorts of streets—Jewish, negro, and run-down American, or plain slum, the first crowded with long-bearded Jews and their fat wives, so greasy, smelly and generally offensive that they sickened me: rag-pickers, chicken-dealers and feather-sorters all. In their streets the smell of these things, picked or crated chickens, many of them partially decayed, decayed meats and vegetables, half-sorted dirty feathers and rags and I know not what else, was sickening in hot weather. In the negro streets—or rather alleys, for they never seemed to occupy any general thoroughfare—were rows or one-, two-, three- and four-story shacks or barns of frame or brick crowded into back yards and with thousands of blacks of the most shuffling and idle character hanging about. In these hot days of June, July and August they seemed to do little save sit or lie in the shade of buildings in this vicinity and swap yarns or contemplate the world with laughter or in silence. Occasionally there was a fight, a murder or a low love affair among them which justified my time here. In addition, there were those other streets of soggy, decayed Americans—your true slum—filled with as low and cantankerous a population of whites as one would find anywhere, a type of animal dangerous to the police themselves, for they could riot and kill horribly and were sullen at best. Invariably the police traveled here in pairs, and whenever an alarm from some policeman on his beat was turned in from this region a sergeant and all the officers in the station at the time would set forth to the rescue, sometimes as many as eight or ten in a police wagon, with orders, as I myself have heard them given, "to club the —— heads off them" or "break their —— bones, but bring them in here. I'll fix 'em"; in response to which all the stolid Irish huskies would go forth to battle, returning frequently with a whole vanload of combatants or alleged combatants, all much the worse for the contest.

There was an old fat Irish sergeant of about fifty or fifty-five, James King by name, who used to amuse me greatly. He ruled here like a potentate under the captain, whom I rarely saw. The latter had an office to himself in the front of the station and rarely came out, seeming always to be busy with bigwigs of one type and another. With the sergeant, however, I became great friends. His place was behind the central desk, in the front of which were two light standards and on the surface of which were his blotter and reports of different kinds. Behind the desk was his big tilted swivel chair, with himself in it, stout, perspiring, coatless, vestless, collarless, his round head and fat neck beady with sweat, his fat arms and hands moist and laid heavily over his protuberant stomach. According to him, he had been at this work exactly eight years, and before that he had "beat the sidewalk," as he said, or traveled a beat.

"Yes, yes, 'tis a waarm avenin'," he would begin whenever

I arrived and he was not busy, which usually he was not, "an' there's naathin' for ye, me lad. But ye might just as well take a chair an' make yerself comfortable. It may be that something will happen, an' again maybe it won't. Ye must hope fer the best, as the sayin' is. 'Tis a bad time fer any trouble to be breakin' out though, in all this hot weather," and then he would elevate a large palmleaf fan which he kept near and begin to fan himself, or swig copiously from a pitcher of ice-water.

Here then he would sit, answering telephone calls from headquarters or marking down reports from the men on their beats or answering the complaints of people who came in hour after hour to announce that they had been robbed or their homes had been broken into or that some neighbor was making a nuisance of himself or their wives or husbands or sons or daughters wouldn't obey them or stay in at night.

"Yes, an' what's the matter now?" he would begin when one of these would put in an appearance.

Perhaps it was a man who would be complaining that his wife or daughter would not stay in at night, or a woman complaining so of her husband, son or daughter.

"Well, me good woman, I can't be helpin' ye with that. This is no court av laaw. If yer husband don't support ye, er yer son don't come in av nights an' he's a minor, ye can get an order from the judge at the Four Courts compellin' him. Then if he don't mind ye' and ye waant him arrested er locked up, I can help ye that way, but not otherwise. Go to the Four Courts."

Sometimes, in the case of a parent complaining of a daughter's or son's disobedience, he would relent a little and say: "See if ye can bring him around here. Tell him that the captain waants to see him. Then if he comes I'll see what I can do fer ye. Maybe I can scare him a bit."

Let us say they came, a shabby, overworked mother or father leading a recalcitrant boy or girl. King would assume a most ferocious air and after listening to the complaint of the parent as if it were all news to him would demand: "What's ailin' ye? Why can't ye stay in nights? What's the matter with ye that ye can't obey yer mother? Don't ye know it's agin the laaw fer a minor to be stayin' out aafter ten at night? Ye don't? Well, it is, an' I'm tellin' ye now. D'ye waant me t'lock ye up? Is that what ye're looking fer? There's a lot av good iron cells back there waitin' fer ye if ye caan't behave yerself. What're ye goin' t'do about it?''

Possibly the one in error would relent a little and begin arguing with the parent, charging unfairness, cruelty and the like.

''Here now, don't ye be taalkin' to yer mother like that! Ye're not old enough to be doin' that. An' what's more, don't let me ketch ye out on the streets er her complainin' to me again. If ye do I'll send one av me men around to bring ye in. This is the last now. D'ye waant to spend a few nights in a cell? Well, then! Now be gettin' out av here an' don't let me hear any more about ye. Not a word. I've had enough now. Out with ye!''

And he would glower and grow red and pop-eyed and fairly roar, shoving them tempestuously out—only, after the victim had gone, he would lean back in his chair and wipe his forehead and sigh: '' 'Tis tough, the bringin' up av childern, hereabouts especially. Ye can't be blamin' them fer waantin' to be out on the streets, an' yet ye can't let 'em out aither, exactly. It's hard to tell what to do with 'em. I've been taalkin' like that fer years now to one an' another. 'Tis all the good it does. Ye can't do much fer 'em hereabouts.''

It was during this period, this summer time and fall, that I came in contact with some of the most interesting characters, newspaper men especially, flotsam and jetsam who drifted in here from other newspaper centers and then drifted out again, newspaper men so intelligent and definite in some respects that they seemed worthy of any position or station in life and yet so indifferent and errant or so poorly placed in spite of their efforts and capacities as to cause me to despair for the reward of merit anywhere—intellectual merit, I mean. For some of these men while fascinating were the rankest kind of failures, drunkards, drug fiends, hypochondriacs. Many of them had stayed too long in the profession, which is a young man's game at best, and others had wasted their opportunities dreaming of a chance fortune no doubt and then had taken to drink or drugs. Still others, young men like myself, drifters and uncertain as to their future, were just finding out how unprofitable the newspaper game was and in consequence were cynical, waspish and moody.

I am not familiar with many professions and so cannot say whether any of the others abound in this same wealth of eccentric capacity and understanding, or offer as little reward. Certainly all the newspaper offices I have ever known sparkled with these exceptional men, few of whom ever seemed to do very well, and no paper I ever worked on paid wages anywhere near equal to the services rendered or the hours exacted. It was always a hard, driving game, with the ash-heap as the reward for the least weakening of energy or ability; and at the same time these newspapers were con-stantly spouting editorially about kindness, justice, charity, a full reward for labor, and were getting up fresh-air funds and so on for those not half as deserving as their employees, but —and this is the point—likely to bring them increased cir-culation. In the short while I was in the newspaper profes-sion I met many men who seemed to be thoroughly sound intellectually, quite free, for the most part, from the nar-row, cramping conventions of their day, and yet they never seemed to get on very well.

I remember one man in particular, Clark I think his name was, who arrived on the scene just about this time and who fascinated me. He was so able and sure of touch mentally and from an editorial point of view, and yet financially and in every material way he was such a failure. He came from Kansas City or Omaha while I was on the *Republic* and had worked in many, many places before that. He was a stocky, dark, clerkly figure, with something of the manager or owner or leader about him, a most shrewd and capable-looking per-son. And when he first came to the *Republic* he seemed des-tined to rise rapidly and never to want for anything, so much self-control and force did he appear to have. He was a hard worker, quiet, unostentatious, and once I had gained his confidence, he gradually revealed a tale of past position and comfort which, verified as it was by Wandell and Williams, was startling when contrasted with his present position. Although he was not much over forty he had been editor or managing editor of several important papers in the West but had lost them through some primary disaster which had caused him to take to drink—his wife's unfaithfulness, I believe—and his inability in recent years to stay sober for more than three months at a stretch. In some other city he had been an important factor in politics. Here he was, still clean and spruce apparently (when I first saw him, at any rate), going about his work with a great deal of energy, writing the most satisfactory newspaper stories; and then, once two or three months of such labor had gone by, disappearing. When I inquired of Williams and Wandell as to his whereabouts the former stared at me with his one eye and smiled, then lifted his fingers in the shape of a glass to his mouth. Wandell merely remarked: "Drink, I think. He may show up and he may not. He had a few weeks' wages when he left."

I did not hear anything more of him for some weeks, when suddenly one day, in that wretched section of St. Louis beloved of Dick and Peter as a source of literary material, I was halted by a figure which I assumed to be one of the lowest of the low. A short, matted, dirty black beard concealed a face that bore no resemblance to Clark. A hat that looked as though it might have been lifted out of an ash-barrel was pulled slouchily and defiantly over long uncombed black hair. His face was filthy, as were his clothes and shoes, slimy even. An old brown coat (how come by, I wonder?) was marked by a greenish slime across the back and shoulders, slime that could only have come from a gutter.

"Don't you know me, Dreiser?" he queried in a deep, rasping voice, a voice so rusty that it sounded as though it had not been used for years "—Clark, Clark of the *Republic*. You know me——" and then when I stared in amazement he added shrewdly: "I've been sick and in a hospital. You haven't a dollar about you, have you? I have to rest a little and get myself in shape again before I can go to work."

"Well, of all things!" I exclaimed in amazement, and then: "I'll be damned!" I could not help laughing: he looked so queer, impossible almost. A stage tramp could scarcely have done better. I gave him the dollar. "What in the world are you doing—drinking?" and then, overawed by the memory of his past efficiency and force I could not go on. It was too astonishing.

"Yes, I've been drinking," he admitted, a little defiantly, I thought, "but I've been sick too, just getting out now. I got pneumonia there in the summer and couldn't work. I'll be all right after a while. What's news at the *Republic?*"

"Nothing."

He mumbled something about having played in bad luck, that he would soon be all right again, then ambled up the wretched rickety street and disappeared.

I bustled out of that vicinity as fast as I could. I was so startled and upset by this that I hurried back to the lobby of the Southern Hotel (my favorite cure for all despondent days), where all was brisk, comfortable, gay. Here I purchased a newspaper and sat down in a rocking-chair. Here at least was no sign of poverty or want. In order to be rid of that sense of failure and degradation which had crept over me I took a drink or two myself. That any one as capable as Clark could fall so low in so short a time was quite beyond me. The still strongly puritan and moralistic streak in me was shocked beyond measure, and for days I could do little but contrast the figure of the man I had seen about the *Republic* office with that I had met in that street of degraded gin-mills and tumbledown tenements. Could people really vary so greatly and in so short a time? What must be the nature of their minds if they could do that? Was mine like that? Would it become so? For days thereafter I was wandering about in spirit with this man from gin-mill to gin-mill and lodging-house to lodging-house, seeing him drink at scummy bars and lying down at night on a straw pallet in some wretched hole.

And then there was Rodenberger, strange, amazing Rodenberger, poet, editorial writer and what not, who when I first met him had a little weekly editorial paper for which he raised the money somehow (I have forgotten its name) and in which he poured forth his views on life and art and nature in no uncertain terms. How he could write! (He was connected with some drug company, by birth or marriage, which may have helped to sustain him. I never knew anything definite concerning his private life.) As I view him now, Rodenberger was a man in whom imagination and logic existed in such a confusing, contesting way as to augur fatalism and (from a worldly or material point of view) failure. He was constantly varying between a state of extreme sobriety and vigorous mental energy, and debauches which lasted for weeks and which included drink, houses of prostitution, morphine, and I know not what else.

One sunny summer morning in July or August, I found him standing at the corner of Sixth and Chestnut outside the LaClede drugstore quite stupefied with drink or something.

"Hello, Rody," I called when I saw him. "What's ailing you? You're not drunk again, are you?"

"Drunk," he replied with a slight sardonic motion of the hand and an equally faint curl of the lip, "and what's more, I'm glad of it. I don't have to think about myself, or St. Louis, or you, when I'm drunk. And what's more," and here he interjected another slight motion of the hand and hiccoughed, "I'm taking dope, and I'm glad of that. I got all the dope I want now, right here in my little old vest pocket, and I'm going to take all I want of it," and he tapped the pocket significantly. Then, in a boasting, contentious spirit, he drew forth a white pillbox and slowly opened it and revealed to my somewhat astonished gaze some thirty or forty small while pills, two or three of which he proceeded to lift toward his mouth.

In my astonishment and sympathy and horror I decided to save him if I could, so I struck his hand a smart blow, knocking the pills all over the sidewalk. Without a word of complaint save a feeble "Zat so?" he dropped to his hands and knees and began crawling here and there after them as fast as he could, picking them up and putting them in his mouth, while I, equally determined, began jumping here and there and crushing them under my heels.

"Rody, for God's sake! Aren't you ashamed of yourself? Get up!"

"I'll show you!" he cried determinedly if somewhat recklessly. "I'll eat 'em all! I'll eat 'em all! G—— D—— you!" and he swallowed all that he had thus far been able to collect.

I saw him dead before me in no time at all, or thought I did.

"Here, Johnson," I called to another of our friends who 'came up just then, "help me with Rody, will you? He's drunk, and he's got a box of morphine pills and he's trying to take them. I knocked them out of his hand and now he's eaten a lot of them."

"Here, Rody," he said, pulling him to his feet and holding him against the wall, "stop this! What the hell's the matter with you?" and then he turned to me: "Maybe they're not morphine. Why don't you ask the druggist? If they are we'd better be getting him to the hospital."

"They're morphine all right," gurgled the victim. "Dontcha worry—I know morphine all right, and I'll eat 'em all," and he began struggling with Johnson.

At the latter's suggestion I hurried into the drugstore, the proprietor and clerk of which were friends to all of us, and inquired. They assured me that they were morphine and when I told them that Rodenberger had swallowed about a dozen they insisted that we bring him in and then call an ambulance, while they prepared an emetic of some kind. It happened that the head physician of the St. Louis City Hospital, Dr. Heinie Marks, was also a friend of all newspaper men (what free advertising we used to give him!), and to him I now turned for aid, calling him on the telephone.

"Bring him out! Bring him out!" he said. Then: "Wait; I'll send the wagon."

By this time Johnson, with the aid of the clerk and the druggist, had brought Rodenberger inside and caused him to drink a quantity of something, whereupon we gazed upon him for signs of his approaching demise. By now he was very pale and limp and seemed momentarily to grow more so. To our intense relief, however, the city ambulance soon came and a smart young interne in white took charge. Then we saw Rodenberger hauled away, to be pumped out later and detained for days. I was told afterward by the doctor that he had taken enough of the pills to end him had he not been thoroughly pumped out and treated. Yet within a week or so he was once more up and around, fate, in the shape of myself and Johnson, having intervened. And many a time thereafter he turned up at this selfsame corner as sound and smiling as ever.

Once, when I ventured to reproach him for this and other follies, he merely said:

"All in the day's wash, my boy, all in the day's wash. If I was so determined to go you should have let me alone. Heaven only knows what trouble you have stored up for me now by keeping me here when I wanted to go. That may have been a divine call! But—Kismet! Allah is Allah! Let's go and have a drink!" And we adjourned to Phil Hackett's bar, where we were soon surrounded by fellow-bibbers who spent most of their time looking out through the cool green lattices of that rest room upon the hot street outside.

I may add that Rodenberger's end was not such as might be expected by the moralists. Ten years later he had completely reformed his habits and entered the railroad business, having attained to a considerable position in one of the principal roads running out of St. Louis.

CHAPTER XXXVI

FOR years past during the summer months the *Republic* had been conducting a summer charity of some kind, a fresh-air fund, in support of which it attempted every summer to invent and foster some quick money-raising scheme. This year it had taken the form of that musty old chestnut, a baseball game, to be played between two local fraternities, the fattest men of one called the Owls and the leanest of another known as the Elks. The hope of the *Republic* was to work up interest in this startling novelty by a humorous handling of it so as to draw a large crowd to the baseball grounds. Before I had even heard of it this task had been assigned to two or three others, a new man each day, in the hope of extracting fresh bits of humor, but so far with but indifferent results.

One day, then, I was handed a clipping concerning this proposed game that had been written the preceding day by another member of the staff and which was headed "Blood on the Moon." It purported to narrate the preliminary mutterings and grumblings of those who were to take part in the contest. It was not so much an amusing picture as a news item, and I did not think very much of it; but since I had been warned by Williams that I was about to be called upon to produce the next day's burst, and that it must be humorous, I was by no means inclined to judge it too harshly. . . . The efforts of one's predecessor always appear more forceful as one's own threaten to prove inadequate. A little later Wandell proceeded to outline to me most of the conditions which surrounded this contest. "See if you can't get some fun into it. You must do it. Some one has to. I depend on you for this. Make us laugh," and he smiled a dry, almost frosty smile. "Laugh!" I thought. "Good Lord, how am I to make anybody laugh? I never wrote anything funny in my life!"

Nevertheless, being put to it for this afternoon (he had given me no other assignment, fancying no doubt that I might have a hard time with this), and being the soul of duty, I went to my desk to think it over. Not an idea came to me. It seemed to me that nothing could be duller than this, a baseball game between fat and lean men; yet if I didn't write something it would be a black mark against me and if I did and it proved a piece of trash I should sink equally low in the estimation of my superior. I took my pencil and began scribbling a possible introduction, wondering how one achieved humor when one had it not. After writing aimlessly for a half-hour or so I finally re-examined the texts of my predecessors of previous days and then sought to take the same tack. Only, instead of describing the aspirations and oppositions of the two rival organizations in general terms, I assumed a specific interest and plotting on the part of certain of their chief officers, who even now, as I proceeded to assert and with names and places given in different parts of the city, were spending days and nights devising ways and means of outwitting the enemy. Thoughts of rubber baseball bats, baskets and nets in which flies might be caught, secret electric wiring under the diamond between the bases to put "pep" into the fat runners, seemed to have some faint trace of humor in them, and these I now introduced as being feverishly worked out in various secret places in order that the great game might not be lost. As I wrote, building up purely imaginary characteristics for each one involved (I did not know any of them), I myself began to grow interested and amused. It all seemed so ridiculous, such trash, and yet the worse I made it the better it seemed. At last I finished it, but upon re-reading it I was disturbed by the coarse horse-play of it all. "This will never get by," I thought. "Wandell will think it's rotten." But having by now come to a rather friendly understanding with Williams, I decided to take it over and ask him so that in case I had failed I might try again.

Wearily he eyed me with his one eye, for already he had been editing this for days, then leaned back in his chair and began to read it over. At first he did not seem to be much interested, but after the first paragraph, which he examined with a blank expression, he smiled and finally chortled: "This is pretty good, yes. You needn't worry about it; I think it'll do. Leave it with me." Then he began to edit it. Later in the afternoon when Wandell had come in to give out the evening assignments I saw Williams gather it up and go in to him. After a time he came out smiling, and in a little while Wandell called me in.

"Not bad, not bad," he said, tapping the manuscript lightly. "You've got the right idea, I think. I'll let you do that for a while afternoons until we get up on it. You needn't do anything else—just that, if you do it well enough."

I was pleased, for judging by the time it had taken to do this (not more than two hours) I should have most of my afternoons to myself. I saw visions of a late breakfast, idling in my room, walks after I had done with my work and before I returned to the office. Curiously enough, this trivial thing, undertaken at first in great doubt and with no sense of ability and with no real equipment for it, nevertheless proved for me the most fortunate thing I had thus far done. It was not so much that it was brilliant, or even especially well done, as that what I did fell in with the idle summer mood of the city or with the contesting organizations and the readers of the *Republic*. Congratulatory letters began to arrive. Pleased individuals whose names had been humorously mentioned began to call up the city editor, or the managing editor, or even the editor-in-chief, and voice their approval. In a trice and almost before I knew it, I was a personage, especially in newspaper circles.

"We've got the stuff now, all right," Wandell cackled most violently one evening, at the same time slapping me genially on the shoulder. "This'll do it, I'm sure. A few weeks, and we'll get a big crowd and a lot of publicity. Just you stick to the way you're doing this now. Don't change your style. We've got 'em coming now."

I was really amazed.

And to add to it, Wandell's manner toward me changed. Hitherto, despite his but poorly concealed efforts, he had been distant, brusque, dictatorial, superior. Now of a sudden he was softer, more confidential.

"I have a friend up the street here—Frank Hewe, an awfully nice fellow. He's the second assistant of this or that or the other such company. In one of these comic blurbs of yours don't you think you could ring him in in some way? He's an Elk and I'm sure the mention would tickle him to death."

I saw the point of Mr. Wandell's good nature. He was handing round some favors on his own account.

But since it was easy for me to do it and could not injure the text in any way, and seemed to popularize the paper and myself immensely, I was glad to do it. Each evening, when at six or seven I chose to amble in, having spent the afternoon at my room or elsewhere idling, my text all done in an hour as a rule, my small chief would beam on me most cordially.

"Whatcha got there? Another rib-tickler? Let's see. Well, go get your dinner, and if you don't want to come back go and see a show. There's not much doing tonight anyhow, and I'd like to keep you fresh. Don't stay up too late, and turn me in another good one tomorrow."

So it went.

In a trice and as if by magic I was lifted into an entirely different realm. The ease of those hours! Citizens of local distinction wanted to meet me. I was asked by Wandell one afternoon to come to the Southern bar in order that Colonel So-and-So, the head of this, that or the other thing, as well as some others, might meet me. I was told that this, that and the other person here thought I must be clever, a fool, or a genius. I was invited to a midnight smoker at some country club. The local newspaper men who gathered at the LaClede daily all knew, and finding me in high favor with Phil Hackett, the lessee of the hotel bar whose name I had mentioned once, now laughed with me and drank at my expense— or rather at that of the proprietor, for I was grandly told by him that I "could pay for no drinks there," which kept me often from going there at all. As the days went on I was assured that owing to my efforts the game was certain to be a big success, that it was the most successful stunt the *Republic* had ever pulled and that it would net the fund several thousand dollars.

For four or five weeks then it seemed to me as though I were walking on air. Life was so different, so pleasant these hot, bright days, with everybody pleased with me and my name as a clever man—a humorist!—being bandied about. Some of my new admirers were so pleased with me that they asked me to come to their homes to see them. I was becoming a personage. Hackett of the LaClede having asked me casually one day where I lived, I was surprised that night in my room by a large wicker hamper containing champagne, whiskey and cordials. I transferred it to the office of the *Republic* for the reportorial staff, with my compliments.

My handling of the fat-lean baseball game having established me as a feature writer of some ability, the *Republic* decided to give me another feature assignment. There had been in progress a voting contest which embraced the whole State and which was to decide which of many hundreds of school-teachers, the favorites out of how many districts in the State I cannot now recall, were to be sent to Chicago to see the World's Fair for two or more weeks at the *Republic's* expense. In addition, a reporter or traveling correspondent was to be sent with the party to report its daily doings and that reporter's comments were to be made a daily news feature; and that reporter was to be myself. I was not seeking it, had not even heard of it, but according to Wandell, who was selecting the man for the management, I was the one most likely to give a satisfactory picture of the life at the great Fair as well as render the *Republic* a service in picturing the doings of these teachers. An agent of the business manager was also going along to look after the practical details, and also the city superintendent of schools. I welcomed this opportunity to see the World's Fair, which was then in its heyday and filling the newspapers.

"I don't mind telling you," Wandell observed to me a few days before the final account of the baseball game was to be written, "that your work on this ball game has been good.

Everybody is pleased. Now, there's a little excursion we're going to send up to Chicago, and I'm going to send you along on that for a rest. Mr. ———, our business manager, will tell you all about it. You see him about transportation and expenses.''

"When am I to go?" I asked.

"Thursday. Thursday night."

"Then I don't have to see the ball game?"

"Oh, that's all right. You've done the important part of that. Let some one else write it up."

I smiled at the compliment. I went downstairs and had somebody explain to me what it was the paper was going to do and congratulated myself. Now I was to have a chance to visit the World's Fair, which had not yet opened when I left Chicago. I could look up my father, whom I had neglected since my mother's death, as well as such other members of the family as were still living in Chicago; but, most important, I could go around to the *Globe* there and "blow" to my old confrères about my present success. All I had to do was to go along and observe what the girls did and how they enjoyed themselves and then write it up.

I went up the street humming and rejoicing, and finally landed in the "art department" of my friends.

"I'm being sent to Chicago to the World's Fair," I said gleefully.

"Bully for you," was the unanimous return. "Let's hope you have a good time."

CHAPTER XXXVII

As the time drew near, though, the thought of being a sort of literary chaperon to a lot of school-teachers, probably all of them homely and uninteresting, was not as cheering as it might have been. I wondered how I should manage to be civil and interesting to so many, how I was to extract news out of them. Yet the attitude of the business manager and the managing editor, as well as the editor-in-chief or publisher, Mr. Knapp, to whom I was now introduced by my city editor, was enough to convince me that whatever I thought of it I was plainly rising in their esteem. Although no word was said about any increase in pay, which I still consider the limit of beggarly, pennywise policy, these magnificoes were most cordial, smiled and congratulated me on my work and then turned me over to the man who had the financing of the trip in charge. He reminded me a good deal of a banker or church elder, small, dark, full-whiskered, solemn, affable, and assured me that he was glad that I had been appointed, that I was the ideal man for the place, and that he would see to it that anything I needed to make my trip pleasant would be provided. I could scarcely believe that I was so important.

After asking me to go and see the superintendent of schools, also of the party as guest of the *Republic,* he said he would send to me a Mr. Dean, who would be his agent en route to look after everything—baggage, fares, hotels, meals. The latter came and at once threw a wet blanket over me: he was so utterly dull and commonplace. His clothes, his shoes, his loud tie and his muddy, commonplace intellect all irritated me beyond measure. Something he said—"Now, of course, we all want to do everything we can to please these ladies and make them happy"—irritated me. The usual pastoral, supervisory stuff, I thought, and I at once decided that I did not want him to bother me in any way. "What! Did this horrible bounder assume that he was regulating my conduct on this trip, or that I was going out of my way to accommodate myself to him and his theory of how the trip should be conducted, or to accept him as a social equal? 'We must' indeed!—I, Theodore Dreiser, the well-known newspaper writer of St. Louis! The effrontery! Well, he would get scant attention from me, and the more he let me alone the better it would be for him and all of us!''

And now Wandell also began to irritate me by attempting to give me minute instructions as to just what was wanted and how I was to write it, although, as I understood it, I was now working for the managing editor who was to have the material edited in the telegraph department. Besides, I thought that I was now entitled to a little leeway and discretion in the choice of what I should report. The idea of making it all advertising for the *Republic* and myself a literary wet-nurse to a school party was a little too much.

However, I bustled down to the train that was waiting to carry this party of damsels to Chicago and the World's Fair, a solid Pullman train which left St. Louis at dusk and arrived in Chicago early the next morning. The fifth of the Pullmans was reserved to carry the school-teachers and their chaperons, Mr. Soldan, superintendent of schools, Mr. Dean, the business-manager-representative, and myself. I entered the car wondering of course what the result of such a temporary companionship with so many girls might be. They were all popular, hence beautiful, prize-winners, as I had heard; but my pessimistic mind had registered a somewhat depressing conception of the ordinary school-mistress and I did not expect much.

For once in my life I was agreeably disappointed. These were young, buxom Missouri school-teachers and as attractive as that profession will permit. I was no sooner seated in a gaudy car than one of the end doors opened and there was ushered in by the porter a pretty, rosy-cheeked, black-haired girl of perhaps twenty-four. This was a good beginning. Immediately thereafter there came in a tall, fair girl with light brown hair and blue eyes. Others now entered,

blondes and brunettes, stout and slender, with various inter-
mediate grades or types. Instead of a mounting contempt I
suddenly began to suffer from a sickening sense of inability
to hold my own in the face of so many pretty girls.
What could I do with twenty girls? How write about
them? Maybe the business-manager-representative or the
superintendent would not come on this train and I should
be left to introduce these girls to each other! God!
I should have to find out their names, and I had not thought
to inquire at the office!

Fortunately for my peace of mind a large, rather showily
dressed man with big soft ruddy hands decorated with several
rings and a full oval face tinted with health, now entered by
the front door and beamed cheerfully upon all.

"Ah, here we are now," he began with the impressive air
of one in authority, going up to the first maiden he saw. "I
see you have arrived safely, Miss—ah—C——. I'm glad to
see you again. How are you?" We went on to another:
"And here is Miss W——! Well, I am glad. I read in the
Republic that you had won."

I realized that this was the Professor Soldan so earnestly
recommended to me, the superintendent of schools and one
upon whom I was to comment. I rather liked him.

An engine went puffing and clanging by on a neighboring
track. I gazed out of the window. It seemed essential for
me to begin doing something but I did not know how to begin.
Suddenly the large jeweled hand was laid on my shoulder and
the professor stood over me. "This must be Mr. Dreiser, of
the *Republic*. Your business manager, Mr. ——, phoned
me this morning that you were coming. You must let me
introduce you to all these young ladies. We want to get the
formalities over and be on easy terms."

I bowed heavily for I felt as though I were turning to stone.
The prettiness and sparkle of these girls all chatting and
laughing had fairly done for me. I followed the professor as
one marches to the gallows and he began at one end of the
car and introduced me to one girl after another as though it
were a state affair of some kind. I felt like a boob. I was

flustered and yet delighted by his geniality and the fact that he was helping me over a very ticklish situation. I envied him his ease and self-possession. He soon betook himself elsewhere, leaving me to converse as best I might with a pretty black-haired Irish girl whose eyes made me wish to be agreeable. And now, idiot, I struggled desperately for bright things to say. How did one entertain a pretty girl, anyhow? The girl came to my rescue by commenting on the nature of the contest and the difficulties she had had. She hadn't thought she would win at all. Some others joined in, and before I knew it the train was out of the station and on its way. The porter was closing the windows for the long tunnel, the girls were sinking into comfortable attitudes, and there was a general air of relaxation and good nature. Before East St. Louis was reached a general conversation was in progress, and by the time the train was a half-hour out a party of familiars had gathered in the little bridal chamber, which was at the rear of the car, laughing and gesticulating. But I was not of it, nor was the girl with whom I was chatting.

"Why don't you come back here, Myra?" called a voice.

"Having lots of fun up there?" called another.

"Do come back, for goodness' sake! Don't try to monopolize one whole man."

I felt my legs going from under me. Could this be true? Must I now go back there and try to face six or seven? Stumblingly I followed Myra, and at the door stopped and looked in. It was full of pretty girls, my partner of the moment before now chattering lightly among them. "I'm gone," I thought. "It's all off. Now for the grand collapse and silence! Which way shall I turn? To whom?"

"There's room for one more here," said a Juney blonde, making a place for me.

I could not refuse this challenge. "I'm the one," I said weakly, and sank heavily beside her. She looked at me encouragingly, as did the others, and at a vast expense of energy and will power I managed to achieve a smile. It was pathetic.

"Isn't train-riding just glorious?" exclaimed one of these bright-faced imps exuberantly. "I bet I haven't been on a train twice before in all my life, and just look at me! I do it all right, don't I? I'd just love to travel. I wish I could travel all the time."

"Oh, don't you, though!" echoed the girl who was sitting beside me and whom up to now I had scarcely noticed. "Do you think she looks so nice riding?"

I cannot recall what I answered. It may have been witty—if so it was an accident.

"What do you call the proper surroundings?" put in a new voice in answer to something that was said, which same drew my attention to limpid blue eyes, a Cupid's bow mouth and a wealth of corn-colored hair.

"These," I finally achieved gallantly, gazing about the compartment and at my companions. A burst of applause followed. I was coming to. Yet I was still bewildered by the bouquet of faces about me. Already the idea of the dreary school-teachers had been dissipated: these were prize-winners. Look where I would I seemed to see a new type of prettiness confronting me. It was like being in the toils of those nymphs in the Ring of the Nibelungen, yet I had no desire to escape, wishing to stay now and see how I could "make out" as a Lothario. Indeed at this I worked hard. I did my best to gaze gayly and captivatingly into pretty eyes of various colors. They all gazed amusedly back. I was almost the only man; they were out for a lark. What would you?

"If I had my wishes now I'd wish for just one thing," I volunteered, expecting to arouse curiosity.

"Which one?" asked the girl with the brown eyes and piquant little face who wished to travel forever. Her look was significant.

"This one," I said, running my finger around in a circle to include them all and yet stopping at none.

"We're not won yet, though," said the girl smirkily.

"Couldn't you be?" I asked smartly.

"Not all at once, anyhow. Could we?" she asked, speaking for the crowd.

I found myself poor at repartee. "It will seem all at once, though, when it happens, won't it?" I finally managed to return. "Isn't it always 'so sudden'?" I was surprising myself.

"Aren't you smart!" said the blue-eyed girl beside me.

"Oh, that's clever, isn't it?" said the girl with the corn-colored hair.

I gazed in her direction. Beside her sat a maiden whom I had but dimly noticed. She was in white, with a mass of sunny red hair. Her eyes were almond-shaped, liquid and blue-gray. Her nose was straight and fine, her lips sweetly curved. She seemed bashful and retiring. At her bosom was a bouquet of pink roses, but one had come loose.

"Oh, your flowers!" I exclaimed.

"Let me give you one," she replied, laughing. I had not heard her voice before and I liked it.

"Certainly," I said. Then to the others: "You see, I'll take anything I can get." She drew a rose from her bosom and held it out toward me. "Won't you put it on?" I asked smartly.

She leaned over and began to fasten it. She worked a moment and then looked at me, making, as I thought, a sheep's eye at me.

"You may have my place," said the girl next me, feigning to help her, and she took it.

The conversation waxed even freer after this, although for me I felt that it had now taken a definite turn. . . . I was talking for her benefit. We were still in the midst of this when the conductor passed through and after him Mr. Dean, middle-aged, dusty, assured, advisory.

"These are the people," he said. "They are all in one party." He called me aside and we sat down, he explaining cheerfully and volubly the trouble he was having keeping everything in order. I could have murdered him.

"I'm looking out for the baggage and the hotel bills and all," he insisted. "In the morning we'll be met by a tally-ho and ride out to the hotel."

I was thinking of my splendid bevy of girls and the delightful time I had been having.

"Well, that'll be fine, won't it?" I said wearily. "Is that all?"

"Oh, we have it all planned out," he went on. "It's going to be a fine trip."

I did my best to show that I had no desire to talk, but still he kept on. He wanted to meet the teachers and I had to introduce him. Fortunately he became interested in one small group and I sidled away—only to find my original group considerably reduced. Some had gone to the dressingroom, others were arranging their parcels about their unmade berths. The porter came in and began to make them up. I looked ruefully about me.

"Well, our little group has broken up," I said at last to the girl of my choice as I came up to where she was sitting.

"Yes. It's getting late. But I'm not sleepy yet."

We dropped into an easy conversation, and I learned that she was from Missouri and taught in a little town not far from St. Louis. She explained to me how she had come to win, and I told her how ignorant I had been of the whole affair up to four days ago. She said that friends had bought hundreds of *Republics* in order to get the coupons. It seemed a fine thing to me for a girl to be so popular.

"You've never been to Chicago, then?" I asked.

"Oh no. I've never been anywhere really. I'm just a simple country girl, you know. I've always wanted to go, though."

She fascinated me. She seemed so direct, truthful, sympathetic.

"You'll enjoy it," I said. "It's worth seeing. I was in Chicago when the Fair was being built. My home is there."

"Then you'll stay with your home-folks, won't you?" she asked, using a word for family to which I was not accustomed. It touched a chord of sympathy. I was not very much in touch with my family any more but the way she seemed to look on hers made me wish that I were.

"Well, not exactly. They live over on the west side. I'll go to see them, though."

I was thinking that now I had her out of that sparkling

group she seemed more agreeable than before, much more interesting, more subdued and homelike.

She arose to leave me. "I want to get some of my things before the porter puts them away," she explained.

I stepped out of her way. She tripped up the aisle and I looked after her, fascinated. Of a sudden she seemed quite the most interesting of all those here, simple, pretty, vigorous and with a kind of tact and grace that was impressive. Also I felt an intense something about her that was concealed by an air of supreme innocence and maidenly reserve. I went out to the smokingroom, where I sat alone looking out of the window.

"What a delightful girl," I thought, with a feeling of intense satisfaction. "And I have the certainty of seeing her again in the morning!"

CHAPTER XXXVIII

THE next morning I was awake early, stirred by the thoughts of Chicago, the Fair, Miss W—— (my favorite), as well as the group of attractive creatures who now formed a sort of background for her. One of the characteristics of my very youthful temperament at that time was the power to invest every place I had ever left with a romance and strangeness such as might have attached to something abandoned, say, a thousand or two years before and which I was now revisiting for the first time to find it nearly all done over. So it was now in my attitude toward Chicago. I had been away for only eight or nine months, and still I expected—what did I not expect?—the whole skyline and landscape to be done over, or all that I had known done away with. Going into Chicago I studied every street and crossing and house and car. How sad to think I had ever had to leave it, to leave Alice, my home, my father, all my relatives and old friends! Where was E——, A——, T——, my father? At thought of the latter I was deeply moved, for had I not left him about a year before and without very much ceremony at the time I had chosen to follow the fortunes of my sister C——? Now that I looked back on it all from the vantage point of a year's work I was much chastened and began to think how snippy and unkind I had been. Poor, tottering, broken soul, I thought. I could see him then as he really was, a warm, generous and yet bigoted and ignorant soul, led captive in his childhood to a brainless theory and having no power within himself to break that chain, and now wandering distrait and forlorn amid a storm of difficulties: age, the death of his wife, the flight of his children, doubt as to their salvation, poverty, a declining health.

I can see him now, a thin grasshopper of a man, brooding wearily with those black-brown Teutonic eyes of his, as sad as failure itself. What thoughts! What moods! He was very much like one of those old men whom Rembrandt has portrayed, wrinkled, sallow, leathery. My father's peculiarly German hair and beard were always carefully combed and brushed, the hair back over his forehead like Nietzsche's, the beard resting reddishly on his chest. His clothes were always loose and ill-fitting, being bought for durability, not style, or made over from abandoned clothes of some one—my brother Paul or my sister M——'s husband. He always wore an old and very carefully preserved black derby hat, very wide of brim and out of style, which he pulled low over his deep-set weary eyes. I always wondered where and when he had bought it. On this trip I offered to buy him a new one, but he preferred to use the money for a mass for the repose of my good mother's soul! Under his arm or in one of his capacious pockets was always a Catholic prayerbook from which he read prayers as familiar to him as his own hands, yet from the mumbling repetition of which he extracted some comfort, as does the Hindu from meditating upon space or time. In health he was always fluttering to one or another of a score of favorite Catholic churches, each as commonplace as the other, and there, before some trashy plaster image of some saint or virgin as dead or helpless as his own past, making supplication for what?—peace in death, the reconversion and right conduct of his children, the salvation of his own and my mother's soul? Debts were his great misery, as I had always known. If one died and left unpaid an old bill of some kind one had to stay in purgatory so much longer!

Riding into Chicago this morning I speculated as to the thinness of his hands as I had known them, the tremulousness of his inquiries, the appeal in his sad resigned eyes, whence all power to compel or convince had long since gone. In the vast cosmic flight of force, flowing from what heart we know not but in which as little corks our suns and planets float, it is possible that there may be some care, an equation, a balancing of the scales of suffering and pleasure. I hope so. If not I know not the reason for tears or those emotions with which so many of us salve the memory of seemingly immedicable ills. If immedicable, why cry?

I sought Miss W——, who was up before me and sitting beside her section window. I was about to go and talk with her when my attention was claimed by other girls. This bevy could not very well afford to see the attention of the only man on board so easily monopolized. There were so many pretty faces among them that I wavered. I talked idly among them, interested to see what overtures and how much of an impression I might make. My natural love of womankind made them all inviting.

When the train drew into Chicago we were met by a tally-ho, which the obliging Mr. Dean had been kind enough to announce to each and every one of us as the train stopped. The idea of riding to the World's Fair in such a thing and with this somewhat conspicuous party of school-teachers went very much against the grain. Being very conscious of my personal dignity in the presence of others and knowing the American and middle-West attitude toward all these new and persistently derided toys and pleasures of the effete East and England, I was inclined to look upon this one as out of place in Chicago. Besides, a canvas strip on the coach advertising the nature of this expedition infuriated me and seemed spiritually involved with the character of Mr. Dean. That bounder had done this, I was sure. I wondered whether the sophisticated and well-groomed superintendent of schools would lend himself to any such thing when plainly it was to be written up in the *Republic*, but since he did not seem to mind it I was mollified; in fact, he took it all with a charming gayety and grace which eventually succeeded in putting my own silly provincialism and pride to rout. He sat up in front with me and the driver discussing philosophy, education, the Fair, a dozen things, during which I made a great pretense at wise deductions and a wider reading than I had ever had.

Once clear of the depot and turning into Adams Street, we were off behind six good horses through as interesting a business section as one might wish to see, its high buildings (the earliest and most numerous in America) and its mass of congested traffic making a brisk summer morning scene. I was reëngaged by Michigan Avenue, that splendid boulevard with its brief vista of the lake, which was whipped to cotton-tops this bright morning by a fresh wind, and then the long residence-lined avenue to the south with its wealth of new and pretentious homes, its smart paving and lighting, its crush of pleasure traffic hurrying townward or to the Fair. Within an hour we were assigned rooms in a comfortable hotel near the Fair grounds, one of those hastily and yet fairly well constructed buildings which later were changed into flats or apartments. One wall of this hotel, as I now discovered, the side on which my room was, faced a portion of the Fair grounds, and from my windows I could see some of its classic façades, porticoes, roofs, domes, lagoons. All at once and out of nothing in this dingy city of six or seven hundred thousand which but a few years before had been a wilderness of wet grass and mud flats, and by this lake which but a hundred years before was a lone silent waste, had now been reared this vast and harmonious collection of perfectly constructed and snowy buildings, containing in their delightful interiors the artistic, mechanical and scientific achievements of the world. Greece, Italy, India, Egypt, Japan, Germany, South America, the West and East Indies, the Arctics—all represented! I have often thought since how those pessimists who up to that time had imagined that nothing of any artistic or scientific import could possibly be brought to fruition in America especially in the middle West, must have opened their eyes as I did mine at the sight of this realized dream of beauty, this splendid picture of the world's own hope for itself. I have long marveled at it and do now as I recall it, its splendid Court of Honor, with its monumental stateliness and simple grandeur; the peristyle with its amazing grace of columns and sculptured figures; the great central arch with its triumphal quadriga; the dome of the Administration Building with its daring nudes; the splendid groupings on the Agricultural Building, as well as those on the Manufacturers' and Women's buildings. It was not as if many minds had labored toward this great end, or as if the great raw city which did not quite understand itself as yet had endeavored to make a great show, but rather as though some brooding spirit of beauty, inherent possibly in some directing over-soul, had waved a magic wand quite as might have Prospero in *The Tempest* or Queen Mab in *A Midsummer Night's Dream,* and lo, this fairyland.

In the morning when I came down from my room I fell in with Miss W—— in the diningroom and was thrilled by the contact. She was so gay, good-natured, smiling, unaffected. And with her now was a younger sister of whom I had not heard and who had come to Chicago by a different route to join her. I was promptly introduced, and we sat down at the same table. It was not long before we were joined by the others, and then I could see by the exchange of glances that it was presumed that I had fallen a victim to this charmer of the night before. But already the personality of the younger sister was appealing to me quite as much as the elder. She was so radiant of humor, freckled, plump, laughing and with such an easy and natural mode of address. Somehow she struck me as knowing more of life than her sister, being more sophisticated and yet quite as innocent.

After breakfast the company broke up into groups of two and three. Each had plans for the day and began talking them over.

We started off finally for the Fair gate and on the way I had an opportunity to study some of the other members of the party and make up my mind as to whether I really preferred her above all. Despite my leaning toward Miss W—— I now discovered that there was a number whose charms, if not superior to those of Miss W——, were greater than I had imagined, while some of those who had attracted me the night before were being modified by little traits of character or mannerism which I did not like. Among them was one rosy black-haired Irish girl whose solid beauty attracted me very much. She was young and dark and robust, with the air of a hoyden. I looked at her, quite taken by her snapping black eyes, but nothing came of it for the moment: we were all becoming interested in the Fair.

Together, then, we drifted for an hour or more in this world of glorious sights, an hour or more of dreaming over the arches, the reflections in the water, the statues, the shadowy throngs by the steps of the lagoons moving like figures in a dream. Was it real? I sometimes wonder, for it is all gone. Gone the summer days and nights, the air, the color, the form, the mood. In its place is a green park by a lake, still beautiful but bereft, a city that grows and grows, ever larger, but harder, colder, grayer.

CHAPTER XXXIX

POSSIBLY it was the brightness and freshness of this first day, the romance of an international fair in America, the snowy whiteness of the buildings against the morning sun, a blue sky and a bluer lake, the lagoons weaving in and out, achieving a lightness and an airiness wholly at war with anything that this Western world had as yet presented, which caused me to be swept into a dream from which I did not recover for months. I walked away a little space with my friend of the night before, learning more of her home and environment. As I saw her now, she seemed more and more natural, winsome, inviting. Humor seemed a part of her, and romance, as well as understanding and patience, a quiet and restful and undisturbed patience. I liked her immensely. She seemed from the first to offer me an understanding and a sympathy which I had never yet realized in any one. She smiled at my humor, appreciated my moods. Returning to my room late in the afternoon I was conscious of a difficult task, what to write that was worth while, and yet so deeply moved by it all that I could have clapped my hands for joy. I wanted to versify or describe it—a mood which youth will understand and maturity smile at, which causes the mind to sing, to set forth on fantastic pilgrimages.

But if I wrote anything worth while I cannot now recall it. I was too eager to loaf and dream and do nothing at all, almost too idle to concentrate on what I had been called upon to do. I sent off something, a thousand or so words of drivel or rapture, and then settled to my real task of seeing the Fair by night and by day. Now that I was here I was cheered by the thought that very soon, within a day or two at most, I should be able to seek out and crow over all my old familiars, Maxwell, Dunlap, Brady, Hutchinson, a considerable group of newspaper men, as well as my brothers A—— and E——, who were here employed somewhere, and my father and several sisters.

For my father, who was now seventy-two years of age, I had, all of a sudden, as I have indicated above, the greatest sympathy. At home, up to my seventeenth or eighteenth birthday, before I got out in the world and began to make my own way, I had found him fussy, cranky, dosed with too much religion; but in spite of all this and the quarrels and bickerings which arose because of it there had always been something tender in his views, charming, poetic and appreciative. Now I felt sorry for him. A little while before and after my mother's death it had seemed to me that he had become unduly wild on the subject of the church and the hereafter, was annoying us all with his persistent preachments concerning duty, economy and the like, the need of living a clean, saving, religious life. Now, after a year out in the world, with a broadening knowledge of very different things, I saw him in an entirely different light. While realizing that he was irritable, crotchety, domineering, I suddenly saw him as just a broken old man whose hopes and ambitions had come to nothing, whose religion, impossible as it was to me, was still a comfort and a blessing to him. Here he was, alone, his wife dead, his children scattered and not very much interested in him any more.

Now that I was here in the city again, I decided that as soon as I could arrange my other affairs I would go over on the west side and look him up and bring him to see the Fair, which of course he had not seen. For I knew that with his saving, worrying, almost penurious disposition he would not be able to bring himself to endure the expense, even though tickets were provided him, of visiting the Fair alone. He had had too much trouble getting enough to live on in these latter years to permit him to enjoy anything which cost money. I could hear him saying: "No, no. I cannot afford it. We have too many debts." He had not always been so but time and many troubles had made the saving of money almost a mania with him.

The next morning, therefore, I journeyed to the west side

(250)

and finally found him quite alone, as it chanced, the other members of the family then living with him having gone out. I shall never forget how old he looked after my year's absence, how his eyelids twitched. After a slightly quizzical and attempted hard examining glance at me his lips twitched and tears welled to his eyes. He was so utterly done for, as he knew, and dependent on the courtesy of his children and life. I cried myself and rubbed his hands and his hair, then told him that I was doing well and had come to take him to see the Fair, that I had tickets—a passbook, no less—and that it shouldn't cost him a penny. Naturally he was surprised and glad to see me, so anxious to know if I still adhered to the Catholic faith and went to confession and communion regularly. In the old days this had been the main bone of contention between us.

"Tell me, Dorsch," he said not two minutes after I arrived, "do you still keep up your church duties?"

When I hesitated for a moment, uncertain what to say, he went on: "You ought to do that, you know. If you should die in a state of mortal sin——"

"Yes, yes," I interrupted, making up my mind to give him peace on this score if I never did another thing in this world, "I always go right along, once every month or six weeks."

"You really do that, do you?" he asked, eyeing me more in appeal than doubt, though judging by my obstinate past he must have doubted.

"Yes," I insisted, "sure. I always go regularly."

"I'm glad of that," he went on hopefully. "I worry so. I think of you and the rest of the children so much. You're a young man now and out in the world, and if you neglect your religious duties——" and he paused as if in a grave quandary. "When you're out like that I know it's hard to think of the church and your duties, but you shouldn't neglect them——"

"Oh, Lord!" I thought. "Now he's off again! This is the same old story—religion, religion, religion!"

"But I do go," I insisted. "You mustn't worry about me."

"I know," he said, with a sudden catch in his voice, "but

I can't help it. You know how it is with the other children: they don't always do right in that respect. Paul is away on the stage; I don't know whether he goes to church any more. A—— and E—— are here, but they don't come here much— I haven't seen them in I don't know how long—months——''

I resolved to plead with E—— and A—— when I saw them.

He was sitting in a big armchair facing a rear window, and now he took my hand again and held it. Soon I felt hot tears on it.

"Pop," I said, pulling his head against me and smoothing it, "you mustn't cry. Things aren't so bad as all that. The children are all right. We'll probably be able to do better and more for you than we've ever done."

"I know, I know," he said after a little while, overcoming his emotion, "but I'm getting so old, and I don't sleep much any more—just an hour or two. I lie there and think. In the morning I get up at four sometimes and make my coffee. Then the days are so long."

I cried too. The long days . . . the fading interests . . . Mother gone and the family broken up. . . .

"I know," I said. "I haven't acted just right—none of us have. I'll write you from now on when I'm away, and send you some money once in a while. I'm going to get you a big overcoat for next winter. And now I want you to come over with me to the Fair. I've tickets, and you'll enjoy it. I'm a press representative now, a traveling correspondent. I'll show you everything."

After due persuasion he got his hat and stick and came with me. We took a car and an elevated road, which finally landed us at the gate, and then, for as long as his strength would endure, we wandered about looking at the enormous buildings, the great Ferris Wheel, the caravels *Nina*, *Pinta* and *Santa Maria* in which Columbus sailed to America, the convent of La Rabida (which, because it related to the Trappists, fascinated him), and finally the German Village on the Midway, as German and *ordentlich* as ever a German would wish, where we had coffee and little German cakes with caraway seeds on them and some pot cheese with red pepper and onions. He was so interested and amused by the vast spectacle that he could do little save exclaim: "By crackie!" "This is now beautiful!" or "That is now wonderful!" In the German village he fell into a conversation with a buxom German *frau* who had a stand there and who hailed from some part of Germany about which he seemed to know, and then all was well indeed. It was long before I could get him away. These delightful visits were repeated only about four times during my stay of two weeks, when he admitted that it was tiring and he had seen enough.

Another morning when I had not too much to do I looked up my brother E——, who was driving a laundry wagon somewhere on the south side, and got him to come out evenings and Sundays, as well as A——, who was connected with an electric plant as assistant of some kind. I recall now, with an odd feeling as to the significance of relationship and family ties generally, how keenly important his and E——'s interests were to me then and how I suffered because I thought they were not getting along as well as they should. Looking in a shoe window in Pittsburgh a year or two later, I actually choked with emotion because I thought that maybe E—— did not earn enough to keep himself looking well. A—— always seemed more or less thwarted in his ambitions, and whenever I saw him I felt sad because, like so many millions of others in this grinding world, he had never had a real chance. Life is so casual, and luck comes to many who sleep and flies from those who try. I always felt that under more advantageous circumstances A—— would have done well. He was so wise, if slightly cynical, full of a laughing humor. His taste for literature and artistic things in general was high, although entirely untrained. Like myself he had a turn for the problems of nature, constantly wondering as to the why of this or that and seeking the answer in a broader knowledge. But long hours of work and poor pay seemed to handicap him in his search. I was sad beyond words about his condition, and urged him to come to St. Louis and try his luck there, which he subsequently did.

(253)

Another thing I did was to visit the old *Globe* office in Fifth Avenue downtown, only to find things in a bad way there. Although Brady, Hutchinson and Dunlap were still there the paper was not paying, was, in fact, in danger of immediate collapse. John B. MacDonald, its financial backer or angel, having lost a fortune in trying to make it pay and win an election with it, was about ready to quit and the paper was on its last legs. Could I get them jobs in St. Louis? Maxwell had gone to the *Tribune* and was now a successful copy-reader there. . . . In my new summer suit and straw hat and with my various credentials, I felt myself to be quite a personage. How much better I had done than these men who had been in the business longer than I had! Certainly I would see what I could do. They must write me. They could find me now at such-and-such a hotel.

The sweets of success!

In the Newspaper Press Association offices in the great Administration Building several of my friends from the press showed up and here we foregathered to talk. Daily in this building at eight or nine or ten at night I filed a report or message about one thousand words long and was pleased to see by the papers that arrived that my text was used about as I wrote it. Loving the grounds of the Fair so much, I browsed there nearly all day long and all evening, escorting now one girl and now another, but principally Miss W—— and her sister. Almost unconsciously I was being fascinated by these two, with my Miss W—— the more; and yet I was not content to confine myself to her but was constantly looking here and there, being lured by a number of the others.

Thus one afternoon, after I had visited the Administration Building and filed my dispatch rather early, Miss W—— having been unable to be with me at the Fair, I returned to the hotel, a little weary of sightseeing, and finding an upper balcony which faced the Fair sat there in a rocker awaiting the return of some of the party. Presently, as I was resting and humming to myself, there came down to the parlor, which adjoined this balcony, that rosy Irish girl, Miss Ginity, who had attracted me the very first morning. She seemed to be seeking that room in order to sing and play, there being a piano here. She was dressed in a close-fitting suit of white linen, which set off her robust little figure to perfection. Her heavy, oily black hair was parted severely in the middle and hung heavily over her white temples. She had a rich-blooded, healthy, aggressive look, not unmarked by desire.

I was looking through the window when she came in and was wondering if she would discover me, when she did. She smiled, and I waved to her to come out. We talked about the Fair and my duties in connection with it. When I explained the nature of my dispatches she wanted to know if I had mentioned her name yet. I assured her that I had, and this pleased her. I had the feeling that she liked me and that I could influence her if I chose.

"What has become of your friend Miss W——?" she finally asked with a touch of malice when I looked at her too kindly.

"I don't know. I haven't seen her since yesterday or the day before," which was not true. "What makes you ask that?"

"Oh, I thought you rather liked her," she said boldly, throwing up her chin and smiling.

"And what made you think it?" I asked calmly. It was in my mind that I could master and deceive her as to this, and I proposed to try.

"Oh, I just thought so. You seemed to like her company."

"Not any more than I do that of others," I insisted with great assurance. "She's interesting, that's all. I didn't think I was showing any preference."

"Oh, I'm just joking," she laughed. "I really don't think anything about it. One of the other girls made the remark."

"Well, she's wrong," I said indifferently.

But I could see that she wasn't joking. I could also see that I had relieved her mind. My pose of indifference had quelled her feeling that I was not wholly free. We sat and talked until dinner, and then I asked her if she would like to go for a stroll in the park, to which she agreed. By now we were obviously drifting toward each other emotionally, and I thought how fine it would be to idle and dream with this girl in the moonlight.

After dinner, when we started out, the air was soft and balmy and the moon was just rising over the treetops in the East. A faint odor of fresh flowers and fresh leaves was abroad and the night seemed to rest in a soothing stillness. From the Midway came the sounds of muffled drums and flutes, vibrant with the passion of the East. Before us were the wide stretches of the park, dark and suggestive of intrigue where groups of trees were gathered in silent, motionless array, in others silvered by a fairy brightness which suggested a world of romance and feeling.

I walked silently on with her, flooded with a voiceless feeling of ecstasy. Now I was surely proving to myself that I was not entirely helpless in the presence of girls. This time of idleness and moonlight was in such smooth consonance with my most romantic wishes. She was not so romantic, but the ardent luxury of her nature appeared to answer to the romantic call of mine.

"Isn't this wonderful?" I said at last, seeking to interest her.

"Yes," she replied, almost practically. "I've been wondering why some of the girls don't come over here at night. It's so wonderful. But I suppose they're tired."

"They're not as strong as you, that's it. You're so vigorous. I was thinking today how healthy you look."

"Were you? And I was just thinking what my mother would say if she knew I was out here with a total stranger."

"You told me you lived in St. Louis, I think?" I said.

"Yes, out in the north end. Near O'Fallon Park."

"Well, then, I'll get to see you when you go back," I laughed.

"Oh, will you?" she returned coquettishly. "How do you know?"

"Well, won't I?"

The thought flashed across my mind that once I had been in this selfsame park with Alice several years before; we had sat under a tree not so very far from here, near a pagoda silvered by the moon, and had listened to music played in the distance. I remembered how I had whispered sweet nothings and kissed her to my heart's content.

"Well, you may if you're good," she replied.

I began jesting with her now. I deliberately descended from the ordinary reaches of my intelligence, anxious to match her own interests with some which would seem allied. I wanted her to like me, although I felt all the while that we were by no means suited temperamentally. She was too commonplace and unimaginative, although so attractive physically.

We sat in silence for a time, and I slipped my hand down and laid hold of her fingers. She did not stir, pretending not to notice, but I felt that she was thrilling also.

"You asked about Miss W——," I said. "What made you do that?"

"Oh, I thought you liked her. Why shouldn't I?"

"It never occurred to you that I might like some one else?"

"Certainly not. Why should I?"

I pressed her fingers softly. She turned on me all at once a face so white and tense that it showed fully the feeling that now gripped her. It was almost as if she were breaking under an intense nervous strain which she was attempting to conceal.

"I thought you might," I replied daringly. "There is some one, you know." I was surprising myself.

"Is there?" Her voice sounded weak. She did not attempt to look at me now, and I was wondering how far I would go.

"You couldn't guess, of course?"

"No. Why should I?"

"Look at me," I said quietly.

"All right," she said with a little indifferent shrug. "I'll look at you. There now; what of it?"

Again that intense, nervous, strained look. Her lips were parted in a shy frightened smile, showing her pretty teeth. Her eyes were touched with points of light where the moonlight, falling over my shoulder, shone upon them. It gave her whole face an eerie, almost spectral paleness, something mystical and insubstantial, which spoke of the brevity and non-endurance of all these things. She was far more wonderful here than ever she could have been in clear daylight.

"You have beautiful eyes," I remarked.

"Oh," she shrugged disdainfully, "is that all?"

"No. You have beautiful teeth and hair—such hair!"

"You mustn't grow sentimental," she commented, not removing her hand.

I slipped my arm about her waist and she moved nervously.

"And you still can't guess who?" I said finally.

"No," she replied, keeping her face from me.

"Then I'll tell you," and putting my free hand to her cheek I turned her face to me.

I studied her closely, and then in a moment the last shred of reluctance and coquetry in her seemed to evaporate. At the touch of my hand on her cheek she seemed to change: the whole power of her ardent nature was rising. At last she seemed to be yielding completely, and I put my lips to hers and kissed her warmly, then pressed her close and held her.

"Now do you know?" I asked after a time.

"Yes," she nodded, and for a proffered kiss returned an ardent one of her own.

I was beside myself with astonishment and delight. For the life of me I could not explain to myself how it was that I had achieved this result so swiftly. Something in the idyllic atmosphere, something in our temperaments, I fancied, made this quick spiritual and material understanding possible, but I wanted to know how. For a time we sat thus in the moon-light, I holding her hand and pressing her waist. Yet I could not feel that I liked her beyond the charm of her physical appearance, but that was enough at present. Physical beauty, with not too much grossness, was all I asked then—youth, a measure of innocence, and beauty. I pretended to have a real feeling for her and to be struck by her beauty, which was not wholly untrue. My feelings, however, as I well knew, were of so light and variable a character that it seemed almost a shame to lure her in this fashion. Why had I done it? It was decidedly unfortunate for her, I now thought, that we two should now meet under the same roof, with Miss W—— and others, perhaps making a third, fourth, or fifth possibly, but I anticipated no troublesome results. I might keep them apart. Anyhow, if I could not, my relationship in either case had not become earnest enough to cause me to worry. I hoped, however, to make it so in the case of Miss W——; Miss Ginity I knew from the first to be only a momentary flame.

CHAPTER XL

As I hoped, there were no ill effects from this little diversion, but by now I was so interested in Miss W——that I felt a little unfair to her. As I look back on it I can imagine no greater error of mind or temperament than that which drew me to her, considering my own variable tendencies and my naturally freedom-loving point of view. But since we are all blind victims of chance and given to far better hind-sight than fore-sight I have no complaint to make. It is quite possible that this was all a part of my essential destiny or development, one of those storm-breeding mistakes by which one grows. Life seems thus often casually to thrust upon one an experience which is to prove illuminating or disastrous.

To pick up the thread of my narrative, I saw Miss Ginity at breakfast, but she showed no sign that we had been out together the previous evening. Instead, she went on her way briskly as though nothing had happened, and this made her rather alluring again in my eyes. When Miss W—— came down I suffered a slight revulsion of feeling: she was so fresh and innocent, so spiritually and mentally above any such quick and compromising relationship as that which I and my new acquaintance had established the night before. I planned to be more circumspect in my relations with Miss Ginity and to pay more attention to Miss W——.

This plan was facilitated by the way in which the various members of the party now grouped and adjusted themselves. Miss W—— and her sister seemed to prefer to go about together, with me as an occasional third, and Miss Ginity and several of her new acquaintances made a second company, with whom I occasionally walked. Thus the distribution of my attentions was in no danger of immediate detection and I went gayly on.

A peculiar characteristic at this time and later was that I never really expected any of these relationships to endure. Marriage might be well enough for the average man but it never seemed to me that I should endure in it, that it would permanently affect my present free relationship with the world. I might be greatly grieved at times in a high emotional way because they could not last, but that was rising to heights of sentiment which puzzled even myself. One of the things which troubled and astonished me was that I could like two, three, and even more women at the same time, like them very much indeed. It seemed strange that I could yearn over them, now one and now another. A good man, I told myself, would not do this. The thought would never occur to him, or if it did he would repress it sternly. Obviously, if not profoundly evil I was a freak and had best keep my peculiar thoughts and desires to myself if I wanted to have anything to do with good people. I should be entirely alone, perhaps even seized upon by the law.

During the next two weeks I saw much of both Miss W—— and Miss Ginity. By day I usually accompanied Miss W—— and her sister from place to place about the grounds and of an evening strolled with Miss Ginity, all the while wondering if Miss W—— really liked me, whether her present feeling was likely to turn to something deeper. I felt a very definite point of view in her, very different from mine. In her was none of the variability that troubled me: if ever a person was fixed in conventional views it was she. One life, one love would have answered for her exactly. She could have accepted any condition, however painful or even degrading, providing she was bolstered up by what she considered the moral law. "To have and to hold, in sickness and in health, in poverty and in riches, until death do us part." I think the full force of these laws must have been imbibed with her mother's milk.

As for Miss Ginity, although she was conventional enough, I did feel that she might be persuaded to relax the moral rule in favor of one at least, and so was congratulating myself upon having achieved an affectional triumph. She may not have been deeply impressed by my physical attraction but there was something about me nevertheless which seemed to hold her. After a few days she left the hotel to visit some friends or relatives, to whom she had to pay considerable attention, but in my box nights or mornings, if by any chance I had not seen her, I would find notes explaining where she could be found in the evening, usually at a drugstore near the park or her new apartment, and we would take a few minutes' stroll in the park. Such a fever of emotion as she displayed at times! "Oh dear!" she would exclaim in an intense hungry way upon seeing me. "Oh, I could hardly wait!" And once in the park she would throw her strong young arms about me and kiss me in a fiery, hungry way. There was one last transport the night before she left for Michigan for a visit, when if I had been half the Don Juan I longed to be we might have passed the boundary line; but lack of courage on my part and inexperience on hers kept us apart.

When I saw her again in St. Louis——
But that is still another story.

CHAPTER XLI

Thus these days sped swiftly and ecstatically by. For once in my life I seemed to be truly and consistently happy, and that in this very city where but a year or two before I had suffered such keen distress. Toward the middle of the second week Miss Ginity left for Michigan, and then I had Miss W—— all to myself. By now I had come to feel an intense interest in her, an elation over the mere thought of being with her. In addition to this joy my mind and body seemed to be responding in some ecstatic fashion to Chicago and the Fair as a whole, the romance and color of it all, the winelike quality of the air, the raw, fresh, young force of the city, so vividly manifested in its sounding streets, its towering new buildings, its far-flung lines of avenues and boulevards, and, by way of contrast, its vast regions of middle and lower class poor. When we lived here as a family I had always thought that poverty was no great hardship. The poor were poor enough, in all conscience, but oh, the singing hope of the city itself! Up, up, and to work! Here were tasks for a million hands. In spite of my attachment to the Fair and Miss Ginity and Miss W—— I was still lured cityward, to visit the streets in which we had once lived or where I had walked so much in the old days, mere journeys of remembrance.

But as I wandered about I realized that the city was not my city any more, that life was a baseless, shifting thing, its seeming ties uncertain and unstable and that that which one day we held dear was tomorrow gone, to come no more. How plain it was, I thought and with some surprise, so ignorant is youth, that even seemingly brisk organizations such as the *Globe* here in Chicago and some others with which I had been connected could wither or disappear completely, one's commercial as well as one's family life be scattered to the four winds. Sensing this, I now felt an intense sense of

loneliness and homesickness, for what I could scarcely say:
for each and every one of past pleasant moments, I presume, our abandoned home in Flournoy Street, now rented
to another; my old desk at the *Globe,* now occupied by another; Alice's former home on this south side; N——'s in
Indiana Street. I was gloomy over having no fixed abode,
no intimates worthy the name here who could soothe and
comfort me in such an hour as this. Curiously enough, at such
moments I felt an intense leaning toward Miss W——, who
seemed to answer with something stable and abiding. I am
at a loss even now to describe it but so it was, and it was
more than anything else a sense of peace and support which
I found in her presence, a something that suggested durability
and warmth—possibly the whole closely-knit family atmosphere which was behind her and upon which she relied. She
would listen, apparently with interest, to all my youthful
and no doubt bragging accounts of my former newspaper
experiences here as well as in St. Louis, which I painted in
high colors with myself as a newspaper man deep in the
councils of my paper. Walking about the Fair grounds one
night I wished to take her hand but so overawed was I by
her personality that I could scarcely muster up the courage
to do it. When I at last did she shyly withdrew her hand,
pretending not to notice.

The same thing happened an evening or two later when
I persuaded her and her sister to accompany me and a
fellow-reporter whom I met in Chicago, to Lincoln Park,
where was a band concert and the playing of a colored
fountain given by the late C. T. Yerkes, then looked upon as
one of the sights of the city. I recall how warm and clear
was the evening, our trip northward on the newly-built "Alley
L," so-called because no public thoroughfare could be secured
for it, how when we got off at Congress Street, where the
enormous store of Siegel, Cooper & Company had only recently
been opened, we there took a surface cable to Lincoln Park.
It was barely dusk when we reached the park, and the fountain did not play until nine; but pending its colored wonders,
we walked along the shore of the lake in the darkness, alone,

her sister and my friend having been swallowed up in the great crowd.

Once near the lake shore we were alone. I found myself desperately interested without knowing how to proceed. It was a state of hypnosis, I fancy, in which I felt myself to be rapturously happy because more or less convinced of her feeling for me, and yet gravely uncertain as to whether she would ever permit herself to be ensnared in love. She was so poised and serene, so stable and yet so tender. I felt foolish, unworthy. Were not the crude brutalities of love too much for her? She might like me now, but the slightest error on my part in word or deed would no doubt drive her away and I should never see her again. I wanted to put my arm about her waist or hold her hand, but it was all beyond me then. She seemed too remote, a little unreal.

Finally, moved by the idyllic quality of it all, I left her and strolled down to the very edge of the lake where the water was lapping the sand. I had the feeling that if she really cared for me she would follow me, but she did not. She waited sedately on the rise above, but I felt all the while that she was drawing toward me intensely and holding me as in a vise. Half-angry but still fascinated, I returned, anything but the master of this situation. In truth, she had me as completely in tow as any woman could wish and was able, consciously or unconsciously, to regulate the progress of this affair to suit herself.

But nothing came of this except a deeper feeling of her exceptional charm. I was more than ever moved by her grace and force. What sobriety! What delicacy of feature! Her big eyes, soft and appealing, her small red mouth, her abundance of red hair, a constant enticement.

Before she left for her home, one of the inland counties about ninety miles from St. Louis, all that was left of the party, which was not many, paid a visit to St. Joe on the Michigan shore, opposite Chicago. It was a deliciously bright and warm Sunday. The steamers were comfortable and the beach at St. Joe perfect, a long coast of lovely white sand with the blue waves breaking over it. En route, because of the size of the party and the accidental arrangement of friends, I was thrown in with R——, the sister of my adored one, and in spite of myself, I found myself being swiftly drawn to her, desperately so, and that in the face of the strong attachment for her sister. There was something so cheering and whole-souled about her point of view, something so provoking and elusive, a veritable sprite of gayety and humor. For some reason, both on the boat and in the water, she devoted herself to me, until she seemed suddenly to realize what was happening to us both. Then she desisted and I saw her no more, or very little of her; but the damage had been done. I was intensely moved by her, even dreaming of changing my attentions; but she was too fond of her sister to allow anything like that. From then on she avoided me, with the sole intent, as I could see, of not injuring her sister.

We returned at night, I with the most troubled feelings about the whole affair, and it was only after I had returned to St. Louis that the old feeling for S—— came back and I began to see and think of her as I had that night in Lincoln Park. Then her charm seemed to come with full force and for days I could think of nothing else: the Fair, the hotel, the evening walks, and what she was doing now; but even this was shot through with the most jumbled thoughts of her sister and Miss Ginity. . . . I leave it to those who can to solve this mystery of the affections. Miss W——, as I understood it, was not to come back to St. Louis until the late autumn, when she could be found in an aristocratic suburb about twenty miles out, teaching of course, whereas Miss Ginity was little more than a half hour's ride from my room.

But, as I now ruefully thought, I had not troubled to look up Alice, although once she had meant so much of Chicago and happiness to me. What kind of man was I to become thus indifferent and then grieve over it?

CHAPTER XLII

To return and take up the ordinary routine of reporting after these crystal days of beauty and romance was anything but satisfactory. Gone was the White City with its towers and pinnacles and the wide blue wash of lake at its feet. After the Fair and the greater city, St. Louis seemed prosaic indeed. Still, I argued, I was getting along here better than I had in Chicago. When I went down to the office I found Wandell poring as usual over current papers. He was always scribbling and snipping, like a little old leathery Punch, in his mussy office. The mere sight of him made me wish that I were through with the newspaper business forever: it brought back all the regularity of the old days. When should I get out of it? I now began to ask myself for the first time. What was my real calling in life? Should I ever again have my evenings to myself? When should I be able to idle and dawdle as I had seen other people doing? I did not then realize how few the leisure class really comprises; I was always taking the evidence of one or two passing before my gaze as indicating a vast company. *I* was one of the unfortunates who were shut out; *I* was one whose life was to be a wretched tragedy for want of means to enjoy it now when I had youth and health!

"Well, did you have a good time?" asked Wandell.

"Yes," I replied dolefully. "That's a great show up there. It's beautiful."

"Any of the girls fall in love with you?" he croaked good-humoredly.

"Oh, it wasn't as bad as that."

"Well, I suppose you're ready to settle down now to hard work. I've got a lot of things here for you to do."

I cannot say that I was cheered by this. It was hard to

have to settle down to ordinary reporting after all these recent glories. It seemed to me as though an idyllic chapter of my life had been closed forever. Thereafter, I undertook one interesting assignment and another but without further developing my education as to the workings of life. I was beginning to tire of reporting, and one more murder or political or social mystery aided me in no way.

I recall, however, taking on a strange murder mystery over in Illinois which kept me stationed in a small countyseat for days, and all the time there was nothing save a sense of hard work about it all. Again, there was a train robbery that took me into the heart of a rural region where were nothing but farmers and small towns. Again there was a change of train service which permitted the distribution of St. Louis newspapers earlier than the Chicago papers in territory which was somehow disputed between them and because of which I was called upon to make a trip between midnight and dawn, riding for hours in the mailcar, and then describing fully this supposedly wonderful special newspaper service which was to make all the inhabitants of this region wiser, kinder, richer because they could get the St. Louis. papers before they could those of Chicago! I really did not think much of it, although I was congratulated upon having penned a fine picture.

One thing really did interest me: A famous mindreader having come to town and wishing to advertise his skill, he requested the *Republic* to appoint a man or a committee to ride with him in a carriage through the crowded downtown streets while he, blindfolded but driving, followed the directing thoughts of the man who should sit on the seat beside him. I was ordered to get up this committee, which I did—Dick, Peter, Rodenberger and myself were my final choice, I sitting on the front seat and doing the thinking while the mindreader raced in and out between cars and wagons, turning sharp corners, escaping huge trucks by a hair only, to wind up finally at Dick's door, dash up the one flight of stairs and into the room (the door being left open for this), and then climb up on a chair placed next to a wardrobe and, as per my thought, all decided on beforehand, take down that peculiar head of Alley Sloper and hand it to me.

Now this thing, when actually worked out under my very eyes and with myself doing the thinking, astounded me and caused me to ponder the mysteries of life more than ever. How could another man read my mind like that? What was it that perceived and interpreted my thoughts? It gave me an immense kick mentally, one that stays by me to this day, and set me off eventually on the matters of psychology and chemic mysteries generaliy. When this was written up as true, as it was, it made a splendid story and attracted a great deal of attention. Once and for all, it cleared up my thoughts as to the power of mind over so-called matter and caused this "committee" to enter upon experiments of its own with hypnotists, spiritualists and the like, until we were fairly well satisfied as to the import of these things. I myself stood on the stomach of a thin hypnotized boy of not more than seventeen years of age, while his head was placed on one chair, his feet on another and no brace of any kind was put under his body. Yet his stomach held me up. But, having established the truth of such things for ourselves, we found no method of doing anything with our knowledge. It was practically useless in this region, and decidedly taboo.

Another individual who interested me quite as might a book or story was a spiritualist, a fat, sluglike Irish type, who came to town about this time and proved to be immensely successful in getting up large meetings, entrance to which he charged. Soon there were ugly rumors as to the orgiastic character of his séances, especially at his home where he advertised to receive interested spiritualists in private. One day my noble and nosy city editor set me to the task of ferreting out all this, with the intention of *sicking* the moralists on the gentleman and so driving him out of town. Was it because Mr. Wandell, interested in morals or at least responding to the local sentiment for a moral city, considered this man a real menace to St. Louis and so wished to be rid of him? Not at all. Mr. Wandell cared no more for Mr. Mooney or the public or its subsurface morals than he cared for the politics of Beluchistan. In the heart of St. Louis at this very time, in Chestnut Street, was a large district devoted to just such orgies as this stranger was supposed to be perpetrating; but this area was never in the public eye, and you could not, for your life, put it there. The public apparently did not want it attacked, or if it did there were forces sufficiently powerful to keep it from obtaining its wishes. The police were supposed to extract regular payments from one and all in this area, as Rodenberger, in the little paper he ran, frequently charged, but this paper had no weight. The most amazing social complications occasionally led directly to one or another of these houses, as I myself had seen, but no comment was ever made on the peculiarity of the area as a whole or its persistence in the face of so much moral sentiment. The vice crusaders never troubled it, neither did the papers or the churches or anybody else. But when it came to Mr. Mooney—well, here was an individual who could be easily and safely attacked, and so—

Mr. Mooney had a large following and many defenders whose animosity or gullibility led them to look upon him as a personage of great import. He was unquestionably a shrewd and able manipulator, one of the finest quacks I ever saw. He would race up and down among the members of his large audience in his spiritualistic "church meetings," his fat waxy eyelids closed, his immense white shirt-front shining, his dress coattails flying like those of a bustling butler or head-waiter, the while he exclaimed: "Is there any one here by the name of Peter? Is there any one here by the name of Augusta? There is an old white-bearded man here who says he has something to say to Augusta. And Peter—Peter, your sister says not to marry, that everything now troubling you will soon come out all right."

He would open these meetings with spiritual invocations of one kind and another and pretend the profoundest religiosity and spirituality when as a matter of fact he was a faker of the most brazen stamp. As Wandell afterward showed me by clippings and police reports from other cities, he had been driven from one city to another, cities usually very far apart so that the news of his troubles might not spread too quickly. His last resting-place had been Norfolk, Virginia, and before that he had been in such widely scattered spots as Liverpool, San Francisco, Sydney, New South Wales. Always he had been immensely successful, drawing large crowds, taking up collections and doing a private séance business which must have netted him a tidy sum. Indeed in private life, as I soon found, he was a gourmet, a sybarite and a riant amorist, laughing in his sleeve at all his touts and followers.

For some time I was unable to gather any evidence that would convict him of anything in a direct way. Once he found the *Republic* to be unfavorable, he became pugnacious and threatened to assault me if I ever came near him or his place or attempted to write up anything about him which was not true! On the other hand, Wandell, being equally determined to catch him, insisted upon my following him up and exposing him. My task was not easy. I was compelled to hang about his meetings, trying to find some one who would tell me something definite against him.

Going to his rooms one day when he was absent, I managed to meet his landlady who, when I told her that I was from the *Republic* and wanted to know something about Mr. Mooney's visitors, his private conduct and so forth, asked me to come in. At once I sensed something definite and important, for I had been there before and had been turned away by this same woman. But today, for some reason she escorted me very secretly to a room on the second floor where she closed and locked the door and then began a long story concerning the peculiar relations which existed between Mr. Mooney and some of his male and female disciples, especially the female ones. She finally admitted that she had been watching Mr. Mooney's rooms through a keyhole. For weeks past there had been various visitors whose comings and goings had meant little to her until they became "so regular," as she said, and Mr. Mooney so particularly engaged with them. Then, since Mr. Mooney's fame had been spreading and the *Republic* had begun to attack him, she had become most watchful and now, as she told me, he was "carrying on" most shamefully with one and another of his visitors, male and female. Just what these relations were she at first refused to state, but when I pointed out to her that unless she could furnish me with other and more convincing proof than her mere word or charge it would all be of small value, she unbent sufficiently to fix on one particular woman, whose card and a note addressed to Mr. Mooney she had evidently purloined from his room. These she produced and turned over to me with a rousing description of the nature of the visits.

Armed with the card and note, I immediately proceeded to the west end where I soon found the house of the lady, determined to see whether she would admit this soft impeachment, whether I could make her admit it. I was a little uncertain then as to how I was to go about it. Suppose I should run into the lady's husband, I thought, or suppose they should come down together when I sent in my card? Or suppose that I charged her with what I knew and she called some one to her aid and had me thrown out or beaten up? Nevertheless I went nervously up the steps and rang the bell, whereupon a footman opened the door.

"Who is it you wish to see?"

I told him.

"Have you an appointment with her?"

"No, but I'm from the *Republic,* and you tell her that it is very important for her to see me. We have an article about her and a certain Mr. Mooney which we propose to print in the morning, and I think she will want to see me about it." I stared at him with a great deal of effrontery. He finally closed the door, leaving me outside, but soon returned and said: "You may come in."

I walked into a large, heavily furnished reception-room, representing the best Western taste of the time, in which I nosed about thinking how fine it all was and wondering how I was to proceed about all this once she appeared. Suppose she proved to be a fierce and contentious soul well able to hold her own, or suppose there was some mistake about this letter or the statement of the landlady! As I was walking up and down, quite troubled as to just what I should say, I heard the rustle of silk skirts. I turned just as a vigorous and well-dressed woman of thirty-odd swept into the room. She was rather smart, bronze-haired, pink-fleshed, not in the least nervous or disturbed.

"You wish to see me?"

"Yes, ma'am."

"About what, please?"

"I am from the *Republic*," I began. "We have a rather startling story about you and Mr. Mooney. It appears that his place has been watched and that you——"

"A story about me?" she interrupted with an air of hauteur, seeming to have no idea of what I was driving at. "And about a Mr. Who? Mooney, you say? What kind of a story is it? Why do you come to me about it? Why, I don't even know the man!"

"Oh, but I think you do," I replied, thinking of the letter and card in my pocket. "As a matter of fact, I know that you do. At the office right now we have a card and a letter of yours to Mr. Mooney, which the *Republic* proposes to publish along with some other matter unless some satisfactory explanation as to why it should not be printed can be made. We are conducting a campaign against Mr. Mooney, as you probably know."

I have often thought of this scene as a fine illustration of the crass, rough force of life, its queer non-moral tangles, bluster, bluff, lies, make-believe. Beginning by accusing me of attempted blackmail, and adding that she would inform her husband and that I must leave the house at once or be thrown out, she glared until I replied that I would leave but that I had her letter to Mr. Mooney, that there were witnesses who would testify as to what had happened between her and Mr. Mooney and that unless she proceeded to see my city editor at once the whole thing would be written up for the next day's paper. Then of a sudden she collapsed. Her face blanched, her body trembled, and she, a healthy, vigorous woman, dropped to her knees before me, seized my hands and coat and began pleading with me in an agonized voice.

(273)

"But you wouldn't do that! My husband! My home! My social position! My children! My God, you wouldn't have me driven out of my own home! If he came here now! Oh, my God, tell me what I am to do! Tell me that you won't do anything—that the *Republic* won't! I'll give you anything you want. Oh, you couldn't be so heartless! Maybe I have done wrong—but think of what will happen to me if you do this!"

I stared at her in amazement. Never had I been the center of such an astonishing scene. On the instant I felt a mingled sense of triumph and extreme pity. Thoughts as to whether I should tell the *Republic* what I knew, whether if I did it would have the cruelty to expose this woman, whether she would or could be made to pay blackmail by any one raced through my mind. I was sorry and yet amused. Always this thought of blackmail, of which I heard considerable in newspaper work but of which I never had any proof, troubled me. If I exposed her, what then? Would Wandell hound her? If I did not would he discover that I was suppressing the news and so discharge me? Pity for her was plainly mingled with a sense of having achieved another newspaper beat. Now, assuredly, the *Republic* could make this erratic individual move on. To her I proceeded to make plain that I personally was helpless, a mere reporter who of himself could do nothing. If she wished she could see Mr. Wandell, who could help her if he chose, and I gave her his home address, knowing that he would not be at his office at this time of day, but hoping to see him myself before she did. Weeping and moaning, she raced upstairs, leaving me to make my way out as best I might. Once out I meditated on this effrontery and the hard, cold work I was capable of doing. Surely this was a dreadful thing to have done. Had I the right? Was it fair? Suppose I had been the victim? Still I congratulated myself upon having done a very clever piece of work for which I should be highly complimented.

The lady must have proceeded at once to my city editor for when I returned to the office he was there; he called me to him at once.

(274)

"Great God! What have you been doing now? Of all men I have ever known, you can get me into more trouble in a half-hour than any other man could in a year! Here I was, sitting peacefully at home, and up comes my wife telling me there's a weeping woman in the parlor who had just driven up to see me. Down I go and she grabs my hands, falls on her knees and begins telling me about some letters we have, that her life will be ruined if we publish them. Do you want to get me sued for divorce?" he went on, cackling and chortling in his impish way. "What the hell are those letters, anyhow? Where are they? What's this story you've dug up now? Who is this woman? You're the damnedest man I ever saw!" and he cackled some more. I handed over the letter and he proceeded to look it over with considerable gusto. As I could see, he was pleased beyond measure.

I told my story, and he was intensely interested but seemed to meditate on its character for some time. What happened after that between him and the woman I was never able to make out. But one thing is sure: the story was never published, not this incident. An hour or two later, seeing me enter the office after my dinner, he called me in and began:

"You leave this with me now and drop the story for the present. There are other ways to get Mooney," and sure enough, in a few days Mr. Mooney suddenly left town. It was a curious procedure to me, but at least Mr. Mooney was soon gone—and——

But figure it out for yourself.

CHAPTER XLIII

Two other incidents in connection with my newspaper work at this time threw a clear light on social crimes and conditions which cannot always be discussed or explained. One of these related to an old man of about sixty-five years of age who was in the coffee and spice business in one of those old streets which bordered on the waterfront. One afternoon in mid-August, when there was little to do in the way of reporting and I was hanging about the office waiting for something to turn up, Wandell received a telephone message and handed me a slip of paper. "You go down to this address and see what you can find out. There's been a fight or something. A crowd has been beating up an old man and the police have arrested him—to save him, I suppose."

I took a car and soon reached the scene, a decayed and tumbledown region of small family dwellings now turned into tenements of even a poorer character. St. Louis had what so large a center as New York has not: alleys or rear passageways to all houses by which trade parcels, waste and the like are delivered or removed. And facing these were old barns, sheds, and tumbledown warrens of houses and flats occupied by poor whites or blacks, or both. In an old decayed and vacant brick barn in one of these alleys there had been only a few hours before a furious scene, although when I arrived it was all over, everything was still and peaceful. All that I could learn was that several hours before an old man had been found in this barn with a little girl of eight or nine years. The child's parents or friends were informed and a chase ensued. The criminal had been surrounded by a group of irate citizens who threatened to kill him. Then the police arrived and escorted him to the station at North Seventh, where supposedly he was locked up.

On my arrival at the station, however, nothing was known

of this case. My noble King knew nothing and when I looked on the "blotter," which supposedly contained a public record of all arrests and charges made, and which it was my privilege as well as that of every other newspaper man to look over, there was no evidence of any such offense having been committed or of any such prisoner having been brought here.

"What became of that attempted assault in K Street?" I inquired of King, who was drowsily reading a newspaper. "I was just over there and they told me the man had been brought here."

He looked up at me wearily, seemingly not interested. "What case? It must be down if it came in here. What case are ye taalkin' about? Maybe it didn't come here."

I looked at him curiously, struck all at once by an air of concealment. He was not as friendly as usual.

"That's funny," I said. "I've just come from there and they told me he was here. It would be on the blotter, wouldn't it? Were you here an hour or two ago?"

For the first time since I had been coming here he grew a bit truculent. "Sure. If it's not on there it's not on there, and that's all I know. If you want to know more than that you'll have to see the captain."

At thought of the police attempting to conceal a thing like this in the face of my direct knowledge I grew irritable and bold myself.

"Where's the captain?" I asked.

"He's out now. He'll be back at four, I think."

I sat down and waited, then decided to call up the office for further instructions. Wandell was in. He advised me to call up Edmonstone at the Four Courts and see if it was recorded, which I did, but nothing was known. When I returned I found the captain in. He was a taciturn man and had small use for reporters at any time.

"Yes, yes, yes," he kept reiterating as I asked him about the case. "Well, I'll tell you," he said after a long pause, seeing that I was determined to know, "he's not here now. I let him go. No one saw him commit the crime. He's an old man with a big wholesale business in Second Street, never arrested before, and he has a wife and grown sons and daughters. Of course he oughtn't to be doin' anything of that kind—still, he claims that he wasn't. Anyhow, no good can come of writin' it up in the papers now. Here's his name and address," and he opened a small book which he drew out of his pocket and showed me that and no more. "Now you can go and talk to him yourself if you want to, but if you take my advice you'll let him alone. I see no good in pullin' him down if it's goin' to hurt his family. But that's as you newspaper men see it."

I could have sympathized with this stocky Irishman more if we had not all been suspicious of the police. I decided to see this old man myself, curiosity and the desire for a good story controlling me. I hurried to a car and rode out to the west end, where, in a well-built street and a house of fair proportions I found my man sitting on his front porch no doubt awaiting some such disastrous onslaught as this and anxious to keep it from his family. The moment he saw me he walked to his gate and stopped me. He was tall and angular, with a grizzled, short, round beard and a dull, unimportant face, a kind of Smith Brothers-coughdrop type. Apparently he was well into that period where one is supposed to settle down into a serene old age and forget all one ever knew of youth. I inquired whether a Mr. So-and-So lived there, and he replied that he was Mr. So-and-So.

"I'm from the *Republic*," I began, "and we have a story regarding a charge that has been made against you today in one of the police stations."

He eyed me with a nervous uncertainty that was almost tremulous. He did not seem to be able to speak at first but chewed on something, a bit of tobacco possibly.

"Not so loud," he said. "Come out here. I'll give you ten dollars if you won't say anything about this," and he began to fumble in one of his waistcoat pockets.

"No, no," I said, with an air of profound virtue. "I can't take money for anything like that. I can't stop anything the paper may want to say. You'll have to see the editor."

All the while I was thinking how like an old fox he was and

that if one did have the power to suppress a story of this kind here was a fine opportunity for blackmail. He might have been made to pay a thousand or more. At the same time I could not help sympathizing with him a little, considering his age and his unfortunate predicament. Of late I had been getting a much clearer light on my own character and idiosyncrasies as well as on those of many others, and was beginning to see how few there were who could afford to cast the stone of righteousness or superior worth. Nearly all were secretly doing one thing and another which they would publicly denounce and which, if exposed, would cause them to be shunned or punished. Sex vagaries were not as uncommon as the majority supposed and perhaps were not to be given too sharp a punishment if strict justice were to be done to all. Yet here was I at this moment yelping at the heels of this errant, who had been found out. At the same time I cannot say that I was very much moved by the personality of the man: he looked to be narrow and close-fisted. I wondered how a business man of any acumen could be connected with so shabby an affair, or being caught could be so dull as to offer any newspaper man so small a sum as ten dollars to hush it up. And how about the other papers, the other reporters who might hear of it—did he expect to buy them all off for ten dollars each? The fact that he had admitted the truth of the charges left nothing to say. I felt myself grow nervous and incoherent and finally left rather discomfited and puzzled as to what I should do. When I returned to the office and told Wandell he seemed to be rather dubious also and more or less disgusted.

"You can't make much out of a case of that kind," he said. "We couldn't print it if you did; the public wouldn't stand for it. And if you attack the police for concealing it then they'll be down on us. He ought to be exposed, I suppose, but—well—— Write it out and I'll see."

I therefore wrote it up in a wary and guarded way, telling what had happened and how the police had not entered the charge, but the story never appeared. Somehow, I was rather glad of it, although I thought the man should be punished.

CHAPTER XLIV

WHILE I was on the *Globe-Democrat* there was a sort of race-track tout, gambler, amateur detective and political and police hanger-on generally, who was a purveyor of news not only to our police and political men but to the sporting and other editors, a sort of Jack-of-all-news or tipster. To me he was both ridiculous and disgusting, loud, bold, uncouth, the kind of creature that begins as bootblack or newsboy and winds up as the president of a racing association or ball team. He claimed to be Irish, having a freckled face, red hair, gray eyes, and rather large hands and feet. In reality he was one of those South Russian Jews who looked so much like the Irish as to be frequently mistaken for them. He had the wit to see that it would be of more advantage to him to be thought Irish than Jewish, and so had changed his name of Shapirowitz to Galvin—"Red" Galvin. One of the most offensive things about him was that his clothes were loud, just such clothes as touts and gamblers affect, hard, bright-checked suits, bright yellow shoes, ties of the most radiant hues, hats of a clashing sonorousness, and rings and pins and cuff-links glistening with diamonds or rubies—the kind of man who is convinced that clothes and a little money make the man, as they quite do in such instances.

Galvin had the social and moral point of view of both the hawk and the buzzard. According to Wood, who early made friends with him quite as he did with the Chinese and others for purposes of study, he was identified with some houses of prostitution in which he had a small financial interest, as well as various political schemes then being locally fostered by one and another group of low politicians who were constantly getting up one scheme and another to mulct the city in some underhanded way. He was a species of political and social grafter, having all the high ideals of a bagnio detective: he began to interest Mr. Tobias Mitchell, who was a creature of an allied if slightly higher type, and the pair became reasonably good friends. Mitchell used him as an assistant to Hazard, Bellairs, Bennett, Hartung and myself: he supplied the paper with stories which we would re-write. I used to laugh at him, more or less to his face, as being a freak, which of course generated only the kindliest of feelings between us. He always suggested to me the type of detective or plain-clothes man who would take money from street-girls, prey on them, as indeed I suspected him of doing.

I wondered how he could make anything out of this news-paper connection since, as Hartung and others told me, he could not write. It was necessary to rewrite his stuff almost entirely. But his great recommendation to Mitchell and others was that he could get news of things where other reporters could not, among the police, detectives and politi-cians, with whom he was evidently hand-in-hand. By reason of his underworld connections many amazing details as to one form and another of political and social jobbery came to light, which doubtless made him invaluable to a city editor.

When some of his stories were given to me to rewrite we were thrown into immediate and clashing contact. Because of his leers and bravado, when he knew he could not write two good sentences in order, I frequently wanted to brain him but took it out in smiles and dry cynical comments. His favorite expressions were "See?" and "I sez tuh him" or "He sez tuh me," always accompanied by a contemptuous wave of a hand or a pugnaciously protruded chin. One of the chief reasons why I hated him was that Dick Wood told me he had once remarked that newspaper work was a beggar's game at best and that *writers grew on trees,* meaning that they were so numerous as to be negligible and not worth considering.

I made the best of these trying situations when I had to do over a story of his, extracting all the information I could and then writing it out, which resulted in some of his stories receiving excellent space in the day's news and made him all the more pugnacious and sure of himself. And at the same time these made him of more value to the paper. However, in due time I left the *Globe-Democrat,* and one day, greatly to my astonishment and irritation, he appeared at the North Seventh Street station as a full-fledged reporter, having been given a regular position by Mitchell and set to doing police work—out of which task at the Four Courts, if I remember rightly, he finally ousted Jock Bellairs, who was given to too much drinking.

To my surprise and chagrin I noticed at once that he was, as if by reason of past intimacies of which I had not the slightest idea, far more en rapport with the sergeants and the captain than I had ever dreamed of being. It was "Charlie" here and "Cap" there. But what roiled me most was that he gave himself all the airs of a newspaper man, swaggering about and talking of this, that and the other story he had written (I having done some of them myself!). The crowning blow was that he was soon closeted with the captain in his room, strolling in and out of that sanctum as if it were his private demesne and giving me the impression of being in touch with realms and deeds of which I was never to have the slightest knowledge. This made me apprehensive lest in these intimacies tales and mysteries should be unfolded that would have their first light in the pages of the *Globe-Democrat* and so leave me to be laughed at as one who could not get the news. I watched the *Globe-Democrat* more closely than ever before for evidence of such treachery on the part of the police as would result in a "scoop" for him, at the same time redoubling my interest in such items as might appear. The consequence was that on more than one occasion I made good stories out of things which Mr. Galvin had evidently dismissed as worthless; and now and then a case into which I had inquired at the stationhouse appeared in the *Globe-Democrat* with details which I had not been able to obtain and concerning which the police had insisted they knew nothing.

For a long time, by dint of energy and a rather plain indication to all concerned that I would not tolerate false dealing, I managed not only to hold my own but occasionally to give my confrère a good beating—as when, for one instance, a negro girl in one of those crowded alleys was cut almost to shreds by an ex-lover armed with a razor, for reasons which, as my investigation proved, were highly romantic. Some seven or eight months before, this girl and her assailant had been living together in Cairo, Illinois, and the lover, who was wildly fond of her, became suspicious and finally satisfying himself that she was faithless set a trap to catch her. He was a coal passer or stevedore, working now on one boat and now on another plying the Mississippi between New Orleans and St. Louis. And one day when she thought he was on a river steamer for a week or two he burst in upon her and found her with another man. Death would have been her portion, as well as that of her lover, had it not been for the interference of friends which permitted the pair to escape.

The man returned to his task as stevedore, working his way from one river city to another. When he came to Memphis, Natchez, New Orleans, Vicksburg or St. Louis, he disguised himself as a peddler selling trinkets and charms and in this capacity walked the crowded negro sections of these cities calling his wares. One of these trips finally brought him to St. Louis, and here on a late August afternoon, ambling up this stifling little alley calling out his charms and trinkets, he had finally encountered her. The girl put her head out of the doorway. Dropping his tray he drew a razor and slashed her cheeks and lips, arms, legs, back and sides, so that when I arrived at the City Hospital she was unconscious and her life despaired of. The lover, abandoning his tray of cheap jewelry, which was later brought to the stationhouse and exhibited, had made good his escape and was not captured, during my stay in St. Louis at least. Her present paramour had also gone his way, leaving her to suffer alone.

Owing possibly to Galvin's underestimate of its romance, this story received only a scant stick as a low dive cutting affray in the *Globe-Democrat*, while in the *Republic* I had turned it into a negro romance which filled all of a column. Into it I had tried to put the hot river waterfronts of the different cities which the lover had visited, the crowded negro quarters of Memphis, New Orleans, Cairo, the bold negro life which two truants such as the false mistress and her lover might enjoy. I had tried to suggest the sing-song sleepiness of the levee boat-landings, the stevedores at their lazy labors, the idle, dreamy character of the slow-moving boats. Even an old negro refrain appropriate to a trinket peddler had been introduced:

"Eyah—Rings, Pins, Buckles, Ribbons!"

The barbaric character of the alley in which it occurred, lined with rickety curtain-hung shacks and swarming with the idle, crooning, shuffling negro life of the South, appealed to me. An old black mammy with a yellow-dotted kerchief over her head, who kept talking of "disha Gawge" and "disha Sam" and "disha Maquatia" (the girl), moved me to a poetic frenzy. From a crowd of blacks that hung about the vacated shack of the lovers after the girl had been taken away I picked up the main thread of the story, the varying characteristics of the girl and her lover, and then having visited the hospital and seen the victim I hurried to the office and endeavored to convince Wandell that I had an important story. At first he was not inclined to think so, negro life being a little too low for local consumption, but after I had entered upon some of the details he told me to go ahead. I wrote it out as well as I could, and it went in on the second page. The next day, meeting Galvin, having first examined the *Globe* to see what had been done there, I beamed on him cheerfully and was met with a snarl of rage.

"You think you're a hell of a feller, dontcha, because yuh can sling a little ink? Yuh think yuh've pulled off sompin swell. Well, say, yuh're not near as much as yuh think yuh are. Wait an' see. I've been up against wordy boys like yuh before, an' I can work all around 'em. All you guys do is to get a few facts an' then pad 'em up. Yuh never get the real stuff, never," and he snapped his fingers under my nose. "Wait'll we get a real case sometime, you an' me, an' I'll show yuh sompin."

He glared at me with hard, revengeful eyes, and he then and there put a fear into me from which I never recovered, although at the time I merely smiled.

"Is that so? That's easy enough to say, now that you're

trimmed, but I guess I'll be right there when the time comes.''

"Aw, go to hell!" he snarled, and I walked off smiling but beginning to wonder nervously just what it was he was going to do to me, and how soon.

CHAPTER XLV

SOME time before this (when I was still working for the *Globe-Democrat*), there had occurred on the Missouri Pacific, about one hundred and fifty miles west of St. Louis a hold-up, the story of which interested me, although I had nothing to do with it. According to the reports, seven lusty and daring bandits, all heavily armed and desperate, had held up an eight-car Pullman and baggage express train between one and two of the morning at a lonely spot, and after overawing the passengers, had compelled the engineer and fireman to dismount, uncouple the engine and run it a hundred paces ahead, then return and help break open the door of the express car. This they did, using a stick of dynamite or giant powder handed them by one of the bandits. And then both were made to enter the express car, where, under the eye of one of the bandits and despite the presence of the express messenger, who was armed yet overawed, they were compelled to blow open the safe and carry forth between twenty and thirty thousand dollars in bills and coin, which they deposited on the ground in sacks and packages for the bandits. Then, if you please, they were compelled to re-enter their engine, back it up and couple it to the train and proceed upon their journey, leaving the bandits to gather up their booty and depart.

Naturally such a story was of great interest to St. Louis, as well as to all the other cities near at hand. It smacked of the lawlessness of the 'forties. All banks, express companies, railroads and financial institutions generally were intensely interested. The whole front page was given to this deed, and it was worth it, although during my short career in journalism in this region no less than a dozen amazing train robberies took place in as many months in the region bounded by the Mississippi and the Rockies, the Canadian line and the Gulf. Four or five of them occurred within a hundred miles of St. Louis.

The truth about this particular robbery was that there had not been seven bandits but just one, an ex-railroad hand, turned robber for this occasion only, and armed, as subsequent developments proved, with but a brace of revolvers, each containing six shots, and a few sticks of fuse-prepared giant powder! Despite the glowing newspaper account which made of this a most desperate and murderous affair, there had been no prowling up and down the aisles of the cars by bandits armed to the teeth, as a number of passengers insisted (among whom was the Governor of the State, his Lieutenant-Governor, several officers of his staff, all returning from a military banquet or feast somewhere). Nor was there any shooting at passengers who ventured to peer out into the darkness. Just this one lone bandit, who was very busy up in the front attending to the robbing. What made this story all the more ridiculous in the light of later developments was that at the time the train stopped in the darkness and the imaginary bandits began to shout and fire shots, and even to rob the passengers of their watches, pins, purses, these worthies of the State, or so it was claimed in guffawing newspaper circles afterward, crawled under their seats or into their berths and did not emerge until the train was well on its way once more. Long before the true story of the lone bandit came out, the presence of the Governor and his staff was well known and had lent luster to the deed and strengthened the interest which later attached to the story of the real bandit.

The St. Louis newspaper files for 1893 will show whether or not I am correct. This lone bandit, as it was later indisputably proved, was nothing more than an ex-farm hand turned railroad hand and then "baggage-smasher" at a small station. Owing to love and poverty he had plotted this astounding coup, which, once all its details were revealed, fascinated the American public from coast to coast. That a lone individual should undertake such an astounding task was uppermost in everybody's mind, including that of our city editors, and to the task of unraveling it they now bent their every effort.

When the robbery occurred I was working for the *Globe-Democrat;* later, when it was discovered by detectives working for the railroad and the express company who the star robber was, I was connected with the *Republic*. Early one afternoon I was shown a telegram from some backwoods town in Missouri—let us say Bald Knob, just for a name's sake—that Lem Rollins (that name will do as well as any other), an ex-employee of the Missouri Pacific, had been arrested by detectives for the road and express company for the crime, and that upon searching his room they had found most of the stolen money. Also, because of other facts with which he had been confronted he had confessed that he and he alone had been guilty of the express robbery. The dispatch added that he had shown the detectives where the remainder of the money lay hidden, and that this very afternoon he would be en route to St. Louis, scheduled to arrive over the St. Louis & San Francisco, and that he would be confined in the county jail here. Imagine the excitement. The burglar had not told how he had accomplished this great feat, and here he was now en route to St. Louis, and might be met and interviewed on the train. From a news point of view the story was immense.

When I came in Wandell exclaimed: "I'll tell you what you do, Dreiser—Lord! I thought you wouldn't come back in time! Here's a St. Louis & San Francisco time-table; according to it you can take a local that leaves here at two-fifteen and get as far as this place, Pacific, where the incoming express stops. It's just possible that the *Globe* and the other papers haven't got hold of this yet—maybe they have, but whatever happens, we won't get licked, and that's the main thing."

I hurried down to the Union Station, but when I asked for a ticket to Pacific, the ticket agent asked "Which road?"

"Are there two?"

"Sure, Missouri Pacific, and St. Louis & San Francisco."

"They both go to the same place, do they?"

"Yes; they meet there."

"Which train leaves first?"

"St. Louis & San Francisco. It's waiting now."

I hurried to it, but the thought of this other road in from Pacific troubled me. Suppose the bandit should be on the other train instead of on this! I consulted with the conductor when he came for my ticket and was told that Pacific was the only place at which these two roads met, one going west and the other southwest from there. "Good," I thought. "Then he is certain to be on this line."

But now another thought came to me: supposing reporters from other papers were aboard, especially the *Globe-Democrat!* I rose and walked forward to the smoker, and there, to my great disgust and nervous dissatisfaction, was Galvin, red-headed, serene, a cigar between his teeth, slumped low in his seat smoking and reading a paper as calmly as though he were bent upon the most unimportant task in the world.

"How now?" I asked myself. "The *Globe* has sent that swine! Here he is, and these country detectives and railroad men will be sure, on the instant, to make friends with him and do their best to serve him. They like that sort of man. They may even give him details which they will refuse to give me. I shall have to interview my man in front of him, and he will get the benefit of all my questions! At his request they may even refuse to let me interview him!"

I returned to my seat nervous and much troubled, all the more so because I now recalled Galvin's threat. But I was determined to give him the tussle of his life. Now we would see whether he could beat me or not—not, if fair play were exercised; of that I felt confident. Why, he could not even write a decent line! Why should I be afraid of him? . . . But I was, just the same.

As the dreary local drew near Pacific I became more and more nervous. When we drew up at the platform I jumped down, all alive with the determination not to be outdone. I saw Galvin leap out, and on the instant he spied me. I never saw a face change more quickly from an expression of ease and assurance to one of bristling opposition and distrust.

How he hated me. He looked about to see who else might dismount, then, seeing no one, he bustled up to the station-agent to see when the train from the west was due. I decided not to trail, and sought information from the conductor, who assured me that the eastbound express would probably be on time, five minutes later.

"It always stops here, does it?" I inquired anxiously.

"It always stops."

As we talked Galvin came back to the platform and stood looking up the track. Our train now pulled out, and a few minutes later the whistle of the express was heard. Now for a real contest, I thought. Somewhere in one of those cars would be the bandit surrounded by detectives, and my duty was to get to him first, to explain who I was and begin my questioning, overawing Galvin perhaps with the ease with which I should take charge. Maybe the bandit would not want to talk; if so I must make him, cajole him or his captors, or both. No doubt, since I was the better interviewer, or so I thought, I should have to do all the talking, and this wretch would make notes or make a deal with the detectives while I was talking. In a few moments the train was rolling into the station, and then I saw my friend Galvin leap aboard and with that iron effrontery and savageness which I always hated in him, begin to race through the cars. I was about to follow him when I saw the conductor stepping down beside me.

"Is that train-robber they are bringing in from Bald Knob on here? I'm from the *Republic,* and I've been sent out here to interview him."

"You're on the wrong road, brother," he smiled. "He's not on here. They're bringing him in over the Missouri Pacific. They took him across from Bald Knob to Denton and caught the train there—but I'll tell you," and he consulted his watch, "you might be able to catch that yet if you run for it. It's only across the field here. You see that little yellow station over there? Well, that's the Missouri Pacific depot. I don't know whether it stops here or not, but it may. It's due now, but sometimes it's a little late. You'll have to run for it though; you haven't a minute to spare."

"You wouldn't fool me about a thing like this, would you?"
I pleaded.

"Not for anything. I know how you feel. If you can get
on that train you'll find him, unless they've taken him off
somewhere else."

I don't remember if I even stopped to thank him. Instead
of following Galvin into the cars I now leaped to the little
path which cut diagonally across this long field, evidently well
worn by human feet. As I ran I looked back once or twice
to see if my enemy was following me, but apparently he
had not seen me. I now looked forward eagerly toward this
other station, but, as I ran, I saw the semaphore arm, which
stood at right angles opposite the station, lower for a clear
track for some train. At the same time I spied a mail-bag
hanging out on an express arm, indicating that whatever this
train was it was not going to stop here. I turned, still uncertain as to whether I had made a mistake in not searching
the other train after all. Supposing the conductor had fooled
me. . . . Supposing the burglar were on there, and Galvin was
already beginning to question him! Oh, Lord, what a beat!
And what would happen to me then? Was it another case
of three shows and no critic? I slowed up in my running,
chill beads of sweat bursting through my pores, but as I did
so I saw the St. Louis & San Francisco train begin to move
and from it, as if shot out of it, leaped Galvin.

"Ha!" I thought. "Then the robber is not on there!
Galvin has just discovered it! He knows now that he is
coming in on this line"—for I could see him running along
the path. "Oh, kind Heaven, if I can beat him to it! If I
can only get on and leave him behind! He has all of a thousand feet still to run, and I am here!"

Desperately I ran into the station, thrust my head in at the
open office window and called:

"When is this St. Louis express due here?"

"Now," he replied surlily.

"Does it stop?"

"No, it don't stop."

"Can it be stopped?"

"It can *not!*"

"You mean that you have no right to stop it?"

"I mean I won't stop it!"

Even as he said this there came the shriek of a whistle in the distance.

"Oh, Lord," I thought. "Here it comes, and he won't let me on, and Galvin will be here any minute!" For the moment I was even willing that Galvin should catch it too, if only I could get on. Think of what Wandell would think if I missed it!

"Will five dollars stop it?" I asked desperately, diving into my pocket.

"No."

"Will ten?"

"It might," he replied crustily.

"Stop it," I urged and handed over the bill.

The agent took it, grabbed a tablet of yellow order blanks which lay before him, scribbled something on the face of one and ran out to the track. At the same time he called to me:

"Run on down the track. Run after it. She won't stop here. She can't. Run on. She'll go a thousand feet before she can slow up."

I ran, while he stood there holding up this thin sheet of yellow paper. As I ran I heard the express rushing up behind me. On the instant it was alongside and past, its wheels grinding and emitting sparks. It was stopping! I should get on, and oh, glory be! Galvin would not! Fine! I could hear the gritty screech of the wheels against the brakes as the train came to a full stop. Now I would make it, and what a victory! I came up to it and climbed aboard, but, looking back, I saw to my horror that my rival had almost caught up and was now close at hand, not a hundred feet behind. He had seen the signal, had seen me running, and instead of running to the station had taken a diagonal tack and followed me. I saw that he would make the train. I tried to signal the agent behind to let the train go, but he had already done so. The conductor came out on the rear platform and I appealed to him.

"Let her go!" I pleaded. "Let her go! It's all right! Go on!"

"Don't that other fellow want to get on too?" he asked curiously.

"No, no, no! Don't let him on!" I pleaded. "I arranged to stop this train! I'm from the *Republic!* He's nobody! He's no right on here!" But even as I spoke up came Galvin, breathless and perspiring, and crawled eagerly on, a leer of mingled triumph and joy at my discomfiture written all over his face. If I had had more courage I would have beaten him off. As it was, I merely groaned. To think that I should have done all this for him!

"Is that so?" he sneered. "You think you'll leave me behind, do you? Well, I fooled you this trip, didn't I?" and his lip curled.

I was beaten. It was an immensely painful moment for me, to lose when I had everything in my own hands. My spirits fell so for the moment that I did not even trouble to inquire whether the robber was on the train. I ambled in after my rival, who had proceeded on his eager way, satisfied that I should have to beat him in the quality of the interview.

CHAPTER XLVI

FOLLOWING Galvin forward through the train, I soon discovered the detectives and their prisoner in one of the forward cars. The prisoner was a most unpromising specimen for so unique a deed, short, broad-shouldered, heavy-limbed, with a squarish, unexpressive, dull face, blue-gray eyes, dark brown hair, big, lumpy, rough hands—just the hands one would expect to find on a railroad or baggage smasher—and a tanned and seamed skin. He had on the cheap nondescript clothes of a laborer; a blue hickory shirt, blackish-gray trousers, brown coat and a red bandanna handkerchief tied about his neck. On his head was a small round brown hat, pulled down over his eyes. He had the still, indifferent expression of a captive bird, and when I came up after Galvin and sat down he scarcely looked at me or at Galvin.

Between him and the car window, to foil any attempt at escape in that direction, and fastened to him by a pair of handcuffs, was the sheriff of the county in which he had been taken, a big, bland, inexperienced creature whose sense of his own importance was plainly enhanced by his task. Facing him was one of the detectives of the road or express company, a short, canny, vulture-like person, and opposite them, across the aisle, sat still another "detective." There may have been still others, but I failed to inquire. I was so incensed at the mere presence of Galvin and his cheap and coarse methods of ingratiating himself into any company, and especially one like this, that I could scarcely speak. "What!" I thought. "When the utmost finesse would be required to get the true inwardness of all this, to send a cheap pig like this to thrust himself forward and muddle what might otherwise prove a fine story! Why, if it hadn't been for me and my luck and my money, he wouldn't be here at all. And he was posing as a reporter—the best man of the *Globe!*"

He had the detective-politician-gambler's habit of simulating an intense interest and enthusiasm which he did not feel, his face wreathing itself into a cheery smile the while his eyes followed one like those of a basilisk, attempting all the while to discover whether his assumed friendship was being accepted at the value he wished.

"Gee, sport," he began familiarly in my presence, patting the burglar on the knee and fixing him with that basilisk gaze, "that was a great trick you pulled off. The papers'll be crazy to find out how you did it. My paper, the *Globe-Democrat*, wants a whole page of it. It wants your picture too. Did you really do it all alone? Gee! Well, that's what I call swell work, eh, Cap?" and now he turned his ingratiating leer on the county sheriff and the other detectives. In a moment or two more he was telling the latter what an intimate friend he was of "Billy" Desmond, the chief of detectives of St. Louis, and Mr. So-and-So, the chief of police, as well as various other detectives and policemen.

"The dull stuff!" I thought. "And this is what he considers place in this world! And he wants a whole page for the *Globe!* He'd do well if he wrote a paragraph alone!"

Still, to my intense chagrin, I could see that he was making headway, not only with the sheriff and the detectives but with the burglar himself. The latter smiled a raw, wry smile and looked at him as if he might possibly understand such a person. Galvin's good clothes, always looking like new, his bright yellow shoes, sparkling rings and pins and gaudy tie, seemed to impress them all. So this was the sort of thing these people liked—and they took him for a real newspaper man from a great newspaper!

Indeed the only time that I seemed to obtain the least grip on this situation or to impress myself on the minds of the prisoner and his captors, was when it came to those finer shades of questioning which concerned just why, for what ulterior reasons, he had attempted this deed alone; and then I noticed that my confrère was all ears and making copious notes. He knew enough to take from others what he could not work out for himself. In regard to the principal or general points, I found that my Irish-Jewish friend was as swift at ferreting out facts as any one, and as eager to know how and why. And always, to my astonishment and chagrin, the prisoner as well as the detectives paid more attention to him than to me. They turned to him as to a lamp and seemed to be immensely more impressed with him than with me, although the main lines of questioning fell to me. All at once I found him whispering to one or other of the detectives while I was developing some thought, but when I turned up anything new, or asked a question he had not thought of, he was all ears again and back to resume the questioning on his own account. In truth, he irritated me frightfully, and appeared to be intensely happy in doing so. My contemptuous looks and remarks did not disturb him in the least. By now I was so dour and enraged that I could think of but one thing that would have really satisfied me, and that was to attack him physically and give him a good beating—although I seriously questioned whether I could do that, he was so contentious, cynical and savage.

However the story was finally extracted, and a fine tale it made. It appeared that up to seven or eight months preceding the robbery, this robber had been first a freight brakeman or yard hand on this road, later being promoted to the position of superior switchman and assistant freight handler. Previous to this he had been a livery stable helper in the town in which he was eventually taken, and before that a farm hand in that neighborhood. About a year before the crime this road, along with many others, had laid off a large number of men, including himself, and reduced the wages of all others by as much as ten per cent. Naturally a great deal of labor discontent ensued. A number of train robberies, charged and traced to dismissed and dissatisfied ex-employees, now followed. The methods of successful train robbing were so clearly set forth by the newspapers that nearly any one so inclined could follow them. Among other things, while working as a freight handler, Lem Rollins had fieard of the many money shipments made by the express companies and the manner in which they were guarded. The Missouri Pacific, for which he worked, was a very popular route for money shipments, both West and East, bullion and bills being in transit all the while between St. Louis and the East, and Kansas City and the West, and although express messengers even at this time, owing to numerous train robberies which had been occurring in the West lately were always well armed, still these assaults had not been without success. The death of firemen, engineers, messengers, conductors and even passengers who ventured to protest, as well as the fact that much money had recently been stolen and never recovered, had not only encouraged the growth of banditry everywhere but had put such an unreasoning fear into most employees of the road as well as its passengers, who had no occasion for risking their lives in defense of the roads, that but few even of those especially picked guards ventured to give the marauders battle. I myself during the short time I had been in St. Louis had helped report three such robberies in its immdiate vicinity, in all of which cases the bandits had escaped unharmed.

But the motives which eventually resulted in the amazing single-handed attempt of this particular robber were not so much that he was a discharged and poor railroad hand unable to find any other form of employment as that in his idleness, having wandered back to his native region, he had fallen in love with a young girl. Here, being hard pressed for cash and unable to make her such presents as he desired, he had first begun to think seriously of some method of raising money, and later, another ex-railroad hand showing up and proposing to rob a train, he had at first rejected it as not feasible, not wishing to tie himself up in a crime, especially with others; still later, his condition becoming more pressing, he had begun to think of robbing a train on his own account.

Why alone—that was the point we were all most anxious to find out—singlehanded, and with all the odds against him? Neither Galvin nor myself could induce him to make this point clear, although, once I raised it, we were both most eager to solve it. "Didn't he know that he could not expect to overcome engineer and fireman, baggage-man and mail-man, to say nothing of the express messenger, the conductor and the passengers?"

Yes, he knew, only he had thought he could do it. Other bandits (so few as three in one case of which he had read) had held up large trains; why not one? Revolver shots fired about a train easily overawed all passengers, as well as the trainmen apparently. It was a life and death job either way, and it would be better for him if he worked it out alone instead of with others. Often, he said, other men "squealed" or they had girls who told on them. I looked at him, intensely interested and moved to admiration by the sheer animal courage of it all, the "gall," the grit, or what you will, imbedded somewhere in this stocky frame.

And how came he to fix on this particular train? I asked. Well, it was this way: Every Thursday and Friday a limited running west at midnight carried larger shipments of money than on other days. This was due to exchanges being made between Eastern and Western banks; but he did not know that. Having decided on one of these trains, he proceeded by degrees to secure first a small handbag, from which he had scraped all evidence of the maker's name, then later, from other distant places, so as to avoid all chance of detection, six or seven fused sticks of giant powder such as farmers use to blow up stumps, and still later, two revolvers holding six cartridges each, some cartridges, and cord and cloth out of which he proposed to make bundles of the money. Placing all this in his bag, he eventually visited a small town nearest the spot which, because of its loneliness, he had fixed on as the ideal place for his crime, and then, reconnoitering it and its possibilities, finally arranged all his plans to a nicety.

Here, as he now told us, just at the outskirts of this hamlet, stood a large water-tank at which this express as well as nearly all other trains stopped for water. Beyond it, about five miles, was a wood with a marsh somewhere in its depths, an ideal place to bury his booty quickly. The express was due at this tank at about one in the morning. The nearest town beyond the wood was all of five miles away, a mere hamlet like this one. His plan was to conceal himself near this tank and when the train stopped, and just before it started again, to slip in between the engine tender and the front baggage car, which was "blind" at both ends. Another arrangement, carefully executed beforehand, was to take his handbag (without the revolvers and sticks of giant powder, which he would carry), and place it along the track just opposite that point in the wood where he wished the train to stop. Here, once he had concealed himself between the engine and the baggage car, and the train having resumed its journey, he would keep watch until the headlight of the engine revealed this bag lying beside the track, when he would rise up and compel the engineer to stop the train. So far, so good.

However, as it turned out, two slight errors, one of forgetfulness and one of eyesight, caused him finally to lose the fruit of his plan. On the night in question, between eight and nine, he arrived on the scene of action and did as he had planned. He put the bag in place and boarded the train. However, on reaching the spot where he felt sure the bag should be, he could not see it. Realizing that he was where he wished to work he rose up, covered the two men in the cab, drove them before him to the rear of the engine, where under duress they were made to uncouple it, then conducted them to the express car door, where he presented them with a stick of giant powder and .ordered them to blow it open. This they did, the messenger within having first refused so to do. They were driven into the car and made to 'blow open the safe, throwing out the packages of bills and coin as he commanded. But during this time, realizing the danger of either trainmen or passengers climbing down from the cars in the rear and coming forward, he had fired a few shots toward the passenger coaches, calling to imaginary companions to keep watch there. At the same time, to throw the fear of death into the minds of both engineer and fireman, he pre tended to be calling to imaginary confrères on the other side of the train to "keep watch over there."

"Don't kill anybody unless you have to, boys," he had said, or "That'll be all right, Frank. Stay over there. Watch that side. I'll take care of these two." And then he would fire a few more shots.

Once the express car door and safe had been blown open and the money handed out, he had compelled the engineer and fireman to come down, recouple the engine, and pull away. Only after the train had safely disappeared did he venture to gather up the various packages, rolling them in his coat, since he had lost his bag, and with this over his shoulder he had staggered off into the night, eventually succeeding in concealing it in the swamp, and then making off for safety himself.

The two things which finally caused his discovery were, first, the loss of the bag, which, after concealing the money, he attempted to find but without success; and, second (and this he did not even know at the time), that in the bag which he had lost he had placed some time before and then forgotten apparently a small handkerchief containing the initials of his love in one corner. Why he might have wished to carry the handkerchief about with him was understandable enough, but why he should have put it into the bag and then forgot it was not clear, even to himself. From the detectives we now learned that the next day at noon the bag was found by other detectives and citizens just where he had placed it, and that the handkerchief had given them their first clue. The wood was searched, without success however, save that footprints were discovered in various places and measured. Again, experts meditating on the crime decided that, owing to the hard times and the laying-off and discharging of employees, some of these might have had a hand in it; and so in due time the whereabouts and movements of each and every one of those who had worked for the road were gone into. It was finally discovered that this particular ex-helper had returned to his native town and had been going with a certain girl, and was about to be married to her. Next, it was discovered that her initials corresponded to those on the handkerchief. Presto, Mr. Rollins was arrested, a search of his room made, and nearly all of the money recovered. Then, being "caught with the goods," he confessed, and here he was being hurried to St. Louis to be jailed and sentenced, while we harpies of the press and the law were gathered about him to make capital of his error.

The only thing that consoled me, however, as I rode toward St. Louis and tried to piece the details of his crime together, was that if I had failed to make it impossible for Galvin to get the story at all, still, when it came to the narration of it, I should unquestionably write a better story, for he would have to tell his story to some one else, while I should be able to write my own, putting in such touches as I chose. Only one detail remained to be arranged for, and that was the matter of a picture. Why neither Wandell nor myself, nor the editor of the *Globe*, had thought to include an artist on this expedition was more a fault of the time than anything else, illustrations for news stories being by no means as numerous as they are today, and the peripatetic photographer having not yet been invented. As we neared St. Louis Galvin began to see the import of this very clearly, and suddenly began to comment on it, saying he "guessed" we'd have to send to the Four Courts afterward and have one made. Suddenly his eyes filled with a shrewd cunning, and he turned to me and said:

"How would it be, old man, if we took him up to the *Globe* office and let the boys make a picture of him—your friends, Wood and McCord? Then both of us could get one right away. I'd say take him to the *Republic*, only the *Globe* is so much nearer, and we have that new flashlight machine, you know" (which was true, the *Republic* being very poorly equipped in this respect). He added a friendly aside to the effect that of course this depended on whether the prisoner and the officers in charge were willing.

"Not on your life," I replied suspiciously and resentfully, "not to the *Globe*, anyhow. If you want to bring him down

(*301*)

to the *Republic,* all right; we'll have them make pictures and you can have one."

"But why not the *Globe?*" he went on. "Wood and Mc-Cord are your friends more'n they are mine. Think of the difference in the distance. We want to save time, don't we? Here it is nearly six-thirty, and by the time we get down there and have a picture taken and I get back to the office it'll be half past seven or eight. It's all right for you, I suppose, because you can write faster, but look at me. I'd just as lief go down there as not, but what's the difference? Besides, the *Globe's* got a much better plant, and you know it. Either Wood or McCord'll make a fine picture, and when we explain to 'em how it is you'll be sure to get one, the same as us—just the same picture. Ain't that all right?"

"No it's not," I replied truculently, "and I won't do it, that's all. It's all right about Dick and Peter—I know what they'll do for me if the paper will let them, but I know the paper won't let them, and besides, you're not going to be able to claim in the morning that this man was brought to the *Globe* first. I know you. Don't begin to try to put anything over on me, because I won't stand for it, see? And if these people do it anyhow I'll make a kick at headquarters, that's all."

For a moment he appeared to be quieted by this and to decide to abandon his project, but later he took it up again, seemingly in the most conciliatory spirit in the world. At the same time, and from now on, he kept boring me with his eyes, a thing which I had never known him to do before. He was always too hang-dog in looking at me; but now of a sudden there was something bold and friendly as well as tolerant and cynical in his gaze.

"Aw, come on," he argued. He was amazingly aggressive. "What's the use being small about it? The *Globe's* nearer. Think what a fine picture it'll make. If you don't we'll have to go clear to the office and send an artist down to the jail. You can't take any good pictures down there tonight."

"Cut it," I replied. "I won't do it, that's all," but even as he talked a strange feeling of uncertainty or confusion began to creep over me. For the first time since knowing him, in spite of all my opposition of this afternoon and before, I found myself not quite hating him but feeling as though he weren't such an utterly bad sort after all. What was so wrong about this *Globe* idea anyhow, I began suddenly to ask myself, in the most insane and yet dreamy way imaginable. Why wouldn't it be all right to do that? Inwardly or downwardly, or somewhere within me, something was telling me that it was all wrong and that I was making a big mistake even to think about it. I felt half asleep or surrounded by clouds which made everything he said seem all right. Still, I wasn't asleep, and now I didn't believe a word he said, but——

"To the *Globe*, sure," I found myself saying to myself in spite of myself, in a dumb, half-numb way. "That wouldn't be so bad. It's nearer. What's wrong with that? Dick or Peter will make a good picture, and then I can take it along," only at the same time I was also thinking, "I shouldn't really do that. He'll claim the credit for having brought this man to the *Globe* office. I'll be making a big mistake. The *Republic* or nothing. Let him come down to the *Republic*."

In the meantime we were entering St. Louis and the station. By then, somehow, he had not only convinced the sheriff and the other officers, but the prisoner. They liked him and were willing to do what he said. I could even see the rural love of show and parade gleaming in the eyes of the sheriff and the two detectives. Plainly, the office of the *Globe* was the great place in their estimation for such an exhibition. At the same time, between looking at me and the prisoner and the officers, he had knitted a fine mental net from which I seemed unable to escape. Even as I rose with these others to leave the train I cried: "No, I won't come in on this! It's all right if you want to bring him down to the *Republic*, or you can take him to the Four Courts, but I'm not going to let you get away with this. You hear now, don't you?" But then it was too late.

Once outside, Galvin laid hold of my arm in an amazingly genial fashion and hung on it. In spite of me, he seemed to be master of the situation and to realize it. Once more he began to plead, and getting in front of me he seemed to do his best to keep my optical attention. From that point on and from that day to this, I have never been able to explain to myself what did happen. All at once, and much more clearly than before, I seemed to see that his plan in regard to the *Globe* was the best. It would save time, and besides, he kept repeating in an almost sing-song way that we would go first to the *Globe* and then to the *Republic*. "You come up with me to the *Globe*, and then I'll go down with you to the *Republic*," he kept saying. "We'll just let Wood or McCord take one picture, and then we'll all go down to your place—see?"

Although I didn't see I went. For the time, nothing seemed important. If he had stayed by me I think he could have prevented my writing any story at all. As it was he was so eager to achieve this splendid triumph of introducing the celebrated bandit into the editorial rooms of the *Globe* first and there having him photographed and introduced to my old chief, that he hailed a carriage, and, the six of us crowding into it, we were bustled off in a trice to the door of the *Globe*, where, once I reached it, and seeing him and the detectives and the bandit hurrying across the sidewalk, I suddenly awoke to the asininity of it all.

"Wait!" I called. "Say, hold on! Cut this! I won't do it! I don't agree to this!" but it was too late. In a trice the prisoner and the rest of them were up the two or three low steps of the main entrance and into the hall, and I was left outside to meditate on the insanity of the thing I had done.

"Great God!" I suddenly exclaimed to myself. "What have I let that fellow do to me? I've been hypnotized, that's what it is! I've allowed him to take a prisoner whom I had in my own hands at one time into the office of our great rival to be photographed! He's put it all over me on this job—and I had him beaten! I had him where I could have shoved him off the train—and now I let him do this to me, and tomorrow there'll be a long editorial in the *Globe* telling how this fellow was brought there first and photographed, and his picture to prove it!'' I swore and groaned for blocks as I walked towards the *Republic*, wondering what I should do.

Distinct as was my failure, it was so easy, even when practically admitting the whole truth, to make it seem as though the police had deliberately worked against the *Republic*. I did not even have to do that but merely recited my protests, without admitting or insisting upon hypnotism, which Wandell would not have believed anyhow. On the instant he burst into a great rage against the police department, seeing apparently no fault in anything I had done, and vowing vengeance. They were always doing this; they did it to the *Republic* when he was on the *Globe*. Wait—he would get even with them yet! Rushing a photographer to the jail, he had various pictures made, all of which appeared with my story, but to no purpose. The *Globe* had us beaten. Although I had slaved over the text, given it the finest turns I could, still there on the front page of the *Globe* was a large picture of the bandit, seated in the sanctum sanctorum of the great G-D, a portion of the figure, although not the head, of its great chief standing in the background, and over it all, in extra large type, the caption:

"LONE TRAIN ROBBER VISITS OFFICE OF GLOBE
TO PAY HIS RESPECTS"

and underneath in italics a full account of how he had willingly and gladly come there.

I suffered tortures, not only for days but for weeks and months, absolute tortures. Whenever I thought of Galvin I wanted to kill him. To think, I said to myself, that I had thought of the two trains and then run across the meadow and paid the agent for stopping the train, which permitted Galvin to see the burglar at all, and then to be done in this way! And, what was worse, he was so gayly and cynically conscious of having done me. When we met on the street one day, his lip curled with the old undying hatred and contempt.

"These swell reporters!" he sneered. "These high-priced

ink-slingers! Say, who got the best of the train robber story, eh?"

And I replied——

But never mind what I replied. No publisher would print it.

CHAPTER XLVII

THINGS like these taught me not to depend too utterly on my own skill. I might propose and believe, but there were things above my planning or powers, and creatures I might choose to despise were not so helpless after all. It fixed my thoughts permanently on the weakness of the human mind as a directing organ. One might think till doomsday in terms of human ideas, but apparently over and above ideas there were forces which superseded or controlled them. . . . My own fine contemptuous ideas might be superseded or set at naught by the raw animal or psychic force of a man like Galvin.

During the next few months a number of things happened which seemed to broaden my horizon considerably. For one thing, my trip to Chicago having revived interest in me in the minds of a number of newspaper men there, and having seemingly convinced them of my success here, I was bombarded with letters from one and another wanting to know whether or not they could obtain work here and whether I could and would aid them. At the close of the Fair in Chicago in October hard times were expected in newspaper circles there, so many men being released from work. I had letters from at least four, one of whom was a hanger-on by the name of Michaelson, of whom more anon, who had attached himself to me largely because I was the stronger and he expected aid of me. I have often thought how frequently this has happened to me—one of my typical experiences, as it is of every one who begins to get along. It is so much easier for the strong to tolerate the weak than the strong. Strength craves sycophancy. We want only those who will swing the censer before our ambitions and desires. Michaelson, or ''Mich,'' was a poor hack who had been connected with a commercial agency where daily reports had to be written out as to the financial and social condition of John Smith the butcher, or George Jones the baker. This led Mich, who was a farm-boy to begin with, to imagine that he could write and that he would like to run a country paper, only he thought to get some experience in the city first. By some process, of which I forget the steps, he fixed on me; and through myself and McEnnis, who was then so friendly to me, had secured a try-out on the *Globe* in Chicago. After I left McEnnis quickly tired of him, and I heard of him next as working for the City Press, an organization which served all newspapers, and paid next to nothing. Next I heard that he was married (having succeeded so well!), and still later he began to bombard me with pleas for aid in getting a place in St. Louis. Also there were letters from much better men: H. L. Dunlap, afterwards chief press advisor of President Taft; an excellent reporter by the name of Brady, whom I have previously mentioned; and a little later, John Maxwell.

Meanwhile, in spite of my great failure in connection with Galvin, my standing with Wandell seemed to rise rather than sink. Believe it or no, I became a privileged character about this institution or its city room, a singular thing in the news-paper profession. Because of specials I was constantly writ-ing for the Sunday paper, I was taken up by the sporting editor, who wanted my occasional help in his work; the drama-tic editor, who wanted my help on his dramatic page, asking me to see plays from time to time; and the managing editor himself, a small, courteous, soft-spoken, red-headed man from Kansas City, who began to invite me to lunch or dinner and talk to me as though I knew much (or ought to) about the world he represented. I was so unfitted for all this intellectu-ally, my hour of stability and feeling for organization and control having not yet arrived, that I scarcely knew how to manage it. I was nervous, shy, poorly spoken, at least in their presence, while inwardly I was blazing with ambition, vanity and self-confidence. I wanted nothing so much as to be alone with my own desires and labors even though I believed all the while that I did not and that I was lonely and neglected!

Unsophisticated as I really was, I began to see Wandell

as but a minor figure in this journalistic world, or but one of many, likely to be here and gone tomorrow, and I swaggered about, taking liberties which months before I should never have dreamed of taking. He talked to me too freely and showed me that he relied on my advice and judgment and admired my work. All out-of-town assignments of any importance were given to me. Occasionally at seven in the evening he would say that he would buy me a drink if I would wait a minute, a not very wise thing to do. Later, after completing one big assignment or another, I would stroll out of the office at, say, eight-thirty or nine without a word or a by-your-leave, and so respectful had he become that instead of calling me down in person he began writing me monitory letters, couched in the most diplomatic language but insisting that I abide by the rules which governed other reporters. But by now I had grown so in my own estimation that I smiled confidently, knowing very well that he would not fire me; my salary was too small. Besides, I knew that he really needed me or some one like me and I saw no immediate rival anywhere, one who would work as hard and for as little. Still I would reform for a time, or would plead that the managing or the dramatic editor had asked me to do thus and so.

"To hell with the managing editor!" he one day exclaimed in a rage. "This is my department. If he wants you to sit around with him let him come to me, or else you first see that you have my consent."

At the same time he remained most friendly and would sit and chat over proposed stories, getting my advice as to how to do them, and as one man after another left him or he wanted to enlarge his staff he would ask me if I knew any one who would make a satisfactory addition. Having had these appeals from Dunlap, Brady and several others still in Chicago, I named first Dunlap (because I felt so sure of his merit), and then these others. To my surprise, he had me write Dunlap to come to work, and when he came and made good, Wandell asked me to bring still others to him. This flattered me very much. I felt myself becoming a power. The result was that after a time five men, three from Chicago and two from other papers in St. Louis, were transferred to the staff of the *Republic* by reason of my recommendation, and that with full knowledge of the fact that I was the one to whom they owed their opportunity. You may imagine the airs which I assumed.

About this time still another thing occurred which lifted me still more in my own esteem. Strolling into the Southern Hotel one evening I chanced to see my old chief, McCullagh, sitting as was his custom near one of the pillars of the lobby reading his evening paper. It had always been such a pleasing and homelike thing in my days at the *Globe* to walk into the lobby around dinner time and see this great chief in his low shoes and white socks sitting and reading here as though he were in his own home. It took away a bit of the loneliness of the city for me for he appeared to have no other home than this and he was my chief. And now, for the first time since I had so ignominiously retired from the *Globe,* I saw him as before, smoking and reading. Hitherto I had carefully avoided this and every other place at such hours as I was likely to encounter him. But now I had grown so conceited that I was not quite so much afraid of him; he was still wonderful to me but I was beginning to feel that I had a future of my own and that I could achieve it, regardless perhaps of the error that had so pained me then. Still I felt to the full all that old allegiance, respect and affection which had dominated me while I was on the *Globe.* He was my big editor, my chief, and there was none other like him anywhere for me, and there never was afterward. Nearing the newsstand, for which I made at sight of him in the hope that I should escape unseen, I saw him get up and come forward, perhaps to secure a cigar or another paper. I flushed guiltily and looked wildly about for some place to hide. It was not to be.

"Good evening, Mr. McCullagh," I said politely as he neared me.

"How d' do?" he returned gutturally but with such an air of sociability as I had never noticed in him before. "How d' do? Well, you're still about, I see. You're on the *Republic,* I believe?"

"Yes, sir," I said. I was so pleased and flattered to think that he should trouble to talk to me at all or to indicate that he knew where I was that I could scarcely contain myself. I wanted to thank him, to apologize, to tell him how wonderful he was to me and what a fool I was in my own estimation, but I couldn't. My tongue was thick.

"You like it over there?"

"Yes, sir. Fairly well, sir." I was as humble in his presence as a jackie is before an officer. He seemed always so forceful and commanding.

"That little matter of those theaters," he began after a pause, turning and walking back to his chair, I following, "—Um! um! I don't think you understand quite how I felt about that. I was sorry to see you go. Um! um!" and he cleared his throat. "It was an unfortunate mistake all around. I want you to know that I did not blame you so much. Um! You might have been relieved of other work. I don't want to take you away from any other paper, but—um!—I want you to know that if you are ever free and want to come back you can. There is no prejudice in my mind against you."

I don't know of anything that ever moved me more. It was wonderful, thrilling. I could have cried from sheer delight. He, my chief, saying this to me! And after all those wretched hours! What a fool I was, I now thought, not to have gone to him personally then and asked his consideration. However, as I saw it, it was too late. Why change now and go back? But I was so excited that I could scarcely speak, and probably would not have known what to say if I had tried. I stood there, and finally blurted out:

"I'm very sorry, Mr. McCullagh. I didn't mean to do what I did. It was a mistake. I had that extra assignment and—"

"O-oh, that's all right—that's all right," he insisted gruffly and as if he wished to be done with it once and for all. "No harm done. I didn't mind that so much. But you needn't have left—that's what I wish you to understand. You could have stayed if you had wanted to."

As I viewed it afterward, my best opportunity for a secure position in St. Louis was here. If I had only known it, or.

knowing, had been quick to take advantage of it, I might have profited greatly. Mr. McCullagh's mood was plainly warm toward me; he probably looked upon me as a foolish and excitable but fairly capable boy whom it would have been his pleasure to assist in the world. He had brought me from Chicago; perhaps he wished me to remain under his eye. . . . Plainly, a word, and I could have returned, I am sure of it, perhaps never to leave. As it was, however, I was so nervous and excited that I took no advantage of it. Possibly he noticed my embarrassment and was pleased. At any rate, as I mumbled my thanks and gratitude for all he had done for me, saying that if I were doing things over I should try to do differently, he interrupted me with:

"Just a moment. It may be that you have some young friend whom you want to help to a position here in St. Louis. If you have, send him to me. I'll do anything I can for him. I'm always glad to do anything I can for young men."

I smiled and flushed and thanked him, but for the life of me I could think of nothing else to say. It was so strange, so tremendous, that this man should want to do anything for me after all the ridiculous things I had done under him that I could only hurry away, out of his sight. Once in the shielding darkness outside I felt better but sad. It seemed as if I had made a mistake, as if I should have asked him to take me back.

"Why, he as much as offered to!" I said to myself. "I can go back there any time I wish, or he'll give me a place for some one else—think of it! Then he doesn't consider me a fool, as I thought he did!"

For days thereafter I went about my work trying to decide whether I should resign from the *Republic* and return to him, only now I seemed so very important here, to myself at least, that it did not seem wise. Wasn't I getting along? Would returning to work under Mitchell be an advantage? I decided not. Also, that I had no real excuse for leaving the *Republic* at present; so I did nothing, waiting to be absolutely sure what I wanted to do. There was a feeling growing in me at this time that I really did not want to stay in

St. Louis at all, that perhaps it would be better for me if I should move on elsewhere. McEnnis, as I recalled, had cautioned me to that effect. Another newspaper man writing me from Chicago and asking for a place (a friend of Dunlap's, by the way), I recommended him and he was put to work on the *Globe-Democrat*. And so my reputation for influence in local newspaper affairs grew.

And in the meantime still other things had been happening to me which seemed to complicate my life here and make me almost a fixture in St. Louis. For one thing, worrying over the well-being of my two brothers, E—— and A——, who were still in Chicago, and wishing to do something to improve their condition, I thought that St. Louis would be as good a place for them as any in which to try their fortunes anew. Both had seemed rather unhappy in Chicago and since I was getting along here I felt that it would be only decent in me to give them a helping hand if I could. The blood-tie was rather strong in me then. I have always had a weakness for members of our family regardless of their deserts or mine or what I thought they had done to me. I had a comfortable floor with ample room for them if I chose to invite them, and I thought that my advice and aid and enthusiasm might help them to do better. There was in me then, and has remained (though in a fading form, I am sorry to say), a sort of home-longing (the German *Heimweh,* no doubt) which made me look back on everything in connection with our troubled lives with a sadness, an ache, a desire to remedy or repair if possible some of the ills and pains that had beset us all. We had not always been unhappy together; what family ever has been? We had quarreled over trivial things, but there had been many happy hours. And now we were separated, and these two brothers were not doing as well as I.

I say it in faint extenuation of all the many hard unkind things I have done in my time, that at the thought of the possible misery some of my brothers and sisters might be enduring, the lacks from which they might be hopelessly suffering, my throat often tightened and my heart ached. Life bears so hard on us all, on many so terribly. What, E——

or A—— longing for something and not being able to afford it! It hurt me far more than any lack of my own ever could. It never occurred to me that they might be wishing to help me; it was always I, hard up or otherwise, wishing that I might do something for them. And this longing in the face of no complaint on their part and no means on mine to translate it into anything much better than wishes and dreams made it all the more painful at times.

My plan was to bring them here and give them a little leisure to look about for some way to better themselves, and then—well, then I should not need to worry about them so much. With this in mind I wrote first to E—— and then A——, and the former, younger and more restless and always more attracted to me than any of the others, soon came on; while A—— required a little more time to think. However, in the course of time he too appeared, and then we three were installed in my rooms, the harboring of my brothers costing me five additional dollars. Here we kept bachelor's hall, gay enough while it lasted but more or less clouded over all the while by their need of finding work.

I had forgotten, or did not know, or the fact did not make a sufficiently sharp impression on me, that this was a panic year (1893) and that there were hundreds of thousands of men out of work, the country over. Indeed, trade was at a standstill, or nearly so. When I first went on the *Republic*, if I had only stopped to remember, many factories were closing down or slowing up, discharging men or issuing scrip of their own wherewith to pay them until times should be better, and some shops and stores were failing entirely. It had been my first experience of a panic and should have made a deep impression on me had I been of a practical turn, for one of my earliest assignments had been to visit some of the owners of factories and stores and shops and ask the cause of their decline and whether better times were in sight. Occasionally even then I read long editorials in the *Republic* or the *Globe* on the subject, yet I could take no interest in them. They were too heavy, as I thought. Yet I can remember the gloom hanging over streets and shops and how solemnly some of the manufacturers spoke of the crisis and the hard times yet in store. There were to be hard times for a year or more.

I recall one old man at this time, very prosy and stiff and conventional, "one of our best business men," who had had a large iron factory on the south side for fifty years and who now in his old age had to shut down for good. Being sent out to interview him, I found him after a long search in one of the silent wings of his empty foundry, walking about alone examining some machinery which also was still. I asked him what the trouble was and if he would resume work soon again.

"Just say that I'm done," he replied. "This panic has finished me. I could go on later, I suppose, but I'm too old to begin all over again. I haven't any money now, and that's all there is to it."

I left him meditating over some tool he was trying to adjust.

In the face of this imagine my gayly inviting my two brothers to this difficult scene and then expecting them to get along in some way, persuading them to throw up whatever places or positions they had in Chicago! Yet in so doing I satisfied an emotional or psychic longing to have them near me and to do something for them, and beyond that I did not think.

In fact it took me years and years to get one thing straight in my poor brain, and that was this: that aside from the economic or practical possibility of translating one's dreams into reality, the less one broods over them the better. Here I was now, earning the very inadequate stipend of eighteen dollars—or it may have been twenty or twenty-two, for I have a dim recollection of having been given at least one raise in pay—yet with no more practical sense than to undertake a burden which I could not possibly sustain. For despite my good intentions I had no surplus wherewith to sustain my brothers, assuming that their efforts proved even temporarily unavailing. All this dream of doing something for them was based on good will and a totally inadequate income. In consequence it could not but fail, as it did, seeing that St. Louis was far less commercially active than Chicago. It was not growing much and there was an older and much more European theory of apprenticeship and continuity in place and type of work than prevailed at that time in the windy city. Work was really very hard to get, especially in manufacturing and commercial lines, and in consequence my two brothers, after only a week or two of pleasuring, which was all I could afford, were compelled to hunt here and there, early and late, without finding anything to do. True, I tried to help them in one way and another with advice as to institutions, lines of work and the like, but to no end.

But before and after they came, how enthusiastically and no doubt falsely I painted the city of St. Louis, its large size, opportunities, beauties, etc., and once they were here I put myself to the task of showing them its charms; but to no avail. We went about together to restaurants, parks, theaters, outlying places. As long as it was new and they felt that there was some hope of finding work they were gay enough and interested and we spent a number of delightful hours together. But as time wore on and fading summer days proved that their dreams and mine were hopeless and they could do no better here than in Chicago if as well, their moods changed, as did mine. The burden of expense was considerable. While paying gayly enough for food and rent, and even laundry, for the three, I began to wonder whether I should be able to endure the strain much longer. Love them as I might in their absence, and happy as I was with them, still it was not possible for me to keep up this pace. I was depriving myself of bare necessities, and I think they saw it. I said nothing, of that I am positive, but after a month or six weeks of trial and failure they themselves saw the point and became unhappy over it. Our morning and evening hours, whenever I could see them in the evening, became less and less gay. Finally A——, with his usual eye for the sensible, announced that he was tired of searching here and was about to return to Chicago. He did not like St. Louis anyhow; it was a "hell of a place," a third-rate city. He was going back where he could get work. And E——, perhaps recalling past joys of which I knew nothing, said he was going also. And so once more I was alone.

Yet even this rough experience had no marked effect on me. It taught me little if anything in regard to the economic struggle. I know now that these two must have had a hard time replacing themselves in Chicago at that time, but the meaning of it did not get to me then. As for E——, some years later I persuaded him to join me in New York, where I managed to keep him by me that time until he became self-supporting.

CHAPTER XLVIII

BECAUSE Miss W—— lived some distance from the city and would remain there until her school season opened, I neglected to write to her; but once September had come and the day of her return was near I began to think of her and soon was as keenly interested as ever. Her simplicity and charm came back to me with great force, and I one day sat down and wrote her a brief letter recalling our Chicago days and asking her how long it would be before she would be returning to St. Louis. I was rather nervous now lest she should not answer.

In due time, however, a note came in which she told me that she expected to be at Florissant, about twenty or twenty-five miles out of St. Louis, by September fifteenth, when her school work would begin, and that she would be in St. Louis shortly afterward to visit an aunt and hoped to see me. There was something about the letter so simple, direct and yet artful that it touched me deeply. As I have said, I really knew nothing of the conditions which surrounded her, and yet from the time I received this letter I sensed something that appealed to me: a rurality and simplicity plus a certain artful daintiness—the power, I suppose, to pose under my glance and yet evade—which held me as in a vise. Beside her, all others seemed harder, bolder, or of coarser fiber.

It does not matter now but as I look back on it there seems to have been more of pure, exalted or frenetic romance in this thing (at first, and even a year or so afterward), than in any mating experience of which I have any recollection, with the possible exception of Alice. Unlike most of my other affairs, this (in the beginning at least) seemed more a matter of pure romance or poetry, a desire to see and be near her. Indeed I could only think of her as a part of some idyllic country scene, of walking or riding with her along some leafy country lane, of rowing a little boat on a stream, of sitting with her under trees in a hammock, of watching her play tennis, of being with her where grass, flowers, trees and a blue sky were. In that idyllic world of the Fair she had seemed well-placed. This must be a perfect love, I thought. Here was your truly sweet, pure girl who inspired a man with a nobler passion than mere lust. I began to picture myself with her in a home somewhere, possibly here in St. Louis, of going with her to church even, for I fancied she was of a strict religious bent, of pushing a baby carriage—indeed, of leading a thoroughly domestic life, and being happy in it!

We fell into a correspondence which swiftly took on a regular form and resulted, on my part, in a most extended correspondence, letters so long that they surprised even myself. I found myself in the grip of a letter-writing fever such as hitherto had never possessed me, writing long, personal, intimate accounts of my own affairs, my work, my dreams, what not, as well as what I thought of her, of the beauty of life as I had seen it with her in Chicago, my theories and imaginings in regard to everything. As I see it now, this was perhaps my first and easiest attempt at literary expression, the form being negligible and yet sufficient to encompass and embody without difficulty all the surging and seething emotions and ideas which had hitherto been locked up in me, bubbling and steaming to the explosion point. Indeed the newspaper forms to which I was daily compelled to confine myself offered no outlet, and in addition, in Miss W—— I had found a seemingly sympathetic and understanding soul, one which required and inspired all the best that was in me. I was now, as I told myself, on the verge of something wonderful, a new life. I must work, save, advance myself and better my condition generally, so as to be worthy of her. . . . At the very same time I was still able to see beauty in other women and the cloying delights of those who would never be able to be as good as she! They might be good enough for me but far beneath her whose eyes were "too pure to behold evil."

In the latter part of September she came to St. Louis and gave me my first delighted sight of her since we had left Chicago. At this time I was at the topmost toss of my adventures in St. Louis. I was, as I now assumed, somebody. By now also I had found a new room in the very heart of the city, on Broadway near the Southern, and was leading a bachelor existence under truly metropolitan circumstances. This room was on the third floor rear of a building which looked out over some nondescript music hall whose glass roof was just below and from whence nightly, and frequently in the afternoon, issued all sorts of garish music hall clatter, including music and singing and voices in monologue or dialogue. One block south were the Southern Hotel, Faust's Restaurant, and the Olympic Theater. In the block north were the courthouse and Dick's old room, which by now he had abandoned, having in spite of all his fine dreams of a resplendent heiress married a girl whom together we had met in the church some months before—a circus-rider! Thereafter he had removed to a prosaic flat on the south side, an institution which seemed to me but a crude and rather pathetic attempt at worthless domesticity.

I should like to report here that something over a year later this first marriage of his terminated in the death of his wife. Later—some two or three years—he indulged in a second most prosaic and inartistic romance—wedding finally, on this occasion, the daughter of a carpenter. And her name—Sopheronisby Boanerga Watkins. And a year or two after this she was burned to death by an exploding oil stove. And this was the man who was bent on capturing an heiress.

In my new room therefore, because it was more of a center, I had already managed to set up a kind of garret salon, which was patronized by Dick and Peter, Rodenberger, Dunlap, Brady and a number of other acquaintances. No sooner was I settled here than Michaelson, whose affairs I had straightened out by getting him a place on the *Republic,* put in an appearance, and also John Maxwell, who because of untoward conditions in Chicago had come to St. Louis to better his fortunes. But more of that later.

In spite of all these friends and labors and attempts at aiding others, it was my affair with Miss W—— which now completely engrossed me. So seriously had I taken this new adventure to heart that I was scarcely able to eat or sleep. Once I knew definitely that she was inclined to like me, as her letters proved, and the exact day of her arrival had been fixed, I walked on air. I had not been able to save much money since I had been on the *Republic* (possibly a hundred dollars all told, and that since my brothers had left), but of that I took forty or fifty and bought a new fall suit of a most pronounced if not startling pattern, the coat being extra long and of no known relation to any current style (an idea of my own), to say nothing of such extras as patent leather shoes, ties, collars, a new pearl-gray hat—all purchased in view of this expected visit for her especial delectation! Although I had little money for what I considered the essentials of courtship—theater boxes, dinners and suppers at the best restaurants, flowers, candy—still I hoped to make an impression. Why shouldn't I? Being a newspaper man and an ex-dramatic editor, to say nothing of my rather close friendship with the present *Republic* critic, I could easily obtain theater tickets, although the exigencies of my work often prevented, as I discovered afterward, my accompanying her for more than an hour at a time.

CHAPTER XLIX

ON the day of her arrival I arrayed myself in my best, armed myself with flowers, candy and two tickets for the theater, and made my way out to her aunt's in one of the simpler home streets in the west end. I was so fearful that my afternoon assignment should prove a barrier to my seeing her that day that I went to her as early as ten-thirty, intending to offer her the tickets and arrange to stop for her afterwards at the theater; or, failing that, to see her for a little while in the evening if my assignments permitted. I was so vain of my standing in her eyes, so anxious to make a good impression, that I was ashamed to confess that my reportorial duties made it difficult for me to see her at all. After my free days in Chicago I wanted her to think that I was more than a mere reporter, a sort of traveling correspondent and feature man, which in a way I was, only my superiors were determined to keep me for some reason in the ordinary reportorial class taking daily assignments as usual. Instead of confessing my difficulties I made a great show of freedom.

I found her in a small tree-shaded, cool-looking brick house, with a brick sidewalk before it and a space of grass on one side. Never did place seem more charming. I stared at it as one might at a shrine. Here at last was the temporary home of my beloved, and she was within!

I knocked, and an attractive slip of a girl (her niece, as I learned) answered. I was shown into a long, dustless, darkened parlor. After giving me time to weigh the taste and affluence of her relatives according to my standards, she arrived, the beloved, the beautiful. In view of many later sadder things, it seems that here at least I might attempt to do her full justice. She seemed exquisite to me then, a trim, agreeable sylph of a girl, with a lovely oval face, stark red hair braided and coiled after the fashion of a Greek head, a clear pink skin, long, narrow, almond-shaped, gray-blue eyes, delicate, graceful hands, a perfect figure, small well-formed feet. There was something of the wood or water nymph about her, a seeking in her eyes, a breath of wild winds in her hair, a scarlet glory to her mouth. And yet she was so obviously a simple and inexperienced country girl, caught firm and fast in American religious and puritanic traditions and with no hint in her mind of all the wild, mad ways of the world. Sometimes I have grieved that she ever met me, or that I so little understood myself as to have sought her out.

I first saw her, after this long time, framed in a white doorway, and she made a fascinating picture. Here, as in Chicago, she seemed shy, innocent, questioning, as one who might fly at the first sound. I gazed in admiration. Despite a certain something in her letters which had indirectly assured me of her affection or her desire for mine, still she held aloof, extending a cool hand and asking me to sit down, smiling tenderly and graciously. I felt odd, out of place, and yet wonderfully drawn to her, passionately interested. What followed by way of conversation I cannot remember now—talk of the Fair, I suppose, some of those we had known, her summer, mine. She took my roses and pinned some of them on, placing the rest in a jar. There was a piano here, and after a time she consented to play. In a moment, it seemed, it was twelve-thirty, and I had to go.

I walked on air. It seemed to me that I had never seen any one more beautiful—and I doubt now that I had. There was no reason to be applied to the thing: it was plain infatuation, a burning, consuming desire for her. If I had lost her then and there, or any time within a year thereafter, I should have deemed it the most amazing affair of my life.

I returned to the office and took some assignment, which I cut short at three-thirty in order to get back to the Grand Opera House to sit beside her. The play was an Irish love drama, with Chauncey Olcott, the singing comedian, in the title rôle. With her beside me I thought it perfect. Love! Ah, love! When the performance was ended I was ready to weep over the torturing beauty of life. Outside we found the matinée crowds, the carriages, the sense of autumn gayety and show in the air. A nearby ice-cream and candy store was crowded to suffocation. Young girls of the better families hummed like bees. Because of my poverty and uncertain station I felt depressed, at the same time pretending to a station which I felt to be most unreal. The mixture of ambition and uncertainty, pride, a gay coaxing in the air, added to the need to return to conventional toil—how these tortured me! Nothing surprises me now more than my driving emotions all through this period. I was as one possessed.

We parted at a street-car—when I wanted a carriage! We met at her aunt's home at eight-thirty, because I saw an opportunity of deliberately evading an assignment. In this simple parlor I dreamed the wildest, the most fantastic dreams. She was the be-all and the end-all of my existence. Now I must work for her, wait for her, succeed for her! Her mediocre piano technique seemed perfect, her voice ideal! Never was such beauty, such color. St. Louis took on a glamour which it had never before possessed. . . . If only this love affair could have gone on to a swift fruition it would have been perfect, blinding.

But all the formalities, traditions, beliefs, of a conventional and puritanic region were in the way. Love, as it is in most places, and despite its consuming blaze, was a slow process. There must be many such visits, I knew, before I could even place an arm about her. I was to be permitted to take her to church, to concerts, the theater, a restaurant occasionally, but nothing more.

The next morning I went to church with her; the next afternoon unavoidable work kept me from her, but that night I shirked and stayed with her until eleven. The next morning, since she had to catch an early train for Florissant, I slept late, but during the next two weeks (she could not come oftener, having to spend one Sunday with her "folks," as she referred to them) I poured forth my amazement and delight on reams of thin paper. I wonder now where they are. Once there was a trunk full.

Perhaps the most interesting effect of this sudden fierce passion was the heightened color it lent to everything. Never before had I realized quite so clearly the charm of life as life, its wondrous singing, its intense appeal. I remember witnessing a hanging about this time, standing beside the murderer when the trap was sprung, and being horrified, sickened to death, yet when I returned to the office and there was a letter from her—the world was perfect once more, no evil or pain in it! I followed up the horrors of a political catastrophe, in which a city treasurer shot himself to escape the law—but a letter from her, and the world was beautiful. A negro in an outlying county assaulted a girl, and I arrived in time to see him lynched, but walking in the wood afterward, away from the swinging body, I thought of her—and life contained not a single ill. Such is infatuation. If I had been alive before, now I was more than alive. I tingled all over with longing and aspiration—to be an editor, a publisher, a playwright—I know not what. The simple homes I had dreamed over before as representing all that was charming and soothing and shielding were now twice as attractive. Love, all its possibilities, paraded before my eyes, a gorgeous, fantastic procession. Love! Love! The charm of a home in which it would find its most appropriate setting! The brooding tenderness of it! Its healing force against the blows of ordinary life! To be married, to have your beloved with you, to have a charming home to which to return of an evening, or at any hour, sick or well! I was young, in good health and spirits. In a few years I should be neither so young nor so vital. Age would descend, cold, gray, thin, passionless. This glorious, glorious period of love, desire, would be gone, and then what? Ah, and then what! If I did not achieve now and soon all that I desired in the way of tenderness, fortune, beauty—now when I was young and could enjoy it—my chance would once and for all be over. I should be helpless. Youth would come no more! Love would come no more! But now—now—life was sounding, singing, urging, teasing; but also it was running away fast, and what was I doing about it? What could I do?

The five months which followed were a period of just such color and mood, the richest period of rank romanticism I have ever endured. At times I could laugh, at others sigh, over the incidents of this period, for there is as little happiness in love as there is out of it, at least in my case. If I had only known myself I might have seen, and that plainly, that it was not any of the charming conventional things which this girl represented but her charming physical self that I craved. The world, as I see it now, has trussed itself up too helplessly with too many strings of convention, religion, dogma. It has accepted too many rules, all calculated for the guidance of individuals in connection with the propagation and rearing of children, the conquest and development of this planet. This is all very well for those who are interested in that, but what of those who are not? Is it everybody's business to get married and accept all the dictates of conventional society—that is, bear and rear children according to a given social or religious theory? Cannot the world have too much of mere breeding? Are two billion wage slaves, for instance, more advantageous than one billion, or one billion more than five hundred million? Or is an unconquered planet less interesting than a conquered one? Isn't the mere *contact of love,* if it produces ideas, experiences, tragedies even, as important as raising a few hundred thousand coal miners, railroad hands or heroes destined to be eventually ground or shot in some contest with autocratic or capitalistic classes? And, furthermore, I am inclined to suspect that the monogamous standard to which the world has been tethered much too harshly for a thousand years or more now is entirely wrong. I do not believe that it is Nature's only or ultimate way of continuing or preserving itself. Nor am I inclined to accept the belief that it produces the highest type of citizen. The ancient world knew little of strict monogamy, and some countries today are still without it. Even in our religious or moralistic day we are beginning to see less and less of its strict enforcement. (Fifty thousand divorces in one State in one year is but a straw.) It is a product, I suspect, of intellectual lethargy or dullness, a mental incapacity for individuality. What

we have achieved is a vast ruthless machine for the propagation of people far beyond the world's need, even its capacity
to support decently. In special cases, where the strong find
themselves, we see more of secret polygamy and polyandry
than is suspected by the dull and the ignorant. Economic
opportunity, plus love or attraction, arranges all this, all the
churches, laws, disasters to the contrary notwithstanding.
Love or desire, where economic conditions permit, will and
does find a way.

Here I was dreaming of all the excellencies of which the
conventionalists prate in connection with home, peace, stability and the like, anxious to put my neck under that yoke,
when in reality what I really wanted, and the only thing
that my peculiarly erratic and individual disposition would
permit, was mental and personal freedom. I did not really
want any such conventional girl at all, and if I had clearly
understood what it all meant I might have been only too glad
to give her up. What I wanted was the joy of possessing her
without any of the hindrances or binding chains of convention and monogamy, but she would none of it. This unsatisfied desire, added to a huge world-sorrow over life itself, the
richness and promise of the visible scene, the sting and urge
of its beauty, the briefness of our days, the uncertainty of our
hopes, the smallness of our capacity to achieve or consume
where so much is, produced an intense ache and urge which
endured until I left St. Louis. I was so staggered by the
promise and the possibilities of life, at the same time growing
more and more doubtful of my capacity to achieve anything,
that I was falling into a profound sadness. Yet I was only
twenty-two, and between these thoughts would come intense
waves of do and dare: I was to be all that I fancied, achieve
all that I dreamed. As a contrast to all these thoughts, fan-
cies, and depressions, I indulged in a heavy military coat
of the most disturbing length, a wide-brimmed Stetson hat,
Southern style, gloves, a cane, soft pleated shirts—a most *outré*
equipment for all occasions including those on which I could
call upon her or take her to a theater or restaurant. I remember one Saturday morning, when I was on my way to see

my lady love and had stopped at the Olympic to secure two seats, meeting a dapper, rather flashy newspaper man. I had on the military coat, and the hat, a pair of bright yellow gloves, narrow-toed patent leather shoes, a ring, a pin, a suit brighter than his own, a cane, and I was carrying a bouquet of roses. I was about to take a street-car out to her place, not being prosperous enough to hire a carriage.

"Well, for —— sake, old man, what's up?" he called, seizing me by the arm. "You're not getting married, are you?"

"Aw, cut the comedy!" I replied, or words to that effect. "Can't a fellow put on any decent clothes in this town without exciting the natives? What's wrong?"

"Nothing, nothing," he replied apologetically. "You look swell. You got on more dog than ever I see a newspaper man around here pull. You must be getting along! How are things at the *Republic,* anyhow?"

We now conversed more affably. He touched the coat gingerly and with interest, felt of the quality of the cloth, looked me up and down, seemingly with admiration—more likely with amazement — shook his head approvingly and said: "Some class, I must say. You're right there, sport, with the raiment," and walked off.

It was in this style that I prosecuted my quest. For my ordinary day's labor I wore other clothes, but sometimes, when stealing a march on my city editor Saturday afternoons or Sundays or evenings, I had to perform a lightning change act in order to get into my finery, pay my visit, and still get back to the office between eleven and twelve, or before six-thirty, in my ordinary clothes. Sometimes I changed as many as three times in one afternoon or evening. My room being near here facilitated this. A little later, when I was more experienced, I aided myself to this speed by wearing all but the coat and hat, an array in which I never presumed to enter the office. Even my ultra impressive suit and my shoes, shirts and ties attracted attention.

"Gee whiz, Mr. Dreiser!" my pet office boy at the *Republic* once remarked to me as I entered in this array, "you certainly look as though you ought to own the paper! The boss don't look like you.''

Wandell, Williams, the sporting editor, the religious editor, the dramatic editor, all eyed me with evident curiosity. ''You certainly are laying it on thick these days,'' Williams genially remarked, beaming on me with his one eye.

As for my lady love—well, I reached the place where I could hold her hand, put my arms about her, kiss her, but never could I induce her to sit upon my lap. That was reserved for a much later date.

CHAPTER L

ALL love transports contain an element of the ridiculous, I presume, but to each how very important. I will pass mine over with what I have already said, save this: that each little variation in her costume, however slight, in her coiffure, or the way she looked or walked amid new surroundings, all seemed to re-emphasize the perfection that I had discovered and was so fortunate as to possess. She gave me her photograph, which I framed in silver and hung in my room. I begged for a lock of her hair, and finding a bit of blue ribbon that I knew belonged to her purloined that. She would not allow me to visit at Florissant, where she taught, being bashful about confessing this new relationship, but nevertheless, on several Sundays when she was at her home "up the State" I visited this glorious region, hallowed by her presence, and tried to decide for myself just where she lived and taught— her sacred rooms! A little later an exposition or State Fair was held in the enormous exposition building at Fourteenth and Olive streets, and here, when the Sousa concerts were first on, and later when the gay Veiled Prophets festivities began (a sort of Roman Harvest rejoicing, winding up with a great parade and ball), I saw more of her than ever before. It was during this time, in a letter, that she confessed that she loved me. Before this, however, seeing that I made no progress in any other way, being allowed no intimacy beyond an occasional stolen kiss, I had proposed to her and been accepted with a kind of morbid formalism. I had had to ask her in the most definite way and be formally accepted as her affianced husband. Thereafter I squandered my last cent to purchase a diamond ring at wholesale, secured through a friend on the *Globe*, and then indeed I felt myself set up in the world, as one who was destined to tread the conventional and peaceful ways of the majority.

Yet in spite of my profound infatuation I was still able to see beauty in other women and be moved by it. The chemical attractions and repulsions which draw us away from one and to another are beginning to be more clearly understood in these days and to undermine our more formal notions of stability and order, but even at that time this variation in myself might have taught me to look with suspicion on my own emotions. I think I did imagine that I was a scoundrel in harboring lusts after other women, when I was so deeply involved with this one, but I told myself that I must be peculiarly afflicted in this way, that all men were not so, that I myself should and probably would hold myself in check eventually, etc.; all of which merely proves how disjointed and non-self-understanding can be the processes of the human mind. Not only do we fail to see ourselves as others see us but we have not the faintest conception of ourselves as we really are.

An incident which might have proved to me how shallow was the depth of my supposed feeling, and that it was nothing more than a strong sex-desire, was this: One night about twelve a telephone message to the *Republic* stated that on a branch extension of one of the car lines, about seven or eight miles from the city, a murder had just been committed. Three negroes entering a lone "Owl" car, which ran from the city terminus to a small village had shot and killed the conductor and fired on the motorman. A young girl who had been on board, the only passenger, had escaped by the front door and had not since been heard of—or so the telephone message stated. As I happened to be in the office at the time, the story was assigned to me.

By good luck I managed to catch a twelve o'clock theater car and arrived at the end of the line at twelve-forty, where I learned that the body of the dead man had been transferred to his home at some point farther out, and that a posse of male residents of the region had already been organized and were now helping the police to search this country round for the negroes. When I asked about the girl who had been on board one of the men at the barn exclaimed: "Sure, she's a wonder! You want to tell about her. She hunted up a house, borrowed a horse, and notified everybody along the route. She's the one that first phoned the news.''

Here was a story indeed. Midnight, a murder, dark woods, lonely country. A girl flees from three murderous, drunken negroes, borrows a horse, and tells all the countryside. What more could a newspaper man want? I was all ears. Now if she were only good-looking!

I now realized that my first duty was not so much to see the body of the dead man and interview his wife, although that was an item not to be neglected, or the motorman who had escaped with his life, although he was here and told me all that had happened quite accurately, but this girl, this heroine, who, they said, was no more than seventeen or eighteen.

The car in which the murder had been committed was here in the barn. The blood-stains of the victim were still to be seen on the floor. I took this car, which was now carrying a group of detectives, a doctor and some other officials, to the dead man's house, or to the house of the girl, I forget which. When I arrived there I discovered that a large comfortable residence some little distance beyond the home of the dead man was the scene of all news and activity, for here it was that the body of the conductor had been carried, and from here the girl had taken a horse and ridden far and wide to call others to her aid. When I hurried up to the door she had returned and was holding a sort of levee. The large living-room was crowded, and in the center, under the flare of a hanging lamp, was this maiden, rather pretty, with her hair brushed straight back from her forehead, and her face alight with the intensity of her recent experiences and actions. I drew near and surveyed her over the shoulders of the others as she talked, finally getting close enough to engage her in direct conversation, as was my duty. She was very simple in manner and speech—not quite the dashing heroine I had imagined yet attractive enough. For my benefit, and possibly for the dozenth time, she narrated all that had befallen her from the time she boarded the car until she had leaped

(332)

from the front step after the shot and hid in the wood, finding her way to this house eventually and borrowing a horse to notify others, because, for one thing, there was no telephone here, and for another there was no man at home at the time who could have gone for her. With a kind of naïf enthusiasm she explained to me that once the shot had been fired and the conductor had fallen face down in the car (he had come in to rebuke these boisterous blacks, who were addressing bold remarks to her), she was cold with fright, but that after she had left the car she felt calmer and determined to do some· thing to aid in the capture of the murderers. Hiding behind bushes, she had seen the negroes dash out of the rear door of the car and run back along the track into the darkness, and had then hurried in the other direction, coming to this house and summoning aid. . . . It was a fine story, her ride in the darkness and how people rose to come out and help her. I made copious notes in my mind, took her name and address, visited the conductor's wife, who was a little distance away, and then hurried to the nearest telephone to communicate my news.

During this conversation with the girl I made an impression on her. As we talked I had drawn quite close and my enthusiasm for her deed had drawn forth various approving smiles and exclamations. When I took her address I said I should like to know more of her, and she smiled and said: "Well, you can see me any time tomorrow." This was Saturday night.

The *Republic* at this time had instituted what it called a "reward for heroism" medal to be given to whosoever should perform a truly heroic deed during the current year within the city or its immediate suburbs. Thinking over this girl's deed as I went along, and wondering how I should proceed in the matter of retaining her interest, I thought of this medal and asked myself why it should not be given to her. She was certainly worthy of it. Plainly she was a hero, riding thus in the darkness and in the face of such a crime—and good-looking too!—and eighteen! After I had reached the office and written a most glowing account of all this for the late edition, I decided to speak to Wandell the next day, and did. He fell in with the idea at once.

"A fine idea," he squeaked shrilly. "Bully—we'll do that! You'll have to go back, though, and see whether she'll accept it. Sometimes these people won't stand for all this notoriety stuff, you know. But if she does—— By the way," he asked quickly, "is she good-looking?"

"Sure," I replied enthusiastically. "She's very good-looking—a beauty, I think."

"Well, if that's the case all the better. She must be made to give you a picture. Don't let her crawl out of that, even if you have to bring her down here or take her to a photographer. If she accepts I'll order the medal tomorrow, and you can write the whole thing up. It'll make a fine Sunday feature, eh? Dreiser's girl hero! What!"

This medal idea was just the thing to take me back to her, the excuse I needed and one that ought to bring her close to me if anything could. For the time being, I had forgotten all about Miss W—— and her charms. She came into my mind, but it was so all-important for me to follow up this new interest—one that I could manage quite as well as not, along with the other. I dressed in my very best clothes the next morning, excluding the amazing coat, and sallied forth to find my heroine. After considerable difficulty I managed to place her in a very simple home on what had once been a farm. Her father, who opened the door, was a German of the most rigid and austere mien—a Lutheran, I think—her mother a simple and pleasant-looking fat *hausfrau*. In the garish noon light my heroine was neither so melodramatic nor so poignant as she had seemed the night before. There was something less alive and less delicate in her composition, mental and physical, and yet she was by no means dull. Perhaps she lacked the excitement and the crowd. She had a peculiar mouth, a little wide but sweet, and a most engaging smile. Incidentally, it now developed that she had a younger sister, darker, more graceful, almost more attractive than herself.

The two of them, as I soon found upon entering into conversation, offered that same problem in American life that so many children of foreign-born parents do. Although by no means poor, they were restless, if not unhappy, in their state. The old German father was one of those stern religionists and moralists who plainly had always held, or tried to hold, his two children in severest check. At the same time, as was obvious, this keen strident American life was calling to them as never had his fatherland to him. They were both intensely alive and eager for adventure. Never before, apparently, had they seen a reporter, never been so close to a really truly thrilling tragedy. And Gunda—that was my heroine's name—had actually been a part of it—how, she could now scarcely think. Her parents were not at all stirred by her triumph or the publicity that attached to it. In spite of the fact that her father owned this property and was sufficiently well-placed to maintain her in school or idleness (American style), she was already a clerk in one of the great stores of the city, and her sister was also preparing to go to work, having just left school.

I cannot tell how, but in a few moments we three were engaged in a most ardent conversation. There was an old fireplace in this house with some blazing wood in it, and before this we sat and laughed and chattered, while I explained just what was wanted. Their mother and father did not even remain in the room. I could see that the younger sister was for urging Gunda on to any gayety or flirtation, and was herself eager to share in one. It ended by my suggesting that they both come down to dinner with me some evening—a suggestion which they welcomed with enthusiasm but explained that it would have to be done under the rose. Their father was so old-fashioned that he would not allow them to take up with any one so swiftly, would not even allow them to have any beaux in the house. But they could meet me, and stay in town all night with friends. Gunda laughed, and the younger sister clapped her hands for joy.

I made a most solemn statement of what was wanted to the parents, secured two photographs of Gunda, and departed, having arranged to see them the following Wednesday at seven at one of the prominent corners of the city.

CHAPTER LI

CONCERNING these two girls and their odd, unsophisticated, daring point of view and love of life, I have always had the most confused feelings. They were crazy and starving for something different from what they knew. What had become of all the staid and dull sobriety of their parents in this queer American atmosphere? The old people had no interest in or patience with any such restlessness. As for their two girls, it would have been as easy to seduce one or both of them, in the happy, seeking mood in which they met me, as to step off a car. Plainly they liked me, both of them. My conquest was so easy that it detracted from the charm. The weaker sex, in youth at least, has to be sought to be worth while. I began to question whether .I should proceed in this matter as fast as they seemed to wish.

Now that they had made friends with me, I liked them both. When we met the following Wednesday evening, and I had taken them to a commonplace restaurant, I was a little puzzled to know what to do with them, rarely having a whole evening to myself. Finally I invited them to my room, wondering if they would come. It seemed a great adventure to me, most daring, but I could not quite make up my mind which of the two I preferred. Just the same they came with me, looking on the proceeding as a great and delicious adventure. As we came along Broadway in the dark after dinner they hung on my arms, laughing and jesting at what their parents would think, and when we went up the dimly lighted stair, an old, wide, squeaky flight, they chortled over the fun and mystery of it all. The room was nothing much—the same old books, hangings and other trifles—but it seemed to please them greatly. What pleased them most was the fact that one could go and come without attracting any attention. They browsed about at first, and I, never having been con-

(336)

fronted by just this situation before and being still backward, did little or nothing save discuss generalities. The one I had most favored (the heroine) was more retiring than the younger, less feverish but still gay. I could only be with them from seven to ten-thirty, but they intimated that they would come again when they could stay as late as I chose. The suggestion was too obvious and I lost interest. Soon I told them I had to go back to the office and took them to a car. A few days later I took the medal to Gunda at the store, where she received it with much pleasure, asking where I had been and when she was to see me again. I made an appointment for another day, which I never kept. It meant, as I reasoned it out, that I should have to go further with her and her sister, but not being sufficiently impelled or courageous I dropped the whole matter. Then, because Miss W—— now seemed more significant than ever, I returned to her with a fuller devotion than ever before.

Owing to a driving desire to get on, to do something, to be more than I was and have all the pleasures I craved at once, there now set in a period of mental dissatisfaction and unrest which eventually took me out of St. Louis and the West, and resulted in a period of stress and distress. Sometimes I really believe that certain lives are predestined to undergo a given group of experiences, else why the unconscionable urge to move and be away which drives some people like the cuts of a lash? Aside from the question of salary, there was, as I see it now, little reason for the fierce and gnawing pains that assailed me, and toward the last even this question of salary was not a factor; for my employers, learning that I was about to leave, were quick enough to offer me more money as well as definite advancement. By then, however, my self-dissatisfaction had become so great that nothing short of a larger salary and higher position than they could afford to give me would have detained me. Toward the last I seemed to be obsessed by the idea of leaving St. Louis and going East. New York—or, at least other cities east of this one, seemed to call me far more than anything the West had to offer.

And now, curiously, various things seemed to combine to drive or lure me forth, things as clear in retrospect as they were indistinguishable and meaningless then. One of these forces, aside from that of being worthy of my new love and lifting her to some high estate which then possessed me, was John Maxwell who had done me such an inestimable service in Chicago when I was trying to break into the newspaper business, and who had now arrived on the scene with the hope of connecting with St. Louis journalism. Fat, cynical, Cyclopean John! Was ever a more Nietzschean mind in a more amiable body! His doctrine of ruthless progress, as I now clearly saw, was so tall and strident, whereas his personal modus operandi was so compellingly genial, human, sympathetic. He was forever talking about burning, slaying, shoving people out of one's path, doing the best thing by oneself and the like, while at the same time actually extending a helping hand to almost everybody and doing as little to advantage himself personally as any man I ever knew. It was all theory, plus an inherent desire to expound. His literary admirations were of a turgidly sentimental or romantic character, as, for instance, Jean Valjean of *Les Misérables,* and the good bishop; *Père Goriot, Camille,* poor Smike in *Nicholas Nickleby;* and, of all things, and yet quite like him in judgment, the various novels of Hall Caine (*The Bondman, The Christian, The Deemster*).

"My boy!" he used to say to me, with a fat and yet wholly impressive vehemence that I could not help admiring whether I agreed with him or not, "that character of Jean Valjean is one of the greatest in the world—a masterpiece—and I'll tell you why—" and he would then begin to enlarge upon the moral beauty of Valjean carrying the wounded Marius through the sewer, his taking up and caring for the poor degraded mother, abandoned by the students of Paris, his gentle and forgiving attitude toward all poverty and crime.

The amusing thing about all this was, of course, that in the next breath he would reiterate that all men were dogs and thieves, that in all cases one had to press one's advantage to the limit and trust nobody, that one must burn, cut,

(*338*)

slay, if one wished to succeed. Once I said to him, still under the delusion that the world might well be full of tenderness, charity, honesty and the like: "John, you don't really believe all that. You're not as hard as you say."

"The hell I'm not! The trouble with you is that you don't know me. You're just a cub yet, Theodore," and his face wore that adorable, fat, cynical smirk, "full of college notions of virtue and charity, and all that guff. You think that because I helped you a little in Chicago all men are honest, kind, and true. Well, you'll have to stow that pretty soon. You're getting along now, and whatever you think other people ought to do you'll find it won't be very convenient to do it yourself—see?" And he smirked angelically once more. To me, in spite of what he said, he seemed anything but hard or mean.

Being in hard lines, he had come to St. Louis, not at my suggestion but at that of Dunlap and Brady, both of whom no doubt assured him that I could secure him a position instanter. I began to think what if anything I could do to help him, but so overawed was I still by his personality that I felt that nothing would do for him less than a place as copy-reader or assistant city editor—and that was a very difficult matter indeed, really beyond my local influence. I was too young and too inexperienced to recommend anybody for such a place, although my Chicago friends had come to imagine that I could do anything here. I had the foolish notion that John would speak to me about it, but so sensitive was he, I presume, on the subject of what was due from me to him that he thought (I am merely guessing) that I should bestir myself without any direct word. He had been here for days, I later learned, without even coming near me. He had gone to a hotel, and in a few days sent word by Dunlap, with whom he was now on the most intimate terms, that he was in town and looking for a place. I assume now that it was but the part of decency for me to have hurried to call on him, but so different was my position now and so hurried was I with a number of things that I never even thought of doing it at once. I fancied that he would come to the office with Dunlap, or that a day or two would make no difference. At the end of the second day after Dunlap spoke to me of his being here the latter said: "Don't you want to come along with me and see John?"

I was delighted at the invitation and that same evening followed Dunlap to John's hotel room. It was a curious meeting, full of an odd diffidence on my part and I know not what on his. From others he had gathered the idea that I was successful here and therefore in a position to be uppish, whereas I was really in a most humble and affectionate frame of mind toward him. He met me with a most cynical, leering expression, which by no means put me at ease. He seemed at once reproachful, antagonistic and contemptuous.

"Well," he began at once, "I hear you're making a big hit down here, Theodore. Everything's coming your way now, eh?"

"Oh, not so good as that, John," I said. "I don't think I've done so wonderfully well. I hear you want to stay here; have you found anything yet?"

"Not a thing," he smiled. "I haven't been trying very hard, I guess."

I told him what I knew of St. Louis, how things went generally, and offered to give him letters or personal introductions to McCullagh, a managing editor on the *Chronicle,* to Wandell, and several others. He thanked me, and then I invited him to come and live in my room, which he declined at the time, taking instead a room next door to mine on the same floor—largely because it was inexpensive and central and not, I am sure, because it was near me. Here he stayed nearly a month, during which time he doubtless made efforts to find something to do, which I also did. Suddenly he was gone, and a little later, and much to my astonishment, Dunlap informed me that he had concluded that I had been instrumental in keeping him from obtaining work here! This he had deduced not so much from anything he knew or had heard, but by some amazing process of reversal; since I was much beholden to him and in a position to assist him, I, by some perversion of nature, would resent his coming and would do everything in my power to keep him out!

No event in my life ever gave me a queerer sense of being misunderstood and defeated. Of all the people I knew, I would rather have aided Maxwell than any one else. Because I felt so sure that I could not recommend him for anything good enough for him, I felt ashamed to try. I did the little I could, but after a while he left without bidding me good-by.

But before he went there were many gatherings in his room or mine, and always he assumed the same condescending and bantering tone toward me that he had used in Chicago, which made me feel as though he thought my present standing a little too good for me. And yet at times, in his more cheerful moods, he seemed the same old John, tender, ranting, filled with a sincere desire for the welfare of any untutored beginner, and only so restless and irritable now because he was meshed in financial difficulties.

At that, he attempted to do me one more service, which, although I did not resent it very much, I completely misunderstood. This was in regard to Miss W——, whose photograph he now saw and whose relation to me he gathered to be serious, although what he said related more to my whole future than to her. One day he walked into my room and saw the picture of my love hanging on the wall. He paused first to examine it.

"Who's this?" he inquired curiously.

I can see him yet, without coat or waistcoat, suspenders down, his fat stomach pulled in tightly by the waistband of his trousers, his fat face pink with health, his hair tousled on his fine round head.

"That's the girl I'm engaged to," I announced proudly. "I'm going to marry her one of these days when I get on my feet." Then, lover-like, I began to expatiate on her charms, while he continued to study the photograph.

"Have you any idea how old she is?" he queried, looking up with that queer, cynical, unbelieving look of his.

"Oh, about my age."

"Oh hell!" he said roughly. "She's older than that. She's five or six years older than you. What do you want to get married for anyhow? You're just a kid yet. Everything's before you. You're only now getting a start. Now you want to go and tie yourself up so you can't move!''

He ambled over to the window and stared out. Then he sank comfortably into one of my chairs, while I uttered some fine romantic bosh about love, a home, not wanting to wander around the world all my days alone. As I talked he contemplated me with one of those audacious smirky leers of his, as irritating and disconcerting an expression as I have seen on any face.

''Oh hell, Theodore!'' he remarked finally, as if to sweep away all I had said. Then after a time he added, as if addressing the world in general: ''If there's a bigger damn fool than a young newspaper man in or out of love, let me know. Here you are, just twenty-one, just starting out. You come down here from Chicago and get a little start, and the first thing you want to do is to load yourself up with a wife, and in a year or so two or three kids. Now I know damned well,'' he went on, no doubt noting the look of easy toleration on my part, ''that what I'm going to say won't make you like me any better, but I'm going to say it anyhow. You're like all these young newspaper scouts: the moment you get a start you think you know it all. Well, Theodore, you've got a long time to live and a lot of things to learn. I had something to do with getting you into this game, and that's the only reason I'm talking to you now. I'd like to see you go on and not make a mistake. In the first place you're too young to get married, and in the second, as I said before, that girl is five years older than you if she's a day. I think she's older,'' and he went over and re-examined the picture, while I spluttered, insisting that he was crazy, that she was no more than two years older if so much. ''Along with this,'' he went on, completely ignoring my remarks, ''she's one of these middle-West girls, all right for life out here but no good for the newspaper game or you. I've been through all that myself. Just remember, my boy, that I'm ten years older than you. She belongs to some church, I suppose?''

''Methodist,'' I replied ruefully.

''I knew it! But I'm not knocking her; I'm not saying

that she isn't pretty and virtuous, but I do say that she's older than you, and narrow. Why, man, you don't know your own mind yet. You don't know where you'll want to go or what you'll want to do. In ten years from now you'll be thirty-two, and she'll be thirty-seven or more, believing and feeling things that will make you tired. You'll never agree with her—or if you do, so much the worse for you. What she wants is a home and children and a steady provider, and what you really want is freedom to go and do as you please, only you don't know it.

"Now I've watched you, Theodore, and I hear what people down here say about you, and I think you have something ahead of you if you don't make a fool of yourself. But if you marry now—and a conventional and narrow woman at that, one older than you—you're gone. She'll cause you endless trouble. In three or four years you'll have children, and you'll get a worried, irritated point of view. Take my advice. Run with girls if you want to, but don't marry. Now I've said my say, and you can do as you damned please."

He smirked genially and condescendingly once more, and I felt very much impressed and put down. After all, I feared, in spite of my slushy mood, that what he said was true, that it would be best for me to devote myself solely to work and study and let women alone. But also I knew that I couldn't.

The next time my beloved came to the city I decided to sound her on the likelihood of my changing, differing. We were walking along a leaf-strewn street, the red, brown, yellow and green leaves thick on the brick walk, of a gray November afternoon.

"And what would you do then?" I asked, referring to my fear of changing, not caring for her any longer.

She meditated for a while, kicking the leaves and staring at the ground without looking up. Finally she surveyed me with clear appealing blue-gray eyes.

"But you won't," she said. "Let's not think of anything like that any more. We won't, will we?"

Her tone was so tender and appealing that it moved me tremendously. She had this power over me, and retained it for years, of appealing to my deepest emotions. I felt so sorry for her—for life—even then. It was as if all that Maxwell had said was really true. She was different, older; she might never understand me. But this craving for her—what to do about that? All love, the fiercest passions, might cool and die out, but how did that help me then? In the long future before me should I not regret having given her up, never to have carried to fruition this delicious fever? I thought so.

For weeks thereafter my thoughts were colored by the truth of all John had said. She would never give herself to me without marriage, and here I was, lonely and financially unable to take her, and spiritually unable to justify my marriage to her even if I were. The tangle of life, its unfairness and indifference to the moods and longings of any individual, swept over me once more, weighing me down far beyond the power of expression. I felt like one condemned to carry a cross, and very unwilling and unhappy in doing it. The delirious painful meetings went on and on. I suffered untold tortures from my desires and my dreams. And they were destined never to be fulfilled. . . . Glorious fruit that hangs upon the vine too long, and then decays!

Another thing that happened at this time and made a great impression, tending more firmly than even Maxwell's remarks to alter my point of view and make me feel that I must leave St. Louis and go on, was the arrival in the city of my brother Paul, who, as the star of a claptrap melodrama entitled "The Danger Signal," now put in an appearance. He was one of my four brothers now out in the world making their own way and of them all by far the most successful. I had not seen him since my newspaper days in Chicago two years before. He was then in another play, "The Tin Soldier," by the reigning farceur, Hoyt. *His* had not been the leading rôle at that time, but somehow his skill as a comedian had pushed him into that rôle. Previously he had leading parts in such middle-class plays as "A Midnight Bell," "The Two Johns" and other things of that sort, as well as being an end man in several famous minstrel shows.

Now in this late November or early December, walking along South Sixth Street in the region of the old Havlin Theater, where all the standard melodramas of the time played, I was startled to see his face and name staring at me from a billboard. "Ah," I thought, "my famous brother! Now these people will know whether our family amounts to anything or not! Wait'll they hear he is my brother!"

His picture on the billboard recalled so many pleasant memories of him, his visits home, his kindness to and intense love for my mother, how in my tenth year he had talked of my being a writer (Heaven only knows why), and how once on one of his visits home, when I was fourteen, he had set me to the task of composing a humorous essay which he felt sure I could write! Willingly and singingly I essayed it, but when I chose the ancient topic of the mule and its tendency to kick his face fell, and he tried to show me in the gentlest way possible how hackneyed that was and to put me on the track of doing something original. . . . Now after all this time, and scarcely knowing whether or not he knew I was here, I was to see him once more, to make clear to him my worldly improvement. I do not say it to boast, but I honestly think there was more joy in the mere thought of seeing him again than there was in showing him off and getting a little personal credit because of his success.

CHAPTER LII

As I look back upon my life now I realize clearly that of all the members of our family subsequent to my mother's death, the only one who, without quite understanding me, still sympathized with my intellectual and artistic point of view—and that most helpfully and at times practically—was my brother Paul. Despite the fact that all my other brothers were much better able intellectually than he to appreciate the kind of thing I was tending toward mentally, his was the sympathy that buoyed me up. I do not think he understood, even in later years (long after I had written *Sister Carrie*, for instance), what I was driving at. His world was that of the popular song, the middle-class actor or comedian, the middle-class comedy, and such humorous esthetes of the writing world as Bill Nye, Petroleum V. Nasby, and the authors of the *Spoopendyke Papers* and *Samantha at Saratoga*. As far as I could make out—and I say this in no lofty, condescending spirit—he was full of simple middle-class romance, middle-class humor, middle-class tenderness, and middle-class grossness—all of which I am very free to say I admire. After all, we cannot all be artists, statesmen, generals, thieves or financiers. Some of us, the large majority, have to be just plain everyday middle-class, and a very comfortable state it is under any decent form of government.

But there is so very much more to be said of him, things which persistently lift him in my memory to a height far more appealing and important than hundreds of greater and surer fame. For my brother was a humorist of so tender and delicate a mold that to speak of him as a mere middle-class artist or middle-class thinker and composer, would be to do him a gross injustice and miss the entire significance and flavor of his being. His tenderness and sympathy, a very human appreciation of the weakness and errors as well as the toils and tribulations of most of us, was his most outstanding and engaging quality and gave him a very definite force and charm. Admitting that he had an intense, possibly an undue fondness for women (I have never been able to discover just where the dividing line is to be drawn in such matters), a frivolous, childish, horse-play sense of humor at times, still he had other qualities that were positively adorable. That sunny disposition, that vigorous, stout body and nimble mind, those smiling sweet blue eyes, that air of gayety and well-being that was with him nearly all the time, even at the most trying times! Life seemed to bubble in him. Hope sprang upward like a fountain. You felt in him a capacity to do (in his limited field), an ability to achieve, whether he was succeeding at the moment or not. Never having the least power to interpret anything in a high musical way, still he was always full of music of a tender, sometimes sad, sometimes gay kind, the ballad-maker of a nation. For myself, I was always fascinated by this skill of his, the lovable art that attempts to interpret sorrow and pleasure in terms of song, however humble. And on the stage, how, in a crude way, by mere smile and gesture, he could make an audience laugh! I have seen houses crowded to the ceiling with middle- or lower-class people, shop girls and boys, factory hands and the like, who tittered continuously at his every move. He seemed to radiate a kind of comforting sunshine and humor without a sharp edge or sting (satire was entirely beyond him), a kind of wilding asininity, your true clown in cap and bells, which caused even my morbid soul to chortle by the hour. Already he was a composer of a certain type of melodramatic and tearful yet land-sweeping songs (*The Letter That Never Came, The Pardon Came Too Late, I Believe It for My Mother Told Me So, The Bowery*). (Let those who wish to know him better read of him in *Twelve Men: My Brother Paul.*)

Well, this was my brother Paul, the same whom I have described as stout, gross, sensual, and all of these qualities went hand-in-hand. I have no time here for more than the briefest glimpse, the faintest echo. I should like to write a book about him—the wonderful, the tender! But now he was coming to St. Louis, and in my youthful, vainglorious way I was determined to show him what I was. He should be introduced to Peter, Dick and Rodenberger, my cronies. I would have a feast in my room after the theater in his honor. I would give another, a supper at Faust's, then the leading restaurant of St. Louis, of a gay Bohemian character, and invite Wandell, Dunlap, my managing editor (I can never think of his name), Bassford, the dramatic editor, and Peter, Dick and Rodenberger. I proposed to bring my love to his theater some afternoon or evening and introduce him to her.

I hurried to the office of the *Globe* to find Dick and Peter and tell them my news and plans. They were very much for whatever it was I wanted to do, and eager to meet Paul of course. Also, within the next twenty-four hours I had written to Miss W——, and told Wandell, Bassford, the managing editor and nearly everybody else. I dropped in at Faust's to get an estimate on the kind of dinner I thought he would like, having the head-waiter plan it for me, and then eagerly awaited his arrival.

Sunday morning came, and I called at the theater at about eleven, and found him on the stage of this old theater entirely surrounded by trunks and scenery. There was with him at the moment a very petite actress, the female star of the company, who, as I later learned, was one of his passing flames. He was stout as ever, and dressed in the most engaging Broadway fashion: a suit of good cloth and smart cut, a fur coat, a high hat and a gold-headed cane—in short, all the earmarks of prosperity and comfort. What a wonderful thing he and this stage world, even this world of claptrap melodrama, seemed to me at the time. I felt on the instant somehow as though I were better established in the world than I thought, to be thus connected with one who traveled all over the country. The whole world seemed to come closer because of him.

"Hello!" he called, plainly astonished. "Where'd you come from?" and then seeing that I was better dressed and poised mentally than he had ever known me, he looked me over in an odd, slightly doubting way, as a stranger might, and then introduced me to his friend. Seeing him apparently pleased by my arrival and eager to talk with me, she quickly excused herself, saying she had to go on to her hotel; then he fell to asking me questions as to how I came to be here, how I was getting along. I am sure he was slightly puzzled and possibly disturbed by my sharp change from a shy, retiring boy to one who examined him with the chill and weighing eye of the newspaper man. To me, all of a sudden, he was not merely one whom I had to like because he was my brother or one who knew more about life than I—rather less, I now thought, quickly gathering his intellectual import, but because of his character solely. I might like or dislike that as I chose. He reminded me now a great deal of my mother, and I could not help recalling how loving and generous he had always been with her. Instantly he appealed to me as the simple, home-loving mother-boy that he was. It brought him so close to me that I was definitely and tenderly drawn to him. I could feel how fine and generous he really was. Even then although I doubt very much whether he liked me at first, finding me so brash and self-sufficient, still, so simple and communistic were the laws by which his charming mind worked, he at once accepted me as a part of the family and so of himself, a brother, one of mother's boys. How often have I heard him say in regard to some immediate relative concerning whom an acrimonious debate might be going forward, "After all, he's your brother, isn't he?" or "She's your sister," as though mere consanguinity should dissolve all dissatisfactions and rages! Isn't there something humanly sweet about that, in the face of all the cold, decisive conclusions of this world?

CHAPTER LIII

WELL, such was my brother Paul and now he was here. Never before was he so much my dear brother as now. So generally admirable was 'he that I should have liked him quite as much had he been no relative. After a few moments of explanation as to my present state I offered to share my room with him for the period of his stay, but he declined. Then I offered to take him to lunch, but he was too hurried or engaged. He agreed to come to my room after the show, however, and offered me a box for myself and my new friends. So much faith did I have in the good sense of Peter, Dick and Rodenberger, their certainty of appreciating the charm of a man like Paul, that I brought them to the theater this same night, although I knew the show itself must be a mess. There was a scenic engine in this show, with a heroine lying across the rails! My dear brother was a comic switchman or engineer in this act, evoking roars of low-brow laughter by his antics and jokes.

I shall never forget how my three friends took all this. Now that he was actually here they were good enough to take him into their affectionate consideration on my account, almost as though he belonged to them. He was "Dreiser's brother Paul," even "Dear old Paul" afterwards. Because working conditions favored us that night we all three descended on the Havlin together, sitting in the box while the show was in progress but spending all the intermissions in Paul's dressingroom or on the back of the stage. Having overcome his first surprise and possibly dislike of my brash newspaper manner, he was now all smiles and plainly delighted with my friends, Rodenberger and Peter, especially the latter, appealing to him as characters not unlike himself, individuals whom he could understand. And in later years, when I was in New York, he was always asking after them and singing their praises. Dick also came in for a share of his warm affection, but in a slower way. He thought Dick amusing but queer, like a strange animal of some kind. On subsequent tours which took him to St. Louis he was always in touch with these three. Above all things, the waggish grotesqueries of McCord's mind moved him immensely. Peter's incisive personality and daring unconventionality seemed to fascinate Paul. "Wonderful boy, that," he used to say to me, almost as though he were confiding a deep secret. "You'll hear from him yet, mark my word. You can't lose a kid like that." And time proved quite plainly that he was right.

During the play Paul sang one of his own compositions, *The Bowery*. It was an exceptional comic song, quite destructive of the good name of the Bowery forever, so much so that ten years later the merchants and property owners of that famous thoroughfare petitioned to have the name of the street changed, on the ground that the jibes involved in the song had destroyed its character as an honest business street forever. So much for the import of a silly ballad, and the passing song-writer. What are the really powerful things in this world anyhow?

After the show we all adjourned to some scowsy music hall in the vicinity of this old theater, which Dick insisted by reason of its very wretchedness would amuse Paul, although I am sure it did not (he was never a satirist). And thence to my room, where I had the man who provided the midnight lunch for the workers at the *Globe* spread a small feast. I had no piano, but Paul sang, and Peter gave an imitation of a street player who could manipulate at one and the same time a drum, mouth-organ and accordion. We had to beat my good brother on the back to keep him from choking.

But it was during a week of breakfasts together that the first impressive conversations in regard to New York occurred, conversations that finally imbued me with the feeling that I should never be quite satisfied until I had reached there. Whether this was due to the fact that I now told him about my present state and ambitions or dreams and my somewhat remarkable success here, or that he was now coming to the place where he was able to suggest ways and means and at the same time indulge the somewhat paternalistic streak in himself, I do not know, but during the week he persisted in the most florid descriptions of New York and my duty to go there, its import to me intellectually and otherwise; and finally he convinced me that I should never reach my true intellectual stature unless I did. Other places might be very good, he insisted, they all had their value, but there was only one place where one might live in a keen and vigorous way, and that was New York. It was *the* city, the only cosmopolitan city, a wonder-world in itself. It was great, wonderful, marvelous, the size, the color, the tang, the beauty.

He went on to explain that the West was narrow, slow, not really alive. In New York one might always do, think and act more freely than anywhere else. The air itself was tonic. All really ambitious people, people who were destined to do or be anything, eventually drifted there—editors, newspaper men, actors, playwrights, song-writers, musicians, money-makers. He pointed to himself as a case in point, how he had ventured there, a gawky stripling doing a monologue, and how one Harry Minor, now of antique "Bowery Theater" fame, had seized on him, carried him along and forwarded him in every way. Some one was certain to do as much for me, for any one of ability. In passing, he now confided that only recently, from having been the star song-writer for a well-known New York music publisher (Willis Woodward), he had succeeded, with two other men, in organizing a music publishing company in which he had a third interest, and which was to publish his songs as well as those of others and was pledged to pay him an honest royalty (a thing which he insisted had not so far been done) as well as a full share as partner. In addition, under the friendly urging of an ambitious manager, he was now writing a play, to be known as "The Green Goods Man," in which within a year or two he would appear as star. Also he reminded me that our sister E——, who had long since moved to New York (as early as 1885), was now living in West Fifteenth Street, where she would be glad to receive me. He was always in New York in the summer, living with this sister. "Why not come down there next summer when I am there off the road, and look it over?"

As he talked, New York came nearer than ever it had before, and I could see the light of conviction and enthusiasm in his eye. It was plain, now that he had seen me again, that he wanted me to succeed. My friends had already sung my praises to him, although he himself could see that I was fast emerging from my too shy youth. St. Louis might be well enough, and Chicago—but New York! New York! One who had not seen it but who was eager to see the world could not help but sniff and prick up his ears.

It was during this week that I gave the supper previously mentioned, and took my fiancée to meet my brother. I am satisfied that she liked him, or was rather amused by him, not understanding the least detail of his life or the character of the stage, while the sole comment that I could get out of him was that she was charming but that if he were in my place he would not think of marrying yet—a statement which had more light thrown on it years later by his persistent indifference to if not dislike of her, although he was always too courteous and mindful of others to express himself openly to me. . . . All of which is neither here nor there.

My glorious supper turned out to be somewhat of a failure. Without knowing it, I was trying to harmonize elements which would not mix, at least not on such a short notice. The true Bohemianism and at the same time exclusive camaraderie of such youths as Peter, Dick and Rodenberger, and the rather stilted intellectual sufficiency of my editorial friends and superiors of the *Republic*, and the utter innocence and naïveté of Paul himself, proved too much. The dinner was stilted, formal, boring. My dear brother was as barren of intellectual interests as a child. No current problem such as might have interested these editorial men had the smallest interest for him or had ever been weighed by him. He could not discuss them, although I fancy if we had turned to prize-fighters or baseball heroes or comic characters in general he would have done well enough. Indeed his and their thoughts were so far apart that they found him all but dull. On the other hand, Peter, Dick and Rodenberger finding Paul delightful were not in the least interested in the others, looking upon them as executives and of no great import. Between these groups I was lost, not knowing how to harmonize them. Struck all at once by the ridiculousness and futility of my attempt, I could not talk gayly or naturally, and the more I tried to bring things round the worse they became. Finally I was on pins and needles, until the whole thing was saved by Wandell remembering early that he had something to do at the office. Seizing their opportunity, the managing editor and the dramatic editor went with him. The others and I now attempted to rally, but it was too late. A half hour later we broke up, and I accompanied my brother to his hotel door. He made none but pleasant comments, but it was all such a fizzle that I could have wept.

By Sunday morning he was gone again, and then my life settled into its old routine, apparently—only it did not. Now more than ever I felt myself to be a flitting figure in this interesting but humdrum local world, comfortable enough perhaps but with no significant future for me. The idea of New York as a great and glowing center had taken root.

Some other things tended to move me from St. Louis. Only recently Michaelson, who had come to St. Louis to obtain my aid in securing a place, had been harping on the advantage of being a country editor, the ease of the life, its security. He was out of work and eager to leave the city. I think he was convinced that I was financially in a position to buy a half interest in some fairly successful country paper (which I was not), while he took the other half interest on time. Anyway I had been thinking of this as a way of getting out of the horrible grind of newspaperdom; only this mood of my brother seemed to reach down to the very depths of my being, depths hitherto not plumbed by anything, and put New York before me as a kind of ultimate certainty. I must go there at some time or other! meanwhile it might be a good thing for me to run a country paper. It might make me some money, give me station and confidence. . . .

At the same time, in the face of my growing estimate of myself, backed by the plaudits of such men as Peter and Dick (who were receiving twice my salary), to say nothing of the assurance of my brother that I had that mysterious thing, personality, I was always cramped for cash, and there was no sign on the part of my employers that I would ever be worth very much more to them. Toward the very last, as I have said, they changed, but then it was too late. I might write and write, page specials every week, assignments of all kinds, theatrical and sport reviews at times—and still, after all the evidence that I could be of exceptional service to them, twenty-two or -three dollars was all I could get. And dogging my heels was Michaelson, a cheerful, comforting soul in the main, but a burden. It has always been a matter of great interest to me to observe how certain types, parasites, barnacles, decide that they are to be aided or strengthened by another, and without a "by-your-leave" or any other form or courtesy to "edge in," bring their trunk, and make themselves at home. Although I never really liked Michaelson very much, here he was, idling about, worrying about a job or his future, living in my room toward the last, eating his meals (at least his breakfasts) with me, and talking about the country, the charm, ease and profit of editing a country newspaper!

Now, of all the people in this dusty world, I can imagine no one less fitted than myself, temperamentally or in any other way, to edit a country paper. The intellectual limitations of such a world! My own errant disposition and ideas, my contempt for and revolt against the standardized and clock-work motions and notions of the average man and woman! In six months I should have been arrested or drummed out by the preacher, the elders, and all the other worthies for miles around. Let sleeping dogs lie. The louder all conventionalists snore the better—for me anyhow.

But here I was listening to Michaelson's silly drivel and

wondering if a country newspaper might not offer an escape from the humdrum and clamlike existence into which I seemed to have fallen. From December on this cheerful mediocrity, of about the warmth and intelligence of a bright collie, was telling me daily how wonderful I was and that I "ought to get out of here and into something which would really profit me and get me somewhere"—into the editorship of a country weekly!

What jocular fates trifled with my sense of the reasonable or the ridiculous at this time I do not know, but I was interested—largely, I presume, because I was too wandering and nebulous to think of anything else to do. This cheerful soul finally ended by indicating a paper—the Weekly Something of Grand Rapids, Ohio (not Michigan), near his father's farm (see pp. 247-255, *A Hoosier Holiday*), which, according to him, was just the thing and should offer a complete solution for all our material and social aspirations in this world. By way of this paper, or some other of its kind, one might rise to any height, political or social, state or national. I might become a state assemblyman from my county, a senator, a congressman, or United States senator! When you owned a country paper you were an independent person (imagine the editor of a country paper being independent of the conventions of his community!), not a poor harried scribe on a city paper, uncertain from week to week whether you were to be retained any longer. There were the delights of a country life, the sweet simplicity of a country town, away from the noise and streets and gaudy, shabby nothingness of a great city. . . . As I listened to the picture of his native town, his father's farm, the cows, pigs, chickens, how we could go there and live for a while, my imagination mounted to a heaven of unadulterated success, peace, joy. In my mind I had already rented or bought a small vine-clad cottage in Grand Rapids, Ohio, where, according to Michaelson, was a wonderful sparkling rapids to be seen glimmering in the moonlight, a railroad which went into Toledo within an hour, fertile farmland all about, both gas and oil recently struck, making the

(356)

farmers prosperous and therefore in the mood for a first-class newspaper such as we would edit. Imagine sparkling rapids glimmering in the moonlight listed as a financial asset of a country paper!

CHAPTER LIV

My thoughts being now turned, if vaguely, to the idea of rural life and editing a country newspaper, although I really did not believe that I could succeed at that, I talked and talked, to Michaelson, to my future wife, to Dick and Peter, in a roundabout, hinting way, developing all sorts of theories as to the possible future that awaited me. To buoy up my faith in myself, I tried to make Miss W—— feel that I was a personage and would do great things. . . . How nature would ever get on without total blindness, or at least immense credulity on the part of its creatures, I cannot guess. Certainly if women in their love period had any more sense than the men they would not be impressed with the boshy dreams of such swains as myself. Either they cannot help themselves or they must want to believe. Nature must want them to believe. How the woman who married me could have been impressed by my faith in myself at this period is beyond my reasoning, and yet she was impressed, or saw nothing better in store for her than myself.

That she was so impressed, and that I, moved by her affection for me or my own desire to possess her, was impelled to do something to better my condition, was obvious. Hints thrown out at the *Republic* office, to my sponsor Wandell in particular, that I might leave producing nothing, I decided sometime during January and February, 1893, to take up Michaelson's proposition, although I did not see how, other than by gross luck, it could come to anything. Neither of us had any money to speak of, and yet we were planning to buy a country newspaper. For a few days before starting we debated this foolish matter and then I sent him to his home town to look over the field there and report, which he immediately did, writing most glowing accounts of an absolutely worthless country paper there, which he was positive we could secure for a song and turn into a paying proposition at once. I cannot say that I believed this, and yet I went because I felt the need of something different. And all the time the tug of that immense physical desire toward my beloved which, were there any such thing as sanity in life, might have been satisfied without any great blow to society, was holding me as by hooks of steel. It was this conflict between the need to go and the wish to stay that tortured me. Yet I went. I had the pain of separating from her in this mood, realizing that youth was slipping away, that in the uncertainty of all things there might never be a happy fruition to our love (and there was not). And yet I went.

I bade her a final farewell the Sunday night before my departure. I hinted at all sorts of glorious achievements as well as all possible forms of failure. Lover-wise, I was tremendously impressed with the sterling worth and connections of this girl, the homely, conventional and prosaic surroundings. My unfitness for fulfilling her dreams tortured me. As I could plainly see, she was for life as it had been lived by billions, by those who interpret it as a matter of duty, simplicity, care and thrift. I think she saw before her a modest home in which would be children, enough money to clothe them decently, enough money to entertain a few friends, and eventually to die and be buried respectably. On the other hand, I was little more than a pulsing force, with no convictions, no definite theories or plans. In my sky the latest cloud of thought or plan was the great thing. Not I but destiny, over which I had no control, had me in hand. I felt, or thought I felt, the greatest love . . . while within me was a voice which said: ''What a liar! What a pretender! You will satisfy yourself, make your own way as best you can. Each new day will be a clean slate for you, no least picture of the past thereon—none, at least, which might not be quickly wiped away. Any beautiful woman would satisfy you.'' Still I suffered torture for her and myself, and left the next day, lacerated by the postponement, the defeated desire for happiness in love.

My attitude on leaving the *Republic* was one of complete

indifference, coupled with a kind of satisfaction at the last moment that, after having seemed previously totally indifferent to my worth, the city editor, the managing editor, and even the publisher, seemed suddenly to feel that if I could be induced to stay I might prove of greater value to them than thus far I had—from a cash point of view. And so they made a hearty if belated effort to detain me. Indeed on my very sudden announcement only a few days before my departure that I was going, my city editor expressed great regret, asked me not to act hastily, told me he proposed to speak to the editor-in-chief. But this did not interest me any more. I was down on the *Republic* for the way it had treated me. Why hadn't they done something for me months ago? That afternoon as I was leaving the building on an assignment, the managing editor caught me and wanted to know of my plans, said if I would stay he believed that soon a better place in the editorial department could be made for me. Having already written Michaelson that I would soon join him, however, I now felt it impossible not to leave. The truth is I really wanted to go and now that I had brought myself to this point, I did not want to retreat. Besides, there was a satisfaction in refusing these belated courtesies. The editor said that if I were really going the publisher would be glad to give me a general letter of introduction which might stand me in good stead in other cities. True enough, on the Monday on which I left, having gone to the office to say farewell, I was met by the publisher, who handed me a letter of introduction. It was of the "To whom it might concern" variety and related my labors and capacities in no vague words. I might have used this letter to advantage in many a strait, but never did. Rather, by some queer inversion of thought, I concluded that it was somewhat above my capacity, said more for me than I deserved, and might secure for me some place which I could not fill. For over a year I carried it about in my pocket, often when I was without a job and with only a few dollars in my pockets, and still I did not use it. Why, I have often wondered since. Little as I should understand such a thing in another, so little do I now understand this in myself.

CHAPTER LV

THAT evening at seven I carried my bags down to the great Union Station, feeling that I was a failure. Other men had money; they need not thus go jerking about the world seeking a career. So many youths and maids had all that was needful to their ease and comfort arranged from the beginning. They did not need to fret about the making of a bare living. The ugly favoritism of life which piles comforts in the laps of some while snatching the smallest crumb of satisfaction from the lips of others was never more apparent to me. I was in a black despair, and made short work of getting into my berth. For a long time I stared at dark fields flashing by, punctuated by lamps in scattered cottages, the gloomy and lonely little towns of Illinois and Indiana. Then I slept.

I was aroused by a ray of sunshine in my eyes. I lifted one of my blinds and saw the cornfields of Northern Ohio, the brown stumps of last year's crop protruding through the snow. Commonplace little towns, the small brown or red railway stations with the adjoining cattle-runs, and tall gas-well derricks protruding out of dirty, snowless soil, made me realize that I was approaching the end of my journey. I found that I had ample time to shave, dress and breakfast in the adjoining buffet—a thing I proposed to do if it proved the last pretentious, liberal, courageous deed of my life.

For I was not too well provided with cash, and was I not leaving civilization? Though I had but a hundred dollars, might not my state soon be much worse? I have often smiled since over the awe in which I then held the Pullman car, its porter, conductor, and all that went with it. To my inexperienced soul it seemed to be the acme of elegance and grandeur. Could life offer anything more than the privilege of riding about the world in these mobile palaces? And here was I this sunny winter morning with enough money to indulge in a breakfast in one of these grand ambling chambers, though if I kept up this reckless pace there was no telling where I should end.

I selected a table adjoining one at which sat two drummers who talked of journeys far and wide, of large sales of binders and reapers and the condition of trade. They seemed to me to be among the most fortunate of men, high up in the world as positions go, able to steer straight and profitable courses for themselves. Because they had half a broiled spring chicken, I had one, and coffee and rolls and French fried potatoes, as did they, feeling all the while that I was indulging in limitless grandeur. At one station at which the train stopped some poor-looking farmer boys in jeans and "galluses" and wrinkled hats looking up at me with interest as I ate, I stared down at them, hoping that I should be taken for a millionaire to whom this was little more than a wearisome commonplace. I felt fully capable of playing the part and so gave the boys a cold and repressive glance, as much as to say, Behold! I assured myself that the way to establish my true worth was to make every one else feel small by comparison.

The town of Grand Rapids lay in the extreme northwestern portion of Ohio on the Maumee, a little stream which begins somewhere west of Fort Wayne, Indiana, and runs northeast to Toledo, emptying into Lake Erie. The town was traversed by this one railroad, which began at St. Louis and ended at Toledo, and consisted of a number of small frame houses and stores, with a few brick structures of one and two stories. I had not arranged with Michaelson that he should meet me at any given time, having been uncertain as to the time of my departure from St. Louis, and so I had to look him up. As I stepped down at the little depot I noted the small houses with snow-covered yards, the bare trees and the glimpse of rolling country which I caught through the open spaces between. There was the river, wide and shallow, flowing directly through the heart of the town and tumbling rapidly and picturesquely over gray stones. I was far more concerned as to whether I should sometime be able to write a poem or a story about this river than I was to know if a local weekly could subsist here. And after the hurry and bustle of St. Louis, the town did not impress me. I felt now that I had made a dreadful mistake and wondered why I had been so foolish as to give up the opportunities suggested by my friends on the *Republic*, and my sweetheart, when I might have remained and married her under the new editorial conditions proffered me.

Yet I walked on to the main corner and inquired where my friend lived, then out a country road indicated to me as leading toward his home. I found an old rambling frame house, facing the Maumee River, with a lean-to and kitchen and springhouse, corncribs, a barn twice the size of the house, and smaller buildings, all resting comfortably on a rise of ground. Apple and pear trees surrounded it, now leafless in the wind. A curl of smoke rose from the lean-to and told me where the cookstove was. As I entered the front gate I felt the joy of a country home. It told of simple and plain things, food, warmth, comfort, minds content with routine. Michaelson appeared at the door and greeted me most enthusiastically. He introduced me to his family with the exuberant youthfulness of a schoolboy.

I met the father, a little old dried-up quizzical man, who looked at me over his glasses in a wondering way and rubbed his mouth with the back of his hand. I met the mother, small, wizened, middle-aged, looking as though she had gone through a thousand worries. Then I met Michaelson's wife, a dark, chubby, brown-skinned woman, stocky and not over-intelligent. They asked me to make myself at home, listened to an account of my experiences in getting there, and then Michaelson volunteered to show me about the place.

My mind revolted at the thought of such a humdrum life as this for myself, though I was constantly touched by its charm—for others. I followed the elder Mrs. Michaelson into the lean-to and watched her cook, went with Michaelson to the barn to look over the live stock and returned to talk with Michaelson senior about the prospects of the Republican party in Ohio. He was much interested in a man named

(363)

McKinley, a politician of Ohio, who had been a congressman for years and who was now being talked of as the next candidate of the Republican party for the Presidency. I had scarcely heard of him up to that time, but I gave my host my opinion, such as it was. We sat about the big drum sheet-iron stove, heated by natural gas, then but newly discovered and piped in that region. After dinner I proposed to my friend that we go into the village and inspect the printing plant which he had said was for sale. We walked along the road discussing the possibilities, and it seemed to me as we walked that he was not as enthusiastic as he had been in St. Louis.

"I've been looking at this fellow's plant," he said vaguely, "and I don't know whether I want to give him two hundred down for it. He hasn't got anything. That old press he has is in pretty bad shape, and his type is all worn down."

"Can we get it for two hundred?" I asked innocently.

"Sure, two hundred down. I wouldn't think of giving him more. All he wants now is enough to get out of here, some one to take it off his hands. He can't run it."

We went to the office of the *Herald*, a long dark loft over a feed store, and found there a press and some stands of type, and a table before the two front windows, which looked west. The place was unlighted except by these windows and two in the back, and contained no provision for artificial light except two or three tin kerosene lamps. Slazey, the youthful editor, was not in. We walked about and examined the contents of the room, all run down. The town was small and slow, and even an idealist could see that there was small room here for a career.

Presently the proprietor returned, and I saw a sad specimen of the country editor of those days: sleepy, sickly-looking, with a spare, gaunt face and a head which had the appearance of an egg with the point turned to the back. His hair was long and straight and thin, the back part of it growing down over his dusty coat-collar. He wore a pair of baggy trousers of no shape or distinguishable color, and his coat and waistcoat were greasy. He extended a damp, indifferent hand to me.

"I hear you want to sell out," I said.

"Yes, I'm willing to sell," he replied sadly.

"Do you mind showing us what you have here?"

He went about mechanically, and pointed out the press and type and some paper he had on hand.

"Let me see that list of subscribers you showed me the other day," said Michaelson, who now seemed eager to convince himself that there might be something in this affair.

Slazey brought it out from an old drawer and together we examined it, spreading it out on the dusty table and looking at the names checked off as paid. There were not more than a thousand. Some of them had another mark beside the check, and this excited my curiosity.

"What's this cross here for?"

"That's the one that's paid for this year."

"Isn't this this year's list?"

"No. I just thought I'd check up the new payments on the old list. I haven't had time to make out a new one."

Our faces fell. The names checked with a cross did not aggregate five hundred.

"I'll tell you what we'd better do," observed Michaelson heavily, probably feeling that I had become suddenly depressed. "Suppose we go around and see some of the merchants and ask them if they'll support us with advertising?"

I agreed, feeling all the while that the whole venture was ridiculous, and together we went about among the silent stores, talking with conservative men, who represented all that was discouraging and wearisome in life. Here they stood all day long calculating in pennies and dimes, whereas the city merchant counted in hundreds and thousands. It was dispiriting. Think of living in a place like this, among such people!

"I might give a good paper my support," said one, a long, lean, sanctimonious man who looked as though he had narrow notions and a firm determination to rule in his small world. "But it's mighty hard to make a paper that would suit this community. We're religious and hard-working here, and we like the things that interest religious and hard-working people.

Course if it was run right it might pay pretty well, but I dunno as 'twould neither. You never can tell."

I saw that he would be one hard customer to deal with anyhow. If there were many like him—— The poor, thin-blooded, calculating world which he represented frightened me.

"How much advertising do you think you could give to a paper that was 'run' right?"

"Well, that depends," he said gloomily and disinterestedly. "I'd have to see how it was run first. Some weeks I might give more than others."

Michaelson nudged me and we left.

"I forgot to tell you," he said, "that he's a Baptist and a Republican. He'd expect you to run it in favor of those institutions if you got his support. But all the men around town won't feel that way."

In the dusty back room of a drugstore we found a chemist who did not know whether a weekly newspaper was of any value to him, and could not contribute more than fifty cents a week in advertising if it were. The proprietor of the village hotel, a thick-set, red-faced man with the air of a country evil-doer, said that he did not see that a local newspaper was particularly valuable to him. He might advertise, but it would be more as a favor than anything else.

I began to sum up the difficulties of our position. We should be handicapped, to begin with, by a wretched printing outfit. We should be beholden to a company of small, lean-living, narrow men who would take offense at the least show of individuality and cut us off entirely from support. We should have to busy ourselves gathering trivial items of news, dunning hard-working, indifferent farmers for small amounts of money, and reduce all our thoughts and ambitions to the measure of this narrow world. I saw myself dying by inches. It gave me the creeps. Youth and hope were calling.

"I don't see this," I said to myself. "It's horrible. I should die." To Michaelson I said: "Suppose we give up our canvassing for today?"

"We might as well," he replied. "There's a paper over at Bowling Green for sale, and it's a better paper. We might go over in a day or two and look at it. We might as well go home now."

I agreed, and we turned down a street that led to the road, meditating. I knew nothing of my destiny, but I knew that it had little to do with this. These great wide fields, many of them already sown to wheat under the snow, these hundreds of oil or gas-well derricks promising a new source of profit to many, the cleanly farmhouses and neatly divided farms all appealed to me, but this world was not for me. I was thinking of something different, richer, more poignant, less worthy possibly, more terrible, more fruitful for the moods and the emotions. What could these bleak fields offer? I thought of St. Louis, the crowded streets, the vital offices of the great papers, their thrashing presses, the hotels, the theaters, the trains. What, bury myself here? I thought of the East—New York possibly, at least Cleveland, Buffalo, Pittsburgh, Philadelphia.

"I like the country, but it's a hard place to make a living, isn't it?" I finally said.

"Yes," he assented gloomily. "I've never been able to get anything out of it—but I haven't done very well in the city either."

I sensed the mood of an easily defeated man.

"I'm so used to the noise and bustle of the streets that these fields seem lonely," I said.

"Yes, but you might get over that in time, don't you think?"

Never, I thought, but did not say so; instead I said: "That's a beautiful sky, isn't it?" and he looked blankly to where a touch of purple was creeping into the background of red and gold.

We reached the house at dusk. Going through the gate I said: "I don't see how I can go into this with you, Mich. There isn't enough in it."

"Well, don't worry about it any more tonight. I'd rather the girl wouldn't know. We'll talk it over in the morning."

CHAPTER LVI

DISHEARTENING as this village and country life might seem as a permanent field of endeavor, it was pleasing enough as a spectacle or as the scene of a vacation. Although it was late February when I came and there was snow on the ground, a warm wind came in a day or two and drove most of it away. A full moon rose every night in the east and there was a sense of approaching Spring. Before the charming old farmhouse flowed the wonderful little Maumee River, dimpling over stones and spreading out wide, as though it wished to appear much more than it was. There is madness in moonlight, and there is madness in that chemical compound which is youth. Here in this simple farming region, once free of the thought that by any chance I might be compelled to remain here, I felt strangely renewed and free as a bird, though at the same time there was an undercurrent of sadness, not only for myself but for life itself, the lapse and decay of things, the impossibility of tasting or knowing more than a fraction of the glories and pleasures that are everywhere outspread. Although I had not had a vacation in years, I was eager to be at work. The greatness of life, its possibilities, the astounding dreams of supremacy which might come true, were calling to me. I wanted to be on, to find what life had in store for me; and yet I wanted to stay here for a while.

Mich's father, as well as his mother and wife, interested me intensely, for they were simple, industrious, believing. They were good Baptists or Methodists or Presbyterians. The grizzled little old farmer who had built up this place or inherited a part and added the rest, was exactly like all the other farmers I have ever known: genial, kindly, fairly tolerant, curious as to the wonders of the world without, full of a great faith in America and its destiny, sure that it is the

(368)

greatest country in the world, and that there has never been one other like it. That first night at supper, and the next morning at breakfast, and all my other days here, the old man questioned me as to life, its ways, my beliefs or theories, and I am positive that he was delighted to have me there, for it was winter and he had little to do besides read his paper.

The newspaper of largest circulation in this region was the *Blade* of Toledo, which he read assiduously. The mother and daughter-in-law did most of the work. The mother was forever busy cooking breakfast or dinner, cleaning the rooms, milking, making butter and cheese, gathering eggs from a nearby hennery. Her large cellar was stocked with jellies, preserved fruit, apples, potatoes and other vegetables. There was an ample store of bacon, salt pork and beef. I found that no fresh meat other than chicken was served, but the meals were delightful and plentiful, delicious biscuits and jelly, fresh butter, eggs, ham, bacon, salt pork or cured beef, and the rarely absent fried chicken, as well as some rabbits which Mich shot. During my stay he did nothing but idle about the barn, practicing on a cornet which he said had saved his lungs at a time when he was threatened with consumption. But his playing! I wonder the cure did not prove fatal. I noted the intense interest of Mich's father in what the discovery of gas in this region would do for it. He was almost certain that all small towns hereabout would now become prosperous manufacturing centers. There would be work for all. Wages would go up. Many people would soon come here and become rich. This of course never came true at all. The flow of natural gas soon gave out and the oil strikes were not even rivals of some nearby fields.

All this talk was alien to my thoughts. I could not fix my interest on trade and what it held in store for anybody. I knew it must be so and that America was destined to grow materially, but somehow the thing did not interest me. My thoughts leaped to the artistic spectacle such material prosperity might subsequently present, not to the purely material phase of the prosperity itself. Indeed I could never think of the work being done in any factory or institution without passing from that work to the lives behind it, the crowds of commonplace workers, the great streets which they filled, the bare homes, and the separate and distinct dramas of their individual lives. I was tremendously interested by the rise of various captains of industry then already bestriding America, their opportunities and pleasures, the ease and skill with which they organized "trusts" and combinations, their manipulations of the great railroads, oil and coal fields, their control of the telegraph and the telephone, their sharp and watchful domination of American politics; but only as drama. Grover Cleveland was President, and his every deed was paining the Republicans quite as much as it was gratifying the Democrats, but I could already see that the lot of the underdog varied little with the much-heralded changes of administration— and it was the underdog that always interested me more than the upper one, his needs, his woes, his simplicities. Here, as elsewhere, I could see by talking to Mich and his father, men became vastly excited, paraded and all but wept over the results of one election or another, city, State or national, but when all was said and done and America had been "saved," or the Constitution "defended" or "wrecked," the condition of the average man, myself included, was about as it had been before.

The few days I spent here represented an interlude between an old and a new life. I have always felt that in leaving St. Louis I put my youth behind me; that which followed was both sobering and broadening. But on this farm, beside this charming river, I paused for a few days and took stock of my life thus far, and it certainly seemed pointless and unpromising. I thought constantly and desperately of my future, the uncertainty of it, and yet all the while my eye was fixed not upon any really practical solution for me but rather upon the pleasures and luxuries of life as enjoyed by others, the fine houses, the fine clothes, the privilege of traveling, of sharing in the amusements of the rich and the clever. Here I was, at the foot of the ladder, with not the least skill for making money, compelled to make my way upward as best I might, and yet thinking in terms of millions always. However much I might earn in journalism, I had sense enough to know that it would yield me little or nothing. After some thought, I decided that I would move on to some other city, where I would get into the newspaper business for a while and then see what I should see.

Indeed I never saw Mich but once again.

But Toledo. This was my first free and unaided flight into the unknown. I found here a city far more agreeable than St. Louis, which, being much greater in size, had districts which were positively appalling for their poverty and vice; whereas here was a city of not quite 100,000, as clean and fresh as any city could be. I recall being struck with clean asphalt pavements, a canal or waterway in which many lake vessels were riding, and houses and stores, frame for the most part, which seemed clean if not quite new. The first papers I bought, the *Blade* and the *Bee*, were full of the usual American small city bluster together with columns and columns about American politics and business.

Before seeking work I decided to investigate the town. I was intensely interested in America and its cities, and wondered, in spite of my interest in New York, which I would select for my permanent resting-place. When was I to have a home of my own? Would it be as pleasing as one of these many which here and elsewhere I saw in quiet rows shaded by trees, many of them with spacious lawns and suggestive of that security and comfort so dear to the mollusc-like human heart? For, after security, nothing seems to be so important or so desirable to the human organism as rest, or at least ease. The one thing that the life force seems to desire to escape is work, or at any rate strife. One would think that man had been invented against his will by some malign power and was being harried along ways and to tasks against which his soul revolted and to which his strength was not equal.

As I walked about the streets of this city my soul panted for the seeming comfort and luxury of them. The well-kept lawns, the shuttered and laced windows! The wonder of evening fires in winter! The open, cool and shadowy doors in summer! Swings and hammocks on lawns and porches! The luxury of the book and rocker! Somehow in the stress of my disturbed youth I had missed most of this.

After a day of looking about the city I applied to the city editor of the leading morning paper, and encountered one of the intellectual experiences of my life. At the city editorial desk in a small and not too comfortable room sat a small cherubic individual, with a complexion of milk and cream, light brown hair and a serene blue eye, who looked me over quizzically, as much as to say: "Look what the latest breeze has wafted in." His attitude was neither ·antagonistic nor welcoming. He was so assured that I half-detected on sight the speculative thinker and dreamer. Yet in the rôle of city editor in a mid-West manufacturing town one must have an air if not the substance of commercial understanding and ability, and so my young city editor seemed to breathe a determination to be very executive and forceful.

"You're a St. Louis newspaper man, eh?" he said, eyeing me casually. "Never worked in a town of this size, though? Well, the conditions are very different. We pay much attention to small items—make a good deal out of nothing," and he smiled. "But there isn't a thing I can see now, nothing beyond a three- or four-day job which you wouldn't want, I'm sure."

"How do you know I wouldn't?"

"Well, I'll tell you about it. There's a street-car strike on and I could use a man who had nerve enough to ride around on the cars the company is attempting to run and report how things are. But I'll tell you frankly: it's dangerous. You may be shot or hit with a brick."

I indicated my willingness to undertake this and he looked at me in a mock serious and yet approving way. He took me on and I went about the city on one car-line and another, studying the strange streets, expecting and fearing every moment that a brick might be shied at me through the window or that a gang of irate workingmen would board the car and beat me up. But nothing happened, not a single threatening workman anywhere; I so reported and was told to write it up and make as much of the "story" as possible. Without knowing anything of the merits of the case, my sympathies were all with the workingmen. I had seen enough of strikes, and of poverty, and of the quarrels between the money-lords and the poor, to be all on one side. As was the custom in all news-paper offices with which I ever had anything to do, where labor and capital were concerned I was told to be neutral and not antagonize either side. I wrote my "story" and it was published in the first edition. Then, at the order of this same youth, I visited some charity bazaar, where all the im-portant paintings owned in the city were being exhibited, and wrote an account which was headed, "As in Old Toledo," with all the silly chaff about "gallants and ladies gay," after which I spread my feet under a desk, being interested to talk more with the smiling if indifferent youth who had em-ployed me.

The opportunity soon came, for apparently he was as much interested in me as I in him. He came over after I had sub-mitted my second bit of copy and announced that it was en-tirely satisfactory. A man from the composing-room entered and commented on the fact that James Whitcomb Riley and Eugene Field were billed to lecture in the city soon. I remarked that I had once seen Field in the office of the *News* in Chicago, which brought out the fact that my city editor had once worked in Chicago, had been a member of the White-chapel Club, knew Field, Finley Peter Dunne, Brand Whit-lock, Ben King and others. At mention of the magic name of Ben King, author of "If I Should Die Tonight" and "Jane Jones," the atmosphere of Chicago of the time of the White-chapel Club and Eugene Field and Ben King returned. At once we fell into a varied and gay exchange of intimacies.

It resulted in an enduring and yet stormy and disillusion-ing friendship. If he had been a girl I would have married him, of course. It would have been inevitable. We were in-tellectual affinities. Our dreams were practically identical, though we approached them from different angles. He was the sentimentalist in thought, though the realist in action; I was the realist in thought and the sentimentalist in action. He took me out to lunch, and we stayed nearly three hours. He took me to dinner, and to do so was compelled to call up his wife and say he had to stay in town. He had dreams of becoming a poet and novelist, I of becoming a playwright. Before the second day had gone he had shown me a book of fairy-tales and some poems. I became enamored of him, the victim of a delightful illusion.

Because he liked me he wanted me to stay on. There was no immediate place, he said, but one might open at any time. Having very little money, I could not see my way to that, but I did try to get a place on the rival paper. That failing, he suggested that although I wander on toward Cleveland and Buffalo I stand ready to come back if he telegraphed for me. Meanwhile we reveled in that wonderful possession, intellectual affection. I thought him wonderful, perfect, great; he thought—well, I have heard him tell in after years what he thought. Even now at times he fixes me with hungry, welcoming eyes.

CHAPTER LVII

WHETHER I should go East or West suddenly became a question with me. I had the feeling that I might do better in Detroit or some point west of Chicago, only the nearness of such cities as Cleveland, Buffalo, Pittsburgh and those farther east deterred me; the cost of reaching them was small, and all the while I should be moving toward my brother in New York. And so, after making inquiry at the office of the *Bee* for a possible opening and finding none, and learning from several newspaper men that Detroit was not considered a live journalistic town, I decided to travel eastward, and bought a ticket to Cleveland.

Riding in sight of the tumbling waves of Lake Erie, I was taken back in thought to my days in Chicago and all those who had already dropped out of my life forever. What a queer, haphazard, disconnected thing this living was! Where should I be tomorrow, what doing—the next year—the year after that? Should I ever have any money, any standing, any friends? So I tortured myself. Arriving in Cleveland at the close of a smoky gray afternoon, I left my bag at the station and sought a room, then walked out to see what I should see. I knew no one. Not a friend anywhere within five hundred miles. My sole resource my little skill as a newspaper worker. Buying the afternoon and morning papers, I examined them with care, copying down their editorial room addresses, then betook me to a small beanery for food.

The next morning I was up early, determined to see as much as I could, to visit the offices of the afternoon papers before noon, then to look in upon the city editors of the two or three morning papers. The latter proved not very friendly and there appeared to be no opening anywhere. But I determined to remain here for a few days studying the city as a city and visiting the same editors each day or as often as they would endure me. If nothing came of it within a week, and no telegram came from my friend H—— in Toledo calling me back, I proposed to move on; to which city I had not as yet made up my mind.

The thing that interested me most about Cleveland then was that it was so raw, dark, dirty, smoky, and yet possessed of one thing: force, raucous, clattering, semi-intelligent force. America was then so new industrially, in the furnace stage of its existence. Everything was in the making: fortunes, art, social and commercial life. The most impressive things were its rich men, their homes, factories, clubs, office buildings and institutions of commerce and pleasure generally; and this was as true of Cleveland as of any other city in America.

Indeed the thing which held my attention, after I had been in Cleveland a day or two and had established myself in a somber room in a somber neighborhood once occupied by the very rich, were those great and new residences in Euclid Avenue, with wide lawns and iron or stone statues of stags and dogs and deer, which were occupied by such rich men as John D. Rockefeller, Tom Johnson, and Henry M. Flagler. Rockefeller only a year or two before had given millions to revivify the almost defunct University of Chicago, then a small Baptist college, and was accordingly being hailed as one of the richest men of America. He and his satellites and confrères were already casting a luster over Cleveland. They were all living here in Euclid Avenue, and I was interested to look up their homes, envying them their wealth of course and wishing that I were famous or a member of a wealthy family, and that I might some day meet one of the beautiful girls I thought must be here and have her fall in love with and make me rich. Physically or artistically or materially, there was nothing to see but business: a few large hotels, like those of every American city, and these few great houses. Add a few theaters and commonplace churches. All American cities and all the inhabitants were busy with but one thing: commerce. They ate, drank and slept trade. In my wanderings I found a huge steel works and a world of low, smoky, pathetic little hovels about it. Although I was not as yet given to reasoning about

(376)

the profound delusion of equality under democracy, this evidence of the little brain toiling for the big one struck me with great force and produced a good deal of speculative thought later on.

The paper with which I was eventually connected was the Cleveland *Leader,* which represented all that was conservative in the local life. Wandering into its office on the second or third day of my stay, I was met at the desk of the city editor by a small, boyish-looking person of a ferret-like countenance, who wanted to know what I was after. I told him, and he said there was nothing, but on hearing of the papers with which I had been connected and the nature of the work I had done he suggested that possibly I might be able to do something for the Sunday edition. The Sunday editor proved to be a tall, melancholy man with sad eyes, a sallow face, sunken cheeks, narrow shoulders and a general air of weariness and depression.

"What is it, now, you want?" he asked slowly, looking up from his musty rolltop desk.

"Your city editor suggested that possibly you might have some Sunday work for me to do. I've had experience in this line in Chicago and St. Louis."

"Yes," he said not asking me to sit down. "Well, now, what do you think you could write about?"

This was a poser. Being new to the city I had not thought of any particular thing, and could not at this moment. I told him this.

"There's one thing you might write about if you could. Did you ever hear of a new-style grain-boat they are putting on the Lakes called——"

"Turtle-back?" I interrupted.

"Turtle-back?" went on the editor indifferently. "Well, there's one here now in the harbor. It's the first one to come here. Do you think you could get up something on that?"

"I'm sure I could. I'd like to try. Do you use pictures?"

"You might get a photo or two; we could have drawings made from them."

I started for the door, eager to be about this, when he said: "We don't pay very much: three dollars a column."

That was discouraging, but I was filled with the joy of doing something. On my way out I stopped at the business office and bought a copy of the last Sunday issue, which proved to be a poor makeshift composed of a half-dozen articles on local enterprises and illustrated with a few crude drawings. I read one or two of them, and then looked up my waterfront boat. I found it tied up at a dock adjoining an immense railroad yard and near an imposing grain elevator. Finding nobody about, I nosed out the bookkeeper of the grain elevator, who told me that the captain of the boat had gone to the company's local office in a nearby street. I hastened to the place, and there found a bluff old lake captain in blue, short, stout, ruddy, coarse, who volunteered, almost with a "Heigh!" and a "Ho!" to tell me something about it.

"I think I ought to know a little something about 'em—I sailed the first one that was ever sailed out of the port of Chicago."

I listened with open ears. I caught a disjointed story of plans and specifications, Sault Ste. Marie, the pine woods of Northern Michigan, the vast grain business of Chicago and other lake ports, early navigation on the lakes, the theory of a bilge keel and a turtle-back top, and all strung together with numerous "y'sees" and "so nows." I made notes, on backs of envelopes, scraps of paper, and finally on a pad furnished me by the generous bookkeeper. I carried my notes back to the paper.

The Sunday editor was out. I waited patiently until half-past four, and then, the light fading, gave up the idea of going with a photographer to the boat. I went to a faded green baize-covered table and began to write my story. I had no sooner done a paragraph or two than the Sunday editor returned, bringing with him an atmosphere of lassitude and indifference. I went to him to explain what I had done.

"Well, write it up, write it up. We'll see," and he turned away to his papers.

I labored hard at my story, and by seven or eight o'clock

had ground out two thousand words of description which had more of the bluff old captain in it than of the boat. The Sunday editor took it when I was through, and shoved it into a pigeon-hole, telling me to call in a day or two and he would let me know. I thought this strange. It seemed to me that if I were working for a Sunday paper I should work every day. I called the next day, but Mr. Loomis had not read it. The next day he said the story was well enough written, though very long. "You don't want to write so loosely. Stick to your facts closer."

This day I suggested a subject of my own, "the beauty of some of the new suburbs," but he frowned at this as offering a lot of free advertising to real estate men who ought to be made to pay. Then I proposed an article on the magnificence of Euclid Avenue, which was turned down as old. I then spoke of a great steel works which was but then coming into the city, but as this offered great opportunity to all the papers he thought poorly of it. He compromised a day or two later by allowing me to write up a chicken-farm which lay outside the city.

Of course this made a poor showing for me at the cashier's desk. At the end of the second week I was allowed to put in a bill for seven dollars and a half. I had not realized that I was wasting so much time. I appealed to all the editors again for a regular staff position, but was told there was no opening. It began to look as if I should have to leave Cleveland soon, and I wondered where I should go next—Buffalo or Pittsburgh, both equally near.

CHAPTER LVIII

FINDING Cleveland hopeless for me, I one day picked up and left. Then came Buffalo, which I reached toward the end of March. Aside from the Falls I found it a little tame, no especial snap to it—not as much as I had felt to be characteristic of Cleveland. What interest there was for me I provided myself, wandering about in odd drear neighborhoods, about grain elevators and soap factories and railroad yards and manufacturing districts. Here, as in Cleveland, I could not help but see that in spite of our boasted democracy and equality of opportunity there was as much misery and squalor and as little decent balancing of opportunity against energy as anywhere else in the world. The little homes, the poor, shabby, colorless, drear, drab little homes with their grassless "yards," their unpaved streets, their uncollected garbage, their fluttering, thin-flamed gas-lamps, the crowds of ragged, dirty, ill-cared-for children! Near at hand was always the inevitable and wretched saloon, not satisfying a need for pleasure in a decent way but pandering to the lowest and most conniving and most destroying instincts of the lowest politicians and heelers and grafters and crooks, while the huge financial and manufacturing magnates at the top with their lust for power and authority used the very flesh of the weaker elements for purposes of their own. It was the saloon, not liquor, which brought about the prohibition folly. I used to listen, as a part of my reportorial duties, to the blatherings of thin-minded, thin-blooded, thin-experienced religionists as well as to those of kept editorial writers, about the merits and blessings and opportunities of our noble and bounteous land; but whenever I encountered such regions as this I knew well enough that there was something wrong with their noble maunderings. Shout as they might, there was here displayed before my very eyes ample evidence that somewhere there was a screw loose in the "Fatherhood of Man—Brotherhood of God" machinery.

After I had placed myself in a commonplace neighborhood near the business center, I canvassed the newspaper offices and their editors. Although I had in my pocket that letter from the publisher of the St. Louis *Republic* extolling my virtues as a reporter and correspondent, so truly vagrom was my mood and practical judgment that I did not present it to any one. Instead I merely mooned into one office after another (there were only four papers here), convinced before entering that I should not get anything—and I did not. One young city editor, seeming to take at least an interest in me, assured me that if I would remain in Buffalo for six weeks he could place me; but since I had not enough money to sustain myself so long I decided not to wait. Ten days spent in reconnoitering these offices daily, and I concluded that it was useless to remain longer. Yet before I went I determined to see at least one thing more: the Falls.

Therefore one day I traveled by trolley to Niagara and looked at that tumbling flood, then not chained or drained by turbine water-power sluices. I was impressed, but not quite so much as I had thought I should be. Standing out on a rock near the greatest volume of water under a gray sky, I was awed by the downpour and then became dizzy and felt as though I were being carried along whether I would or not. Farther upstream I stared at the water as it gathered force and speed, wondering how I should feel if I were in a small canoe and fighting it for my life. Behind the falls were great stalagmites and stalactites of ice and snow still standing from the cold of weeks before. I recalled that Blondel, a famous French swimmer of his day, had ten years before swum these fierce and angry waters below the Falls. I wondered how he had done it, so wildly did they leap, huge wheels of water going round and round and whitecaps leaping and spitting and striking at each other.

When I returned to Buffalo I congratulated myself that if I had got nothing else out of my visit to Buffalo, at least I had gained this.

CHAPTER LIX

I now decided that Pittsburgh would be as good a field as any, and one morning seeing a sign outside a cut-rate ticket-broker's window reading "Pittsburgh, $5.75," I bought a ticket, returned to my small room to pack my bag, and departed. I arrived at Pittsburgh at six or seven that same evening.

Of all the cities in which I ever worked or lived Pittsburgh was the most agreeable. Perhaps it was due to the fact that my stay included only spring, summer and fall, or that I found a peculiarly easy newspaper atmosphere, or that the city was so different physically from any I had thus far seen; but whether owing to one thing or another certainly no other newspaper work I ever did seemed so pleasant, no other city more interesting. What a city for a realist to work and dream in! The wonder to me is that it has not produced a score of writers, poets, painters and sculptors, instead of—well, how many? And who are they?

I came down to it through the brown-blue mountains of Western Pennsylvania, and all day long we had been winding at the base of one or another of them, following the bed of a stream or turning out into a broad smooth valley, crossing directly at the center of it, or climbing some low ridge with a puff-puff-puff and then clattering almost recklessly down the other slope. I had never before seen any mountains. The sight of sooty-faced miners at certain places, their little oil and tow tin lamps fastened to their hats, their tin dinner-pails on their arms, impressed me as something new and faintly reminiscent of the one or two small coal mines about Sullivan, Indiana, where I had lived when I was a boy of seven. Along the way I saw a heavy-faced and heavy-bodied type of peasant woman, with a black or brown or blue or green skirt and a waist of a contrasting color, a headcloth or neckerchief of still another, trailed by a few children of equally solid proportions, hanging up clothes or doing something else about their miserable places. These were the much-maligned hunkies just then being imported by the large manufacturing and mining and steel-making industries of the country to take the place of the restless and less docile American working man and woman. I marveled at their appearance and number, and assumed, American-fashion, that in their far-off and unhappy lands they had heard of the wonderful American Constitution, its guaranty of life, liberty and the pursuit of happiness, as well as of the bounteous opportunities afforded by this great land, and that they had forsaken their miseries to come all this distance to enjoy these greater blessings.

I did not then know of the manufacturers' foreign labor agent with his lying propaganda among ignorant and often fairly contented peasants, painting America as a country rolling in wealth and opportunity, and then bringing them here to take the places of more restless and greatly underpaid foreigners who, having been brought over by the same gay pictures, were becoming irritated and demanded more pay. I did not then know of the padrone, the labor spy, the company store, five cents an hour for breaker children, the company stockade, all in full operation at this time. All I knew was that there had been a great steel strike in Pittsburgh recently, that Andrew Carnegie, as well as other steel manufacturers (the Olivers, for one), had built fences and strung them with electrified barbed wire in order to protect themselves against the "lawless" attacks of "lawless" workingmen.

I also knew that a large number of State or county or city paid deputy sheriffs and mounted police and city policemen had been sworn in and set to guarding the company's property and that H. C. Frick, a leading steel manager for Mr. Carnegie, had been slightly wounded by a desperado named Alexander Berkman, who was inflaming these workingmen, all foreigners of course, lawless and unappreciative of the great and prosperous steel company which was paying them reasonable wages and against which they had no honest complaint.

Our mid-Western papers, up to the day of Cleveland's election in 1892 and for some time after, had been full of the merits of this labor dispute, with long and didactic editorials, intended in the main to prove that the workingman was not so greatly underpaid, considering the type of labor he performed and the intelligence he brought to his task; that the public was not in the main vastly interested in labor disputes, both parties to the dispute being unduly selfish; that it would be a severe blow to the prosperity of the country if labor disputes were too long continued; that unless labor was reasonable in its demands capital would become disheartened and leave the country. I had not made up my mind that the argument was all on one side, although I knew that the aver-'age man in America, despite its great and boundless opportunities, was about as much put upon and kicked about and underpaid as any other. This growing labor problem or the general American dissatisfaction with poor returns upon efforts made crystallized three years later in the Free Silver campaign and the "gold parades." The "full dinner-pail" was then invented as a slogan to counteract the vast economic unrest, and the threat to close down and so bring misery to the entire country unless William McKinley was elected was also freely posted. Henry George, Father McGlynn, Herr Most, Emma Goldman, and a score of others were abroad voicing the woes of hundreds of thousands who were supposed to have no woes.

At that time, as I see it now, America was just entering upon the most lurid phase of that vast, splendid, most lawless and most savage period in which the great financiers were plotting and conniving at the enslavement of the people and belaboring each other. Those crude parvenu dynasties which now sit enthroned in our democracy, threatening its very life with their pretensions and assumptions, were then in their very beginning. John D. Rockefeller was still in Cleveland; Flagler, William Rockefeller, H. H. Rogers, were still comparatively young and secret agents; Carnegie was still in Pittsburgh, an iron master, and of all his brood of powerful children only Frick had appeared; William H. Vanderbilt and Jay Gould had only recently died; Cleveland was President, and Mark Hanna was an unknown business man in Cleveland. The great struggles of the railroads, the coal companies, the gas companies, to overawe and tax the people were still in abeyance, or just being born. The multi-million-aire had arrived, it is true, but not the billionaire. On every hand were giants plotting, fighting, dreaming; and yet in Pittsburgh there was still something of a singing spirit.

When I arrived here and came out of the railway station, which was directly across the Monongahela River from the business center, 'I was impressed by the huge walls of hills that arose on every hand, a great black sheer ridge rising to a height of five or six hundred feet to my right and enclosing this river, on the bosom of which lay steamboats of good size. From the station a pleasingly designed bridge of fair size led to the city beyond, and across it trundled in unbroken lines street-cars and wagons and buggies of all sizes and descrip-tions. The city itself was already smartly outlined by lights, a galaxy climbing the hills in every direction, and below me as I walked out upon this bridge was an agate stream reflecting the lights from either shore. Below this was another bridge, and upstream another. The whole river for a mile or more was suddenly lit to a rosy glow, a glow which, as I saw upon turning, came from the tops of some forty or fifty stacks belching a deep orange-red flame. At the same time an enor-mous pounding and crackling came from somewhere, as though titans were at work upon subterranean anvils. I stared and admired. I felt that I was truly adventuring into a new and strange world. I was glad now that I had not found work in Toledo or Cleveland or Buffalo.

The city beyond the river proved as interesting as the river cliffs and forges about the station. As I walked along I dis-covered the name of the street (Smithfield), which began at the bridge's end and was lined with buildings of not more than three or four stories although it was one of the principal streets of the business center. At the bridge-head on the city side stood a large smoke-colored stone building, which later I discovered was the principal hotel, the Monongahela, and beyond that was a most attractive and unusual postoffice build-

ing. I came to a cross street finally (Fifth Avenue), brightly
lighted and carrying unusual traffic, and turned into it. I
found this central region to be most puzzlingly laid out, and
did not attempt to solve its mysteries. Instead, I entered
a modest restaurant in a side street. Later I hunted up a
small hotel, where I paid a dollar for a room for the night. I
retired, speculating as to how I should make out here. Something about the city drew me intensely. I wished I might
remain for a time. The next morning I was up bright and
early to look up the morning papers and find out the names of
the afternoon papers. I found that there were four: the
Dispatch and *Times,* morning papers, and the *Gazette-Tele-
graph* and *Leader,* afternoon. I thought them most interesting and different from those of other cities in which I had
worked.

"Andy Pastor had his right hand lacerated while at work in the
23-inch mill yesterday."
"John Kristoff had his right wrist sprained while at work in the
140-inch mill yesterday."
"Joseph Novic is suffering from contused wounds of the left wrist
received while at work in the 23-inch mill yesterday."
"A train of hot metal, being hauled from a mixing-house to open
hearth No. 2, was side-swiped by a yard engine near the 48-inch mill.
The impact tilted the ladles of some of the cars and the hot metal
spilled in a pool of water along the track. Antony Brosak, Constan-
tine Czernik and Kafros Maskar were seriously wounded by the exploding metal."

Such items arrested my attention at once; and then such
names as Squirrel Hill, Sawmill Run, Moon Run, Hazelwood,
Wind Gap Road, Braddock, McKeesport, Homestead, Swissvale, somehow made me wish to know more of this region.

The *Dispatch* was Republican, the *Times* Democratic. Both
were evidently edited with much conservatism as to local news.
I made haste to visit the afternoon newspaper offices, only to
discover that they were fully equipped with writers. I then
proceeded in search of a room and finally found one in Wylie
Avenue, a curious street that climbed a hill to its top and
then stopped. Here, almost at the top of this hill, in an old
yellow stonefront house the rear rooms of which commanded
a long and deep canyon or "run," I took a room for a week.
The family of this house rented rooms to several others, clerks

who looked and proved to be a genial sort, holding a kind of court on the front steps of an evening.

I now turned to the morning papers, going first to the *Times*, which had its offices in a handsome building, one of the two or three high office buildings in the city. The city editor received me graciously but could promise nothing. At the *Dispatch*, which was published in a three-story building at Smithfield and Diamond streets, I found a man who expressed much more interest. He was a slender, soft-spoken, one-handed man. On very short acquaintance I found him to be shrewd and canny, gracious always, exceedingly reticent and uncommunicative and an excellent judge of news, and plainly holding his job not so much by reason of what he put into his paper as by what he kept out of it. He wanted to know where I had worked before I came to Pittsburgh, whether I had been connected with any paper here, whether I had ever done feature stuff. I described my experiences as nearly as I could, and finally he said that there was nothing now but he was expecting a vacancy to occur soon. If I could come around in the course of a week or ten days (I drooped sadly)—well, then, in three or four days, he thought he might do something for me. The salary would not be more than eighteen the week. My spirits fell at that, but his manner was so agreeable and his hope for me so keen that I felt greatly encouraged and told him I would wait a few days anyhow. My friend in Toledo had promised me that he would wire me at the first opening, and I was now expecting some word from him. This I told to this city editor, and he said: "Well, you might wait until you hear from him anyhow." A thought of my possible lean purse did not seem to occur to him, and I marveled at the casual manner in which he assumed that I could wait.

Thereafter I roamed the city and its environs, and to my delight found it to be one of the most curious and fascinating places I had ever seen. From a stationery store I first secured a map and figured out the lay of the town. At a glance I saw that the greater part of it stretched eastward along the tongue of land that was between the Allegheny and the Monongahela, and that this was Pittsburgh proper. Across the Allegheny, on the north side, was the city of Allegheny, an individual municipality but so completely connected with Pittsburgh as to be identical with it, and connected with it by many bridges. Across the Monongahela, on the south side, were various towns: Mt. Washington, Duquesne, Homestead. I was interested especially in Homestead because of the long and bitter contest between the steel-workers and the Carnegie Company, which for six months and more in 1892 had occupied space on the front page of every newspaper in America.

Having studied my map I explored, going first across the river into Allegheny. Here I found a city built about the base of high granite hills or between ridges in hollows called "gaps" or "runs" with a street or car-line clambering and twisting directly over them. A charming park and boulevard system had been laid out, with the city hall, a public market and a Carnegie public library as a center. The place had large dry-goods and business houses.

On another day I crossed to the south side and ascended by an inclined plane, such as later I discovered to be one of the transportation features of Pittsburgh, the hill called Mt. Washington, from the top of which, walking along an avenue called Grand View Boulevard which skirted the brow of the hill, I had the finest view of a city I have ever seen. In later years I looked down upon New York from the heights of the Palisades and the hills of Staten Island; on Rome from the Pincian Gardens; on Florence from San Miniato; and on Pasadena and Los Angeles from the slopes of Mt. Lowe; but never anywhere have I seen a scene which impressed me more than this: the rugged beauty of the mountains, which encircle the city, the three rivers that run as threads of bright metal, dividing it into three parts, the several cities joined as one, their clambering streets presenting a checkered pattern emphasized here and there by the soot-darkened spires of churches and the walls of the taller and newer and cleaner office buildings.

As in most American cities of any size, the skyscraper was just being introduced and being welcomed as full proof of the growth and wealth and force of the city. No city was complete without at least one: the more, of course, the grander.

Pittsburgh had a better claim to the skyscraper as a commercial necessity than any other American city that I know. The tongue of land which lies between the Allegheny and the Monongahela, very likely not more than two or three square miles in extent, is still the natural heart of the commercial life for fifty, a hundred miles about. Here meet the three large rivers, all navigable. Here, again, the natural runs and gaps of the various hills about, as well as the levels which pursue the banks of the streams and which are the natural vents or routes for railroad lines, street-cars and streets, come to a common center. Whether by bridges from Allegheny, the south bank of the Ohio or the Monongahela, or along the shores of the Allegheny or Monongahela within the city of Pittsburgh itself, all meet somewhere in this level tongue; and here, of necessity, is the business center. So without the tall building, I cannot see how one-tenth of the business which would and should be normally transacted here would ever come about.

CHAPTER LX

BARRING two or three tall buildings, the city of Pittsburgh was then of a simple and homelike aspect. A few blackened church spires, a small dark city hall and an old market-place, a long stretch of blast furnaces, black as night, and the lightly constructed bridges over the rivers, gave it all an airy grace and charm.

Since the houses up here were very simple, mostly working-men's cottages, and the streets back followed the crests of hills twisting and winding as they went and providing in consequence the most startling and effective views of green hills and mountains beyond, I decided that should I be so fortunate as to secure work I would move over here. It would be like living in a mountain resort, and most inexpensively.

I descended and took a car which followed the Monongahela upstream to Homestead, and here for the first time had a view of that enormous steel plant which only recently (June to December, 1892) had played such a great part in the industrial drama of America. The details of the quarrel were fairly fresh in my mind: how the Carnegie Steel Company had planned, with the technicalities of a wage-scale readjustment as an excuse, to break the power of the Amalgamated Steel Workers, who were becoming too forceful and who were best organized in their plant, and how the Amalgamated, resenting the introduction of three hundred Pinkerton guards to "protect" the plant, had attacked them, killing several and injuring others, and so permitting the introduction of the State militia, which speedily and permanently broke the power of the strikers. They could only wait then and starve, and so they had waited and starved for six months, when they finally returned to work, such of them as would be received. When I reached there in April, 1894, the battle was already fifteen months past, but the feeling was still alive. I did not then know what it was about this town of Homestead that was so depressing, but in the six months of my stay here I found that it was a compound of a sense of defeat and sullen despair. The men had not forgotten. Even then the company was busy, and had been for months, importing Poles, Hungarians, Lithuanians, to take the places of the ousted strikers. Whole colonies were already here, housed under the most unsatisfactory conditions, and more were coming. Hence the despair of those who had been defeated.

Along the river sprawled for a quarter of a mile or more the huge low length of the furnaces, great black bottle-like affairs with rows of stacks and long low sheds or buildings paralleling them, sheds from which came a continuous hammering and sputtering and the glow of red fire. The whole was shrouded by a pall of gray smoke, even in the bright sunshine. Above the plant, on a slope which rose steeply behind it, were a few moderately attractive dwellings grouped about two small parks, the trees of which were languishing for want of air. Behind and to the sides of these were the spires of several churches, those soporifics against failure and despair. Turning up side streets one found, invariably, uniform frame houses, closely built and dulled by smoke and grime, and below, on the flats behind the mill, were cluttered alleys so unsightly and unsanitary as to shock me into the belief that I was once more witnessing the lowest phases of Chicago slum-life, the worst I had ever seen. The streets were mere mud-tracks. Where there were trees (and there were few) they were dwarfed and their foliage withered by a metallic fume which was over all. Though the sun was bright at the top of the hill, down here it was gray, almost cloudy, at best a filtered dull gold haze.

The place held me until night. I browsed about its saloons, of which there was a large number, most of them idle during the drift of the afternoon. The open gates of the mill held my interest also, for through them I could see furnaces, huge cranes, switching engines, cars of molten iron being hauled to and fro, and mountains of powdered iron ore and scrap iron piled here and there awaiting the hour of new birth in the smelting vats. When the sun had gone down, and I had watched a shift of men coming out with their buckets and coats over their arms, and other hundreds entering in a rush, I returned to the city with a sense of the weight and breadth and depth of huge effort. Here bridges and rail and plate steel were made for all the world. But of all these units that dwelt and labored here scarce a fraction seemed even to sense a portion of the meaning of all they did. I knew that Carnegie had become a multi-millionaire, as had Phipps and others, and that he was beginning to give libraries, that Phipps had already given several floral conservatories, and that their "lobbies" in Congress were even then bartering for the patronage of the government on their terms; but the poor units in these hovels at Homestead—what did they know?

On another day I explored the east end of Pittsburgh, which was the exclusive residence section of the city and a contrast to such hovels and deprivations as I had witnessed at Homestead and among the shacks across the Monongahela and below Mt. Washington. Never in my life, neither before nor since, in New York, Chicago or elsewhere, was the vast gap which divides the rich from the poor in America so vividly and forcefully brought home to me. I had seen on my map a park called Schenley, and thinking that it might be interesting I made my way out a main thoroughfare called (quite appropriately, I think) Fifth Avenue, lined with some of the finest residences of the city. Never did the mere possession of wealth impress me so keenly. Here were homes of the most imposing character, huge, verandaed, tree-shaded, with immense lawns, great stone or iron or hedge fences and formal gardens and walks of a most ornate character. It was a region of well-curbed, well-drained and well-paved thoroughfares. Even the street-lamps were of a better design than elsewhere, so eager was a young and democratic municipality to see that superior living conditions were provided for the rich. There were avenues lined with well-cropped trees, and at every turn one encountered expensive carriages, their horses jingling silver or gold-gilt harness, their front seats occupied by one or two footmen in livery, while reclining was Madam or Sir, or both, gazing condescendingly upon the all too comfortable world about them.

In Schenley Park was a huge and interesting arboretum or botanical garden under glass, a most oriental affair given by Phipps of the Carnegie Company. A large graceful library of white limestone, perhaps four or five times the size of the one in Allegheny, given by Andrew Carnegie, was in process of construction. And he was another of the chief beneficiaries of Homestead, the possessor of a great house in this region, another in New York and still another in Scotland, a man for whom the unwitting "Pinkertons" and contending strikers had been killed. Like huge ribbons of fire these and other names of powerful steel men—the Olivers, Thaws, Fricks, Thompsons—seemed to rise and band the sky. It seemed astonishing to me that some men could thus rise and soar about the heavens like eagles, while others, drab sparrows all, could only pick among the offal of the hot ways below. What were these things called democracy and equality about which men prated? Had they any basis in fact? There was constant palaver about the equality of opportunity which gave such men as these their chance, but I could not help speculating as to the lack of equality of opportunity these men created for others once their equality at the top had made them. If equality of opportunity had been so excellent for them why not for others, especially those in their immediate care? True, all men had not the brains to seize upon and make use of that which was put before them, but again, not all men of brains had the blessing of opportunity as had these few men. Strength, as I felt, should not be too arrogant or too forgetful of the accident or chance by which it had arrived. It might do something for the poor—pay them decent living wages, for instance. Were these giants planning to subject their sons and daughters to the same "equality of opportunity" which had confronted them at the start and which they were so eager to recommend to the attention of others? Not at all. In this very neighborhood I passed an exclusive private school for girls, with great grounds and a beautiful wall— another sample of equality of opportunity.

On the fourth day of my stay here I called again at the *Dispatch* office and was given a position, but only after the arrival of a telegram from Toledo offering me work at eighteen a week. Now I had long since passed out of the eighteen-dollar stage of reporting, and this was by no means a comforting message. If I could show it to the *Dispatch* city editor, I reasoned, it would probably hasten his decision to accept me, but also he might consider eighteen dollars as a rate of pay acceptable to me and would offer no more. I decided not to use it just then but to go first and see if anything had come about in my favor.

"Nothing yet," he said on seeing me. "Drop around to-morrow or Saturday. I'm sure to know then one way or the other."

I went out and in the doorway below stood and meditated. What was I to do? If I delayed too long my friend in Toledo would not be able to do anything for me, and if I showed this message it would fix my salary at a place below that which I felt I deserved. I finally hit upon the idea of changing the eighteen to twenty-five and went to a telegraph office to find some girl to rewrite it for me. Not seeing a girl I would be willing to approach, I worked over it myself, carefully erasing and changing until the twenty-five, while a little forced and scraggly, looked fairly natural. With this in my pocket I returned to the *Dispatch* this same afternoon, and told the city editor with as great an air of assurance as I could achieve that I had just received this message and was a little uncertain as to what to do about it. "The fact is," I said, "I have started from the West to go East. New York is my eventual goal, unless I find a good place this side of it. But I'm up against it now and unless I can do something here I might as well go back there for the present. I wouldn't show you this except that I must answer it tonight."

He read it and looked at me uncertainly. Finally he got up, told me to wait a minute, and went through a nearby door. In a minute or two he returned and said: "Well, that's all right. We can do as well as that, anyhow, if you want to stay at that rate."

"All right," I replied as nonchalantly as I could. "When do I start?"

"Come around tomorrow at twelve. I may not have anything for you, but I'll carry you for a day or two until I have."

I trotted down the nearby steps as fast as my feet would carry me, anxious to get out of his sight so that I might congratulate myself freely. I hurried to a telegraph office to reject my friend's offer. To celebrate my cleverness and success I indulged in a good meal at one of the best restaurants. Here I sat, and to prepare myself for my work examined that day's *Dispatch*, as well as the other papers, with a view to unraveling their method of treating a feature or a striking piece of news, also to discover what they considered a feature. By nine or ten I had solved that mystery as well as I could, and then to quiet my excited nerves I walked about the business section, finally crossing to Mt. Washington so as to view the lighted city at night from this great height. It was radiantly clear up there, and a young moon shining, and I had the pleasure of looking down upon as wonderful a night panorama as I have ever seen, a winking and fluttering field of diamonds that outrivaled the sky itself. As far as the eye could see were these lamps blinking and winking, and overhead was another glistering field of stars. Below was that enormous group of stacks with their red tongues waving in the wind. Far up the Monongahela, where lay Homestead and McKeesport and Braddock and Swissvale, other glows of red fire indicated where huge furnaces were blazing and boiling in the night. I thought of the nest of slums I had seen at Homestead, of those fine houses in the east end, and of Carnegie with his libraries, of Phipps with his glass conservatories. How to get up in the world and be somebody was my own thought now, and yet I knew that wealth was not for me. The best I should ever do was to think and dream, standing aloof as a spectator.

The next day I began work on the *Dispatch* and for six months was a part of it, beginning with ordinary news reporting, but gradually taking up the task of preparing original column features, first for the daily and later for the Sunday issue. Still later, not long before I left, I was by way of being an unpaid assistant to the dramatic editor, and a traveling correspondent.

What impressed me most was the peculiar character of the city and the newspaper world here, the more or less somnolent nature of its population (apart from the steel companies and their employees) and the genial and sociable character of the newspaper men. Never had I encountered more intelligent or helpful or companionable albeit cynical men than I found here. They knew the world, and their opportunities for studying public as well as private impulses and desires and contrasting them with public and private performances were so great as to make them puzzled if not always accurate judges of affairs and events. One can always talk to a newspaper man, I think, with the full confidence that one is talking to a man who is at least free of moralistic mush. Nearly everything in connection with those trashy romances of justice, truth, mercy, patriotism, public profession of all sorts, is already and forever gone if they have been in the business for any length of time. The religionist is seen by them for what he is: a swallower of romance or a masquerader looking to profit and preferment. Of the politician, they know or believe but one thing: that he is out for himself, a trickster artfully juggling with the moods and passions and ignorance of the public. Judges are men who have by some chance or other secured good positions and are careful to trim their sails according to the moods and passions of the strongest element in any community or nation in which they chance to be. The arts are in the main to be respected, when they are not frankly confessed to be enigmas.

In a very little while I came to be on friendly terms with the men of this and some other papers, men who, because of their intimate contact with local political and social conditions, were well fitted to enlighten me as to the exact economic and political conditions here. Two in particular, the political and labor men of this paper were most helpful. The former, a large, genial, commercial-drummer type, who might also have made an excellent theatrical manager or promoter, provided me with a clear insight into the general cleavage of local and State politics and personalities. I liked him very much. The other, the labor man, was a slow, silent, dark, square-shouldered and almost square-headed youth, who drifted in and out of the office irregularly. He it was who attended, when permitted by the working people themselves, all labor meetings in the city or elsewhere, as far east at times as the hard coal regions about Wilkes-Barre and Scranton. As he himself told me, he was the paper's sole authority for such comments or assertions as it dared to make in connection with the mining of coal and the manufacture of steel. He was an intense sympathizer with labor, but not so much with organized as with unorganized workers. He believed that labor here had two years before lost a most important battle, one which would show in its contests with money in the future: which was true. He pretended to know that there was a vast movement on foot among the moneyed elements in America to cripple if not utterly destroy organized labor, and to that end he assured me once that all the great steel and coal and oil magnates were in a conspiracy to flood the country with cheap foreign labor, which they had lured or were luring here by all sorts of dishonest devices; once here, these immigrants were to be used to break the demand of better-paid and more intelligent labor. He pretended to know that in the coal and steel regions thousands had already been introduced and more were on their way, and that all such devices as showy churches and schools for defectives, etc., were used to keep ignorant and tame those already here.

"But you can't say anything about it in Pittsburgh," he said to me. "If I should talk I'd have to get out of here. The papers here won't use a thing unfavorable to the magnates in any of these fields. I write all sorts of things, but they never get in."

He read the *Congressional Record* daily, as well as various radical papers from different parts of the country, and was constantly calling my attention to statistics and incidents which proved that the workingman was being most unjustly put upon and undermined; but he never did it in any urgent or disturbed manner. Rather, he seemed to be profoundly convinced that the cause of the workers everywhere in America was hopeless. They hadn't the subtlety and the force and the innate cruelty of those who ruled them. They were given to religious and educational illusions, the parochial school and church paper, which left them helpless. In the course of time, because I expressed interest in and sympathy for these people, he took me into various mill slums in and near the city to see how they lived.

CHAPTER LXI

I WENT with him first to Homestead, then to some tenements there, later to some other mill districts nearer Pittsburgh, the name of which I have forgotten. What astonished me, in so far as the steel mills were concerned, was the large number of furnaces going at once, the piles, mountains, of powdered iron ore ready to be smelted, the long lines of cars, flat, box and coal cars, and the nature and size and force of the machinery used to roll steel. The work, as he or his friends the bosses showed me, was divided between the "front" and the "back." Those working at the front of the furnace took care of the molten ore and slag which was being "puddled." The men at the back, the stock and yard men, filled huge steel buckets or "skips" suspended from traveling cranes with ore, fuel and limestone, all of which was piled near at hand; this material was then trundled to a point over the mouth of the melting-vats, as they were called, and "released" via a movable bottom. At this particular plant I was told that the machinery for handling all this was better than elsewhere, the company being richer and more progressive. In some of the less progressive concerns the men filled carts with raw material and then trundled them around to the front of a hoist, which was at the back of the furnace, where they were lifted and dumped into the furnaces. But in this mill all a man had to do to fill a steel bucket with raw material was to push one of those steel buckets suspended from a trolley under a chute and pull a rod, when the "stock" tumbled into it. From these it was trundled, by machinery, to a point over the furnace. The furnaces were charged or fed constantly by feeders working in twelve-hour shifts, so that there was little chance to rest from their labors. Their pay was not more than half of that paid to the men at the "front" because it was neither so hard nor so skillful, although it looked hard enough to me.

The men at the front, the puddlers, were the labor princes of this realm and yet among the hardest worked. A puddling or blast furnace was a brick structure like an oven, about seven feet high and six feet square, with two compartments, one a receptacle into which pigiron was thrown, the other a fuel chamber where the melting heat was generated. The drafts were so arranged that the flame swept from the fuel chamber directly upon the surface of the iron. From five to six hundred pounds of pigiron were put into each furnace at one time, after which it was closed and sufficient heat applied to melt down the iron. Then the puddler began to work it with an iron rod through a hole in the furnace door, so as to stir up the liquid and bring it in contact with the air. As the impurities became separated from the iron and rose to the top as slag, they were tipped out through a center notch. As it became freer from impurities, a constantly higher temperature was required to keep the iron in a liquid condition. Gradually it began to solidify in granules, much as butter forms in churning. Later it took on or was worked into large malleable balls or lumps or rolls like butter, three to any given "charge" or furnace. Then, while still in a comparatively soft but not molten condition, these were taken out and thrown across a steel floor to a "taker" to be worked by other machinery and other processes.

Puddling was a full-sized man's job. There were always two, and sometimes three, to a single furnace, and they took turns at working the metal, as a rule ten minutes to a turn. No man could stand before a furnace and perform that backbreaking toil continually. Even when working by spells a man was often nearly exhausted at the end of his spell. As a rule he had to go outside and sit on a bench, the perspiration running off him. The intensity of the heat in those days (1893) was not as yet relieved by the device of shielding the furnace with water-cooled plates. The wages of these men was in the neighborhood of three dollars a day, the highest then paid. Before the great strike it had been more.

But the men who most fascinated me were the "roughers" who, once the puddler had done his work and thrown his lump of red-hot iron out upon an open hearth, and another man had taken it and thrown it to a "rougher," fed it into a second machine which rolled or beat it into a more easily handled and workable form. The exact details of the process escape me now, but I remember the picture they presented in those hot, fire-lighted, noisy and sputtering rooms. Agility and even youth were at a premium, and a false step possibly meant death. I remember watching two men in the mill below Mt. Washington, one who pulled out billet after billet from furnace after furnace and threw them along the steel floor to the "rougher," and the latter, who, dressed only in trousers and a sleeveless flannel shirt, the sweat pouring from his body and his muscles standing out in knots, took these same and, with the skill and agility of a tight-rope performer, tossed them into the machine. He was constantly leaping about thrusting the red billets which came almost in a stream into or between the first pair of rolls for which they were intended. And yet before he could turn back there was always another on the floor behind him. The rolls into which he fed these billets were built in a train, side by side in line, and as they went through one pair they had to be seized by a "catcher" and shoved back through the next. Back and forth, back and forth they went at an ever increasing speed, until the catcher at the next to the last pair of rolls, seizing the end of the rod as it came through, still red-hot, described with it a fiery circle bending it back again to enter the last roll, from which it passed into water. It was wonderful.

And yet these men were not looked upon as anything extraordinary. While the places in which they worked were metal infernos and their toil of the most intense and exacting character, they were not allowed to organize to better their condition. The recent great victory of the steel magnates had settled that. In that very city and elsewhere, these magnates were rolling in wealth. Their profits were tumbling in so fast that they scarcely knew what to do with them. Vast libraries and universities were being built with their gifts. Immense mansions were crowded with art and historic furniture. Their children were being sent to special schools to be taught how to be ladies and gentlemen in a democracy which they contemned; and on the other hand, these sweating men were being denied an additional five or ten cents an hour and the right to organize. If they protested or attempted to drive out imported strike-breakers they were fired and State or Federal troops were called in to protect the mills. They could not organize then, and they are not organized now.

My friend Martyn, who was intensely sympathetic toward them, was still more sympathetic toward the men who were not so skillful, mere day laborers who received from one dollar to one-sixty-five at a time when two a day was too little to support any one. He grew melodramatic as he told me where these men lived and how they lived, and finally took me in order that I might see for myself. Afterward, in the course of my reportorial work, I came upon some of these neighborhoods and individuals, and since they are all a part of the great fortune-building era, and illustrate how democracy works in America, and how some great fortunes were built, I propose to put down here a few pictures of things that I saw. Wages varied from one to one-sixty-five a day for the commonest laborer, three and even four a day for the skilled worker. Rents, or what the cheaper workers, who constituted by far the greater number, were able to pay, varied from two-fifteen per week, or eight-sixty per month, to four-seventy-two per week, or twenty per month.

And the type of places they could secure for this! I recall visiting a two-room tenement in a court, the character of which first opened my eyes to the type of home these workers endured. This court consisted of four sides with an open space in the center. Three of these sides were smoke-grimed wooden houses three stories in height; the fourth was an ancient and odorous wooden stable, where the horses of a contractor were kept. In the center of this court stood a circular wooden building or lavatory with ten triangular compartments, each opening into one vault or cesspool. Near this was one hydrant, the only water-supply for all these homes or rooms. These two conveniences served twenty families, Polish, Hungarian, Slavonic, Jewish, Negro, of from three to five people each, living in the sixty-three rooms which made up the three grimy sides above mentioned. There were twenty-seven children in these rooms, for whom this court was their only playground. For twenty housewives this was the only place where they could string their wash-lines. For twenty tired, sweaty, unwashed husbands this was, aside from the saloon, the only near and neighborly recreation and companionship center. Here of a sweltering summer night, after playing cards and drinking beer, they would frequently stretch themselves to sleep.

But this was not all. As waste pipes were wanting in the houses, heavy tubs of water had to be carried in and out, and this in a smoky town where a double amount of washing and cleaning was necessary. When the weather permitted, the heavy washes were done in the yard. Then the pavement of this populous court, covered with tubs, wringers, clothes baskets and pools of soapy water, made a poor playground for children. In addition to this, these lavatories must be used, and in consequence a situation was created which may be better imagined than explained. Many of the front windows of these apartments looked down on this center, which was only a few yards from the kitchen windows, creating a neat, sanitary and uplifting condition. While usually only two families used one of these compartments, in some other courts three or four families were compelled to use one, giving rise to indifference and a sense of irresponsibility for their condition. While all the streets had sewers and by borough ordinance these outside vaults must be connected with them, still most of them were flushed only by waste water, which flowed directly into them from the yard faucet. When conditions became unbearable the vaults were washed out with a hose attached to the hydrant, but in winter, when there was danger of freezing, this was not always possible. There was not one indoor closet in any of these courts.

But to return to the apartment in question. The kitchen

was steaming with vapor from a big washtub set on a chair in the middle of the room. The mother, who had carried the water in, was trying to wash and at the same time keep the older of her two babies from tumbling into the tub of scalding water that was standing on the floor. On one side of the room was a huge puffy bed, with one feather tick to sleep on and another for covering. Near the window was a sewing-machine, in a corner a melodeon, and of course there was the inevitable cookstove, upon which was simmering a pot of soup. To the left, in the second room, were one boarder and the man of the house asleep. Two boarders, so I learned, were at work, but at night would be home to sleep in the bed now occupied by one boarder and the man of the house. The little family and their boarders, taken to help out on the rent, worked and lived so in order that Mr. Carnegie might give the world one or two extra libraries with his name plastered on the front, and Mr. Frick a mansion on Fifth Avenue.

It was to Martyn and his interest that I owed still other views. He took me one day to a boardinghouse in which lived twenty-four people, all in two rooms, and yet, to my astonishment and confusion, it was not so bad as that other court, so great apparently is the value of intimate human contact. Few of the very poor day laborers, as Martyn explained to me, who were young and unmarried, cared how they lived so long as they lived cheaply and could save a little. This particular boardinghouse in Homestead was in a court such as I have described, and consisted of two rooms, one above the other, each measuring perhaps 12x20. In the kitchen at the time was the wife of the boarding boss cooking dinner. Along one side of the room was an oilcloth-covered table with a plank bench on each side; above it was a rack holding a long row of white cups, and a shelf with tin knives and forks. Near the up-to-date range, the only real piece of furniture in the room, hung the buckets in which all mill men carried their noon or midnight meals. A crowd of men were lounging cheerfully about, talking, smoking and enjoying life, one of them playing a concertina. They were making the most of a brief spell before their meal and departure for work.

In the room above, as the landlord cheerfully showed us, were double iron bedsteads set close together and on them comfortables neatly laid.

In these two rooms lived, besides the boarding boss and his wife, both stalwart Bulgarians, and their two babies, twenty men. They were those who handled steel billets and bars, unloaded and loaded trains, worked in cinder pits, filled steel buckets with stock, and what not. They all worked twelve hours a day, and their reward was this and what they could save over and above it out of nine-sixty per week. Martyn said a good thing about them at the time: "I don't know how it is. I know these people are exploited and misused. The mill-owners pay them the lowest wages, the landlords exploit these boardinghouse keepers as well as their boarders, and the community which they make by their work don't give a damn for them, and yet they are happy, and I'll be hanged if they don't make me happy. It must be that just work is happiness," and I agreed with him. Plenty of work, something to do, the ability to avoid the ennui of idleness and useless, pensive, futile thought!

There was another side that I thought was a part of all this, and that was the "vice" situation. There were so many girls who walked the streets here, and back of the *Dispatch* and postoffice buildings, as well as in the streets ranged along the Monongahela below Smithfield (Water, First and Second), were many houses of disrepute, as large and flourishing an area as I had seen in any city. As I learned from the political and police man, the police here as elsewhere "protected" vice, or in other words preyed upon it.

CHAPTER LXII

In the meantime I was going about my general work, and an easy task it proved. My city editor, cool, speculative, diplomatic soul, soon instructed me as to the value of news and its limitations here. "We don't touch on labor conditions except through our labor man," he told me, "and he knows what to say. There's nothing to be said about the rich or religious in a derogatory sense: they're all right in so far as we know. We don't touch on scandals in high life. The big steel men here just about own the place, so we can't. Some papers out West and down in New York go in for sensationalism, but we don't. I'd rather have some simple little feature any time, a story about some old fellow with eccentric habits, than any of these scandals or tragedies. Of course we do cover them when we have to, but we have to be mighty careful what we say."

So much for a free press in Pittsburgh, A. D. 1893!

And I found that the city itself, possibly by reason of the recent defeat administered to organized labor and the soft pedal of the newspapers, presented a most quiescent and somnolent aspect. There was little local news. Suicides, occasional drownings, a wedding or death in high society, a brawl in a saloon, the enlargement of a steel plant, the visit of a celebrity or the remarks of some local pastor, provided the pabulum on which the local readers were fed. Sometimes an outside event, such as the organization by General Coxey, of Canton, Ohio, of his "hobo" army, at that time moving toward Washington to petition congress against the doings of the trusts; or the dictatorial and impossible doings of Grover Cleveland, opposition President to the dominant party of the State; or the manner in which the moribund Democratic party of this region was attempting to steal an office or share in the spoils—these and the grand comments of gentlemen in high financial positions here and elsewhere as to the outlook for prosperity in the nation or the steel mills or the coal fields, occupied the best places in the newspapers. For a great metropolis as daring, forceful, economically and socially restless as this, it seemed unbelievable that it could be so quiescent or say so little about the colossal ambitions animating the men at the top. But when it came to labor or the unions, their restlessness or unholy anarchistic demands, or the trashy views of a third-rate preacher complaining of looseness in dress or morals, or an actor voicing his views on art, or a politician commenting on some unimportant phase of our life, it was a very different matter. These papers were then free enough to say their say.

I recall that Thomas B. Reed, then Speaker of the House, once passed through the city and stopped off to visit some friendly steel magnate. I was sent to interview him and obtain his views as to "General" Coxey's army, a band of poor mistaken theorists who imagined that by marching to Washington and protesting to Congress they could compel a trust-dictated American Senate and House to take cognizance of their woes. This able statesman—and he was no fool, being at the time in the councils and favor of the money power and looked upon as the probable Republican Presidential nominee —pretended to me to believe that a vast national menace lay in such a movement and protest.

"Why, it's the same as revolution!" he ranted, washing his face in his suite at the Monongahela, his suspenders swaying loosely about his fat thighs. "It's an unheard-of proceeding. For a hundred years the American people have had a fixed and constitutional and democratic method of procedure. They have their county and State and national conventions, and their power of instructing delegates to the same. They can write any plank they wish into any party platform, and compel its enforcement by their votes. Now comes along a man who finds something that doesn't just suit his views, and instead of waiting and appealing to the regular party councils, he organizes an army and proceeds to march on Washington."

"But he has been able to muster only three or four hundred men all told," I suggested mildly. "He doesn't seem to be attracting many followers."

"The number of his followers isn't the point," he insisted. "If one man can gather an army of five hundred, another can gather an army of ten or five hundred thousand. That means revolution."

"Yes," I ventured. "But what about the thing of which they are complaining?"

"It doesn't matter what their grievance is," he said somewhat testily. "This is a government of law and prescribed political procedure. Our people must abide by that."

I was ready to agree, only I was thinking of the easy manner in which delegates and elected representatives everywhere were ignoring the interests if not the mandates of the body politic at large and listening to the advice and needs of financiers and trust-builders. Already the air was full of complaints against monopoly. Trusts and combinations of every kind were being organized, and the people were being taxed accordingly. All property, however come by, was sacred in America. The least protest of the mass anywhere was revolutionary, or at least the upwellings of worthless and never-to-be-countenanced malcontents. I could not believe this. I firmly believed then, as I do now, that the chains wherewith a rapidly developing financial oligarchy or autocracy meant to bind a liberty-deluded mass were then and there being forged. I felt then, as I do now, that the people of that day should have been more alive to their interests, that they should have compelled, at Washington or elsewhere, by peaceable political means if possible, by dire and threatening uprisings if necessary, a more careful concern for their interests than any congressman or senator or governor or President, at that time or since, was giving them. As I talked to this noble chairman of the House my heart was full of these sentiments, only I did not deem it of any avail to argue with him. I was a mere cub reporter and he was the Speaker of the House of Representatives, but I had a keen contempt for the enthusiasm he manifested for law. When it came to what the money barons wished, the manufacturers and trust organizers hiding behind a huge and extortionate tariff wall, he was one of their chief guards and political and congressional advocates. If you doubt it look up his record.

But it was owing to this very careful interpretation of what was and what was not news that I experienced some of the most delightful newspaper hours of my life. Large features being scarce, I was assigned to do ''city hall and police, Allegheny,'' as the assignment book used to read, and with this mild task ahead of me I was in the habit of crossing the Allegheny River into the city of Allegheny, where, ensconced in a chair in the reporters' room of the combined city hall and central police station or in the Carnegie Public Library over the way, or in the cool, central, shaded court of the Allegheny General Hospital, with the head interne of which I soon made friends, I waited for something to turn up. As is usual with all city and police and hospital officials everywhere, the hope of favorable and often manufactured publicity animating them, I was received most cordially. All I had to do was to announce that I was from the *Dispatch* and assigned to this bailiwick, and I was informed as to anything of importance that had come to the surface during the last ten or twelve hours. If there was nothing—and usually there was not—I sat about with several other reporters or with the head interne of the hospital, or, having no especial inquiry to make, I crossed the street to Squire Daniels, whose office was in the tree-shaded square facing this civic center, and here (a squire being the equivalent of a petty police magistrate), inquired if anything had come to his notice.

Squire Daniels, a large, bald, pink-faced individual of three hundredweight, used of a sunny afternoon these warm Spring days to sit out in front of his office, his chair tilted against his office wall or a tree, and, with three or four cronies, retail the most delicious stories of old-time political characters and incidents. He was a mine of this sort of thing and an immense favorite in consequence with all the newspaper men and politicians. I was introduced to him on my third or fourth day in Allegheny as he was sitting out on his tilted chair, and he surveyed me with a smile.

"From the *Dispatch*, eh? Well, take a chair if you can find one; if you can't, sit on the curb or in the doorway. Many's the man I seen from the *Dispatch* in my time. Your boss, Harry Gaither, used to come around here before he got to be city editor. So did your Sunday man, Funger. There ain't much news I can give you, but whatever there is you're welcome to it. I always treat all the boys alike," and he smiled. Then he proceeded with his tale, something about an old alderman or politician who had painted a pig once in order to bring it up to certain prize specifications and so won the prize, only to be found out later because the "specifications" wore off. He had such a zestful way of telling his stories as to compel laughter.

And then directly across the street to the east from the city hall was the Allegheny Carnegie library, a very handsome building which contained, in addition to the library, an auditorium in which had been placed the usual "one of the largest" if not "the largest" pipe organ in the world. This organ had one advantage: it was supplied with a paid city organist, who on Sundays, Wednesdays and Saturdays entertained the public with free recitals, and so capable was he that seats were at a premium and standing-room only the rule unless one arrived far ahead of time. This manifestation of interest on the part of the public pleased me greatly and somehow qualified, if it did not atone for, Mr. Carnegie's indifference to the welfare of his employees.

But I was most impressed with the forty or fifty thousand volumes so conveniently arranged that one could walk from stack to stack, looking at the labels and satisfying one's interest by browsing in the books. The place had most comfortable window-nooks and chairs between stacks and in alcoves. One afternoon, having nothing else to do, I came here and by the merest chance picked up a volume entitled *The Wild Ass's Skin* by the writer who so fascinated Wandell—Honoré de Balzac. I examined it curiously, reading a preface which shimmered with his praise. He was the great master of France. His *Comédie Humaine* covered every aspect of the human welter. His interpretations of character were exhaustive and exact. His backgrounds were abundant, picturesque, gorgeous. In Paris his home had been turned into a museum, and contained his effects as they were at the time of his death.

I turned to the first page and began reading, and from then on until dusk I sat in this charming alcove reading. A new and inviting door to life had been suddenly thrown open to me. Here was one who saw, thought, felt. Through him I saw a prospect so wide that it left me breathless—all Paris, all France, all life through French eyes. Here was one who had a tremendous and sensitive grasp of life, philosophic, tolerant, patient, amused. At once I was personally identified with his Raphael, his Rastignac, his Bixiou, his Bianchon. With Raphael I entered the gaming-house in the Palais Royal, looked despairingly down into the waters of the Seine from the Pont Royal, turned from it to the shop of the dealer in antiques, was ignored by the perfect young lady before the shop of the print-seller, attended the Taillefer banquet, suffered horrors over the shrinking skin. The lady without a heart was all too real. It was for me a literary revolution. Not only for the brilliant and incisive manner with which Balzac grasped life and invented themes whereby to present it, but for the fact that the types he handled with most enthusiasm and skill—the brooding, seeking, ambitious beginner in life's social, political, artistic and commercial affairs (Rastignac, Raphael, de Rubempre, Bianchon)—were, I thought, so much like myself. Indeed, later taking up and consuming almost at a sitting *The Great Man from the Provinces, Père Goriot, Cousin Pons, Cousin Bette*, it was so easy to identify myself with the young and seeking aspirants. The brilliant and intimate pictures of Parisian life, the exact flavor of its politics, arts, sciences, religions, social goings to and fro impressed me so as to accomplish for me what his imaginary magic skin had done for his Raphael: transfer me bodily and without defect or lack to the center as well as the circumference of the world which he was describing. I knew his characters as well as he did, so magical was his skill. His grand and somewhat pompous philosophical deductions, his easy and offhand disposition of all manner of critical, social, political, historical, religious problems, the manner in which he assumed as by right of genius intimate and irrefutable knowledge of all subjects, fascinated and captured me as the true method of the seer and the genius. Oh, to possess an insight such as this! To know and be a part of such a cosmos as Paris, to be able to go there, to work, to study, suffer, rise, and even end in defeat if need be, so fascinatingly alive were all the journeys of his puppets! What was Pittsburgh, what St. Louis, what Chicago?—and yet, in spite of myself, while I adored his Paris, still I was obtaining a new and more dramatic light on the world in which I found myself. Pittsburgh was not Paris, America was not France, but in truth they were something, and Pittsburgh at least had aspects which somehow suggested Paris. These charming rivers, these many little bridges, the sharp contrasts presented by the east end and the mill regions, the huge industries here and their importance to the world at large, impressed me more vividly than before. I was in a workaday, begrimed, and yet vivid Paris. Taillefer, Nucingen, Valentin were no different from some of the immense money magnets here, in their ease, luxury, power, at least the possibilities which they possessed.

Coming out of the library this day, and day after day thereafter, the while I rendered as little reportorial service as was consistent with even a show of effort, I marveled at the physical similarity of the two cities as I conceived it, at the chance for pictures here as well as there. American pictures here, as opposed to French pictures there. And all the while I was riding with Lucien to Paris, with his mistress, courting Madame Nucingen with Rastignac, brooding over the horror of the automatically contracting skin with Raphael, poring over his miseries with Goriot, practicing the horrible art of prostitution with Madame Marneffe. For a period of four or five months I ate, slept, dreamed, lived him and his characters and his views and his city. I cannot imagine a greater joy and inspiration than I had in Balzac these Spring and Summer days in Pittsburgh. Idyllic days, dreamy days, poetic days, wonderful days, the while I ostensibly did ''police and city hall'' in Allegheny.

CHAPTER LXIII

It would be unfair to myself not to indicate that I rendered an adequate return for the stipend paid me. As a matter of fact, owing to the peculiar character of the local news conditions, as well as my own creative if poorly equipped literary instincts at the time, I was able to render just such service as my employers craved, and that with scarcely a wrench to my mental ease. For what they craved, more than news of a dramatic or disturbing character, was some sort of idle feature stuff which they could use in place of news and still interest their readers. The Spring time, Balzac, the very picturesque city itself, my own idling and yet reflective disposition, caused me finally to attempt a series of mood or word pictures about the most trivial matters—a summer storm, a spring day, a visit to a hospital, the death of an old switchman's dog, the arrival of the first mosquito—which gave me my first taste of what it means to be a creative writer.

The city editor asked me one day if I could not invent some kind of feature, and I sat down and thought of one theme and another. Finally I thought of the fly as a possible subject for an idle skit. Being young and ambitious, and having just crawled out of a breeding-pit somewhere, he alighted on the nearest fence or windowsill, brushed his head and wings reflectively and meditated on the chances of a livelihood or a career. What would be open to a young and ambitious fly in a world all too crowded with flies? There were barns, of course, and kitchens and horses and cows and pigs, but these fields were overrun, and this was a sensitive and cleanly and meditative fly. Flying about here and there to inspect the world, he encountered within a modest and respectable home a shiny pate which seemed to offer a rather polished field of effort and so on.

This idle thing which took me not more than three-quarters

of an hour to write and which I was almost afraid to submit, produced a remarkable change in the attitude of the office, as well as in my life and career. We had at this time as assistant city editor a small, retiring, sentimental soul, Jim Israels, who was one of the most gracious and approachable and lovable men I have ever known. He it was to whom I turned over my skit. He took it with an air of kindly consideration and helpfulness.

"Trying to help us out, are you?" he said with a smile, and then added when I predicated its worthlessness: "Well, it's not such an easy thing to turn out that stuff. I hope it's something the chief will like."

He took it and, as I noticed, for I hung about to see, read it at once, and I saw him begin to smile and finally chuckle.

"This thing's all right," he called. "You needn't worry. Gaither'll be pleased with this, I know," and he began to edit it.

I went out to walk and think, for I had nothing to do except wander over to Allegheny to find out if anything had turned up.

When I returned at six I was greeted by my city editor with a smile and told that if I would I could do that sort of thing as much as I liked. "Try and get up something for tomorrow, will you?" I said I would try. The next day, a Spring rain descending with wonderful clouds and a magnificent electrical display, I described how the city, dry and smoky and dirty, lay panting in the deadening heat and how out of the west came, like an answer to a prayer, this sudden and soothing storm, battalion upon battalion of huge clouds riven with great silvery flashes of light, darkening the sun as they came; and how suddenly, while shutters clapped and papers flew and office windows and doors had to be closed and signs squeaked and swung and people everywhere ran to cover, the thousands upon thousands who had been enduring the heat heaved a sigh of gratitude. I described how the steel tenements, the homes of the rich, the office buildings, the factories, the hospitals and jails changed under these conditions, and then ventured to give specific incidents and pictures of animals and men.

This was received with congratulations, especially from the assistant editor, who was more partial to anything sentimental than his chief. But I, feeling that I had hit upon a vein of my own, was not inclined to favor the moods of either but to write such things as appealed to me most. This I did from day to day, wandering out into the country or into strange neighborhoods for ideas and so varying my studies as my mood dictated. I noticed, however, that my more serious attempts were not so popular as the lighter and sillier things. This might have been a guide to me, had I been so inclined, leading to an easy and popular success; but by instinct and observation I was inclined to be interested in the larger and more tragic phases of life. Mere humor, such as I could achieve when I chose, seemed always to require for its foundation the most trivial of incidents, whereas huge and massive conditions underlay tragedy and all the more forceful aspects of life.

But what pleased and surprised me was the manner in which these lighter as well as the more serious things were received and the change they made in my standing. Hitherto I was merely a newcomer being tested and by no means secure in my hold on this position. Now, of a sudden, my status was entirely changed. I was a feature man, one who had succeeded where others apparently had failed, and so I was made more than welcome. To my surprise, my city editor one day asked me whether I had had my lunch. I gladly availed myself of a chance to talk to him, and he told me a little something of local journalistic life, who the publisher of this paper was, his politics and views. The assistant editor asked me to dinner. The Sunday editor, the chief political reporter, the chief city hall and police man grew friendly; I went to lunch or dinner with one or the other, was taken to the Press Club after midnight, and occasionally to a theater by the dramatic man. Finally I was asked to contribute something to the Sunday papers, and later still asked to help the dramatic man with criticisms.

I was a little puzzled and made quite nervous though not

vain by this sudden change. The managing editor came to talk familiarly with me, and after him the son of the publisher, fresh from a European trip. But when he told me how interested he was in the kind of thing I was doing and that he wished he "could write like that," I remember feeling a little envious of him, with his fine clothes and easy manner. An invitation to dine at his home soothed me in no way. I never went. There was some talk of sending me to report a proposed commercial conference (at Buffalo, I believe), looking to the construction of a ship canal from Erie or Buffalo to Pittsburgh, but it interested me not at all. I had no interest in those things, really not in newspaper work, and yet I scarcely knew what I wanted to do if not that. One thing is sure: I had no commercial sense whereby I might have profited by all this. After the second or third sketch had been published there was a decided list in my direction, and I might have utilized my success. Instead, I merely mooned and dreamed as before, reading at the Carnegie Library, going out on assignments or writing one of these sketches and then going home again or to the Press Club. I gathered all sorts of data as to the steel magnates—Carnegie, Phipps and Frick especially—their homes, their clubs, their local condescensions and superiorities. The people of Pittsburgh were looked upon as vassals by some of these, and their interviews on returning from the seashore or the mountains partook of the nature of a royal return.

I remember being sent once to the Duquesne Club to interview Andrew Carnegie, fresh from his travels abroad, and being received by a secretary who allowed me to stand in the back of a room in which Mr. Carnegie, short, stocky, bandy-legged, a grand air of authority investing him, was addressing the élite of the city on the subject of America and its political needs. No note-taking was permitted, but I was later handed a typewritten address to the people of Pittsburgh and told that the *Dispatch* would be allowed to publish that. And it did. I smiled then, and I smile now, at the attitude of press, pulpit, officials of this amazing city of steel and iron where one and all seemed so genuflective and boot-licking, and yet seemed not to profit to any great degree by the presence of these magnates, who were constantly hinting at removing elsewhere unless they were treated thus and so—as though the life of a great and forceful metropolis depended on them alone.

CHAPTER LXIV

IT was about this time that I began to establish cordial relations with the short, broad-shouldered, sad-faced labor reporter whom I have previously mentioned. At first he appeared to be a little shy of me, but as time passed and I seemed to have established myself in the favor of the paper, he became more friendly. He was really a radical at heart, but did not dare let it be known here. Often of a morning he would spend as much as two hours with me, discussing the nature of coal-mining and steel-making, the difficulty of arranging wage conditions which would satisfy all the men and not cause friction; but in the main he commented on the shrewd and cunning way in which the bosses were more and more overreaching their employees, preying upon their prejudices by religious and political dodges, and at the same time misusing them shamefully through the company store, the short ton, the cost of mining materials, rent. At first, knowing nothing about the situation, I was inclined to doubt whether he was as sound in these matters as he seemed to be. Later, as I grew in personal knowledge, I thought he might be too conservative, so painful did many of the things seem which I saw with my own eyes and his aid.

About this time several things conspired to stir up my feelings in regard to New York. The Pittsburgh papers gave great space to New York events and affairs, much more than did most of the mid-Western papers. There was a millionaire steel colony here which was trying to connect itself with the so-called ''Four Hundred'' of New York, as well as the royal social atmosphere of England and France; and the comings and goings and doings of these people at Newport, New York, Bar Harbor, London and Paris were fully chronicled. Occasionally I was sent to one or another of these great homes to ask about the details of certain marriages or proposed trips, and would find the people in the midst of the most luxurious preparations. One night, for instance, I was sent to ask a certain steel man about the rumored resumption or extension of work in one of the mills. His house was but a dot on a great estate, the reaching of which was very difficult. I found him about ten o'clock at night stepping into a carriage to be driven to the local station, which was at the foot of the grounds. Although I was going to the same station in order to catch a local back to the city, he did not ask me to accompany him. Instead he paused on the step of his carriage to say that he could not say definitely whether the work would be done or not. He was entirely surrounded by bags, a gun, a fishing basket and other paraphernalia, after which of course a servant was looking. When he was gone I walked along the same road to the same station, and saw him standing there. Another man came up and greeted him.

"Going down to New York, George?" he inquired.

"No, to the Chesapeake. My lodge man tells me ducks are plentiful there now, and I thought I'd run down and get a few."

The through train, which had been ordered to stop for him, rolled in and he was gone. I waited for my smoky local, marveling at the comfort and ease which had been already attained by a man of not more than forty-five years of age.

But there were other things which seemed always to talk to me of New York, New York. I picked up a new weekly, the *Standard*, one evening, and found a theatrical paper of the most pornographic and alluring character which pretended to report with accuracy all the gayeties of the stage, the clubs, the tenderloins or white-light districts, as well as society of the racier and more spendthrift character. This paper spoke only of pleasure: yacht parties, midnight suppers, dances, scenes behind the stage and of blissful young stars of the theatrical, social and money worlds. Here were ease and luxury! In New York, plainly, was all this, and I might go there and by some fluke of chance taste of it. I studied this paper by the hour, dreaming of all it suggested.

(*419*)

And there was *Munsey's*, the first and most successful of all the ten-cent magazines then coming into existence and being fed to the public by the ton. I saw it first piled in high stacks before a news and book store in Pittsburgh. The size of the pile of magazines and the price induced a cursory examination, although I had never even heard of it before. Poor as it was intellectually—and it was poor—it contained an entire section of highly-coated paper devoted to actresses, the stage and scenes from plays, and still another carrying pictures of beauties in society in different cities, and still another devoted to successful men in Wall Street. It breathed mostly of New York, its social doings, its art and literary colonies. It fired me with an ambition to see New York.

A third paper, *Town Topics*, was the best of all, a paper most brilliantly edited by a man of exceptional literary skill (C. M. S. McLellan). It related to exclusive society in New York, London and Paris, the houses, palaces, yachts, restaurants and hotels, the goings and comings of the owners; and although it really poked fun at all this and other forms of existence elsewhere, still there was an element of envy and delight in it also which fitted my mood. It gave one the impression that there existed in New York, Newport and elsewhere (London principally) a kind of Elysian realm in which forever basked the elect of fortune. Here was neither want nor care.

How I brooded over all this, the marriages and rumors of marriages, the travels, engagements, feasts such as a score of facile novelists subsequently succeeded in picturizing to the entertainment and disturbance of rural America. For me this realm was all flowers, sunshine, smart restaurants, glistering ballrooms, ease, comfort, beauty arrayed as only enchantment or a modern newspaper Sunday supplement can array it. And while I knew that back of it must be the hard contentions and realities such as everywhere hold and characterize life, still I didn't know. In reading these papers I refused to allow myself to cut through to the reality. Life must hold some such realm as this, and spiritually I belonged to it. But I was already twenty-three, and what had I accomplished? I wished most of all now to go to New York and enter the realm pictured by these papers. Why not? I might bag an heiress or capture fortune in some other way. I must save some money, I told myself. Then, financially fortified, against starvation at least, I might reconnoiter the great city and—who knows?—perhaps conquer. Balzac's heroes had seemed to do so, why not I? It is written of the Dragon God of China that in the beginning it swallowed the world.

And to cap it all about this time I had a letter from my good brother, in which he asked me how long I would be "piking" about the West when I ought to be in New York. I should come this summer, when New York was at its best. He would show me Broadway, Manhattan Beach, a dozen worlds. He would introduce me to some New York newspaper men who would introduce me to the managers of the *World* and the *Sun*. (The mere mention of these papers, so overawed was I by the fames of Dana and Pulitzer, frightened me.) I ought to be on a paper like the *Sun*, he said, since to him Dana was the greatest editor in New York. I meditated over this, deciding that I would go when I had more money. I then and there started a bank account, putting in as much as ten or twelve dollars each week, and in a month or two began to feel that sense of security which a little money gives one.

Another thing which had a strange psychologic effect on me at the time, as indeed it appeared to have on most of the intelligentsia of America, was the publication in *Harper's* this spring and summer of George Du Maurier's *Trilby*. I have often doubted the import of novel-writing in general, but viewing the effect of that particular work on me as well as on others one might as well doubt the import of power or fame or emotion of any kind. The effect of this book was not so much one of great reality and insight such as Balzac at times managed to convey, but rather of an exotic mood or perfume of memory and romance conveyed by some one who is in love with that memory and improvising upon it as musicians do upon a theme. Instanter I saw Paris and Trilby and the Jew with his marvelous eyes. Trilby being hypnotized and carried away from Little Billee seemed to me then of the essence of great tragedy. I myself fairly suffered, walking about and dreaming, the while I awaited the one or two final portions. I was lost in the beauty of Paris, the delight of studio life, and resented more than ever, as one might a great deprivation, the need of living in a land where there was nothing but work.

And yet America and this city were fascinating enough to me. But because of the preponderant influence of foreign letters on American life it seemed that Paris and London must be so much better since every one wrote about them. Like Balzac's *Great Man from the Provinces*, this book seemed to connect itself with my own life and the tragedy of not having the means to marry at this time, and of being compelled to wander about in this way unable to support a wife. At last I became so wrought up that I was quite beside myself. I pictured myself as a Little Billee who would eventually lose by poverty, as he by trickery, the thing I most craved: my Western sweetheart. Meditating on this I vented some of my misery in the form of sentimental vaporizings in my feature articles, which were all liked well enough but which seemed merely to heighten my misery. Finally, some sentimental letters being exchanged between myself and my love, I felt an uncontrollable impulse to return and see her and St. Louis before I went farther away perhaps never to return. The sense of an irrecoverable past which had pervaded *Trilby* had, I think, something to do with this, so interfused and interfusing are all thoughts and moods. At any rate, having by now considerable influence with this paper, I proposed a short vacation, and the city editor, wishing no doubt to propitiate me, suggested that the paper would be glad to provide me with transportation both ways. So I made haste to announce a grand return, not only to my intended but to Mc-Cord, Wood and several others who were still in St. Louis.

CHAPTER LXV

As one looks back on youth so much of it appears ridiculous and maundering and without an essential impulse or direction, and yet as I look at life itself I am not sure but that indirection or unimportant idlings are a part of life's method. We often think we are doing some vastly important thing, whereas in reality we are merely marking time. At other times, when we appear to be marking time we are growing or achieving at a great rate; and so it may have been with me. Instead of pushing on to New York, I chose to return to St. Louis and grasp one more hour of exquisite romance, drink one more cup of love. And whether it profited me save as pleasure is profit I cannot tell. Only, may not pleasure be the ultimate profit?

This trip to St. Louis was for me a most pivotal and deranging thing, probably a great mistake. At that time, of course, I could not see that. Instead, I was completely lost in the grip of a passion that subsequently proved detrimental or devastating. The reality which I was seeking to establish was a temporary contact only. Any really beautiful girl or any idyllic scene could have done for me all the things that this particular girl and scene could do, only thus far I had chanced to meet no other who could displace her. And in a way I knew this then, only I realized also that one beautiful specimen was as good a key to the lock of earthly delights as another. . . . Only there were so many locks or chambers to which one key would fit, and how sad, in youth at least, not to have all the locks, or at least a giant illusion as to one!

This return began with a long hot trip in July to St. Louis, and then a quick change in the Union Station there at evening which brought me by midnight to the small town in the back·

woods of Missouri, near which she lived. It was hot. I recall the wide hot fields and small wooden towns of Southern Ohio and Indiana and this Missouri landscape in the night—the frogs, the katydids, the summer stars. I ached and yearned, not so much over her as over youth and love and the evanescence of all material fires. The spirit of youth cried and sang at the same time.

The little cottages with their single yellow light shining in the fields through which this dusty train ran! The perfumed winds!

At last the train stopped and left me standing at midnight on a wooden platform with no one to greet me. The train was late. A liveryman who was supposed to look after me did not. At a lone window sat the telegraph operator, stationmaster, baggage-agent all in one, a green shield shading his eyes. Otherwise the station was bare and silent save for the katydids in some weeds near at hand and some chirping treetoads. The agent told me that a hotel was a part of this station, run by this railroad. Upstairs, over the baggage and other rooms, were a few large barn-like sleeping chambers, carpetless, dusty, cindery, the windows curtainless and broken in places, and save for some all but slatless shutters unshielded from the world and the night. I placed a chair against my door, my purse under my pillow, my bag near at hand. During the night several long freights thundered by, their headlights lighting the room; yet, lying on a mattress of straw and listening to the frogs and katydids outside, I slept just the same. The next morning I tied a handkerchief over my eyes and slept some more, arising about ten to continue my journey.

The home to which I was going was part of an old decayed village, once a point on a trail or stage-coach route, once the prospective capital of the State, but now nothing. A courthouse and some quaint tree-shaded homes were all but lost or islanded in a sea of corn. I rode out a long, hot, dusty road and finally up a long tree-shaded lane to its very end, where I passed through a gate and at the far end came upon a worn, faded, rain-rotted house facing a row of trees in a wide lawn. I felt that never before had I been so impressed with a region and a home. It was all so simple. The house, though old and decayed, was exquisite. The old French windows— copied from where and by whom?—reaching to the grass; the long graceful rooms, the cool hall, the veranda before it, so very Southern in quality, the flowers about every window and door! I found a home in which lived a poverty-stricken and yet spiritually impressive patriarch, a mother who might serve as an American tradition so simple and gracious was she, sisters and brothers who were reared in an atmosphere which somehow induced a gracious, sympathetic idealism and consideration. Poor as they were, they were the best of the families here. The father had been an office-holder and one of the district leaders in his day, and one of his sons still held an office. A son-in-law was the district master of this entire congressional district, which included seven counties, and could almost make or break a congressman. All but three daughters were married, and I was engaged to one of the remaining ones. Another, too beautiful and too hoyden to think of any one in particular, was teaching school, or playing at it. A farm of forty acres to the south of the house was tilled by the father and two sons.

Elsewhere I have indicated this atmosphere, but here I like to touch on it again. We Americans have home traditions or ideals, created as much by song and romance as anything else: *My Old Kentucky Home, Suwanee River*. Despite any willing on my part, this home seemed to fulfill the spirit of those songs. There was something so sadly romantic about it. The shade of the great trees moved across the lawn in stately and lengthening curves. A stream at the foot of the slope leading down from the west side of the house dimpled and whimpered in the sun. Birds sang, and there were golden bees about the flowers and wasps under the eaves of the house. Hammocks of barrel-staves, and others of better texture, were strung between the trees. In a nearby barn of quaint design were several good horses, and there were cows in the field adjoining. Ducks and geese solemnly padded to and fro between the house and the stream. The air was redolent of corn, wheat, clover, timothy, flowers.

To me it seemed that all the spirit of rural America, its idealism, its dreams, the passion of a Brown, the courage and patience and sadness of a Lincoln, the dreams and courage of a Lee or a Jackson, were all here. The very soil smacked of American idealism and faith, a fixedness in sentimental and purely imaginative American tradition, in which I, alas! could not share. I was enraptured. Out of its charms and sentiments I might have composed an elegy or an epic, but I could not believe that it was more than a frail flower of romance. I had seen Pittsburgh. . . . I had seen Lithuanians and Hungarians in their "courts" and hovels. I had seen the girls of that city walking the streets at night. This profound faith in God, in goodness, in virtue and duty that I saw here in no wise squared with the craft, the cruelty, the brutality and the envy that I saw everywhere else. These parents were gracious and God-fearing, but to me they seemed asleep. They did not know life—could not. These boys and girls, as I soon found, respected love and marriage and duty and other things which the idealistic American still clings to.

Outside was all this other life that I had seen of which apparently these people knew nothing. They were as if suspended in dreams, lotus eaters, and my beloved was lost in this same romance. I was thinking of her beauty, her wealth of hair, the color of her cheeks, the beauty of her figure, of what she might be to me. She might have been thinking of the same thing, possibly more indirectly, but also she was thinking of the dignity and duty and sanctity of marriage. For her, marriage and one love were for life. For myself, whether I admitted it or not, love was a thing much less stable. Indeed I was not thinking of marriage at all, but rather whether I could be happy here and now, and how much I could extract out of love. Or perhaps, to be just to myself, I was as much a victim of passion and romance as she was, only to the two of us it did not mean the same thing. Unconsciously I identified her with the beauty of all I saw, and at the same time felt that it was all so different from anything

I knew or believed that I wondered how she would fit in with the kind of life toward which I was moving. How overcome this rigidity in duty and truth?

Both of us being inflamed, it was the most difficult thing for me to look upon her and not crave her physically, and, as she later admitted, she felt the same yearning toward me. At the time, however, she was all but horrified at a thought which ran counter to all the principles impressed upon her since early youth. There was thus set up between us in this delightful atmosphere a conflict between tradition and desire. The hot faint breezes about the house and in the trees seemed to whisper of secret and forbidden contact. The perfumes of the thickly grown beds of flowers, the languorous sultry heat of the afternoon and night, the ripening and blooming fields beyond, the drowsy, still, starry nights with their hum of insects and croak of frogs and the purrs and whimpers and barks of animals, seemed to call for but one thing. There was about her an intense delight in living. No doubt she longed as much to be seized as I to seize her, and yet there was a moral elusiveness which added even more to the chase. I wished to take her then and not wait, but the prejudices of a most careful rearing frightened and deterred her. And yet I shall always feel that the impulse was better than the forces which confuted and subsequently defeated it. For then was the time to unite, not years later when, however much the economic and social and religious conditions which are supposed to surround and safeguard such unions had been fulfilled, my zest for her, and no doubt hers in part for me, had worn away.

Love should act in its heat, not when its bank account is heavy. The chemic formula which works to reproduce the species, and the most vital examples at that, is not concerned with the petty local and social restraints which govern all this. Life if it wants anything wants children, and healthy ones, and the weighing and binding rules which govern their coming and training may easily become too restrictive. Nature's way is correct, her impulses sound. The delight of possessing my fiancée then would have repaid her for her fears, and me for ruthlessness if I had taken her. A clearer and a better grasp of life would have been hers and mine. The coward sips little of life, the strong man drinks deep. Old prejudices must always fall, and life must always change. It is the law.

CHAPTER LXVI

AND so this romance ended for me. At the time, of course, I did not know it; on leaving her I was under the impression that I was more than ever attached to her. In the face of this postponement, life took on a grayer and more disappointing aspect. To be forced to wait when at that moment, if ever, was the time!

And yet I told myself that better days were surely in store. I would return East and in some way place myself so that soon we might be reunited. It was a figment of hope. By the time I was finally capable of maintaining her economically, my earlier mood had changed. That hour which we had known, or might have known, had gone forever. I had seen more of life, more of other women, and although even then she was by no means unattractive the original yearning had vanished. She was now but one of many, and there were those who were younger and more sophisticated, even more attractive.

And yet, before I left her, what days! The sunshine! The lounging under the trees! The drowsy summer heat! The wishing for what might not be! Having decided that her wish was genuine and my impulse to comply with it wise, I stood by it, wishing that it might be otherwise. I consoled myself thinly with the thought that the future must bring us together, and then left, journeying first to St. Louis and later to New York. For while I was here that letter from my brother which urged me once more to come to New York was forwarded to me. Just before leaving Pittsburgh I had sent him a collection of those silly "features" I had been writing, and he also was impressed. I must come to New York. Some metropolitan paper was the place for me and my material. Anyhow, I would enjoy visiting there in the summer time more than later. I wired him that I would arrive at a certain time, and then set out for St. Louis and a visit among my old newspaper friends there.

(429)

I do not know how most people take return visits, but I have often noted that it has only been as I have grown older and emotionally less mobile that they have become less and less significant to me. In my earlier years nothing could have been more poignant or more melancholy than my thoughts on any of these occasions. Whenever I returned to any place in which I had once lived and found things changed, as they always were, I was fairly transfixed by the oppressive sense of the evanescence of everything; a mood so hurtful and dark and yet with so rich if sullen a luster that I was left wordless with pain. I was all but crucified at realizing how unimportant I was, how nothing stayed but all changed. Scenes passed, never to be recaptured. Moods came and friendships and loves, and were gone forever. Life was perpetually moving on. The beautiful pattern of which each of us, but more especially myself, was a part, was changing from day to day, so that things which were an anchor and a comfort and delight yesterday were tomorrow no more. And though perhaps innately I desired change, or at least appropriate and agreeable changes for myself, I did not wish this other, this exterior world to shift, and that under my very eyes.

The most haunting and disturbing thought always was that hourly I was growing older. Life was so brief, such a very little cup at best, and so soon, whatever its miserable amount or character, it would be gone. Some had strength or capacity or looks or fortune, or all, at their command, and then all the world was theirs to travel over and explore. Beauty and ease were theirs, and love perhaps, and the companionship of interesting and capable people; but I, poor waif, with no definite or arresting skill of any kind, not even that of commerce, must go fumbling about looking in upon life from the outside, as it were. Beautiful women, or so I argued, were drawn to any but me. The great opportunities of the day in trade and commerce were for any but me. I should never have a fraction of the means to do as I wished or to share in the life that I most craved. I was an Ishmael, a wanderer.

(430)

In St. Louis I was oppressed beyond words. Of the news-paper men who had been living on the same floor with me in Broadway there was not one left. At the *Globe-Democrat* already reigned a new city editor. My two friends, Wood and McCord, while delighted to see me, told me of those who had already gone and seemed immersed in many things that had arisen since I had gone and were curious as to why I should have returned at all. I hung about for a day or two, wondering all the while why I did so, and then took the train going East.

Of all my journeys thus far this to New York was the most impressive. It took on at once, the moment I left St. Louis, the character of a great adventure, for it was all unknown and enticing. For years my mind had been centered on it. True to the law of gravitation, its pull was in proportion to its ever increasing size. As a boy in Indiana, and later in Chicago, I had read daily papers sent on from New York by my sister E——, who lived there. In Chicago, owing to a rivalry which existed on Chicago's part (not on New York's, I am sure), the papers were studded with invidious comments which, like all poorly based criticism, only served to emphasize the salient and impressive features of the greater city. It had an elevated road that ran through its long streets on stilts of steel and carried hundreds of thousands if not millions in the miniature trains drawn by small engines. It was a long, heavily populated island surrounded by great rivers, and was America's ocean door to Europe. It had the great Brooklyn Bridge, then unparalleled anywhere, Wall Street, Jay Gould, Cornelius Vanderbilt, a huge company of millionaires. It had Tammany Hall, the Statue of Liberty, unveiled not so many years before (when I was a boy in Southern Indiana), Madison Square Garden, the Metropolitan Opera House, the Horse Show. It was the center and home of fashionable society, of all fixed and itinerant actors and actresses. All great theatrical successes began there. Of papers of largest circulation and greatest fame, it had nearly all. As an ignorant understrapper I had often contended, and that noisily, with various passing atoms of New York, as condescending as I was ignorant and stubborn, as to the relative merits of New York and Chicago, New York and St. Louis! There could not be so much difference! There were many great things in these minor places! Some day, surely, Chicago would outstrip New York! . . . Well, I lived to see many changes and things, but not that. Instead I saw the great city grow and grow, until it stood unrivaled, for size and force and wealth at least, anywhere.

And now after all these tentative adventurings I was at last to enter it. Although I was moderately well-placed in Pittsburgh and not coming as a homeless, penniless seeker, still even now I was dreadfully afraid of it—why, I cannot say. Perhaps it was because it was so immense and mentally so much more commanding. Still I consoled myself with the thought that this was only a visit and I was to have a chance to explore it without feeling that I had to make my way then and there.

I recall clearly the hot late afternoon in July when, after stopping off at Pittsburgh to refresh myself and secure a change of clothing, I took the train for New York. I noted with eager, hungry eyes a succession of dreary forge and mining towns, miles of blazing coke ovens paralleling the track and lighting these regions with a lurid glow after dusk, huge dark hills occasionally twinkling with a feeble light or two. I spent a half-wakeful night in the berth, dreaming and meditating in a nervous chemic way. Before dawn I was awake and watching our passage through Philadelphia, then Trenton, New Brunswick, Metuchen, Menlo Park, Rahway, Elizabeth and Newark. Of all of these, save only Menlo Park, the home of Edison, who was then invariably referred to by journalists and paragraphers as "The Wizard of Menlo Park," I knew nothing.

As we neared New York at seven the sky was overcast, and at Newark it began to drizzle. When I stepped down it was pouring, and there at the end of a long trainshed, the immense steel and glass affair that once stood in Jersey City opposite Cortlandt Street of New York, awaited my fat and smiling brother, as sweet-faced and gay and hopeful as a child. At once, he began as was his way, a patter of jests and inquiries as to my trip, then led me to a ferry entrance, one of a half dozen in a row, through which, as through the proscenium arch of a stage, I caught my first glimpse of the great Hudson. A heavy mist of rain was suspended over it through which might be seen dimly the walls of the great city beyond. Puffing and squatty tugs, as graceful as fat ducks, attended by overhanging plumes of smoke, chugged noisily in the foreground of water. At the foot of the outline of the city beyond, only a few skyscrapers having as yet appeared, lay a fringe of ships and docks and ferry houses. No ferry boat being present, we needs must wait for one labeled Desbrosses, as was labeled the slip in which we stood.

But I was talking to my brother and learning of his life here and of that of my sister E——, with whom he was living. The ferry boat eventually came into the slip and discharged a large crowd, and we, along with a vast company of commuters and travelers, entered it. Its center, as I noted, was stuffed with vehicles of all sizes and descriptions, those carrying light merchandise as well as others carrying coal and stone and lumber and beer. I can recall to this hour the odor of ammonia and saltpeter so characteristic of the ferry boats and ferry houses, the crowd in the ferry house on the New York side waiting to cross over once we arrived there, and the miserable little horse-cars, then still trundling along West Street and between Fourteenth and Broadway and the ferries, and Gansevoort Market. These were drawn by one horse, and you deposited your fare yourself.

And this in the city of elevated roads!

But the car which we boarded had two horses. We traveled up West Street from Desbrosses to Christopher and thence along that shabby old thoroughfare to Sixth Avenue and Fourteenth Street, where we changed. At first, aside from the sea and the boats and the sense of hugeness which goes with immense populations everywhere, I was disappointed by the seeming meanness of the streets. Many of them were still paved with cobblestones, like the oldest parts of St. Louis and Pittsburgh. The buildings, houses and stores alike, were for the most part of a shabby red in color and varying in height from one to six stories, most of them of an aged and contemptible appearance. This was, as I soon learned from my serene and confident brother, an old and shabby portion of the city. These horse-cars, in fact, were one of the jokes of the city, but they added to its variety. "Don't think that they haven't anything else. This is just the New York way. It has the new and the old mixed. Wait'll you're here a little while. You'll be like everybody else—there'll be just one place: New York."

And so it proved after a time.

The truth was that the city then, for the first time in a half century if not longer, was but beginning to emerge from a frightful period of misrule at the hands of as evil a band of mercenaries as ever garroted a body politic. It was still being looted and preyed upon in a most shameful manner. Graft and vice stalked hand-in-hand. Although Tammany Hall, the head and center of all the graft and robbery and vice and crime protection, had been delivered a stunning blow by a reform wave which had temporarily ousted it and placed reform officials over the city, still the grip of that organization had not relaxed. The police and all minor officials, as well as the workmen of all departments were still, under the very noses of the newly elected officials, perhaps with their aid, collecting graft and tribute. The Reverend Doctor Parkhurst was preaching, like Savonarola, the destruction of these corruptions of the city.

When I arrived, the streets were not cleaned or well-lighted, their ways not adequately protected or regulated as to traffic. Uncollected garbage lay in piles, the while the city was paying enormous sums for its collection; small and feeble gas-jets fluttered, when in other cities the arc-light had for fifteen years been a commonplace. As we dragged on, on this slow-moving car, the bells on the necks of the horses tinkling rhythmically, I stared and commented.

"Well, you can't say that this is very much."

"My boy," cautioned my good and cheerful brother, "you haven't seen anything yet. This is just an old part of New

York. Wait'll you see Broadway and Fifth Avenue. We're just coming this way because it's the quickest way home."

When we reached Fourteenth Street and Sixth Avenue I was very differently impressed. We had traveled for a little way under an elevated road over which trains thundered, and as we stepped down I beheld an impressively wide thoroughfare, surging even at this hour in the morning with people. Here was Macy's, and northward stretched an area which I was told was the shopping center of the vast metropolis: Altman's, Ehrich's, O'Neill's, Adams', Simpson-Crawford's, all huge stores and all in a row lining the west side of the street. We made our way across Fifteenth Street to the entrance of a narrow brownstone apartment house and ascended two flights, waiting in a rather poorly-lighted hall for an answer to our ring. The door was eventually opened by my sister, whom I had not seen since my mother's death four years before. She had become stout. The trim beauty for which a very few years before she had been notable had entirely disappeared. I was disappointed at first, but was soon reassured and comforted by an inherently kindly and genial disposition, which expressed itself in much talking and laughing.

"Why, Theodore, I'm so glad to see you! Take off your things. Did you have a pleasant trip? George, here's Theodore. This is my husband, Theodore. Come on back, you and Paul," so she rattled on.

I studied her husband, whom I had not seen before, a dark and shrewd and hawklike person who seemed to be always following me with his eyes. He was an American of middle-Western extraction but with a Latin complexion and Latin eyes.

E——'s two children were brought forward, a boy and a girl four and two years of age respectively. A breakfast table was waiting, at which Paul had already seated himself.

"Now, my boy," he began, "this is where you eat real food once more. No jerkwater hotels about this! No Pittsburgh newspaper restaurants about this! Ah, look at the biscuit! Look at the biscuit!" as a maid brought in a creamy plateful. "And here's steak—steak and brown gravy and biscuit! Steak and brown gravy and biscuit!" He rubbed his hands in joy. "I'll bet you haven't seen anything like this since you left home. Ah, good old steak and gravy!" His interest in food was always intense.

"It's been many a day since I've had such biscuit and gravy, E——," I observed.

" 'It's been many a day since I've had such biscuit and gravy, E——,' " mocked my brother.

"Get out, you!" chimed in my sister. "Just listen to him, the old snooks! I can't get him out of the kitchen, can I, George? He's always eating. 'It's been many a day——' Ho! Ho!"

"I thought you were dieting?" I inquired.

"So I am, but you don't expect me not to eat this morning, do you? I'm doing this to welcome you."

"Some welcome!" I scoffed.

Our chatter became more serious as the first glow of welcome wore off. During it all I was never free of a sense of the hugeness and strangeness of the city and the fact that at last I was here. And in this immense and far-flung thing my sister had this minute nook. From where I sat I could hear strange moanings and blowings which sounded like foghorns.

"What is that noise?" I finally asked, for to me it was eerie.

"Boats—tugs and vessels in the harbor. There's a fog on," explained H——, E——'s husband.

I listened to the variety of sounds, some far, some near, some mellow, some hoarse. "How far away are they?"

"Anywhere from one to ten miles."

I stopped and listened again. Suddenly the full majesty of the sea sweeping about this island at this point caught me. The entire city was surrounded by water. Its great buildings and streets were all washed about by that same sea-green salty flood which I had seen coming over from Jersey City, and beyond were the miles and miles of dank salt meadows, traversed by railroads. Huge liners from abroad were even now making their way here. At its shores were ranged in rows great vessels from Europe and all other parts of the world, all floating quietly upon the bosom of this great river. There were tugs and small boats and sailing vessels, and beyond all these, eastward, the silence, the majesty, the deadly earnestness of the sea.

"Do you ever think how wonderful it is to have the sea so close?" I asked.

"No, I can't say that I do," replied my brother-in-law.

"Nor I," said my sister. "You get used to all those things here, you know."

"It's wonderful, my boy," said my brother, as usual helpfully interested. He invariably seemed to approve of all my moods and approaches to sentiment, and, like a mother who admires and spoils a child, was anxious to encourage and indulge me. "Great subject, the sea."

I could not help smiling, he was so naïf and simple and intellectually innocent and sweet.

"It's a great city," I said suddenly, the full import of it all sweeping over me. "I think I'd like to live here."

"Didn't I tell you! Didn't I tell you!" exclaimed my brother gayly. "They all fall for it! Now it's the ocean vessels that get him. You take my advice, my boy, and move down here. The quicker the better for you."

I replied that I might, and then tried to forget the vessels and their sirens, but could not. The sea! The sea! And this great city! Never before was I so anxious to explore a city, and never before so much in awe of one either. It seemed so huge and powerful and terrible. There was something about it which made me seem useless and trivial. Whatever one might have been elsewhere, what could one be here?

CHAPTER LXVII

My sister's husband having something to do with this narrative, I will touch upon his history as well as that of my sister. In her youth E—— was one of the most attractive of the girls in our family. She never had any intellectual or artistic interests of any kind; if she ever read a book I never heard of it. But as for geniality, sympathy, industry, fair-mindedness and an unchanging and self-sacrificing devotion to her children, I have never known any one who could rival her. With no adequate intellectual training, save such as is provided by the impossible theories and teachings of the Catholic Church, she was but thinly capacitated to make her way in the world.

At eighteen or nineteen she had run away and gone to Chicago, where she had eventually met H——, who had apparently fallen violently in love with her. He was fifteen years older than she and moderately well versed in the affairs of this world. At the time she met him he was the rather successful manager of a wholesale drug company, reasonably well-placed socially, married and the father of two or three children, the latter all but grown to maturity. They eloped, going direct to New York.

This was a great shock to my mother, who managed to conceal it from my father although it was a three-days' wonder in the journalistic or scandal world of Chicago. Nothing more was heard of her for several years, when a dangerous illness overtook my mother in Warsaw and E—— came hurrying back for a few days' visit. This was followed by another silence, which was ended by the last illness and death of my mother in Chicago, and she again appeared, a distrait and hysteric soul. I never knew any one to yield more completely to her emotions than she did on this occasion; she was almost fantastic in her grief. During all this time she had been living in New York, and she and her husband were supposed to be well off. Later, talking to Paul in St. Louis, I gathered that H——, while not so successful since he had gone East, was not a bad sort and that he had managed to connect himself with politics in some way, and that they were living comfortably in Fifteenth Street. But when I arrived there I found that they were by no means comfortable. The Tammany administration, under which a year or two before he had held an inspectorship of some kind, had been ended by the investigations of the Lexow Committee, and he was now without work of any kind. Also, instead of having proved a faithful and loving husband, he had long since wearied of his wife and strayed elsewhere. Now, having fallen from his success, he was tractable. Until the arrival of my brother Paul, who for reasons of sympathy had agreed to share the expenses here during the summer season, he had induced E—— to rent rooms, but for this summer this had been given up. With the aid of my brother and some occasional work H—— still did they were fairly comfortable. My sister if not quite happy was still the devoted slave of her children and a most pathetically dependent housewife. Whatever fires or vanities of her youth had compelled her to her meteoric career, she had now settled down and was content to live for her children. Her youth was over, love gone. And yet she managed to convey an atmosphere of cheer and hopefulness.

My brother Paul was in the best of spirits. He held a fair position as an actor, being the star in a road comedy and planning to go out the ensuing fall in a new one which he had written for himself and which subsequently enjoyed many successful seasons on the road. In addition, he was by way of becoming more and more popular nationally as a song-writer. Also as I have said, he had connected himself as a third partner in a song-publishing business which was to publish his own and other songs, and this, despite its smallness, was showing unmistakable signs of success.

The first thing he did this morning was to invite me to come and see this place, and about noon we walked across Fifteenth Street and up Sixth Avenue, then the heart of the shopping district, to Twentieth Street and thence east to between Fifth Avenue and Broadway, where in a one-time fashionable but now decayed dwelling, given over to small wholesale ventures, his concern was housed on the third floor. This was almost the center of a world of smart shops near several great hotels: the Continental, Bartholdi, and the Fifth Avenue. Next door were Lord & Taylor. Below this, on the next corner, at Nineteenth and Broadway, was the Gorham Company, and below that the Ditson Company, a great music house, Arnold, Constable & Company and others. There were excellent restaurants and office buildings crowding out an older world of fashion. I remember being impressed with the great number of severe brownstone houses with their wide flights of stone steps, conservatories and porte-cochères. Fifth Avenue and Twentieth Street were filled with handsome victorias and coaches.

Going into my brother's office I saw a sign on the door which read: *Howley, Haviland & Company,* and underneath, *Wing & Sons, Pianos.*

"Are you the agent for a piano?" I inquired.

"Huh-uh. They let us have a practice piano in return for that sign."

When I met his partners I was impressed with the probability of success which they seemed to suggest and which came true. The senior member, Howley, was a young, small, goggle-eyed hunchback with a mouthful of protruding teeth, and hair as black as a crow, and piercing eyes. He had long thin arms and legs which, because of his back, made him into a kind of spider of a man, and he went about spider-wise, laughing and talking, yet always with a heavy "Scutch" burr.

"We're joost aboot gettin' un our feet here nu," he said to me, his queer twisted face screwed up into a grimace of satisfaction and pride, "end we hevn't ez yet s'mutch to show ye. But wuth a lettle time I'm a-theenkin' ye'll be seein' theengs a-lookin' a leetle bether."

I laughed. "Say," I said to Paul when Howley had gone about some work, "how could you fail with him around? He's as smart as a whip, and they're all good luck anyhow." I was referring to the superstition which counts all hunchbacks as lucky to others.

"Yes," said my brother. "I know they're lucky, and he's as straight and honest as they make 'em. I'll always get a square deal here," and then he began to tell me how his old publisher, by whom Howley had been employed, had "trimmed" him, and how this youth had put him wise. Then and there had begun this friendship which had resulted in this partnership.

The space this firm occupied was merely one square room, twenty by twenty, and in one corner of this was placed the free "try-out" piano. In another, between two windows, two tables stood back to back, piled high with correspondence. A longer table was along one side of a wall and was filled with published music, which was being wrapped and shipped. On the walls were some wooden racks or bins containing "stock," the few songs thus far published. Although only a year old, this firm already had several songs which were beginning to attract attention, one of them entitled *On the Sidewalks of New York*. By the following summer this song was being sung and played all over the country and in England, an international "hit." This office, in this very busy center, cost them only twenty dollars a month, and their "overhead expeenses," as Howley pronounced it, were "juist nexta nothin'." I could see that my good brother was in competent hands for once.

And the second partner, who arrived just as we were sitting down at a small table in a restaurant nearby for lunch, was an equally interesting youth whose personality seemed to spell success. At this time he was still connected as "head of stock," whatever that may mean, with that large wholsesale and retail music house the Ditson Company, at Broadway and Eighteenth Street. Although a third partner in this new concern, he had not yet resigned his connection with the other and was using it, secretly of course, to aid him and his firm in disposing of some of their wares. He was quite young, not more than twenty-seven, very quick and alert in manner, very short of speech, avid and handsome, a most attractive and clean-looking man. He shot out questions and replies as one might bullets out of a gun. "Didy'seeDrake?" "What 'd'esay?" "AnynewsfromBaker?" "Thedevily'say!" "Y' don'tmeanit!"

I was moved to study him with the greatest care. Out of many anywhere, I told myself, I would have selected him as a pushing and promising and very self-centered person, but by no means disagreeable. Speaking of him later, as well as of Howley, my brother once said: "Y'see, Thee, New York's the only place you could do a thing like this. This is the only place you could get fellows with their experience. Howley used to be with my old publisher, Woodward, and he's the one that put me wise to the fact that Woodward was trimming me. And Haviland was a friend of his, working for Ditson."

From the first, I had the feeling that this firm of which my brother was a part would certainly be successful. There was something about it, a spirit of victory and health and joy in work and life, which convinced me that these three would make a go of it. I could see them ending in wealth, as they did before disasters of their own invention overtook them. But that was still years away and after they had at least eaten of the fruits of victory.

As a part of this my initiation into the wonders of the city Paul led me into what he insisted was one of the wealthiest and most ornate of the Roman Churches in New York, St. Francis Xavier in Sixteenth Street, from which he was subsequently buried. Standing in this, he told me of some Jesuit priest there, a friend of his, who was comfortably berthed and "a good sport into the bargain, Thee, a bird." However, having had my fill of Catholicism and its ways, I was not so much impressed, either by his friend or his character. But Sixth Avenue in this sunshine did impress me. It was the crowded center of nearly all the great stores, at least five, each a block in length, standing in one immense line on one side of the street. The carriages! The well-dressed people! Paul pointed out to me the windows of Altman's on the west side of the street at Eighteenth and said it was the most exclusive store in America, that Marshall Field & Company of Chicago was as nothing, and I had the feeling from merely looking at it that this was true; it was so well-arranged and spacious. Its windows, in which selected materials were gracefully draped and contrasted, bore out this impression. There were many vehicles of the better sort constantly pausing at its doors to put down most carefully dressed women and girls. I marveled at the size and wealth of a city which could support so many great stores all in a row.

Because of the heat my brother insisted upon calling a hansom cab to take us to Fourteenth and Broadway, where we were to begin our northward journey. Just south of Union Square at Thirteenth Street was the old Star Theater of which he said: "There you have it. That used to be Lester Wallack's Theater twenty years ago—the great Lester Wallack. There was an actor, my boy, a great actor! They talk about Mansfield and Barrett and Irving and Willard and all these other people today. All good, my boy, all good, but not in it with him, Theodore, not in it. This man was a genius. And he packed 'em too. Many a time I've passed this place when you couldn't get by the door for the crowd." And he proceeded to relate that in the old days, when he first came to New York, all the best part of the theatrical district was still about and below Union Square—Niblo's, the old London on the Bowery, and what not.

I listened. What had been had been. It might all have been very wonderful but it was so no longer, all done and gone. I was new and strange, and wished to see only what was new and wonderful now. The sun was bright on Union Square *now*. This was a newer world in which we were living, he and I, this day. The newest wave of the sea invariably obliterates the one that has gone before. And that was only twenty years ago and it has all changed again.

North of this was the newer Broadway—the Broadway of the current actor, manager and the best theaters—and fresh, smart, gay, pruned of almost every trace of poverty or care. Tiffany's was at Fifteenth and Broadway, its windows glittering with jewels; Brentano's, the booksellers, were at Sixteenth on the west side of Union Square; and Sarony, the photographer, was between Fifteenth and Sixteenth, a great gold replica of his signature indicating his shop. The Century Company, to which my brother called my attention as an institution I might some day be connected with, so great was his optimism and faith in me, stood on the north side of Union Square at Seventeenth. At Nineteenth and Broadway were the Gorham Company, and Arnold, Constable & Company. At Twentieth was Lord & Taylor's great store, adjoining the old building in which was housed my brother's firm. Also, at this street, stood the old Continental Hotel, a popular and excellent restaurant occupying a large portion of its lower floor which became a part of my daily life later. At Twenty-first Street was then standing one of the three great stores of Park & Tilford. At Twenty-third, on the east side of the street, facing Madison Square, was another successful hotel, the Bartholdi, and opposite it, on the west side, was the site of the Flatiron Building.

Across Madison Square, its delicate golden-brown tower soaring aloft and alone, no huge buildings then as now to dwarf it, stood Madison Square Garden, Diana, her arrow pointed to the wind, giving naked chase to a mythic stag, her mythic dogs at her heels, high in the blue air above. The west side of Broadway, between Twenty-third and Twenty-fourth, was occupied by the Fifth Avenue Hotel, the home, as my brother was quick to inform me, of Senator Platt, the Republican boss of the State, who with Croker divided the political control of the State and who here held open court, the famous "Amen Corner," where his political henchmen were allowed to ratify all his suggestions. It was somewhere within. Between Twenty-fifth and Twenty-sixth on the same side of the street were two more hotels, the Albemarle and the Hoffman House. Just north of this, at Twenty-seventh and Broadway, on the east side of the street and running through to Fifth Avenue, was Delmonico's. Into this we now ventured, my good brother hailing genially some acquaintance who happened to be in charge of the floor at the moment. The waiter who served us greeted him familiarly. I stared in awe at its pretentious and ornate furniture, its noble waiters and the something about it which seemed to speak of wealth and power. How easily five cents crooks the knee to five million!

A block or two north of this was the old Fifth Avenue Theater, then a theater of the first class but later devoted to vaudeville. At Twenty-ninth was the Gilsey House, one of the earliest homes of this my Rialto-loving brother. At Thirtieth and Broadway, on the east side, stood Palmer's Theater, famous for its musical and beauty shows. At Thirty-first and Broadway, on the west side of the street, stood Augustus Daly's famous playhouse, its façade suggestive of older homes remodeled to this new use. And already it was coming to be *passé*. Weber & Fields' had not even appeared. And in my short span it appeared and disappeared and became a memory! Between Twenty-eighth and Thirty-fourth were several more important hotels: The Grand, The Imperial; and between Thirty-third and Thirty-fourth streets, in Sixth Avenue, was the old Manhattan Theater, at that time the home of many successes, but also, like Daly's, drawing to the end of a successful career.

In Thirty-fourth, west of Broadway (later a part of the Macy store site), was Koster & Bial's Music Hall, managed by a man who subsequently was to become widely known but who was then only beginning to rise, Oscar Hammerstein. And around the corner, in Broadway at Thirty-fifth, was a very successful theater, the Herald Square, facing the unique and beautiful *Herald* building. Beyond that in Thirty-fifth, not many feet east of Sixth Avenue, was the Garrick, or the Lyceum as it was then known, managed by Daniel Frohman. Above these, at Thirty-sixth, on the west side, was the Marlborough, at which later, in his heyday, my brother chose to live. At Thirty-eighth, on the southeast corner, stood the popular and exclusive Normandie, one of the newer hotels, and at the northeast corner of this same intersection, the new and imposing Knickerbocker Theater. At Thirty-ninth was the far-famed Casino, with its choruses of girls, the Mecca of all night-loving Johnnies and rowdies; and between Thirty-ninth and Fortieth, on the west side, the world-famed Metropolitan

(445)

Opera House, still unchanged save for a restaurant in its northern corner. At Fortieth over the way stood the Empire Theater, with its stock company, which included the Drews, Favershams and what not; and in this same block was the famous Browne's Chop House, a resort for Thespians and night-lovers. At Forty-second and Broadway, the end of all Rialto-dom for my brother, and from which he turned sadly and said: "Well, here's the end," stood that Mecca of Meccas, the new Hotel Metropole, with its restaurant opening on three streets, its leathern seats backed to its walls, its high open windows, an air of super-wisdom as to all matters pertaining to sport and the theater pervading it. This indeed was the extreme northern limit of the white-light district, and here we paused for a drink and to see and be seen.

How well I remember it all—the sense of ease and well-being that was over this place, and over all Broadway; the loud clothes, the bright straw hats, the canes, the diamonds, the hot socks, the air of security and well-being, assumed by those who had won an all-too-brief hour in that pretty, petty world of make-believe and pleasure and fame. And here my good brother was at his best. It was "Paul" here and "Paul" there. Already known for several songs of great fame, as well as for his stage work and genial personality, he was welcomed everywhere.

And then, ambling down the street in the comforting shade of its west wall, what amazing personalities, male and female, and so very many of them, pausing to take him by the hand, slap him on the back, pluck familiarly at his coat lapel and pour into his ear or his capacious bosom magnificent tales of successes, of great shows, of fights and deaths and love affairs and tricks and scandals. And all the time my good brother smiled, laughed, sympathized. There were moments with prizefighters, with long-haired Thespians down on their luck and looking for a dime or a dollar, and bright petty upstarts of the vaudeville world. Retired miners and ranchmen out of the West, here to live and recount their tales of hardships endured, battles won, or of marvelous winnings at cards, trick-eries in racing, prizefighting and what not, now ambled by or stopped and exchanged news or stories. There was talk of what "dogs" or "swine" some people were, what liars, scoundrels, ingrates; as well as the magnificent, magnanimous, "God's own salt" that others were. The oaths! The stories of women! My brother seemed to know them all. I was amazed. What a genial, happy, well-thought-of successful man!

CHAPTER LXVIII

ALL this while of course there had been much talk as to the character of those we met, the wealth and fashion that purchased at Tiffany's or at Brentano's, those who loafed at the Fifth Avenue, the Hoffman House, the Gilsey, the Normandie. My brother had friends in many of these hotels and bars. A friend of his was the editor of the *Standard*, Roland Burke Hennessy, and he would take me up and introduce me. Another was the political or sporting man of the *Sun* or *World* or *Herald*. Here came one who was the manager of the Casino or the Gilsey! One was a writer, a playwright, a songwriter or a poet! A man of facile friendships, my brother! As we passed Twenty-third Street he made it plain that here was a street which had recently begun to replace the older and more colossal Sixth Avenue, some of the newer and much smarter stores—Best's, Le Boutillier's, McCreery's, Stern Brothers'—having built here.

"This is really the smart street now, Thee, this and a part of Fifth Avenue about Twenty-third. The really exclusive stores are coming in here. If you ever work in New York, as you will, you'll want to know about these things. You'll see more smart women in here than in any other shopping street," and he called my attention to the lines of lacquered and befurred and beplushed carriages, the harness of the horses aglitter with nickel and gilt.

Passing Daly's he said: "Now here, my boy, is a manager. He makes actors, he don't hire them. He takes 'em and trains 'em. All these young fellows and girls who are making a stir," and he named a dozen, among whom I noted such names as those of Maude Adams, Willie Collier, Drew and Faversham, "worked for him. And he don't allow any nonsense. There's none of that upstage stuff with him, you bet. When you work for him you're just an ordinary employee and you do what he tells you, not the way you think you ought to do. I've watched him rehearse, and I know, and all these fellows tell the same story about him. But he's a gentleman, my boy, and a manager. Everybody knows that when he finishes with a man or a woman they can act.''

At Thirty-third Street he waved his hand in the direction of the Waldorf, which was then but the half of its later size. "Down there's the Waldorf. That's the place. That's the last word for the rich. That's where they give the biggest balls and dinners, there and at Delmonico's and the Netherland.'' And after a pause he continued: "Some time you ought to write about these things, Thee. They're the limit for extravagance and show. The people out West don't know yet what's going on, but the rich are getting control. They'll own the country pretty soon. A writer like you could make 'em see that. You ought to show up some of these things so they'd know.''

Youthful, inexperienced, unlettered, the whole scroll of this earthly wallow a mere guess, I accepted that as an important challenge. Maybe it ought to be shown up. . . . As though picturing or indicating life has ever yet changed it! But he, the genial and hopeful, always fancied that it might be so—and I with him.

When he left me this day at three or four, his interest ended because the wonders of Broadway had been exhausted, I found myself with all the great strange city still to be explored. Making inquiry as to directions and distances, I soon found myself in Fifth Avenue at Forty-second Street. Here, represented by mansions at least, was that agglomeration of wealth which, as I then imagined, solved all earthly ills. Beauty was here, of course, and ease and dignity and security, that most wonderful and elusive thing in life. I saw, I admired, and I resented, being myself poor and seeking.

Fifth Avenue then lacked a few of the buildings which since have added somewhat to its impressiveness—the Public Library, the Metropolitan Museum façade at Eighty-second Street, as well as most of the great houses which now face Central Park north of Fifty-ninth Street. But in their place was something that has since been lost and never will be again : a line of quiet and unpretentious brownstone residences which, crowded together on spaces of land no wider than twenty-five feet, still had about them an air of exclusiveness which caused one to hesitate and take note. Between Forty-second and Fifty-ninth Street there was scarcely a suggestion of that coming invasion of trade which subsequently, in a period of less than twenty years, changed its character completely. Instead there were clubs, residences, huge quiet and graceful hotels such as the old Plaza and the Windsor, long since destroyed, and the very graceful Cathedral of St. Patrick. All the cross streets in this area were lined uniformly with brownstone or red brick houses of the same height and general appearance, a high flight of steps leading to the front door, a side gate and door for servants under the steps. Nearly all of these houses were closely boarded up for the summer. There was scarcely a trace of life anywhere save here or there where a servant lounged idly at a side gate or on the front steps talking to a policeman or a cabman.

At Fiftieth Street the great church on its platform was as empty as a drum. At Fifty-ninth, where stood the Savoy, the Plaza, and the Netherland, as well as the great home of Cornelius Vanderbilt, it was all bare as a desert. Lonely handsome cabs plupped dismally to and fro, and the father or mother of the present Fifth Avenue bus, an overgrown closed carriage, rolled lonesomely between Washington Square and One Hundred and Tenth Street. Central Park had most of the lovely walks and lakes which grace it today, but no distant skyline. Central Park West as such had not even appeared. That huge wall that breaks the western sky now was wanting. Along this dismal thoroughfare there trundled a dismal yellow horse-car trailing up a cobble-paved street bare of anything save a hotel or two and some squatter shanties on rocks, with their attendant goats.

But for all that, keeping on as far north as the Museum, I was steadily more and more impressed. It was not beautiful, but perhaps, as I thought, it did not need to be. The congestion of the great city and the power of a number of great names were sufficient to excuse it. And ever and anon would come a something—the Gould home at Sixty-first, the Havemeyer and Astor residences at Sixty-sixth and Sixty-eighth, the Lenox Library at Seventy-second—which redeemed it. Even the old red brick and white stone Museum, now but the central core of the much larger building, with its attendant obelisk, had charm and dignity. So far I wandered, then took the bus and returned to my sister's apartment in Fifteenth Street.

If I have presented all this mildly it was by no means a mild experience for me. Sensitive to the brevity of life and what one may do in a given span, vastly interested in the city itself, I was swiftly being hypnotized by a charm more elusive than real, more of the mind than the eye perhaps, which seized upon and held me so tensely nevertheless that soon I was quite unable to judge sanely of all this and saw its commonplace and even mean face in a most roseate light. The beauty, the hope, the possibilities that were here! It was not a handsome city. As I look back on it now, there was much that was gross and soggy and even repulsive about it. It had too many hard and treeless avenues and cross streets, bare of anything save stone walls and stone or cobble pavements and wretched iron lamp-posts. There were regions that were painfully crowded with poverty, dirt, despair. The buildings were too uniformly low, compact, squeezed. Outside the exclusive residence and commercial areas there was no sense of length or space.

But having seen Broadway and this barren section of Fifth Avenue, I could not think of it in a hostile way, the magnetism of large bodies over small ones holding me. Its barrenness did not now appall me, nor its lack of beauty irritate. There was something else here, a quality of life and zest and security and ease for some, cheek by jowl with poverty and longing and sacrifice, which gives to life everywhere its keenest most pathetic edge. Here was none of that eager clattering snap so characteristic of many of our Western cities, which, while it arrests at first, eventually palls. No city that I had ever seen had exactly what this had. As a boy, of course, I had invested Chicago with immense color and force, and it was there, ignorant, American, semi-conscious, seeking, inspiring. But New York was entirely different. It had the feeling of gross and blissful and parading self-indulgence. It was as if self-indulgence whispered to you that here was its true home; as if, for the most part, it was here secure. Life here was harder perhaps, for some more aware, more cynical and ruthless and brazen and shameless, and yet more alluring for these very reasons. Wherever one turned one felt a consciousness of ease and gluttony, indifference to ideals, however low or high, and coupled with a sense of power that had found itself and was not easily to be dislodged, of virtue that has little idealism and is willing to yield for a price. Here, as one could feel, were huge dreams and lusts and vanities being gratified hourly. I wanted to know the worst and the best of it.

During the few days that I was permitted to remain here, I certainly had an excellent sip. My brother, while associated with the other two as a partner, was so small a factor so far as his firm's internal economy was concerned that he was not needed as more than a hand-shaker on Broadway, one who went about among vaudeville and stage singers and actors and song-composers and advertised by his agreeable personality the existence of his firm and its value to them. And it was that quality of geniality in him which so speedily caused his firm to grow and prosper. Indeed he was its very breath and life. I always think of him as idling along Broadway in the summer time, seeing men and women who could sing songs and writers who could write them, and inducing them by the compelling charm of his personality, to resort to his firm. He had a way with people, affectionate, reassuring, intimate. He was a magnet which drew the young and the old, the sophisticated and the unsophisticated, to his house. Gradually, and because of him and his fame, it prospered mightily, and yet I doubt if ever his partners understood how much he meant to them. His house was young and unimportant, yet within a year or two it had forged its way to the front, and this was due to him and none other. The rest was merely fair commercial management of what he provided in great abundance.

While he waited for his regular theatrical season to resume, he was most excellently prepared to entertain one who might be interested to see Broadway. This night, after dinner at my sister's, he said, "Come on, sport," and together, after promising faithfully to be back by midnight, we ambled forth, strolling across Fifteenth Street to Sixth Avenue and then taking a car to Thirty-third Street, the real center of all things theatrical at the time. Here, at Broadway and Thirty-fifth, opposite the *Herald* building and the Herald Square Theater, stood the Hotel Aulic, a popular rendezvous for actors and singers, with whom my brother was most concerned. And here they were in great number, the sidewalks on two sides of the building alive with them, a world of glittering, spinning flies. I recall the agreeable summer evening air, the bright comforting lights, the open doors and windows, the showy clothes, the laughter, the jesting, the expectorating, the back-slapping geniality. It was wonderful, the spirit and the sense of happiness and ease. Men do at times attain to happiness, paradise even, in this shabby, noisome, worthless, evanescent, make-believe world. I have seen it with mine own eyes.

And here, as in that more pretentious institution at Forty-second Street, the Metropole, my brother was at ease. His was by no means the trade way of a drummer but rather that of one who, like these others, was merely up and down the street seeing what he might. He drank, told idle tales, jested unwearyingly. But all the while, as he told me later, he was really looking for certain individuals who could sing or play and whom in this roundabout and casual way he might interest in the particular song or instrumental composition he was then furthering. "And you never can tell," he said. "You might run into some fellow who would be just the one to write a song or sing one for you."

CHAPTER LXIX

THE next day I was left to myself, and visited City Hall, Brooklyn Bridge, Wall Street and the financial and commercial sections.

I, having no skill for making money and intensely hungry for the things that money would buy, stared at Wall Street, a kind of cloudy Olympus in which foregathered all the gods of finance, with the eyes of one who hopes to extract something by mere observation. Physically it was not then, as it is today, the center of a sky-crowded world. There were few if any high buildings below City Hall, few higher than ten stories. Wall Street was curved, low-fronted, like Oxford Street in London. It began, as some one had already pointed out, at a graveyard and ended at a river. The house of J. P. Morgan was just then being assailed for its connection with a government gold bond issue. The offices of Russell Sage and George Gould (the son), as well as those of the Standard Oil Company below Wall in Broadway, and those of a whole company of now forgotten magnates, could have been pointed out by any messenger boy, postman or policeman. What impressed me was that the street was vibrant with something which, though far from pleasing, craft, greed, cunning, niggardliness, ruthlessness, a smart swaggering ease on the part of some, and hopeless, bedraggled or beaten aspect on the part of others, held my interest as might a tiger or a snake. I had never seen such a world. It was so busy and paper-bestrewn, messenger and broker bestridden, as to make one who had nothing to do there feel dull and commonplace. One thought only of millions made in stocks over night, of yachts, orgies, travels, fames and what not else. Since that time Wall Street has become much tamer, less significant, but then one had a feeling that if only one had a tip or a little skill one might become rich; or that, on the other hand, one might be torn to bits and that here was no mercy.

I arrived a little before noon, and the ways were alive with messenger boys and young clerks and assistants. On the ground was a mess of papers, torn telegrams and letters. Near Broad and Wall streets the air was filled with a hum of voices and typewriter clicks issuing from open windows. Just then, as with the theatrical business later, and still later with the motion picture industry, it had come to be important to be in the street, however thin one's connection. To say "I am in Wall Street" suggested a world of prospects and possibilities. The fact that at this time, and for twenty years after, the news columns were all but closed to suicides and failures in Wall Street, so common were they, illustrates how vagrant and unfounded were the dreams of many.

But the end of Wall Street as the seat of American money domination might even then have been foretold. The cities of the nation were growing. New and by degrees more or less independent centers of finance were being developed. In the course of fifteen years it had become the boast of some cities that they could do without New York in the matter of loans, and it was true. They could; and today many enterprises go west, not east, for their cash. In the main, Wall Street has degenerated into a second-rate gamblers' paradise. What significant Wall Street figures are there today?

On one of my morning walks in New York I had wandered up Broadway to the *Herald* Building and looked into its windows, where were visible a number of great presses in full operation, much larger than any I had seen in the West, and my brother had recalled to me the fact that James Gordon Bennett, owner and editor of the *Herald*, had once commissioned Henry M. Stanley, at that time a reporter on the paper, to go to Africa to find Livingstone. And my good brother, who romanticized all things, my supposed abilities and possibilities included, was inclined to think that if I came to New York some such great thing might happen to me.

On another day I went to Printing House Square, where I stared at the *Sun* and *World* and *Times* and *Tribune* buildings, all facing City Hall Park, sighing for the opportunities that they represented. But I did not act. Something about them overawed me, especially the *World*, the editor of which had begun his career in St. Louis years before. Compared with the Western papers with which I had been connected, all New York papers seemed huge, the tasks they represented editorially and reportorially much more difficult. True, a brother of a famous playwright with whom I had worked in St. Louis had come East and connected himself with the *World*, and I might have called upon him and spied out the land. He had fortified himself with a most favorable record in the West, as had I, only I did not look upon mine as so favorable somehow. Again, a city editor once of St. Louis was now here, city editor of one of the city's great papers, the *Recorder*, and another man, a Sunday editor of Pittsburgh, had become the Sunday editor of the *Press* here. But these appeared to me to be exceptional cases. I reconnoitered these large and in the main rather dull institutions with the eye of one who seeks to take a fortress. The editorial pages of all of these papers, as I had noticed in the West, bristled with cynical and condescending remarks about that region, and their voices representing great circulation and wealth gave them amazing weight in my eyes. Although I knew what I knew about the subservience of newspapers to financial interests, their rat-like fear of religionists and moralists, their shameful betrayal of the ordinary man at every point at which he could possibly be betrayed yet still having the power, by weight of lies and pretense and make-believe, to stir him up to his own detriment and destruction, I was frightened by this very power, which in subsequent years I have come to look upon as the most deadly and forceful of all in nature: the power to masquerade and betray.

There was about these papers an air of assurance and righteousness and authority and superiority which overawed and frightened me. To work on the *Sun*, the *Herald*, the *World!* How many cubs, from how many angles of our national life, were constantly and hopefully eying them from the very same sidewalks or benches in City Hall Park, as the ultimate solution of all their literary, commercial, social, political problems and ambitions. The thousands of pipe-smoking collegians

(*456*)

who have essayed the *Sun* alone, the scullion Danas, embryo Greeleys and Bennetts!

I decided that it would be best for me to return to Pittsburgh and save a little money before I took one of these frowning editorial offices by storm, and I did return, but in what a reduced mood! Pittsburgh, after New York and all I had seen there! And in this darkly brooding and indifferent spirit I now resumed my work. A sum of money sufficient to sustain me for a period in New York was all that I wished now.

And in the course of the next four months I did save two hundred and forty dollars, enduring deprivations which I marvel at even now—breakfast consisting of a cruller and a cup of coffee; dinners that cost no more than a quarter, sometimes no more than fifteen cents. In the meantime I worked as before only to greater advantage, because I was now more sure of myself. My study of Balzac and these recent adventures in the great city had so fired my ambition that nothing could have kept me in Pittsburgh. I lived on so little that I think I must have done myself some physical harm which told against me later in the struggle for existence in New York.

At this time I had the fortune to discover Huxley and Tyndall and Herbert Spencer, whose introductory volume to his *Synthetic Philosophy* (*First Principles*) quite blew me, intellectually, to bits. Hitherto, until I had read Huxley, I had some lingering filaments of Catholicism trailing about me, faith in the existence of Christ, the soundness of his moral and sociologic deductions, the brotherhood of man. But on reading *Science and Hebrew Tradition* and *Science and Christian Tradition*, and finding both the Old and New Testaments to be not compendiums of revealed truth but mere records of religious experiences, and very erroneous ones at that, and then taking up *First Principles* and discovering that all I deemed substantial—man's place in nature, his importance in the universe, this too, too solid earth, man's very identity save as an infinitesimal speck of energy or a "suspended equation" drawn or blown here and there by larger forces in which he moved quite unconsciously as an atom—all questioned and dissolved into other and less understandable things, I was completely thrown down in my conceptions or non-conceptions of life.

Up to this time there had been in me a blazing and unchecked desire to get on and the feeling that in doing so we did get somewhere; now in its place was the definite conviction that spiritually one got nowhere, that there was no hereafter, that one lived and had his being because one had to, and that it was of no importance. Of one's ideals, struggles, deprivations, sorrows and joys, it could only be said that they were chemic compulsions, something which for some inexplicable but unimportant reason responded to and resulted from the hope of pleasure and the fear of pain. Man was a mechanism, undevised and uncreated, and a badly and carelessly driven one at that.

I fear that I cannot make you feel how these things came upon me in the course of a few weeks' reading and left me numb, my gravest fears as to the unsolvable disorder and brutality of life eternally verified. I felt as low and hopeless at times as a beggar of the streets. There was of course this other matter of necessity, internal chemical compulsion, to which I had to respond whether I would or no. I was daily facing a round of duties which now more than ever verified all that I had suspected and that these books proved. With a gloomy eye I began to watch how the chemical—and their children, the mechanical—forces operated through man and outside him, and this under my very eyes. Suicides seemed sadder since there was no care for them; failures the same. One of those periodic scandals breaking out in connection with the care of prisoners in some local or state jail, I saw how self-interest, the hope of pleasure or the fear of pain caused jailers or wardens or a sheriff to graft on prisoners, feed them rotten meat, torture them into silence and submission, and then, politics interfering (the hope of pleasure again and the fear of pain on the part of some), the whole thing hushed up, no least measure of the sickening truth breaking out in the subservient papers. Life could or would do nothing for those whom it so shamefully abused.

Again, there was a poor section, one street in the East Pittsburgh district, shut off by a railroad at one end (the latter erecting a high fence to protect itself from trespass) and by an arrogant property owner at the other end; those within were actually left without means of ingress and egress. Yet instead of denouncing either or both, the railroads being so powerful and the citizen prosperous and within his "rights," I was told to write a humorous article but not to "hurt anybody's feelings." Also before my eyes were always those regions of indescribable poverty and indescribable wealth previously mentioned, which were always carefully kept separate by the local papers, all the favors and compliments and commercial and social aids going to those who had, all the sniffs and indifferences and slights going to those who had not; and when I read Spencer I could only sigh. All I could think of was that since nature would not or could not do anything for man, he must, if he could, do something for himself; and of this I saw no prospect, he being a product of these self-same accidental, indifferent and bitterly cruel forces.

And so I went on from day to day, reading, thinking, doing fairly acceptable work, but always withdrawing more and more into myself. As I saw it then, the world could not understand me, nor I it, nor men each other very well. Then a little later I turned and said that since the whole thing was hopeless I might as well forget it and join the narrow, heartless, indifferent scramble, but I could not do that either, lacking the temperament and the skill. All I could do was think, and since no paper such as I knew was interested in any of the things about which I was thinking, I was hopeless indeed. Finally, in late November, having two hundred and forty dollars saved, I decided to leave this dismal scene and seek the charm of the great city beyond, hoping that there I might succeed at something, be eased and rested by some important work of some kind.

CHAPTER LXX

My departure was accelerated by a conversation I had one day with the political reporter of whom I have spoken but whose name I have forgotten. By now I had come to be on agreeable social terms with all the men on our staff, and at midnight it was my custom to drift around to the Press Club, where might be found a goodly company of men who worked on the different papers. I found this political man here one night. He said: "I can't understand why you stay here. Now I wouldn't say that to any one else in the game for fear he'd think I was plotting to get him out of his job, but with you it's different. There's no great chance here, and you have too much ability to waste your time on this town. They won't let you do anything. The steel people have this town sewed up tight. The papers are muzzled. All you can do is to write what the people at the top want you to write, and that's very little. With your talent you could go down to New York and make a place for yourself. I've been there myself, but had to come back on account of my family. The conditions were too uncertain for me, and I have to have a regular income. But with you it's different. You're young, and apparently you haven't any one dependent on you. If you do strike it down there you'll make a lot of money, and what's more you might make a name for yourself. Don't you think it's foolish for you to stay here? Don't think it's anything to me whether you go or stay. I haven't any ax to grind, but I really wonder why you stay."

I explained that I had been drifting, that I was really on my way to New York but taking my time about it. Only a few days before I had been reading of a certain Indo-English newspaper man, fresh out of India with his books and short stories, who was making a great stir. His name was Rudyard Kipling, and the enthusiasm with which he was being received made me not jealous but wishful for a career for myself. The tributes to his brilliance were so unanimous, and he was a mere youth as yet, not more than twenty-seven or -eight. He was coming to America, or was even then on his way, and the wonder of such a success filled my mind. I decided then and there that I would go, must go, and accordingly gave notice of my intention. My city editor merely looked at me as much as to say, ''Well, I thought so,'' then said: ''Well, I think you'll do better there myself, but I'm not glad to have you go. You can refer to us any time you want to.''

On Saturday I drew my pay at noon and by four o'clock had once more boarded the express which deposited me in New York the following morning at seven. My brother had long since left New York and would not be back until the following Spring. I had exchanged a word or two with my sister and found that she was not prospering. Since Paul had left she had been forced to resort to letting rooms, H—— not having found anything to do. I wired her that I was coming, and walked in on her the next morning.

My sister, on seeing me again, was delighted. I did not know then, and perhaps if I had I should not have been so pleased, that I was looked upon by her as the possible way out of a very difficult and trying crisis which she and her two children were then facing. For H——, from being a one-time fairly resourceful and successful and aggressive man, had slipped into a most disconcerting attitude of weakness and all but indifference before the onslaughts of the great city.

My brother Paul, being away, saw no reason why he should be called upon to help them, since H—— was as physically able as himself. Aside from renting their rooms there was apparently no other source of income here, at least none which H—— troubled to provide. He appeared to be done for, played out. Like so many who have fought a fair battle and then lost, he had wearied of the game and was drifting. And my sister, like so many of the children of ordinary families the world over, had received no practical education or training and knew nothing other than housework, that profitless trade. In consequence, within a very short time after my arrival, I found myself faced by one of two alternatives: that of retiring and leaving her to shift as best she might (a step which, in view of what followed, would have been wiser but which my unreasoning sympathy would not permit me to do), or of assisting her with what means I had. But this would be merely postponing the day of reckoning for all of them and bringing a great deal of trouble upon myself. For, finding me willing to pay for my room and board here, and in addition to advance certain sums which had nothing to do with my obligations, H—— felt that he could now drift a little while longer and so did, accepting through his wife such doles as I was willing to make. My sister, fumbling, impractical soul, flowing like water into any crevice of opportunity, accepted this sacrifice on my part.

But despite these facts, which developed very slowly, I was very much alive to the possibilities which the city then held for me. At last I was here. I told myself I had a comfortable place to stay and would remain, and from this vantage point I could now sally forth and reconnoiter the city at my leisure. And as in all previous instances, I devoted a day or two to rambling about, surveying the world which I was seeking to manipulate to my advantage, and then on the second or third afternoon began to investigate those newspaper offices with which I was most anxious to connect.

I can never forget the shock I received when on entering first the *World*, then the *Sun*, and later the *Herald*, I discovered that one could not so much as get in to see the city editor, that worthy being guarded by lobby or anteroom, in which were posted as lookouts and buffers or men-at-arms as cynical and contemptuous a company of youths and hall boys as it has ever been my lot to meet. They were not only self-sufficient, but supercilious, scoffing and ribald. Whenever I entered one of these offices there were two or three on guard, sometimes four or five in the *World* office, wrestling for the possession of an ink-well or a pencil or an apple, or slapping each other on the back. But let a visitor arrive with an inquiry of some kind, and these young banditti would cease their personal brawling long enough at least to place themselves as a barricade between the newcomer and the door to the editorial sanctum, whereupon would ensue the following routine formula, each and every one of them chewing gum or eating an apple.

"Whoja wanta see?"

"The city editor."

"Wha'ja wanta see him about?"

"A job."

"No vacancies. No; no vacancies today. He says to say no vacancies today, see? You can't go in there. He says no vacancies."

"But can't I even see him?"

"No; he don't wanta see anybody. No vacancies."

"Well, how about taking my name in to him?"

"Not if you're lookin' for a job. He says no vacancies."

The tone and the manner were most disconcerting. To me, new to the city and rather overawed by the size of the buildings as well as the reputation of the editors and the publications themselves, this was all but final. For a little while after each rebuff I did not quite see how I was to overcome this difficulty. Plainly they were overrun with applicants, and in so great a city why would they not be? But what was I to do? One must get in or write or call up on the telephone, but would any city editor worthy the name discuss a man's fitness or attempt to judge him by a telephone conversation or a letter?

Rather dourly and speculatively, therefore, after I had visited four or five of these offices with exactly the same result in each instance, I went finally to City Hall Park, which fronted the majority of them—the *Sun*, the *Tribune*, the *Times*, the *World*, the *Press*—and stared at their great buildings. About me was swirling the throng which has always made that region so interesting, the vast mass that bubbles upward from the financial district and the regions south of it and crosses the plaza to Brooklyn Bridge and the elevated roads (the subways had not come yet). About me on the benches of the park was, even in this gray, chill December weather, that large company of bums, loafers, tramps, idlers, the flotsam and jetsam of the great city's whirl and strife to be seen there today. I presume I looked at them and then considered myself and these great offices, and it was then that the idea of *Hurstwood* was born. The city seemed so huge and cruel. I recalled gay Broadway of the preceding summer, and the baking, isolated, exclusive atmosphere of Fifth Avenue, all boarded up. And now I was here and it was winter, with this great newspaper world to be conquered, and I did not see how it was to be done. At four in the afternoon I dubiously turned my steps northward along the great, bustling, solidly commercial Broadway to Fifteenth Street, walking all the way and staring into the shops. Those who recall *Sister Carrie's* wanderings may find a taste of it here. In Union Square, before Tiffany's, I stared at an immense Christmas throng. Then in the darkness I wandered across to my sister's apartment, and in the warmth and light there set me down thinking what to do. My sister noticed my mood and after a little while said:

"You're worrying, aren't you?"

"Oh no, I'm not," I said rather pretentiously.

"Oh yes, you are too. You're wondering how you're going to get along. I know how you are. We're all that way. But you mustn't worry. Paul says you can write wonderfully. You've only been here a day or two. You must wait until you've tried a little while and then see. You're sure to get along. New York isn't so bad, only you have to get started."

I decided that this was true enough and proposed to give myself time to think.

CHAPTER LXXI

BUT the next day, and the next, and the next brought me no solution to the problem. The weather had turned cold and for a time there was a slushy snow on the ground, which made the matter of job-hunting all the worse. Those fierce youths in the anterooms were no more kindly on the second and fifth days than they had been on the first. But by now, in addition to becoming decidedly dour, I was becoming a little angry. It seemed to me to be the height of discourtesy, not to say rank brutality, for newspapers, and especially those which boasted a social and humanitarian leadership of their fellows in American life, to place such unsophisticated and blatant and ill-trained upstarts between themselves and the general public, men and women of all shades and degrees of intelligence who might have to come in contact with them. H. L. Mencken has written: ''The average American newspaper, especially the so-called better sort, has the intelligence of a Baptist evangelist, the courage of a rat, the fairness of a prohibitionist boob-bumper, the information of a high-school janitor, the taste of a designer of celluloid valentines, and the honor of a police-station lawyer.'' Judging by some of my experiences and observations, I would be willing to subscribe to this. The unwarranted and unnecessary airs! The grand assumption of wisdom! The heartless and brutal nature of their internal economies, their pandering to the cheapest of all public instincts and tendencies in search of circulation!

After several days I made up my mind to see the city editor of these papers, regardless of hall boys. And so, going one day at one o'clock to the *World*, I started to walk right in, but, being intercepted as usual, lost my courage and retreated. However, as I have since thought, perhaps this was fortunate, for going downstairs I meditated most grievously as to my failure, my lack of skill and courage in carrying out my intention. So thoroughly did I castigate myself that I recovered my nerve and returned. I reëntered the small office, and finding two of the youths still on hand and waiting to intercept me, brushed them both aside as one might flies, opened the much-guarded door and walked in.

To my satisfaction, while they followed me and by threats and force attempted to persuade me to retreat, I gazed upon one of the most interesting city reportorial and editorial rooms that I have ever beheld. It was forty or fifty feet wide by a hundred or more deep, and lighted, even by day in this gray weather, by a blaze of lights. The entire space from front to back was filled with desks. A varied company of newspaper men, most of them in shirt-sleeves, were hard at work. In the forward part of the room, near the door by which I had entered, and upon a platform, were several desks, at which three or four men were seated—the throne, as I quickly learned, of the city editor and his assistants. Two of these, as I could see, were engaged in reading and marking papers. A third, who looked as though he might be the city editor, was consulting with several men at his desk. Copy boys were ambling to and fro. From somewhere came the constant click-click-click of telegraph instruments and the howl of "Coppee!" I think I should have been forced to retire had it not been for the fact that as I was standing there, threatened and pleaded with by my two adversaries, a young man (since distinguished in the journalistic world, Arthur Brisbane) who was passing through the room looked at me curiously and inquired courteously:

"What is it you want?"

"I want," I said, half-angered by the spectacle I was making and that was being made of me, "a job."

"Where do you come from?"

"The West."

"Wait a moment," he said, and the youths, seeing that I had attracted his attention, immediately withdrew. He went toward the man at the desk whom I had singled out as the city editor, and turned and pointed to me. "This young man wants a job. I wish you would give him one."

The man nodded, and my remarkable interrogator, turning to me, said, "Just wait here," and disappeared.

I did not know quite what to think, so astonished was I, but with each succeeding moment my spirits rose, and by the time the city editor chose to motion me to him I was in a very exalted state indeed. So much for courage, I told myself. Surely I was fortunate, for had I not been dreaming for months—years—of coming to New York and after great deprivation and difficulty perhaps securing a position? And now of a sudden here I was thus swiftly vaulted into the very position which of all others I had most craved. Surely this must be the influence of a star of fortune. Surely now if I had the least trace of ability, I should be in a better position than I had ever been in before. I looked about the great room, as I waited patiently and delightedly, and saw pasted on the walls at intervals printed cards which read: *Accuracy, Accuracy, Accuracy! Who? What? Where? When? How? The Facts—The Color—The Facts!* I knew what those signs meant: the proper order for beginning a newspaper story. Another sign insisted upon *Promptness, Courtesy, Geniality!* Most excellent traits, I thought, but not as easy to put into execution as comfortable publishers and managing editors might suppose.

Presently I was called over and told to take a seat, after being told: "I'll have an assignment for you after a while." That statement meant work, an opportunity, a salary. I felt myself growing apace, only the eye and the glance of my immediate superior was by no means cheering or genial. This man was holding a difficult position, one of the most difficult in newspaperdom in America at the time, and under one of the most eccentric and difficult of publishers, Joseph Pulitzer.

This same Pulitzer, whom Alleyne Ireland subsequently characterized in so brilliant a fashion as to make this brief sketch trivial and unimportant save for its service here as a link in this tale, was a brilliant and eccentric Magyar Jew, long since famous for his journalistic genius. At that time he must have been between fifty-five and sixty years of age, semi-dyspeptic and half-blind, having almost wrecked himself physically, or so I understood, in a long and grueling struggle to ascend to preeminence in the American newspaper world. He was the chief owner, as I understood, of not only the New York *World* but the St. Louis *Post-Dispatch*, the then afternoon paper of largest circulation and influence in that city. While I was in St. Louis the air of that newspaper world was surcharged or still rife with this remarkable publisher's past exploits—how once, when he was starting in the newspaper world as a publisher, he had been horsewhipped by some irate citizen for having published some derogatory item, and, having tamely submitted to the castigation, had then rushed into his sanctum and given orders that an extra should be issued detailing the attack in order that the news value might not be lost to the counting-room. Similarly, one of his St. Louis city or managing editors (one Colonel Cockerill by name, who at this very time or a very little later was still one of the managing editors of the New York *World*) had, after conducting some campaign of exposure against a local citizen by order of his chief, and being confronted in his office by the same, evidently come to punish him, drawn a revolver and killed him.

That was a part of what might have been called the makings of this great newspaper figure. Here in New York, after his arrival on the scene in 1884, at which time he had taken over a moribund journal called the *World*, he had literally succeeded in turning things upside down, much as did William Randolph Heart after him, and as had Charles A. Dana and others before him. Like all aggressive newspaper men worthy the name, he had seized upon every possible vital issue and attacked, attacked, attacked—Tammany Hall, Wall Street (then defended by the *Sun* and the *Herald*), the house of Morgan, some phases of society, and many other features and conditions of the great city. For one thing, he had cut the price of his paper to one cent, a move which was reported to have infuriated his conservative and quiescent rivals, who were getting two, three and five and who did not wish to be disturbed in their peaceful pursuits. The *Sun* in particular, which had been *made* by the brilliant and daring eccentricity

(468)

of Dana and his earlier radicalism, and the *Herald*, which originally owed its growth and fame to the monopoly-fighting skill of Bennett, were now both grown conservative and mutually attacked him as low, vulgar, indecent and the like, an upstart Jew whose nose was in every putrescent dunghill, ratting out filth for the consumption of the dregs of society. But is it not always so when any one arises who wishes to break through from submersion or nothingness into the white light of power and influence? Do not the resultant quakes always infuriate those who have ceased growing or are at least comfortably quiescent and who do not wish to be disturbed?

Just the same, this man, because of his vital, aggressive, restless, working mood, and his vaulting ambition to be all that there was to be of journalistic force in America, was making a veritable hell of his paper and the lives of those who worked for him. And although he himself was not present at the time but was sailing around the world on a yacht, or living in a villa on the Riviera, or at Bar Harbor, or in his town house in New York or London, you could feel the feverish and disturbing and distressing ionic tang of his presence in this room as definitely as though he were there in the flesh. Air fairly sizzled with the ionic rays of this black star. Of secretaries to this editor-publisher and traveling with him at the time but coming back betimes to nose about the paper and cause woe to others, there were five. Of sons, by no means in active charge but growing toward eventual control, two. Of managing editors, all slipping about and, as the newspaper men seemed to think, spying on each other, at one time as many as seven. He had so little faith in his fellow-man, and especially such of his fellow-men as were so unfortunate as to have to work for him, that he played off one against another as might have the council of the Secret Ten in Venice, or as did the devils who ruled in the Vatican in the Middle Ages. Every man's hand, as I came to know in the course of time, was turned against that of every other. All were thoroughly distrustful of each other and feared the incessant spying that was going on. Each, as I was told and as to a certain extent one could feel, was made to believe that he was the important one, or might be, presuming that he could prove that the others were failures or in error. Proposed editorials, suggestions for news features, directions as to policy and what not, were coming in from him every hour via cable or telegraph. Nearly every issue of any importance was being submitted to him by the same means. He was, as described by this same Alleyne Ireland, undoubtedly semi-neurasthenic, a disease-demonized soul, who could scarcely control himself in anything, a man who was fighting an almost insane battle with life itself, trying to be omnipotent and what not else, and never to die.

But in regard to the men working here how sharp a sword of disaster seemed suspended above them by a thread, the sword of dismissal or of bitter reprimand or contempt. They had a kind of nervous, resentful terror in their eyes as have animals when they are tortured. All were either scribbling busily or hurrying in or out. Every man was for himself. If you had asked a man a question, as I ventured to do while sitting here, not knowing anything of how things were done here, he looked at you as though you were a fool, or as though you were trying to take something away from him or cause him trouble of some kind. In the main they bustled by or went on with their work without troubling to pay the slightest attention to you. I had never encountered anything like it before, and only twice afterwards in my life did I find anything which even partially approximated it, and both times in New York. After the peace and ease of Pittsburgh—God! But it was immense, just the same—terrific.

CHAPTER LXXII

AFTER I had waited an hour or so, a boy came up and said: "The city editor wants to see you." I hurried forward to the desk of that Poohbah, who merely handed me a small clipping from another paper giving an account of some extra-terrestrial manifestations that had been taking place in a graveyard near Elizabeth, and told me to "see what there is in that." Unsophisticated as I was as to the ways of the metropolis, and assuming, Western-fashion, that I might ask a question of my new chief, I ventured a feeble "Where is that?" For my pains I received as contemptuous a look as it is possible for one human being to give another.

"Back of the directory! Back of the directory!" came the semi-savage reply, and not quite realizing what was meant by that I retired precipitately, trying to think it out.

Almost mechanically I went to the directory, but fumbling through that part of it which relates to streets and their numbers I began to realize that Elizabeth was a town and not a street. At a desk near the directory I noticed a stout man of perhaps forty, rotund and agreeable, who seemed to be less fierce and self-centered than some of the others. He had evidently only recently entered, for he had kicked off a pair of overshoes and laid a greatcoat over a chair beside him and was scribbling.

"Can you tell me how I can get to Elizabeth?" I inquired of him.

"Sure," he said, looking up and beginning to chuckle. "I haven't been in the city very long myself, but I know where that is. It's on the Jersey Central, about twelve miles out. You'll catch a local by going down to the Liberty Street ferry. I heard him tell you 'Back of the directory,'" he added genially. "You mustn't mind that—that's what they always tell you here, these smart alecks," and he chuckled, very much like my friend McCord. "They're the most inconsiderate lot I ever went up against, but you have to get used to it. Out where I came from they'll give you a civil answer once in a while, but here it's 'Back of the directory,' " and he chuckled again.

"And where do you come from?" I asked.

"Oh, Pittsburgh originally," he said, which same gave me a spiritual lift, "but I haven't been in the game for several years. I've been doing press agent work for a road show, one of my own," and he chuckled again. "I'm not a stranger to New York exactly, but I am to this paper and this game down here."

I wanted to stay longer and talk to him, but I had to hurry on this my first assignment in New York. "Is this your desk?" I asked.

"No; they haven't deigned to give me one yet," and he chuckled again. "But I suppose I will get one eventually—if they don't throw me out."

"I hope I'll see you when I get back."

"Oh, I'll be around here, if I'm not out in the snow. It's tough, isn't it?" and he turned to his work again. I bustled out through that same anteroom where I had been restrained, and observed to my pestiferous opponents: "Now just take notice, Eddie. I belong here, see? I work here. And I'll be back in a little while."

"Oh, dat's all right," he replied with a grin. "We gotta do dat. We gotta keep mosta dese hams outa here, dough. Dat's de orders we got."

"Hams?" I thought. "They let these little snips speak of strangers as hams! That's New York for you!"

I made the short dreary commuters' trip to Elizabeth. When I found my graveyard and the caretaker thereof, he said there was no truth in the story. No man by the name of the dead man mentioned had ever been buried there. No noises or appearances of any kind had been recorded. "They're always publishing things like that about New Jersey," he said. "I wish they'd quit it. Some newspaper fellow just wanted to earn a little money, that's all."

(472)

I tramped back, caught a train and reached the office at eight. Already most of the assignments had been given out. The office was comparatively empty. The city editor had gone to dinner. At a desk along a wall was a long, lean, dyspeptic-looking man, his eyes shaded by a green shield, whom I took to be the night editor, so large was the pile of "copy" beside him, but when I ventured to approach him he merely glared sourly. "The city desk's not closed yet," he growled. "Wait'll they come back."

I retired, rebuffed again.

Presently one of the assistants reappeared and I reported to him. "Nothing to it, eh?" he observed. "But there ought to be some kind of a josh to it." I did not get him. He told me to wait around, and I sought out an empty desk and sat down. The thing that was interesting me was how much I should be paid per week. In the meanwhile I contented myself with counting the desks and wondering about the men who occupied them, who they were, and what they were doing. To my right, against the north wall, were two roll-top desks, at one of which was seated a dapper actor-like man writing and posting. He was arrayed in a close-fitting gray suit, with a bright vest and an exceedingly high collar. Because of some theatrical programs which I saw him examining, I concluded that he must be connected with the dramatic department, probably *the* dramatic critic. I was interested and a little envious. The dramatic department of a great daily in New York seemed a wonderful thing to me.

After a time also there entered another man who opened the desk next the dramatic critic. He was medium tall and stocky, with a mass of loose wavy hair hanging impressively over his collar, not unlike the advance agent of a cure-all or a quack Messiah. His body was encased in a huge cape-coat which reached to his knees after the best manner of a tragedian. He wore a large, soft-brimmed felt, which he now doffed rather grandiosely, and stood a big cane in the corner. He had the look and attitude of a famous musician, the stage-type, and evidently took himself very seriously. I put him down as the musical critic at least, some great authority of whom I should hear later.

Time went by, and I waited. Through the windows from where I was sitting I could see the tops of one or two buildings, one holding a clock-face lighted with a green light. Being weary of sitting, I ventured to leave my seat and look out to the south. Then for the first time I saw that great night panorama of the East River and the bay with its ships and docks, and the dark mass of buildings in between, many of them still lighted. It was a great scene, and a sense of awe came over me. New York was so vast, so varied, so rich, so hard. How was one to make one's way here? I had so little to offer, merely a gift of scribbling; and money, as I could see, was not to be made in that way.

The city editor returned and told me to attend a meeting of some committee which looked to the better lighting and cleaning of a certain district. It was all but too late, as I knew, and if reported would be given no more than an inch of space. I took it rather dejectedly. Then fell the worst blow of all. "Wait a minute," he said, as I moved to depart. "I wanted to tell you. I can't make you a reporter yet—there is no vacancy on our regular staff. But I'll put you on space, and you can charge up whatever you get in at seven-and-a-half a column. We allow fifty cents an hour for time. Show up tomorrow at eleven, and I'll see if anything turns up."

My heart sank to my shoes. No reportorial staff with which I had ever been connected had been paid by space. I went to the meeting and found that it was of no importance, and made but one inch, as I discovered next morning by a careful examination of the paper. And a column of the paper measured exactly twenty-one inches! So my efforts this day, allowing for time charged for my first trip, had resulted in a total of one dollar and eighty-six cents, or a little less than street-sweepers and snow-shovelers were receiving.

But this was not all. Returning about eleven with this item, I ventured to say to the night editor now in charge: "When does a man leave here?"

"You're a new space man, aren't you?"

"Yes, sir."

"You have the late watch tonight."

"And how late is that?"

"Until after the first edition is on the press," he growled.

Not knowing when that was I still did not venture to question him but returned to another reporter working near at hand, who told me I should have to stay until three. At that time my green-shaded mentor called, "You might as well go now," and I made my way to the Sixth Avenue L and so home, having been here since one o'clock of the preceding day. The cheerful face of my sister sleepily admitting me was quite the best thing that this brisk day in the great city had provided.

CHAPTER LXXIII

THE next morning, coming down at eleven I encountered my friend of the day before, whom I found looking through the paper and checking up such results as he had been able to achieve. "Tst! Tst!" he clicked to himself as he went over the pages, looking high and low for a minute squib which he had managed to get in. Looking around and seeing me near at hand, he said: "Positively, this is the worst paper in New York. I've always heard it was, and now I know it. This damned crowd plays favorites. They have an inside ring, a few pets, who get all the cream, and fellows like you and me get the short ends. Take me yesterday: I was sent out on four lousy little stories, and not one amounted to anything. I tramped and rode all over town in the snow, listened to a lot of fools spout, and this morning I have just three little items. Look at that—and that—and that!" and he pointed to check-marks on different pages. They made a total of, say, seven or eight inches, the equivalent in cash of less than three dollars. "And I'm supposed to live on that," he went on, "and I have a boy and a girl in school! How do they figure that a man is to get along?"

I had no consolation to offer him. After a time he resumed: "What they do is to get strangers like us, or any of these down-and-out newspaper men always walking up and down Park Row looking for a job, and get us to work on space because it sounds bigger to a greenhorn. Sure they have space-men here who amount to something, fellows who get big money, but they're not like us. They make as much as seventy-five and a hundred dollars a week. But they're re-write men, old reporters who have too big a pull and who are too sure of themselves to stand for the low salaries they pay here. But they're at the top. We little fellows are told that stuff about space, but all we get is leg-work. If you or I should get hold of a good story don't you ever think they'd let us write it. I know that much. They'd take it away and give it to one of these rewrite fellows. There's one now," and he pointed to a large comfortable man in a light brown overcoat and brown hat who was but now ambling in. "He rewrote one of my stories just the other day. If they wanted you for regular work they'd make you take a regular salary for fear you'd get too much of space. They just keep us little fellows as extras to follow up such things as they wouldn't waste a good man on. And they're always firing a crowd of men every three or four months to keep up the zip of the staff, to keep 'em worried and working hard. I hate the damned business. I told myself in Pittsburgh that I never would get back in it again, but here I am!"

This revelation made me a little sick. So this was my grand job! A long period of drudgery for little or nothing, my hard-earned money exhausted—and then what?

"Just now," he went on, "there's nothing doing around the town or I wouldn't be here. I'm only staying on until I can get something better. It's a dog's life. There's nothing in it. I worked here all last week, and what do you think I made? Twelve dollars and seventy-five cents for the whole week, time included. Twelve dollars and seventy-five cents! It's an outrage!"

I agreed with him. "What is this time they allow?" I asked. "How do they figure—expenses and all?"

"Sure, they allow expenses, and I'm going to figure mine more liberally from now on. It's a little bonus they allow you for the time you work, but you don't get anything anyhow. I'll double any railroad fare I pay. If they don't like it they can get somebody else. But they won't let you do too much of it, and if you can't make a little salary on small stuff they won't keep you even then." He grinned. "Anything big goes to the boys on a salary, and if it's real big the space-men, who are on salary and space also, get the cream. I went out on a story the other afternoon and tramped around in the rain and got all the facts, and just as I was going to sit down and write it—well, I hadn't really got started—one of the managing editors—there are about twenty around here—came up and took it away from me and gave it to somebody else to write. All I got was 'time.' Gee, I was sore! But I don't care," he added with a chuckle. "I'll be getting out of here one of these days."

Being handed this dose of inspiring information, I was in no mood for what followed; although I decided that this series of ills that were now befalling him was due to the fact that he was older than myself and maybe not very efficient, whereas in my case, being young, efficient, etc., etc.—the usual mental bonus youth hands itself—I should do better. But when it came to my assignments this day and the next and the next, and in addition I was "handed" the late watch, my cock sureness began to evaporate. Each day I was given unimportant rumors or verification tales, which came to nothing. So keen was the competition between the papers, especially between the *World* and the *Sun,* or the *World* and the *Herald,* that almost everything suggested by one was looked into and criticized by the others. The items assigned to me this second day were: to visit the city morgue and there look up the body of a young and beautiful girl who was supposed to have drowned herself or been drowned and see if this was true, as another paper had said (and of course she was not beautiful at all); to visit a certain hotel to find out what I could about a hotel beat who had been arrested (this item, although written, was never used); to visit a Unitarian conference called to debate some supposed changes in faith or method of church development, the date for which however had been changed without notice to the papers, for which I was allowed time and carfare. My time, setting aside the long and wearisome hours in which I sat in the office awaiting my turn for an assignment, netted me the handsome sum of two dollars and fifty cents. And all the time in this very paper, I could read the noblest and most elevating discourses about duty, character, the need of a higher sense of citizenship, and what not. I used to frown at the shabby pecksniffery of it, the cheap buncombe that would allow a great publisher to bleed and drive his employees at one end of his house and deliver exordiums as to virtue, duty, industry, thrift, honesty at the other.

However, despite these little setbacks and insights, I was not to be discouraged. The fact that I had succeeded elsewhere made me feel that somehow I should succeed here. Nevertheless, in spite of this sense of efficiency, I was strangely overawed and made more than ordinarily incompetent by the hugeness and force and heartlessness of the great city, its startling contrasts of wealth and poverty, the air of ruthlessness and indifference and disillusion that everywhere prevailed. Only recently there had been a disgusting exposure of the putrescence and heartlessness and brutality which underlay the social structure of the city. There had been the Lexow Investigation with its sickening revelations of graft and corruption, and the protection and encouragement of vice and crime in every walk of political and police life. The most horrible types of brothels had been proved to be not only winked at but preyed upon by the police and the politicians by a fixed and graded monthly tax in which the patrolman, the "roundsman," the captain and the inspector, to say nothing of the district leader, shared. There was undeniable proof that the police and the politicians, even the officials, of the city were closely connected with all sorts of gambling and wire-tapping and bunco-steering, and even the subornation of murder. To the door of every house of prostitution and transient rooming-house the station police captain's man, the *roundsman,* came as regularly as the rent or the gas man, and took more away. "Squealers" had been murdered in cold blood for their squealing. A famous chief of police, Byrnes by name, reputed at that time, far and wide, for his supposed skill in unraveling mysteries, being faced by a saturnalia of crime which he could not solve, had finally in self-defense caused to be arrested, tried, convicted and electrocuted, all upon suborned testimony, an old, helpless, half-witted bum known as Old Shakespeare, whose only crime was that he was worthless and defenseless. But the chief had thereby saved his "reputation." Not far from the region in which my sister lived, although it was respectable enough in its way, tramped count-

(479)

less girls by night and by day looking for men, the great business of New York, and all preyed upon by the police. On several occasions, coming home from work after midnight, I found men lying hatless, coatless, trousers pockets pulled out, possibly their skulls fractured, so inadequate or indifferent or conniving was the so-called police protection.

Nowhere before had I seen such a lavish show of wealth, or, such bitter poverty. In my reporting rounds I soon came upon the East Side; the Bowery, with its endless line of degraded and impossible lodging-houses, a perfect whorl of bums and failures; the Brooklyn waterfront, parts of it terrible in its degradation; and then by way of contrast again the great hotels, the mansions along Fifth Avenue, the smart shops and clubs and churches. When I went into Wall Street, the Tenderloin, the Fifth Avenue district, the East and West sides, I seemed everywhere to sense either a terrifying desire for lust or pleasure or wealth, accompanied by a heartlessness which was freezing to the soul, or a dogged resignation to deprivation and misery. Never had I seen so many down-and-out men—in the parks, along the Bowery and in the lodging-houses which lined that pathetic street. They slept over gratings anywhere from which came a little warm air, or in doorways or cellar-ways. At a half dozen points in different parts of the city I came upon those strange charities which supply a free meal to a man or lodging for the night, providing that he came at a given hour and waited long enough.

And never anywhere had I seen so much show and luxury. Nearly all of the houses along upper Fifth Avenue and its side streets boasted their liveried footmen. Wall Street was a sea of financial trickery and legerdemain, a realm so crowded with sharklike geniuses of finance that one's poor little arithmetic intelligence was entirely discounted and made ridiculous. How was a sniveling scribbler to make his way in such a world? Nothing but chance and luck, as I saw it, could further the average man or lift him out of his rut, and since when had it been proved that I was a favorite of fortune? A crushing sense of incompetence and general inefficiency seemed to settle upon me, and I could not shake it off. Whenever I went out on an assignment—and I was always being sent upon those trivial, shoe-wearing affairs—I carried with me this sense of my unimportance.

CHAPTER LXXIV

IT is entirely possible that, due to some physical or mental defect of my own, I was in no way fitted to contemplate so huge and ruthless a spectacle as New York then presented, or that I had too keen a conception of it at any rate. After a few days of work here I came in touch with several newspaper men from the West—a youth by the name of Graves, another by the name of Elliott, both formerly of Chicago, and a third individual who had once been in St. Louis, Wynne Thomas, brother of the famous playwright, Augustus. All were working on this paper, two of them in the same capacity as myself, the third a staff man. At night we used to sit about doing the late watch and spin all sorts of newspaper tales. These men had wandered from one place to another, and had seen—heavens, what had they not seen! They were completely disillusioned. Here, as in newspaper offices everywhere, one could hear the most disconcerting tales of human depravity and cruelty. I think that in the hours I spent with these men I learned as much about New York and its difficulties and opportunities, its different social strata, its outstanding figures social and political, as I might have learned in months of reporting and reading. They seemed to know every one likely to figure in the public eye. By degrees they introduced me to others, and all confirmed the conclusions which I was reaching. New York was difficult and revolting. The police and politicians were a menace; vice was rampant; wealth was shamelessly showy, cold and brutal. In New York the outsider or beginner had scarcely any chance at all, save as a servant. The city was overrun with hungry, loafing men of all descriptions, newspaper writers included.

After a few weeks of experimenting, however, I had no need of confirmation from any source. An assignment or two having developed well under my handling, and I having reported my success to the city editor, I was allowed to begin to write it, then given another assignment and told to turn my story over to the large gentleman with the gold-headed cane. This infuriated and discouraged me, but I said nothing. I thought it might be due to the city editor's conviction, so far not disturbed by any opportunity I had had, that I could not write.

But one night, a small item about a fight in a tenement house having been given me to investigate, I went to the place in question and found that it was a cheap beer-drinking brawl on the upper East Side which had its origin in the objection of one neighbor to the noise made by another. I constructed a ridiculous story of my own to the effect that the first irritated neighbor was a musician who had been attempting at midnight to construct a waltz, into which the snores, gurgles, moans and gasps of his slumberous next-door neighbor would not fit. Becoming irritated and unable by calls and knocking to arouse his friend and so bring him to silence, he finally resorted to piano banging and glass-breaking of such a terrible character as to arouse the entire neighborhood and cause the sending in of a riot call by a policeman, who thought that a tenement war had broken out. Result: broken heads and an interesting parade to the nearest police station. Somewhere in the text I used the phrase "sawing somnolent wood."

Finding no one in charge of the city editor's desk when I returned, I handed my account to the night city editor. The next morning, lo and behold, there it was on the first page consuming at least a fourth of a column! To my further surprise and gratification, once the city editor appeared I noticed a change of attitude in him. While waiting for an assignment, I caught his eye on me, and finally he came over, paper in hand, and pointing to the item said: "You wrote this, didn't you?" I began to think that I might have made a mistake in creating this bit of news and that it had been investigated and found to be a fiction. "Yes," I replied. Instead of berating me he smiled and said: "Well, it's rather well done. I may be able to make a place for you after a while. I'll see if I can't find an interesting story for you somewhere.''

And true to his word, he gave me another story on this order. In the Hoffman House bar, one of the show-places of the city, there had been a brawl the day before, a fight between a well-known society youth of great wealth who owed the hotel money and would not pay as speedily as it wished, and a manager or assistant manager who had sent him some form of disturbing letter. All the details, as I discovered on reading the item (which had been clipped from the *Herald*), had been fully covered by that paper, and all that remained for me twenty-four hours later was to visit the principals and extract some comments or additions to the tale, which plainly I was expected to revamp in a humorous fashion.

As I have said, humor had never been wholly in my line, and in addition I had by no means overcome my awe of the city and its imposing and much-advertised "Four Hundred." Now to be called upon to invade one of its main hostelries and beard the irate and lofty manager in his den, to say nothing of this young Vanderbilt or Goelet—well—— I told myself that when I reached this hotel the manager would doubtless take a very lofty tone and refuse to discuss the matter—which was exactly what happened. He was infuri-ated to think that he had been reported as fighting. Similarly, should I succeed in finding this society youth's apartment, I should probably be snubbed or shunted off in some cavalier fashion—which was exactly what happened. I was told that my Mr. X. was not there. Then, as a conscientious newspaper man, I knew I should return to the hotel and by cajolery or bribery see if I could not induce some barkeeper or waiter who had witnessed the fight to describe some phase of it that I might use.

But I was in no mood for this, and besides, I was afraid of these New York waiters and managers and society people. Suppose they complained of my tale and denounced me as a faker? I returned to the hotel, but its onyx lobby and bar and its heavy rococo decorations and furniture took my courage away. I lingered about but could not begin my inquiries, and finally walked out. Then I went back to the apartment house in which my youth lived, but still he was not in and I could extract no news from the noble footman who kept the door. I did not see how I was to conjure up humor from the facts in hand. Finally I dropped it as unworthy of me and returned to the office. In doing so I had the feeling that I was turning aside an item by which, had I chosen to fake, I could have furthered myself. I knew now that what my city editor wanted was not merely ''accuracy, accuracy, accuracy,'' but a kind of flair for the ridiculous or the remarkable even though it had to be invented, so that the pages of the paper, and life itself, might not seem so dull. Also I realized that a more experienced man, one used to the ways of the city and acquainted with its interesting and eccentric personalities, might make something out of this and not come to grief; but not I. And so I let it go, realizing that I was losing an excellent opportunity.

And I think that my city editor thought so too. When I returned and told him that I could not find anything interestingly new in connection with this he looked at me as much as to say, ''Well, I'll be damned!'' and threw the clipping on his desk. I am satisfied that if any reporter had succeeded in uncovering any aspect of this case not previously used I should have been dropped forthwith. As it turned out, however, nothing more developed, and for a little time anyhow I was permitted to drag on as before, but with no further favors.

One day, being given a part of a ''badger'' case to unravel, a man and woman working together to divest a hotel man of a check for five thousand dollars, and I having cajoled the lady in the case (then under arrest) into making some interesting remarks as to her part in the affair and badgering in general, I was not allowed to write it but had to content myself with seeing my very good yarn incorporated in another man's story while I took ''time.'' Another day, having developed another excellent tale of a runaway marriage, the girl being of a family of some standing, I was not allowed to write it. I was beginning to see that I was a hopeless failure as a reporter here.

CHAPTER LXXV

THE things which most contributed to my want of newspaper success in New York and eventually drove me, though
much against my will and understanding, into an easier and
more agreeable phase of life were, first, that awe of the grinding and almost disgusting forces of life itself which I found
in Spencer and Huxley and Balzac and which now persistently
haunted me and, due possibly to a depressed physical condition at this time, made it impossible for me to work with any
of the zest that had characterized my work in the West. Next,
there was that astounding contrast between wealth and poverty, here more sharply emphasized than anywhere else in America, which gave the great city a gross and cruel and mechanical look, and this was emphasized not only by the papers
themselves, with their various summaries of investigations
and exposures, but also by my own hourly contact with it—a
look so harsh and indifferent at times as to leave me a little
numb. Again, there was something disillusioning in the sharp
contrast between the professed ideals and preachments of such
a constantly moralizing journal as the *World* and the heartless and savage aspect of its internal economy. Men such as
myself were mere machines or privates in an ill-paid army to
be thrown into any breach. There was no time off for the
space-men, unless it was for all time. One was expected to
achieve the results desired or get out; and if one did achieve
them the reward was nothing.

One day I met an acquaintance and asked about an ex-city
editor from St. Louis who had come to New York, and his
answer staggered me.

"Oh, Cliff? Didn't you hear? Why, he committed suicide
down here in a West Street hotel."

"What was the trouble?" I asked.

"Tired of the game, I guess," he replied. "He didn't

get along down here as well as he had out there. I guess he felt that he was going downhill.''

I walked away, meditating. He had been an excellent newspaper man, as brisk and self-centered as one need be to prosper. The last time I had seen him he was in good physical condition, and yet, after something like a year in New York, he had killed himself.·

However, my mood was not that of one who runs away from a grueling contest. I had no notion of leaving New York, whatever happened, although I constantly speculated as to what I should do when all my money was gone. I had no trade or profession beyond this reporting, and yet I was convinced that there must be something else that I could do. Come what might, I was determined that I would ask no favor of my brother, and as for my sister, who was now a burden on my hands, I was determined that as soon as this burden became too great I would take up her case with my brother Paul, outline all that had been done and ask him to shoulder the difference until such time as I could find myself in whatever work I was destined to do.

But what was it?

One of the things which oppressed me was the fact that on the *World*, as well as on the other papers, were men as young as myself who were apparently of a very different texture, mentally if not physically. Life and this fierce contest which I was taking so much to heart seemed in no wise to disturb them. By reason of temperament and insight perhaps, possibly the lack of it, or, what was more likely, certain fortunate circumstances attending their youth and upbringing, they were part of that oncoming host of professional optimists and yea-sayers, chorus-like in character, which for thirty years or more thereafter in American life was constantly engaged in the pleasing task of emphasizing the possibilities of success, progress, strength and what not for all, in America and elsewhere, while at the same time they were humbly and sycophantically genuflecting before the strong, the lucky, the prosperous. On the *World* alone at this time, to say nothing of the other papers, were at least a dozen, swaggering about in the best of clothes, their manners those of a graduate of Yale or Harvard or Princeton, their minds stuffed with all the noble maxims of the uplifters. There was nothing wrong with the world that could not be easily and quickly righted, once the honest, just, true, kind, industrious turned their giant and selected brains to the task. This newest type of young newspaper man was to have no traffic with evil in any form; he was to concern himself with the Good, the True, the Beautiful. Many of these young men pretended to an intimate working knowledge of many things: society, politics, finance and what not else. Several had evidently made themselves indispensable as ship reporters, interviewers of arriving and departing celebrities, and these were now pointed out to me as men worthy of envy and emulation. One of them had, at the behest of the *World,* crossed the ocean more than once seeking to expose the principals in a growing ship-gambling and bunco scandal. There were those who were in the confidence of the mayor, the governor, and some of the lights in Wall Street. One, a scion of one of the best families, was the paper's best adviser as to social events and scandals. The grand air with which they swung in and out of the office set me beside myself with envy.

And all the time the condition of my personal affairs tended to make me anything but optimistic. I was in very serious financial straits. I sometimes think that I was too new to the city, too green to its psychology and subtlety, to be of any use to a great metropolitan daily; and yet, seeing all I had seen, I should have been worth something. I was only five years distant from the composition of *Sister Carrie,* to say nothing of many short stories and magazine articles. Yet I was haunted by the thought that I was a misfit, that I might really have to give up and return to the West, where in some pathetic humdrum task I should live out a barren and pointless life.

With this probable end staring me in the face, I began to think that I must not give up but must instead turn to letters, the art of short-story writing; only just how to do this I could not see. One of the things that prompted me to try this was the fact that on the *World* at this time were several who had succeeded—David Graham Phillips, James Creelman, then a correspondent for the paper in the war which had broken out between China and Japan, to say nothing of George Cary Eggleston and Reginald de Koven, the latter on the staff as chief musical critic. There was another young man, whose name I have forgotten, who was pointed out to me as a rapidly growing favorite in the office of the *Century*. Then there were those new arrivals in the world of letters: Kipling, Richard Harding Davis, Stephen Crane and some others, whose success fascinated me.

All this was but an irritant to a bubbling chemistry which as yet had found no solution, and was not likely to find one for some time to come. My reading of Spencer and Huxley in no wise tended to clarify and impel my mind in the direction of fiction, or even philosophy. But now, in a kind of ferment or fever due to my necessities and desperation, I set to examining the current magazines and the fiction and articles to be found therein: *Century, Scribner's, Harper's.* I was never more confounded than by the discrepancy existing between my own observations and those displayed here, the beauty and peace and charm to be found in everything, the almost complete absence of any reference to the coarse and the vulgar and the cruel and the terrible. How did it happen that these remarkable persons—geniuses of course, one and all—saw life in this happy roseate way? Was it so, and was I all wrong? Love was almost invariably rewarded in these tales. Almost invariably one's dreams came true, in the magazines. Most of these bits of fiction, delicately phrased, flowed so easily, with such an air of assurance, omniscience and condescension, that I was quite put out by my own lacks and defects. They seemed to deal with phases of sweetness and beauty and success and goodness such as I rarely encountered. There were so many tales of the old South reeking with a poetry which was poetry and little more (George W. Cable; Thomas Nelson Page). In *Harper's* I found such assured writers as William Dean Howells, Charles Dudley Warner, Frank R. Stockton, Mrs. Humphry Ward, and a score of others, all of whom wrote of nobility of character and sacrifice and the greatness of ideals and joy in simple things.

But as I viewed the strenuous world about me, all that I read seemed not to have so very much to do with it. Perhaps, as I now thought, life as I saw it, the darker phases, was never to be written about. Maybe such things were not the true province of fiction anyhow. I read and read, but all I could gather was that I had no such tales to tell, and, however much I tried, I could not think of any. The kind of thing I was witnessing no one would want as fiction. These writers seemed far above the world of which I was a part. Indeed I began to picture them as creatures of the greatest luxury and culture, gentlemen and ladies all, comfortably housed, masters of servants, possessing estates, or at least bachelor quarters, having horses and carriages, and received here, there and everywhere with nods of recognition and smiles of approval.

CHAPTER LXXVI

AND then after a little while, being assigned to do routine work in connection with the East Twenty-seventh Street police station, Bellevue Hospital, and the New York Charities Department, which included branches that looked after the poor-farm, the morgue, an insane asylum or two, a workhouse and what not else, I was called upon daily to face as disagreeable and depressing a series of scenes as it is possible for a human being to witness and which quite finished me. I was compelled to inquire of fat, red-faced sergeants, and door-keepers who reigned in police stations and hospital registry rooms what was new, and, by being as genial and agreeable as possible and so earning their favor, to get an occasional tip as to the most unimportant of brawls. Had I been in a different mental state the thickness and incommunicability of some of these individuals would not have been proof against my arts. I could have devised or manufactured something.

But as it was the nature of this world depressed me so that I could not have written anything very much worth while if I had wanted to. There was the morgue, for instance—that horrible place! Daily from the ever-flowing waters about New York there were recaptured or washed up in all stages and degrees of decomposition the flotsam and jetsam of the great city, its offal, its victims—its what? I came here often (it stood at the foot of East Twenty-sixth Street near Bellevue Hospital) and invariably I found the same old brown-denimed caretaker in charge, a creature so thick and so lethargic and so mentally incompetent generally that it was all I could do to extract a grunt of recognition out of him. Yet, if handed a cigar occasionally or a bag of tobacco, he would trouble to get out of his chair and let you look over a book or ledger containing the roughly jotted down police descriptions, all done in an amazing scrawl, of the height, weight, color of clothes if any, complexion of hair and eyes where these were still distinguishable, probable length of time in water, contents of pockets, jewelry or money if any, etc., which same were to be noted in connection with any mystery or disappearance of a person. And there was always some one "turning up missing." And I noticed, with considerable cynicism, that rarely if ever was there any money or jewelry reported as found by the police. That would be too much to expect.

Being further persuaded via blandishments or tips of one kind and another, this caretaker would lead the way to a shelf of drawers reaching from the floor to the chest-height of a man or higher and running about two sides of the room, and opening those containing the latest arrivals, supposing you were interested to look, would allow you to gaze upon the last of that strange chemical formula which once functioned as a human being here on earth. The faces! The decay! The clothing! I stared in sad horror and promised myself that I would never again look, but duty to the paper compelled me so to do again and again.

And then there was Bellevue itself, that gray-black collection of brick and stone with connecting bridges of iron, which faced, in winter time at least, the gray, icy waters of the East River. I have never been able to forget it, so drear and bleak was it all. The hobbling ghouls of caretakers in their baggy brown cotton suits to be seen wandering here and there or hovering over stoves; the large number of half-well charity patients idling about in gray-green denim, their faces sunken and pinched, their hair poorly combed! And the chipper and yet often coarse and vulgar and always overbearing young doctors and nurses and paid attendants generally! One need but remember that it was the heyday of the most corrupt period of Tammany Hall's shameless political control of New York, Mr. Croker being still in charge. Quite all of those old buildings have since been replaced and surrounded by a tall iron fence and bordered with an attractive lawn. In those days it was a little different: there was the hospital proper, with its various wards, its detention hospital for the criminal or insane, or both, the morgue and a world of smaller pavilions stretching along the riverfront and connected by walks or covered hallways or iron bridges, but lacking the dignity and care of the later structures. There was, too, the dark psychology which attends any badly or foully managed institution, that something which hovers as a cloud over all. And Bellevue at that time had that air and that psychology. It smacked more of a jail and a poorhouse combined than of a hospital, and so it was, I think. At that time it was a seething world of medical and political and social graft, a kind of human hell or sty. Those poor fish who live in comfortable and protected homes and find their little theories and religious beliefs ready-made for them in some overawing church or social atmosphere, should be permitted to take an occasional peep into a world such as this was then. At this very time there was an investigation and an exposure on in connection with this institution, which had revealed not only the murder of helpless patients but the usual graft in connection with food, drugs, clothing, etc., furnished to the patients called charity. Grafting officials and medics and brutes of nurses and attendants abounded, of course. The number of "drunks" and obstreperous or complaining or troublesome patients doped or beaten or thrown out and even killed, and the number and quality of operations conducted by incompetent or indifferent surgeons, was known and shown to be large. One need only return to the legislative investigations of that date to come upon the truth of this.

But the place was so huge and crowded that it was like a city in itself. For one thing, it was a dumping-ground for all the offal gathered by the police and the charity departments, to say nothing of being a realm of "soft snaps" for political pensioners of all kinds. On such days as relatives and friends of charity patients or those detained by the police were permitted to call, the permit room fairly swarmed with people who were pushed and shunted here and there like cattle, and always browbeaten like slaves. I myself, visiting as a stranger subsequently, was often so treated. "Who?

What's his name? What? Whendee come? When? Talk a little louder, can't you? Whatsy matter with your tongue? Over there! Over there! Out that door there!" So we came, procured our little cards, and passed in or out.

And the wretched creatures who were "cured" or written down well enough to walk, and so, before a serious illness had been properly treated and because they were not able to pay, were shunted out into the world of the well and the strong with whom they were supposed to compete once more and make their way. I used to see them coming and going and have talked to scores, men and women who had never had a dollar above their meager needs and who, once illness overtook them, had been swept into this limbo, only to be turned out again at the end of a few weeks or months to make their way as best they might, and really worse off than when they came, for now they were in a weak condition physically as well as penniless, and sometimes, as I noticed, on the day of their going the weather was most inclement. And the old, wrinkled, washed-out clothing doled out to them in which they were to once more wander back to the tenements—to do what? There was a local charity organization at the time, as there is today, but if it acted in behalf of any of these I never saw it. They wandered away west on Twenty-sixth Street and along First and Second Avenue, those drear, dismal, underdog streets—to where?

But by far the most irritating of all the phases of this institution, to me at least, were the various officials and dancing young medics and nurses in their white uniforms, the latter too often engaged in flirting with one another or tennis-playing or reading in some warm room, their feet planted upon a desk the while they smoked and the while the great institution with all its company of miserables wagged its indifferent way. When not actually visiting their patients one could always find them so ensconced somewhere, reading or smoking or talking or flirting. In spite of the world of misery that was thrashing about them they were as comfortable as may be, and to me, when bent upon unraveling the details of some particular case, they always seemed heartless.

"Oh, that old nut? What's interesting about him? Surely you don't expect to dig up anything interesting about him, do you? He's been here three weeks now. No; we don't know anything about him. Don't the records show?" Or, supposing he had died: "I knew he couldn't live. We couldn't give him the necessary attention here. He didn't have any money, and there's too many here as it is. Wanta see an interesting case?" And then one might be led in to some wretch who was out of his mind or had an illusion of some kind. "Funny old duck, eh? But there's no hope. He'll be dead in a week or so."

I think the most sickening thing I ever saw was cash gambling among two young medics and a young nurse in charge of the receiving ward as to whether the next patient to be brought in by the ambulance, which had been sent out on a hurry accident call, would arrive alive or dead.

"Fifty that he's dead!"

"Fifty that he isn't!"

"I say alive!"

"I say dead!"

"Well, hand me that stethoscope. I'm not going to be fooled by looks this time!"

Tearing in came the ambulance, its bell clanging, the hubs of the wheels barely missing the walls of the entryway, and as the stretcher was pulled out and set down on the stone step under the archway the three pushed about and hung over, feeling the heart and looking at the eyes and lips, now pale blue as in death, quite as one might crowd about a curious specimen of plant or animal.

"He's alive!"

"He's dead!"

"I say he's alive! Look at his eyes!" to illustrate which one eye was forced open.

"Aw, what's eatin' you! Listen to his heart! Haven't I got the stetho on it? Listen for yourself!"

The man was dead, but the jangle lasted a laughing minute or more, the while he lay there; then he was removed to the morgue and the loser compelled to "come across" or "fork over."

One of the internes who occasionally went out "on the wagon," as the ambulance was called, told me that once, having picked up a badly injured man who had been knocked down by a car, this same ambulance on racing with this man to the hospital had knocked down another and all but killed him.

"And what did you do about him?" I asked.

"Stopped the boat and chucked him into it, of course."

"On top of the other one?"

"Side by side, sure. It was a little close, though."

"Well, did he die?"

"Yep. But the other one was all right. We couldn't help it, though. It was a life or death case for the first one."

"A fine deal for the merry bystander," was all I could say.

The very worst of all in connection with this great hospital, and I do not care to dwell on it at too great length since it has all been exposed before and the records are available, was this: about the hospital, in the capacity of orderlies, doormen, gatemen, errand boys, gardeners, and what not, were a number of down-and-out ex-patients or pensioners of politicians so old and feeble and generally decrepit mentally and physically as to be fit for little more than the scrap-heap. Their main desire, in so far as I could see, was to sit in the sun or safely within the warmth of a room and do nothing at all. If you asked them a question their first impulse and greatest delight was to say "Don't know" or refer you to some one else. They were accused by the half-dozen reporters who daily foregathered here to be of the lowest, so low indeed that they could be persuaded to do anything for a little money. And in pursuance of this theory there was one day propounded by a little red-headed Irish police reporter who used to hang about there that he would bet anybody five dollars that for the sum of fifteen dollars he could hire old Gansmuder, who was one of the shabbiest and vilest-looking of the hospital orderlies, to kill a man. According to him, and he had his information from one of the policemen stationed in the hospital, Gansmuder was an ex-convict who had done ten years' time for a similar crime. Now old and penniless, he was here finishing up a shameful existence, the pensioner of some politician to whom he had rendered a service perhaps.

At any rate here he was, and, as one of several who heard the boast in the news-room near the gate, I joined in the shout of derision that went up. "Rot!" "What stuff!" "Well, you're the limit, Mickey!" However, as events proved, it was not so much talk as fact. I was not present at the negotiations but from amazed accounts by other newspaper men I learned that Gansmuder, being approached by Finn and one other (Finn first, then the two of them together), agreed for the sum of twenty-five dollars, a part of it to be paid in advance, to lie in wait at a certain street corner in Brooklyn for an individual of a given description and there to strike him in such a way as to dispose of him. Of course the negotiations went no further than this, but somehow, true or no, this one incident has always typified the spirit of that hospital, and indeed of all political New York, to me. It was a period of orgy and crime, and Bellevue and the charities department constituted the back door which gave onto the river, the asylums, the potter's field, and all else this side of complete chemic dissolution.

CHAPTER LXXVII

WHETHER due to a naturally weak and incompetent physique or a mind which unduly tortures itself with the evidences of a none-too-smooth working of the creative impulse and its machinery, or whether I had merely had my fill of reportorial work as such and could endure no more, or whatever else might have been the cause, I finally determined to get out of the newspaper profession entirely, come what might and cost what it might, although just what I was to do once I was out I could not guess. I had no trade or profession other than this, and the thought of editing or writing for anything save a newspaper was as far from me as engineering or painting. I did not think I could write anything beyond newspaper news items, and with this conclusion many will no doubt be glad to agree with me even unto this day.

Yet out of this messy and heartless world in which I was now working I did occasionally extract a tale that was printable, only so low was my credit that I rarely won the privilege of writing it myself. Had I imagined that I could write I might easily have built up stories out of what I saw which would have shocked the souls of the magazine editors and writers, but they would never have been published. They would have been too low, gruesome, drab, horrible, and so beyond the view of any current magazine or its clientele.

Life at that time, outside the dark picture of it presented by the daily papers, must, as I have shown, be all sweetness and gayety and humor. We must discuss only our better selves, and arrive at a happy ending; or if perchance this realer world must be referred to it must be indicated in some cloudy manner which would give it more the charm of shadow than of fact, something used to enhance the values of the lighter and more perfect and beautiful things with which our lives must concern themselves. Marriage, if I read the current magazines correctly, was a sweet and delicate affair, never marred by the slightest erratic conduct of any kind. Love was made in heaven and lasted forever. Ministers, doctors, lawyers and merchants, were all good men, rarely if ever guilty of the shams and subterfuges and trashy aspects of humanity. If a man did an evil thing it was due to his lower nature, which really had nothing to do with his higher —and it was a great concession for the intelligentsia of that day (maybe of this) to admit that he had two natures, one of which was not high. Most of us had only the higher one, our better nature. . . . When I think of the literary and social snobbery and bosh of that day, its utter futility and profound faith in its own goodness, as opposed to facts of its own visible life, I have to smile.

But it never occurred to me that I could write, in the literary sense, and as for editing, I never even thought of it. And yet that was the very next thing I did. I wandered about thinking what I was to do, deciding each day that if I had the courage of a rat I would no longer endure this time-consuming game of reporting, for the pitiful sum which I was allowed to draw. What more could it do for me? I asked myself over and over. Make me more aware of the brutality, subtlety, force, charm, selfishness of life? It could not if I worked a hundred years. Essentially, as I even then saw, it was a boy's game, and I was slowly but surely passing out of the boy stage. Yet in desperation because I saw disappearing the amount which I had saved up in Pittsburgh, and I had not one other thing in sight, I visited other newspaper offices to see if I could not secure, temporarily at least, a better regular salary. But no. Whenever I could get in to see a city or managing editor, which was rare, no one seemed to want me. At the offices of the *Herald, Times, Tribune, Sun,* and elsewhere the same outer office system worked to keep me out, and I was by now too indifferent to the reportorial work and too discouraged really to wish to force myself in or to continue as a reporter at all. Indeed I went about this matter of inquiry more or less perfunctorily, not really believing in either myself or my work. If I had secured a well-paying position I presume that I should have continued. Fortunately or unfortunately, as one chooses to look at such things, I did not; but it seemed far from fortunate then to me.

Finally one Saturday afternoon, having brought in a story which related to a missing girl whose body was found at the morgue and being told to "give the facts to —— and let him write it," I summoned up sufficient courage to say to the assistant who ordered me to do this:

"I don't see why I should always have to do this. I'm not a beginner in this game. I wrote stories, and big ones, before ever I came to this paper."

"Maybe you did," he replied rather sardonically, "but we have the feeling that you haven't proved to be of much use to us."

After this there was nothing to say and but one thing to do. I could not say that I had had no opportunities; but just the same I was terribly hurt in my pride. Without knowing what to do or where to go, I there and then decided that, come what might, this was the end of newspaper reporting for me. Never again, if I died in the fight, would I condescend to be a reporter on any paper. I might starve, but if so—I would starve. Either I was going to get something different, something more profitable to my mind, or I was going to starve or get out of New York.

I went to the assistant and turned over my data, then got my hat and went out. I felt that I should be dismissed eventually anyhow for incompetence and insubordination, so dark was my mood in regard to all of it, and so out I went. One thing I did do; I visited the man who had first ordered the city editor to put me on and submitted to him various clippings of work done in Pittsburgh with the request that he advise me as to where I might turn for work.

"Better try the *Sun*," was his sane advice. "It's a great school, and you might do well over there."

But although I tried I could not get on the *Sun*—not, at least, before I had managed to do something else.

Thus ended my newspaper experiences, which I never resumed save as a writer of Sunday specials, and then under entirely different conditions—but that was ten years later. In the meantime I was now perforce turning toward a world which had never seemed to contain any future for me, and I was doing it without really knowing it. But that is another story. It might be related under some such title as *Literary Experiences*.

N. B. Four years later, having by then established myself sufficiently to pay the rent of an apartment, secure furniture and convince myself that I could make a living for two, I undertook that perilous adventure with the lady of my choice —and that, of course, after the first flare of love had thinned down to the pale flame of duty. Need anything more be said? The first law of convention had been obeyed, whereas the governing forces of temperament had been overridden— and with what results eventually you may well suspect. So much for romance.

THE END